Economic Growth in Prewar Japan

ECONOMIC GROWTH IN PREWAR JAPAN

Takafusa Nakamura

Translated by
Robert A. Feldman

Yale University Press   New Haven and London

Senzenki Nihon Keizai Seichō No Bunseki
  (An Analysis of Economic Growth in Prewar Japan)
by Takafusa Nakamura
Copyright © 1971 by Takafusa Nakamura
Originally published in Japanese by
  IWANAMI SHOTEN, Publishers,
Tokyo, 1971.

Designed by Nancy Ovedovitz and set in VIP Baskerville type.
Printed in the United States of America.

Library of Congress Cataloging in Publication Data

Nakamura, Takafusa, 1925–
  Economic growth in prewar Japan.

  Translation of: Senzenki Nihon keizai seichō no bunseki.
  Includes index.
  1. Japan—Economic conditions—1868–1918.
2. Japan—Economic conditions—1918–1945. I. Title.
HC462.8.N25513 1982   330.952′03   82-50444
  ISBN 0-300-02451-7   AACR2

10   9   8   7   6   5   4   3   2

Contents

Tables

Figures

Preface to the English Edition

It is a tremendous joy to me to see this book, first published ten years ago, now published in English. I only hope that it will aid those with an interest in the Japanese economy to deepen their understanding of Japan's modernization and industrialization processes, and to find clues for thinking about contemporary problems.

But the English version differs from the original Japanese version on several major points. The first is a broadening of content. The introductory chapter has been rewritten with completely revised data and now includes more topics; in addition, chapter 2 now includes a section describing economic growth in the Tokugawa period (1600–1868). These two changes are based on sections of my book *Nihon Keizai: Sono Hatten to Kōzō* (The Japanese Economy: Its Growth and Structure), published by the Tokyo University Press in 1978. I believe that these changes make the present volume newer and richer. I would like to thank Tokyo University Press for allowing the use of these materials.

The second major difference between this book and the original Japanese version is the use of the new data of the *Chōki Keizai Tōkei* (Long-Term Economic Statistics), major portions of which appear in English in Ohkawa et al., *Patterns of Japanese Economic Development*, Yale University Press, 1979. The updating of the tables, figures, and regressions was a difficult task requiring much patience, and was carried out by the book's translator, Robert Feldman. I would like to express my most heartfelt thanks to Mr. Feldman, who served not only as translator but also contributed to significant improvements in the content.

Professor Hugh Patrick of Yale University served as intermediary with Yale University Press in arranging for the translation, and Ms. Marian Ash of Yale Press carried out the tasks involved. Mr. Takao Hori of Iwanami Shoten represented the original publisher in negotiations. I would like to express my thanks to all these people for their help.

One □ An Overview of Growth

GROWTH AND CYCLES

In the period following World War II, economists have gained a new understanding of Japan's high rate of economic growth since the Meiji era (1868–1912). Progress in research was first occasioned by the publication of *Chōki Keizai Tōkei (Long-Term Economic Statistics of Japan* [Tōyō Keizai Shimpō Sha, various years], hereafter cited as LTES). Recently a summary and the main statistics of LTES have been published in English (Ohkawa et al., editors, *Patterns of Japanese Economic Development: A Quantitative Appraisal* [Yale University Press, 1979], hereafter cited as Ohkawa et al. [O]). These national economic accounting estimates were carried out by Kazushi Ohkawa and his group at the Hitotsubashi University Institute of Economic Research. Then, as work taking off in all directions bore fruit, a broad view of Japan's long-term economic development in quantitative terms became possible. These efforts have confirmed that the economic growth rate since the Meiji Restoration was indeed high (see table 1.1), and have at the same time facilitated efforts to elucidate the functional mechanisms of economic development. Using LTES data, this chapter will trace the development of the Japanese economy from the beginning of the Meiji era in 1868 to the outbreak of the Pacific War in 1941.

Quantitative Summary of Economic Growth

Japan's economic growth rate during the Meiji era was around 3% or, more cautiously, between 2.5 and 3.5%. The reason for the ambiguity is that, despite the Ohkawa research group's earlier findings indicating real GNP growth rates of over 3%, recent research points to a rate as low as 2.5%. This author had previously calculated a rate of 3.6% for the Meiji period, but new estimates are as much as one-third lower than that (see table 1.2).

The reasons that the growth rate is so much lower in the new Ohkawa estimates than in the old are as follows. In the new estimates (1) the net product of the tertiary sector in the early years of the Meiji period is

1

Table 1.1. Comparison of National Growth Rates

	Total		Per capita	
	A	B	A	B
United States	4.6*	1.1	2.5	0.6
England	2.1	0.7	—	—
Germany	2.7	1.8	—	—
Italy	1.5	1.7	—	—
Denmark	3.2	1.9	—	—
Norway	2.2	3.0	—	—
Sweden	3.0	2.4	—	—
Japan	†{ 3.6	4.6	2.5	3.6
	‡{ 2.4	3.9	1.3	2.6

Sources: For the United States, Department of Commerce [B], p. 224; for Europe, Mitchell [J], pp. 781–83.

Note: A: 1870–1913, *B:* 1913–38, in percent.

*Average of 1869–78 to 1913. For Japan, rate is for 1887–1913.

†Author's estimates based on unrevised totals from the Hitotsubashi research group's original figures (Nakamura [75], p. 2).

‡Kazushi Ohkawa's revised estimates, from Ohkawa [101] and Ohkawa et al. [O], pp. 256–58.

much higher, and (2) estimated rates of increase in prices since the early Meiji years are higher. Ohkawa himself emphasizes the second reason. The result is seen in table 1.2, where the tertiary sector's real net product for the base period has expanded substantially, thus lowering the growth rate. This author still has doubts, however; the nominal values of tertiary sector output in the early Meiji years may well be overstated. In 1890, 65% of the employed population was in agriculture and forestry, with other occupations taking only 35% (Umemura [168]; Ohkawa et al. [O], p. 392). Even if there were substantial supplementary employment in the tertiary sector, there seems to be an imbalance between this and the structure of income.

Moreover, for agriculture, we must take note of the facts pointed out by James Nakamura. He has shown that early Meiji agricultural product estimates are generally too low, so that, until about the middle of the Meiji period, when the errors are corrected, the growth rate of agricultural product appears higher than it actually was. According to official figures for the beginning of the Meiji period, per capita caloric intake was only 1,350 calories. Nakamura estimates the real level of agricultural product to have been higher on the assumption that per

Table 1.2. Comparison of New and Old Estimates (¥ million)

		Agriculture	Mining and manufacturing	Tertiary industry	Net national product
Nominal					
	Old	432	129	247	803
1888–92		(53.4)	(16.0)	(30.6)	(100)
	New	392	120	432	944
		(41.5)	(12.7)	(45.7)	(100)
	Old	2,757	4,201	7,435	11,483
1932–36		(19.0)	(29.6)	(51.3)	(100)
	New	2,718	4,261	8,491	15,476
		(17.6)	(27.6)	(54.9)	(100)
Real (1934–36 Prices)					
	Old	1,185	367	684	2,235
1888–92		(53.0)	(16.4)	(30.6)	(100)
	New	1,676	358	2,563	4,597
		(36.4)	(7.8)	(55.8)	(100)
	Old	2,870	4,459	7,754	15,083
1932–36		(19.0)	(29.6)	(51.4)	(100)
	New	2,931	4,330	8,781	16,043
		(18.2)	(27.0)	(54.8)	(100)

Source: Ohkawa et al. [100], p. 65.
Note: Figures in parentheses show composition by percent.

capita caloric intake was 1,600 calories. On this basis his estimate of the annual growth rate of the agricultural product index until 1920 comes to a mere 1%. Using this correction, Nakamura then derives a growth rate of 2.8% for real GNP. However, Nakamura's growth rate for agricultural product may be too low since, for example, he ignored higher production of rice because it was substituted for inferior wheat and other grains that had been eaten in larger quantities in earlier years. However, it cannot be denied that Nakamura's work acted as a powerful stimulus for the downward revision of previous estimates. (See James Nakamura [M].)

Such discrepancies arise because data for the Meiji period, particularly for early years, are sparse and of low accuracy; moreover, GNP and GNP deflator estimation always requires many assumptions, which in turn heavily influence the results. The job of preparing historical statistics is of course of basic importance in research on economic history and economic development, and the difficulties must not be taken lightly. In considering Japanese economic growth since the Meiji era, one must regard these basic data as of the utmost importance. Arguments presented in this chapter are based on the Ohkawa group's new set of estimates.

Tables 1.3 and 1.4 give summaries of the estimates of gross national expenditure (GNE) over the long term, and using them we can consider changes in economic growth from period to period. First, looking at the structure of GNP in nominal terms, we see that until the 1910s private consumption was around 75% and government consumption about 6–7%, while capital formation rose gradually from 12 to nearly 20%. The increasing share of government investment in total investment testifies to a rising level of activity in public works such as roads, ports, and railroads and shows that the basic preconditions for economic growth were gradually being provided. The foreign trade accounts show that exports in early years were 6–7% of GNP but gradually rose and were 15–20% from the middle of the Meiji period until the 1930s. This development makes it easy to understand the importance of export markets in GNP growth. The extreme increase in the weight of government investment and consumption in 1905 reflects the armament expansion and the huge costs of the Russo–Japanese War; the repressive effects of this spending on growth can be seen.

Composition of GNP calculated from real data show about the same trends as those derived from nominal data, although private and government consumption are always higher while investment and exports are lower in the earlier years and higher in later years. This is of course the result of differences in deflators, i.e., different long-term changes in the price structure (discussed in greater detail on pp. 94–95). However, the real data are most useful in considering the growth rates of GNE and its components, agricultural product, mining and industrial product, and so forth in different periods.

For convenience, let us separate the prewar period into five subperiods, using as dividers the following years: 1875, 1885, 1900, 1915, 1930, 1940. Part of the reason for this periodization is data constraints, but it is also meaningful from the perspective of Japanese economic development. The year 1875 represents the end of the immediate post-Restoration period and is also the first year for which one can use the basic data source of the Meiji era, the *Bussan Hyō* (Census of Products). The year 1885 marks the end of the period of inflation following the Satsuma Rebellion (1877), and the subsequent Matsukata deflation (1881–84), which attempted to bring the monetary situation under control and establish a new monetary system. Moreover, this era also saw the beginnings of modern industry. During the next period, ending in 1900, modern industry became fairly well established, the gold standard was adopted (1897) based on the gold indemnity from the first Sino– Ja-

Table 1.3. National Income in Current Prices (Five-year moving averages, with percentage composition)

	Amount (¥ million)							Composition (%)						
	Gross national expenditure Y	Personal consumption C	Government consumption C_g	Gross domestic fixed capital formation I_f	Inventory change I_j	Exports E	Imports M	$\frac{C}{Y}$	$\frac{C_g}{Y}$	$\frac{I_f}{Y}$	$\frac{I_j}{Y}$	$\frac{E}{Y}$	$\frac{M}{Y}$	$\frac{I_g}{I_f}$
1885	808	649	62	99	—	52	54	80.3	7.6	12.3	—	6.4	−6.6	19.9
1890	1,028	818	64	148	—	82	84	79.6	6.2	14.4	—	7.9	−8.2	18.0
1895	1,542	1,198	113	268	—	140	179	77.7	7.4	17.4	—	9.1	−11.6	22.6
1900	2,389	1,876	173	381	—	272	314	78.5	7.3	16.0	—	11.4	−13.1	34.3
1905	3,171	2,348	447	484	—	462	571	74.1	14.1	15.3	—	14.6	−18.0	31.2
1910	4,142	3,137	348	733	—	596	672	75.7	8.4	17.7	—	14.4	−16.2	36.0
1915	5,896	4,139	368	1,062	—	1,330	1,003	70.2	6.2	18.0	—	22.6	−17.0	27.2
1920	14,729	10,629	972?	3,016	—	2,739	2,627	72.2	6.6	20.5	—	18.6	−17.8	30.6
1925	15,766	12,237	1,190	2,737	—	2,817	3,215	77.6	7.5	17.4	—	17.9	−20.4	41.2
1930	14,886	10,880	1,655	2,371	—	2,663	2,683	73.1	11.1	15.9	—	17.9	−18.0	46.0
1935	18,552	12,813	2,192	3,604	—	4,162	4,219	69.0	11.8	19.4	—	22.4	−22.7	42.7
1940	31,392	18,071	3,756	9,832	—	6,258	6,426	57.4	11.9	31.2	—	19.9	−20.4	46.4

Source: Ohkawa et al. [O], pp. 251–53; years are calendar years.

Note: Year listed is the middle year of the 5-year period (average) with the exceptions of 1885 being the average of 1885–87 and 1940 the average of 1938–40.

Table 1.4. National Income in Constant Prices (Five-year moving averages and relative composition, 1934–36 prices)

	Amount (¥ million)							Composition (%)					
	Gross national expenditure Y	Personal consumption C	Government consumption C_g	Gross fixed capital formation I_f	Inventory increases I_j	Exports E	Imports M	$\frac{C}{Y}$	$\frac{C_g}{Y}$	$\frac{I_f}{Y}$	$\frac{I_j}{Y}$	$\frac{E}{Y}$	$\frac{M}{Y}$
1885	4,092	3,505	305	356	—	77	151	85.7	7.4	8.7	—	1.9	3.7
1890	4,747	4,112	306	446	—	114	230	86.6	6.4	9.4	—	2.4	4.9
1895	5,592	4,774	478	612	—	160	433	85.4	8.5	10.9	—	2.9	7.7
1900	6,256	5,326	524	716	—	271	581	85.1	8.4	11.4	—	4.3	9.3
1905	6,793	5,418	1,116	793	—	386	919	79.8	16.4	11.7	—	5.7	13.5
1910	7,645	6,183	756	1,166	—	563	1,023	80.9	9.9	15.3	—	7.4	13.4
1915	8,777	6,911	730	1,319	—	1,080	1,263	78.7	8.3	15.0	—	12.3	14.4
1920	11,562	8,808	999	2,364	—	1,259	1,869	76.2	8.6	20.5	—	10.9	16.2
1925	12,319	10,269	1,118	2,179	—	1,411	2,658	83.4	9.1	17.7	—	11.5	21.6
1930	13,958	11,065	1,685	2,360	—	2,210	3,362	79.3	12.1	16.9	—	15.8	24.1
1935	18,105	12,698	2,184	3,352	—	3,924	4,053	70.1	12.1	15.5	—	21.7	22.4
1940	21,839	13,293	2,978	6,454	—	4,032	4,919	60.9	13.6	29.6	—	18.5	22.5

Source and Note: Source and periodization same as for table 1.3.

panese War, and a capitalist economy took shape. The period to 1915, in addition to seeing the final years of Meiji economic development, just preceded the boom of World War I and was the eve of heavy industrialization in such industries as electric power, chemicals, metals, and machinery. The years to 1930, which of course include the start of the world depression and the trough of the gold standard reversion deflation, were the crisis years of the prewar capitalist economy. By 1940 the second Sino–Japanese War had already broken out, but this decade also saw the peak of prewar economic development and the effects of the wartime chemical and heavy industrialization.

With this periodization in mind, let us look at table 1.5. We can immediately see the following facts. Long-term growth over the prewar period was about 3%, with export and import growth up to World War I quite strong, indicating that the pattern of the Japanese economy as a processor dependent on trade had emerged by then. On the other hand it is also clear that there was a great expansion in government expenditures after World War I. Moreover, the growth rate of plant and equipment investment rose remarkably in the 1930s, while growth of consumption was quite low. This pattern of growth resembles that of the postwar high-growth period.

Table 1.5. Growth Rates of GNE Components and of Agricultural and Mining and Manufacturing Production Indexes (Annual percentage rates)

	Y	C	C_g	I_f	E	M	Agricultural production index	Mining and manufacturing production index
1875–85	—	—	—	—	—	—	2.1	3.9
1885–1900	3.1	2.9	3.9	5.1	9.4	10.1	1.6	5.4
1900–15	2.3	1.9	2.2	4.2	9.7	5.3	2.1	5.0
1915–30	3.1	3.2	5.7	4.0	4.9	6.7	0.9	5.1
1930–40	4.6	1.9	5.1	10.6	6.2	3.9	0.5	8.2
1885–1915	2.7	2.4	3.1	4.6	9.5	7.6	1.8	5.1
1915–40	3.7	2.7	5.5	6.6	5.4	5.6	0.7	6.3
1885–1940	3.1	2.5	4.3	5.5	7.6	6.7	1.3	5.7

Sources and Notes: Mining and manufacturing production indexes are from Shinohara [126], pp. 145, 147. Agricultural production indexes are from Umemura [165], pp. 222–23. GNE components are from Ohkawa et al. [O], pp. 302–04. All indexes are provisional.

The Pattern of Cyclical Fluctuation

Another important theme observable from long-term macro data is the pattern of cyclical fluctuation. There are four kinds of such fluctuations, 2–3-year inventory cycles (Kitchin cycles), 7–8-year plant and equipment investment cycles (Juglar cycles), construction cycles of about twice that length (Kuznets cycles), and 50–60-year waves based on technological revolutions (Kondratieff waves). Miyohei Shinohara's classic study [128] shows that prewar cycles in Japan were primarily due to plant and equipment investment, whereas postwar cycles were primarily inventory cycles. Let us begin by examining figures on cyclical fluctuations.

Table 1.6 shows percentage changes from the previous year in gross national product and in private consumption. (Three-year moving averages are used to exclude the shorter term Kitchin cycles and to examine the 7–8-year Juglar cycles.) The table shows that the amplitude of the GNP cycles is slightly higher than that of the private consumption cycles and that a cycle is visable for both about every seven years. The level of the growth rate differs widely for prewar and postwar years, but the cycles do resemble each other after the beginning of the twentieth century.

The cyclical peaks were as follows: the late 1880s, during the first surge in firms' activity; the middle of the 1890s, during the first Sino–Japanese War, the postwar boom, and the second surge in firms' activity; the first half of the 1900s during recovery and the Russo–Japanese War boom; around 1910 during another surge in firms' activity; the latter half of the 1910s, during the frenzied wartime boom of World War I; the small upswing at the end of the 1920s; and the mid-1930s, a time of growth due to increases in exports and internal demand.

The troughs were as follows: for the first cycle, the 1890 panic; the postwar reaction following the first Sino–Japanese War (the first panic of 1897–98); the early 1900s at the time of the second panic, when internal demand fell off as a result of the stagnation of foreign trade and armament expansion around the time of the Boxer Rebellion; the postwar recession of 1907–08 in reaction to the Russo–Japanese War boom; the 1914 panic just after the outbreak of World War I; the early 1920s from the post-World War I panic of 1920 to the Great Kanto Earthquake of 1923; the Financial Panic of 1927; and the downturn of 1930 due to reversion to the gold standard and the worldwide depression.

Let us organize these facts. First, whether looking at three-year averages or annual GNE data, it was only Japan's growth *rate* that rose and fell, there being almost no cases of recessions with negative growth. This contrasts remarkably with foreign countries where negative growth was not at all rare. Thus, Japan's long-term growth rate was relatively high and stable. In Japan's case, as Shinohara has said, there were not abso-

Table 1.6. Growth Rates of Nominal Private Consumption and GNP (Market prices, three-year moving averages)

	Private consumption	GNP		Private consumption	GNP
1888	1.3	2.5	1914	2.8	1.9
1889	6.3	6.2	1915	−0.4	1.5
1890	9.8	9.0	1916	2.0	7.7
			1917	16.0	24.3
1891	9.8	9.5	1918	31.4	34.7
1892	5.3	5.4	1919	41.3	35.0
1893	3.8	4.2	1920	24.1	20.4
1894	3.8	5.7			
1895	9.5	11.7	1921	11.2	7.1
1896	10.8	11.5	1922	0.9	0.3
1897	15.4	13.6	1923	1.4	−2.1
1898	16.1	12.4	1924	2.8	1.5
1899	10.0	11.1	1925	3.2	1.5
1900	7.2	7.1	1926	1.5	2.2
			1927	0.0	1.5
1901	1.6	4.2	1928	−1.7	0.5
1902	3.7	3.1	1929	−1.6	0.6
1903	3.3	3.8	1930	−3.6	−3.3
1904	6.0	7.0			
1905	4.6	6.6	1931	−7.0	−6.7
1906	0.4	6.9	1932	−6.1	−5.9
1907	7.7	7.6	1933	0.0	1.6
1908	8.2	6.7	1934	7.7	8.6
1909	7.1	4.4	1935	8.7	10.1
1910	2.1	1.6	1936	7.0	7.9
			1937	7.9	10.7
1911	4.7	6.1	1938	8.1	13.4
1912	8.5	8.2	1939	10.3	17.4
1913	9.6	8.3	1940	10.5	17.4

Source: Ohkawa et al. [O], table A1.

lute cycles but rather primarily growth *rate* cycles. Second, the cycles in plant and equipment investment were not always of the same scale. There were large-scale booms in the late 1880s, late 1910s, and 1930s, alternating with smaller ones. This suggests that cycles longer than seven years in duration also existed, e.g., Kuznets cycles. To examine this proposition, let us look at table 1.7. To find what is left after seven-year cycles are excluded, each seven years' data were regressed on a time trend, with the coefficient on the trend variable expressing the average

Table 1.7. Trend Growth of GNP and Investment (Seven-year moving trend growth)

	GNP	Investment		GNP	Investment
1888	1.2	5.9	1914	3.8	1.0
1889	0.5	4.6	1915	5.5	6.5
1890	0.2	3.6	1916	6.3	10.5
			1917	6.1	13.6
1891	0.4	3.9	1918	5.1	14.8
1892	0.9	4.6	1919	3.9	11.2
1893	1.1	6.2	1920	2.1	3.4
1894	2.8	8.9			
1895	2.8	10.5	1921	1.0	−1.4
1896	2.4	8.0	1922	1.0	−2.9
1897	2.0	4.3	1923	1.4	−2.4
1898	1.9	2.0	1924	1.9	−0.6
1899	2.0	−1.2	1925	2.9	2.1
1900	1.8	−2.5	1926	3.5	4.3
			1927	3.0	2.8
1901	2.0	−2.8	1928	2.3	0.3
1902	1.7	1.1	1929	2.1	−0.8
1903	1.6	3.4	1930	2.4	0.0
1904	1.6	5.5			
1905	2.0	7.9	1931	3.5	2.3
1906	2.0	7.6	1932	4.9	5.0
1907	2.1	8.3	1933	5.5	8.0
1908	3.2	7.6	1934	5.8	11.3
1909	2.9	7.4	1935	5.5	13.5
1910	2.2	6.3	1936	5.0	15.8
			1937	4.8	16.0
1911	1.8	4.6	1938		
1912	1.8	2.4	1939		
1913	2.4	−0.3	1940		

Source: Ohkawa et al. [O], table A3.

Note: Figures represent trend rate of growth for seven years centered on the year listed.

growth rate for these years. This average rate is assigned to the middle year.

Table 1.7 shows a trough around 1900, with a small peak and trough around 1910; after this, the World War I boom and the stagnation of the 1920s stand out. Viewed in this way, the prewar economy can be said to have experienced the following long cycles.

1. starting with the Matsukata deflation (early 1880s), a growth phase that lasted until establishment of the gold standard (1897);
2. a growth phase from the last half of the twentieth century's first decade until the end of the second. This period is divided into two subperiods by the small decline beginning around 1910;
3. the downturn of the 1920s, with the exception of slight recovery in mid-decade; then, after the panic of 1927, a third growth phase during the 1930s;
4. the period of wartime economy in the late 1930s and early 1940s, and of collapse due to war damage.

These periods seem to be the appropriate ones for historical periodization of the Japanese economy. There probably were similar fluctuations before the Matsukata deflation but they cannot be quantitatively determined with the statistical sources available today.[1]

Capital Stock and Labor Force
The capital stock and the labor force of course play central roles in long-term growth. Table 1.8 shows the changes in these two variables, broken down into primary and nonprimary sectors, along with real net national product. The capital stock increased by more than seven times between 1878 and 1940. At the start of the Meiji era about 74% of the capital stock was in the primary sector but by the outbreak of the Pacific War its share had fallen to 17%. From this we can see just how remarkable was the development of the secondary and tertiary sectors.

During the same time period, population almost doubled. But the employed population rose by only 1.5 times. The reason for this, as seen in the table, is that 72% (15.6 million persons) of the work force was in the primary sector at the beginning of the Meiji era. Roughly 5 million farm households had an average of more than 3 workers apiece. In the secondary and tertiary sectors the number of workers per household was not that high, so that, as these latter sectors expanded, the proportion of the population in the labor force fell. (This proportion will hereafter be called the employment ratio or the labor force ratio.) Moreover, the

1. These cycles of 15 years or more, called Kuznets cycles, were primarily generated by construction activity, according to Fujino [23]. That is, even though there were medium-term Juglar cycles of plant and equipment investment, these were not always of the same magnitude. Empirically, a very large surge in plant and equipment investment based on a boom has usually been followed by a recession that, after recovery, has in turn been followed by another plant and equipment investment expansion, although not on such a large scale as before. In Juglar cycles, strong upswings alternate with weaker ones, the latter primarily consisting of construction. In Japan's case, for example, there was rather little plant and equipment investment by industry in the 1920s from the post-World War I recession onward. But construction activity in the aftermath of the Great Kantō Earthquake made it possible to check the downswing.

Table 1.8. Capital Stock and Labor Force (1934–36 Prices)

	Capital stock (¥ million)			Employees (thousands)			Real net domestic product (¥ million)			Total population (thousands)	Labor force ratio (%)
	All industry	Agriculture, forestry, & fisheries	Other	All industry	Agriculture, forestry, & fisheries	Other	All industry	Agriculture, forestry, & fisheries	Other		
1878	7,219	5,333	1,886	21,754	15,624	6,130	—	—	—	36,166	60.2
1885	7,835	5,425	2,410	22,339	15,654	6,685	3,771	1,590	2,181	38,131	58.3
1890	8,559	5,483	3,075	23,042	15,637	7,405	4,634	1,848	2,786	39,902	57.7
1895	9,550	5,590	3,959	23,724	15,482	8,242	5,301	1,987	3,314	41,557	57.1
1900	11,104	5,699	5,406	24,378	15,853	8,525	5,967	2,071	3,896	43,847	55.6
1905	12,499	5,865	6,634	24,982	15,821	9,161	6,214	1,963	4,251	46,620	53.4
1910	15,362	6,245	9,116	25,475	16,383	9,092	7,427	2,294	5,133	49,184	51.8
1915	18,810	6,541	12,269	26,305	15,615	10,690	8,757	2,691	6,066	52,752	49.9
1920	25,075	6,938	18,137	27,125	14,344	12,781	10,936	2,984	7,952	55,963	48.5
1925	30,286	7,507	22,779	28,105	14,056	14,049	12,986	3,018	9,968	59,737	47.0
1930	36,355	8,244	28,112	29,619	14,648	14,971	13,764	3,130	10,634	64,450	46.0
1935	42,750	8,730	34,019	31,211	14,450	16,761	17,032	3,052	13,980	69,254	45.1
1940	53,779	9,112	44,666	32,500	14,523	17,977	24,417	3,419	20,998	71,933	45.2

Sources: Ohkawa et al. [103], pp. 148–52, 180–81, and Ohkawa et al. [O], pp. 366–68. Labor force data are from appendix to Umemura [167], and Ohkawa et al. [O], pp. 392–93.

Note: Capital stock is total reproducible capital excluding housing (gross capital).

proportion of the population under 15 years of age has been estimated by Yūzō Morita to have been 27.4% in 1871, while the census of 1940 shows 36.0% of the population under 15. The increased proportion of young people in the population in later years is another reason the labor force ratio fell.[2]

These data are arranged more analytically in table 1.9, which shows the capital stock, labor force, and sectoral products with their respective growth rates, average and marginal capital coefficients, and average and marginal labor coefficients. The periodization follows that given earlier for medium-range cycles. From the table we see the following. First, when the growth rate of production is high, the growth rates of both capital stock and of labor force are high. Or perhaps it should be said that high growth of capital stock and labor force result in high growth in production, revealing the intimate relationship between these variables. Second, we see that a fairly stable ratio of production to capital stock has been preserved since the beginning of the twentieth century. Even if the prewar capital coefficient rose somewhat during recessions, it always stayed between two and three. Thus, for one unit of output, more than two units of capital were needed. The average employment coefficient declined steadily from the start of the Meiji period. As for the marginal coefficients, their high variability over the long-term business cycles was only natural. In prosperous times the marginals fell, and in recessions they rose.

As the secondary and tertiary sectors expanded, capital and labor force naturally shifted to these industries. In particular, the similarity between the average capital coefficients for the primary and nonprimary sectors suggests that a good balance was maintained between them. But there were large differences in the employment coefficients of the secondary and tertiary sectors on the one hand and the primary sector on the other.

Money and Prices

Let us now also summarize facts relating to money and prices, which form the backdrop of economic growth. Figure 1.1 shows changes in the money supply since the Meiji era. M_2 (here defined as currency, current deposits, and time deposits; M_1 is currency and current deposits only) was only ¥143 million in 1873 but rose to ¥897 million by 1900, to ¥11 billion by 1920, and finally to ¥42 billion by 1940. Without appropriate increases in the money supply, the development of economic activity is very difficult. However, the effects on society of changes in the value of

2. See Morita [70], p. 414. This book is not well known but is one of the few pieces of first-class scholarship that emerged during the lean scholarly harvest of World War II. Even now it is to be highly recommended.

Table 1.9. Capital Stock, Employed Population, and Real Net Domestic Product: Growth Rates, Capital Coefficients, and Employment Coefficients

	All industry							Primary industry							Nonprimary industry						
	Growth rates							Growth rates							Growth rates						
	K	N	Y'	K/Y'	$\Delta K/\Delta Y'$	N/Y'	$\Delta N/\Delta Y'$	K	N	Y'	K/Y'	$\Delta K/\Delta Y'$	N/Y'	$\Delta N/\Delta Y'$	K	N	Y'	K/Y'	$\Delta K/\Delta Y'$	N/Y'	$\Delta N/\Delta Y'$
1885	—	—	—	2.08	—	5.77	—	—	—	—	3.35	—	9.85	—	—	—	—	1.11	—	3.07	—
1885–1900	2.2	0.5	2.9	1.86	1.49	4.09	0.929	0.3	0.0	1.7	2.75	0.57	7.65	0.414	5.1	1.5	3.8	1.38	1.68	2.26	1.090
1900–13	3.6	0.5	2.5	2.15	2.89	3.15	0.691	0.9	0.3	1.4	2.60	1.80	6.65	1.523	5.7	1.3	2.8	1.96	3.27	1.85	0.907
1913–20	5.1	0.6	4.1	2.29	2.74	2.48	0.436	1.1	−2.0	2.7	2.33	1.00	4.81	−4.185	6.2	4.1	4.4	2.21	2.95	1.82	1.734
1920–30	3.8	0.9	2.3	2.64	3.99	2.15	0.882	1.7	0.2	0.5	2.63	8.95	4.68	2.082	4.7	1.6	2.8	2.66	4.05	1.61	0.957
1930–40	4.0	0.9	5.9	2.20	1.64	1.33	0.270	1.0	−0.1	0.9	2.67	3.00	4.25	−0.432	5.2	1.8	7.2	2.20	1.74	0.96	0.309
1900–20	4.1	0.5	3.1	2.29	2.81	2.48	0.553	1.0	−0.5	1.8	2.33	1.36	4.81	−1.653	5.9	2.3	3.4	2.21	3.10	1.82	1.348
1920–40	3.9	0.9	4.1	2.20	2.13	1.33	0.399	1.3	0.1	0.7	2.67	5.00	4.25	0.411	4.9	1.7	5.0	2.20	2.19	0.96	0.435

Sources: See table 1.8.

Note: Average capital and employment coefficients are for ends of periods listed. K denotes capital stock, N employed population, and Y' real net domestic product.

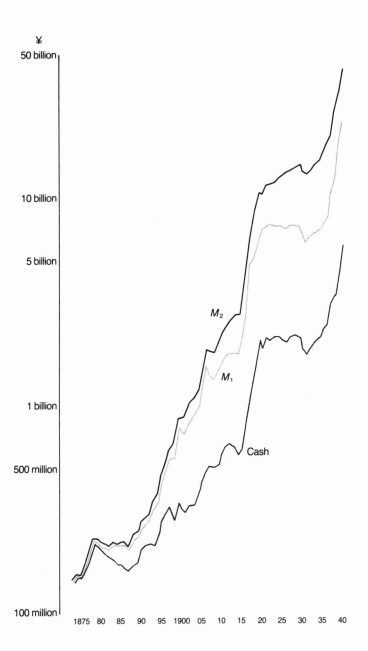

Figure 1.1 Currency, M_1 and M_2. Sources and Notes: Money data are from Asakura and Nishiyama [14], pp. 35–36. Data for deflators are from Ohkawa et al. [O], table A50.

The number listed on the graph is the growth rate g from the equation $x_t = a + gt$, where x is the natural log of the series in question. A separate regression was run for each seven years' data, and the growth rate listed for the middle year. For example, the growth rate from the regression on data from 1897 to 1903 is listed for 1900.

money (i.e., changes in the price level) are quite large. The pace of monetary expansion in Japan has been exceptionally rapid. Although the Matsukata deflation in the 1880s, the recession after the establishment of the gold standard in 1897, and the 10 years after World War I were eras of stagnation in monetary growth, the money supply grew rapidly in all other periods.

To investigate the relationship of the real economy to the money supply, let us look at the ratio of the quantity of money to nominal GNE, i.e., the so-called Marshallian k (see table 1.10). Japan's Marshallian k rose steadily since the middle of the Meiji era, and the growth of k_2 (the ratio of M_2 to GNE) was particularly large. Moreover, with a bit of care, the seven-year plant-and-equipment investment cycles of the prewar period can be seen in the table. When the supply of money is below demand, as during times of deterioration in the balance of payments, the value of k falls, but this coincides with downturns in the business cycle. The recovery in the value of k usually precedes recovery of the general economy. However, the continuous rising trend, especially in the value of k_2, cannot be ignored. This accumulation of money in excess of productive capacity is not unique to Japan, but it cannot be denied that, although the rapid progress of this accumulation was a condition for the expansion of production, it also provided the conditions for price increases.

It is not my intention here to discuss the validity of the quantity theory of money. However, it is certain that an abundant supply of money increases social demands and contributes to rising prices. For example, table 1.11 shows an equation relating M_2 and the GNE deflator (P). No matter what period is used from the Meiji era onward, the regressions show high coefficients of determination, and all the coefficients are highly significant. Moreover, figure 1.2 shows seven-year average growth rates (derived by least squares) for M_2, the GNE deflator, and the consumption deflator. Except for some slight nonconformity in the early Meiji years, the lines always move together. In other words, when short-term leads and lags are excluded, the trends of movement in M_2 and prices agree. The correlation coefficients for the prewar period show the extremely high value of 0.97 for the period from World War I to the Pacific War (1915–40), and also a high figure of 0.83 for 1888 to 1914. This demonstrates that, regardless of the mechanism, the money supply had a crucial effect on the price level in prewar years.

With price levels determined as outlined above, we may now ask what the relationships were among the various types of prices. Although extremely rough, table 1.12 shows the general relationships, giving price indexes for agricultural, forest, and industrial products and for rail transportation and electric power. From the table one can see which

Table 1.10. The Marshallian k (M/GNE)

	k_1 (M_1/GNE)	k_2 (M_2/GNE)		k_1 (M_1/GNE)	k_2 (M_2/GNE)
1885	.27	.28	1914	.37	.59
1886	.27	.28	1915	.41	.64
1887	.25	.26	1916	.46	.70
1888	.26	.28	1917	.48	.73
1889	.24	.26	1918	.45	.74
1890	.24	.26	1919	.43	.70
			1920	.44	.68
1891	.23	.25			
1892	.25	.27	1921	.51	.78
1893	.27	.29	1922	.48	.75
1894	.26	.29	1923	.50	.80
1895	.27	.30	1924	.48	.80
1896	.29	.32	1925	.45	.80
1897	.28	.32	1926	.45	.84
1898	.26	.30	1927	.46	.83
1899	.33	.38	1928	.45	.85
1900	.31	.37	1929	.45	.88
			1930	.46	.94
1901	.30	.36			
1902	.33	.40	1931	.47	.99
1903	.33	.41	1932	.49	1.00
1904	.33	.34	1933	.46	.94
1905	.37	.46	1934	.43	.90
1906	.46	.57	1935	.41	.90
1907	.37	.49	1936	.43	.92
1908	.36	.48	1937	.44	.88
1909	.39	.54	1938	.48	.95
1910	.41	.57	1939	.59	1.07
			1940	.63	1.14
1911	.39	.54			
1912	.38	.54			
1913	.36	.55			

Sources: Asakura and Nishiyama [14], pp. 35–36, for money data, and Ohkawa et al. [O], table A1, for GNE data.

prices increased the most and which the least. The products with the largest price increases were agricultural and forestry products, not only rice but cultivated goods in general. Among industrial products, the prices of chemical products and foods rose most during the prewar years, followed by metals, machinery, and textiles. Railroad fares rose

Table 1.11. Price–Money Regression

	α	β	R^2
1885–1914	0.575	0.445	0.983
	(7.798)	(40.439)	
1915–40	1.680	0.320	0.532
	(2.957)	(5.336)	

Sources: Money data are from Asakura and Nishiyama [14], pp. 35–36, and GNE deflator data from Ohkawa et al. [O], table A50.

Notes: Regression is $\ln P = \alpha + \beta \ln M_2$, where P is the GNE deflator and M_2 is broadly defined money. Figures in parentheses are t-statistics.

the least. And there were large differentials in the growth rates of prices; cultivated agricultural product prices rose more than 5 times while cocoons rose only 2.5 times. Industrial products in general rose 3.5 times, but within this category chemical products rose 4.5 times, food products 4.2 times, and machinery only 2.4 times. Railroad fares rose only 1.75 times. We can view the differences as basically due to relative changes in production costs. The rise in productivity in cocoon farming and textile production was very great in the Meiji era, so the prices of these products climbed relatively slowly even from the beginning. After the 1920s technical progress in heavy and chemical industries was great, and this held their prices down. In farming, where technical change was relatively slow, prices rose remarkably. Owing to these changes in relative prices, the various products were supplied in amounts consistent with social demands, and income in the less progressive sectors was maintained. Thus, over the long run, the price mechanism worked quite well.

INDUSTRIAL STRUCTURE AND OCCUPATIONAL STRUCTURE

Industrial Structure

Next let us outline the industrial structure of the prewar period. Tables 1.13 and 1.14 show data for employed population and net domestic product by sector, respectively.

First, as far as can be seen from the data on employed population, the sector that accounted for the major proportion of workers until 1930 was the primary sector. However, the primary sector did show an increase in number of workers, though only a small one, until 1905; thereafter, the absolute number declined as movement to secondary and tertiary sectors became apparent. Increases in employed population were concentrated in the secondary and tertiary sectors, which accounted for virtually all the increases in total employed population. In the secondary

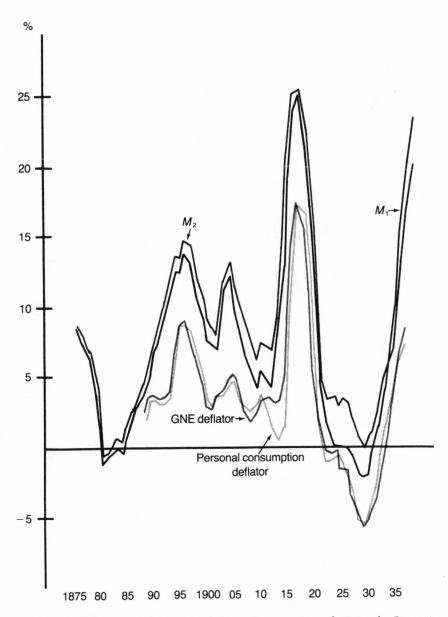

Figure 1.2. Money and Prices: Seven-Year Average Growth Rates in Percent.
Sources: Ohkawa et al. [O] for balance of payments; for specie reserves, Okura
Shō [106], appendix volume, p. 223.

Table 1.12. Price Indexes and Relative Prices by Commodity Groups (1934–36 = 100 for indexes)

Year	Agricultural products				Forest products	Food		Industrial products				High capital intensity products		GNE deflator
	Total	Cultivated goods	Rice	Cocoons		Total products	products	Textiles	Chemicals	Metals	Machinery	Railroad fares	Electric rates	
Index levels														
1880	33.5	30.4	28.6	81.4	37.0	44.1	32.3	72.0	34.6	62.5	62.1	56.7	—	—
1890	27.0	24.3	21.9	67.4	29.3	36.6	27.8	60.5	29.3	42.6	56.4	63.2	—	23.0
1900	47.7	43.7	42.5	62.8	50.6	59.1	45.4	85.2	48.8	70.4	73.7	79.0	—	38.7
1910	62.9	58.9	55.6	82.2	65.3	77.3	70.5	96.2	65.7	69.0	78.8	70.0	125.1	50.1
1920	145.1	134.8	129.7	207.8	178.6	167.7	135.0	228.7	159.5	137.0	127.7	97.1	148.5	139.2
1930	88.3	83.9	76.4	106.2	107.2	100.4	104.1	109.7	100.9	78.1	95.6	103.5	123.3	105.9
1940	160.6	154.4	140.6	202.4	190.7	152.6	135.2	147.2	152.5	179.2	147.6	97.9	98.9	161.3
Terms of trade vs. agriculture														
1880	100	90.8	85.3	243.0	110.4	131.6	96.4	214.9	103.3	186.6	185.4	169.3	—	—
1890	100	90.0	81.1	249.6	108.5	135.6	103.0	224.1	108.5	157.8	208.9	234.1	—	85.2
1900	100	91.6	89.1	131.7	106.1	123.9	95.2	178.6	102.3	147.6	154.5	165.6	—	81.1
1910	100	93.6	88.4	130.7	104.5	122.9	112.1	156.1	104.5	109.7	125.3	111.3	198.9	79.7
1920	100	92.9	89.4	143.2	123.1	115.6	93.0	157.6	109.9	94.4	88.0	66.9	102.3	95.9
1930	100	95.0	86.5	120.3	121.4	113.7	117.9	124.2	114.3	88.5	108.3	117.2	139.6	119.9
1940	100	96.1	87.6	126.0	118.7	95.0	84.2	91.7	95.0	111.6	91.9	61.0	61.6	100.4

Sources: Agricultural and forest product prices are from Ohkawa [99], pp. 165–67, 184; industrial products from ibid., pp. 192–93; railroad and electric rate data also from ibid., pp. 210–11. However, figures for 1940 are geometric averages for 1938–40.

Note: Geometric averages of five years' data; year shown is midyear.

Table 1.13. Employed Population (Thousands)

	Total	Primary	Secondary	Tertiary	Unclassified	Agriculture and forestry only
1872	21,371 (100)	15,525 (72.7)	—	5,846 (27.4)	—	15,525
1885	22,339	15,654 (70.1)	—	6,685 (29.9)	—	15,654
1890	23,042	15,637 (67.8)	—	7,405 (32.1)	—	15,637
1895	23,724	15,482 (65.3)	—	8,242 (34.7)	—	15,482
1900	24,378	15,853 (65.0)	—	8,525 (35.0)	—	15,853
1905	25,061	16,707 (69.5)	3,729 (15.5)	3,618 (15.0)	1,007	16,158
1910	25,475	16,383 (67.1)	4,089 (16.7)	3,943 (16.1)	1,060	15,830
1915	26,305	15,615 (62.5)	4,884 (19.5)	4,501 (18.0)	1,305	15,075
1920	27,260	14,388 (55.3)	6,274 (24.1)	5,355 (20.6)	1,243	13,815
1925	28,105	14,056 (52.4)	6,324 (23.6)	6,432 (24.0)	1,293	13,540
1930	29,619	14,648 (52.1)	6,151 (21.9)	7,331 (26.1)	1,488	14,084
1935	31,211	14,450 (48.7)	6,811 (23.0)	8,410 (28.3)	1,540	13,871
1940	32,500	14,523 (47.7)	8,212 (27.0)	7,728 (25.4)	2,037	13,974

Source: Calculated from Umemura [167].

Notes: Figures shown for 1905 are 1906 data. Primary industry figures for 1872–1900 are for agriculture and forestry only. Compositional figures for 1905–40 exclude unclassified from the total used to calculate the percentages.

Primary sector is agriculture, forestry, and fisheries (maritime) industries. Secondary sector is mining, manufacturing, and construction industries. Tertiary sector is transportation, communications, electricity, gas, waterworks, wholesale and retail trade, banking and finance, services, and public administration.

Figures in parentheses are composition in percent.

Table 1.14. Net Domestic Product by Industry (¥ million)

	Total	Primary	Secondary	Tertiary
1885	750	339	110	301
	(100)	(45.2)	(14.7)	(40.1)
1890	1,024	495	157	371
	(100)	(48.4)	(15.3)	(36.2)
1895	1,329	567	241	521
	(100)	(52.7)	(18.1)	(39.2)
1900	2,177	858	462	857
	(100)	(39.4)	(21.2)	(39.4)
1905	2,669	877	563	1,229
	(100)	(32.9)	(21.1)	(46.1)
1910	3,448	1,119	898	1,431
	(100)	(32.5)	(26.0)	(41.5)
1915	5,765	1,593	1,867	2,305
	(100)	(27.6)	(32.4)	(40.0)
1920	13,363	4,036	3,887	5,440
	(100)	(30.2)	(29.1)	(40.7)
1925	14,896	4,193	4,039	6,664
	(100)	(28.1)	(27.1)	(44.7)
1930	12,311	2,163	3,893	6,255
	(100)	(17.6)	(31.6)	(50.8)
1935	15,709	2,844	5,750	7,115
	(100)	(18.1)	(36.6)	(45.3)
1940	34,664	6,527	16,419	11,718
	(100)	(18.8)	(47.4)	(33.8)

Source: Ohkawa et al. [100], appendix table 8.
Note: Figures in parentheses are composition in percent.

sector the largest increases were, of course, in manufacturing, while the tertiary sector's largest increases were in commercial activities, with transportation and communications second. Another interesting development is the changing shares of the secondary and tertiary sectors. From 1905 to 1920 the secondary sector's share was larger. But in the interwar years from 1920 to 1935, the tertiary sector's share was expanding. Then in 1940, during the war, the secondary sector naturally took priority again.

The data on net domestic product by sector show the share of tertiary industry to have been high in the earliest available data. Even if the data for 1885 are somewhat high, one still cannot deny that tertiary industry already had a large share of net domestic product even in the early Meiji years. Until the Pacific War the tertiary sector's share fluctuated around the 40% level. Its share declined in good times and rose in bad times.

The agricultural sector, which occupied by far the largest portion of the population, produced just under 40% of net product as the twentieth century began, and subsequently its share of product declined to below 20% in 1940. The secondary sector provided less than 10% of product in 1885, rose to about the same level as the primary sector by the time of World War I (both being around 30%), declined a bit in the 1920s, and then reached almost 50% by 1940.

There are many who identify modernization with industrialization, and indeed, the core of modern industry is the factory system of manufacture. However, the above figures force us to recognize the importance of tertiary industry even in a developing economy.

Table 1.15 contrasts the relative positions of heavy industry, defined as the total of chemical, steel, nonferrous metals, and machinery indus-

Table 1.15. Manufacturing Output and Its Composition (¥ million)

	Heavy industry	Food products	Textiles	Total
1885	47.1	119.7	82.1	282.0
	(16.7)	(42.5)	(29.1)	
1890	73.4	156.1	160.0	433.8
	(16.9)	(35.9)	(36.9)	
1895	106.7	219.0	370.7	744.2
	(13.8)	(28.3)	(47.9)	
1900	191.4	429.1	428.5	1,181.2
	(16.2)	(36.3)	(36.3)	
1905	309.9	494.3	458.8	1,420.7
	(21.8)	(34.8)	(32.3)	
1910	434.4	707.6	700.3	2,072.9
	(21.0)	(34.1)	(33.8)	
1915	840.5	784.4	955.1	2,880.3
	(29.2)	(27.2)	(33.2)	
1920	3,202.7	2,285.9	3,286.9	9,579.2
	(33.4)	(23.9)	(34.3)	
1925	2,390.5	2,582.8	3,974.7	10,100
	(23.7)	(25.6)	(39.3)	
1930	2,896	2,206	2,709	8,838
	(32.8)	(25.0)	(30.6)	
1935	6,516	2,461	4,356	14,968
	(43.5)	(16.4)	(29.1)	
1940	19,569	4,058	5,579	33,252
	(58.8)	(12.2)	(16.8)	

Sources: Shinohara [126], and Tsūshō Sangyō Shō Chōsa Tōkei Bu [161].
Note: Figures in parentheses show percentage of total output.

tries, and light industry, represented by food products and textiles. The table shows the share of heavy industry in manufacturing to have reached about 20% by the end of the Meiji era, while that of textiles declined from almost 50% at the end of the nineteenth century to about 30% by 1905 and then stayed there. The food industry produced mostly traditional products like *miso* (bean paste), soy sauce, and *sake* (rice wine) and throughout the prewar period had a share of manufacturing rivaling that of textiles. During World War I the share of heavy industry grew temporarily, but for the most part the Meiji era industrial structure was maintained until 1930 and the coming of the worldwide depression. Then in the 1930s, a sharp change occurred with the rapid expansion of heavy industry. One reason was military demand but we should not

Table 1.16. Net Output per Employee by Industry (¥)

	All industries	Primary sector	Secondary sector		Tertiary sector
1885	34	22	—	61	—
	(1.00)	(0.65)		(1.83)	
1890	44	32	—	71	—
	(1.00)	(0.71)		(1.60)	
1895	56	36	—	92	—
	(1.00)	(0.65)		(1.65)	
1900	89	54	—	154	—
	(1.00)	(0.61)		(1.73)	
1905	107	52	151		340
	(1.00)	(0.49)	(1.42)		(3.19)
1910	135	68	220		363
	(1.00)	(0.50)	(1.63)		(2.68)
1915	219	102	382		512
	(1.00)	(0.47)	(1.74)		(2.34)
1920	490	281	620		1,016
	(1.00)	(0.57)	(1.26)		(2.07)
1925	530	298	639		1,036
	(1.00)	(0.56)	(1.21)		(1.95)
1930	416	148	633		853
	(1.00)	(0.36)	(1.52)		(2.05)
1935	503	196	844		846
	(1.00)	(0.39)	(1.68)		(1.68)
1940	1,067	449	1,999		1,516
	(1.00)	(0.42)	(1.87)		(1.42)

Sources: Calculated from tables 1.13 and 1.14.
Note: Figures in parentheses give ratio of sectoral rate to rate for all industries.

overlook technical progress and a rising demand from society for heavy industrial products. Rather, this period is when the full-scale heavy industrialization so visible in the postwar era began.

Colin Clark's formulation of Petty's law—that the labor force moves from primary industry to more remunerative secondary industry, then to still more remunerative tertiary industry—applies in general to Japanese development. Table 1.16 shows this by using data from tables 1.14 and 1.15 to calculate output per employee in each of these sectors. Certainly in the nineteenth century the secondary and tertiary sectors—predominantly the latter—had much higher income than the primary sector. But after World War I the differences among the sectors shrank, and the secondary sector at times even had output higher than the tertiary, e.g., after 1935. Clark's thesis is that the high productivity in the tertiary sector attracted people to it, but there were some periods when this was not necessarily the case.

Primary Industry, Traditional Industry, and the Labor Market

This section summarizes Japan's prewar occupational structure as related to the industrial structure. As seen previously, the increases in employed population even in the early Meiji years were concentrated in the secondary and tertiary sectors. However, one should not jump to the conclusion that these secondary and tertiary industries consisted entirely of modern manufacturers, banks, or foreign trade companies. Many of these enterprises (such as traditional manufacturers, carpenters, plasterers, rickshaw drivers, small urban shopkeepers, and noodle vendors) were family businesses that at times employed a few hired people. In fact such enterprises continue to exist throughout Japan.

Table 1.17 uses occupational subclass data from the first national census of 1920 and separates the nonprimary labor force into three categories: modern industry, old traditional industry, and new traditional industry. Modern industry includes those industries introduced from abroad after the start of the Meiji era (including railroads, telephone and telegraph, steam-powered shipping, banking, insurance, and foreign trade companies), along with activities dependent on foreign technology (such as medicine and public administration). Old traditional industry includes those industries retaining traditional management methods intact, e.g., carpentry and plastering in the construction trades, wholesale and retail commerce, and cottage industry. New traditional industries are those originally introduced from abroad but for which the technology or management methods were transformed into something approaching those of the traditional, e.g., silk reeling and textile industries, painting, tinsmithing, shoemaking, breadbaking, and so forth.

Table 1.17 shows the employed population in nonprimary industries

Table 1.17. Composition of Employed Population in Industry, 1920

	Employees (thousands)				Composition (total employed population = 100)			
	Modern	Old traditional	New traditional	Total	Modern	Old traditional	New traditional	Total
Primary industry	424.5	14,686.7	—	15,111.1	1.6	53.9	—	55.4
Manufacturing	1,722.9	1,790.8	949.2	4,462.9	6.3	6.6	3.5	16.4
Construction	7.9	665.0	62.1	735.0	0.0	2.4	0.2	2.7
Electricity and gas	92.3	—	—	92.3	0.3	—	—	0.3
Secondary industry	1,823.1	2,455.9	1,011.3	5,290.2	6.7	9.0	3.7	19.4
Commerce	40.4	1,935.5	139.6	2,115.5	0.1	7.1	0.5	7.8
Finance and insurance	94.3	36.2	—	130.5	0.3	0.8	—	0.5
Transportation and communications	482.8	298.7	255.7	1,037.2	1.8	1.1	0.9	3.8
Services	460.6	1,161.2	203.2	1,825.0	1.7	4.3	0.7	6.6
Household servants	—	655.2	—	655.2	—	2.4	—	2.4
Day workers	—	441.4	—	441.4	—	1.6	—	1.6
Public administrators	568.9	—	—	568.9	2.1	—	—	2.1
Tertiary industry total	1,647.1	4,528.2	598.4	6,773.7	6.0	16.6	2.2	24.8
Unidentified	—	—	—	86.0	—	—	—	0.3
Total	3,894.6	21,609.7	1,609.7	27,261.1	14.2	79.5	5.9	100.0
Total excluding primary and unidentified	3,470.2	6,984.1	1,609.7	12,064.0	12.7	25.6	5.9	44.2

Source: Nakamura [76], p. 200, table 2.

in 1920 at slightly more than 12 million persons, or 44% of the total. Within the nonprimary sector the largest proportion were employed in old traditional industries (just under 7 million persons, or about 58% of nonprimary employment), with new traditional industries taking 1.6 million, and modern industries taking only 3.5 million. Let us give some examples from the old traditional industries. In manufacturing, blacksmiths and tinsmiths together numbered 180,000; sawyers and shingle makers, 90,000; coopers 70,000; fitters and joiners, 140,000; workers in construction and related activities, 670,000; those in commerce, 1,940,000; and ricksha, oxcart, and wagon drivers, and other transport workers, 300,000. In addition there were service industry workers such as restaurant keepers, barbers, *geisha,* and household servants. Many of these occupations have disappeared today but the number of self-employed is now far greater than at that time. For example, there are no longer any ricksha drivers but taxi drivers exist instead, and although the number of geisha has declined, bar hostesses have taken their places. Old traditional industries indeed do shrink but new traditional ones often succeed them.

Also, by subtracting employment in modern industry from total nonprimary employment, we can derive traditional industry employment and then trace its trends in the prewar period (see table 1.18). These data for the modern sector do not include banking, foreign trade, and medicine, and thus underestimate modern sector employment. And indeed, table 1.17 shows modern industry employment at 3.47 million in 1920, while table 1.18 shows an average of 3.04 million for 1916–25, or about 430,000 too low. But even with such discrepancies there are not likely to be large errors in reading the long-run trends in traditional employment from table 1.18. The table shows traditional sector employment to have risen greatly at the end of the nineteenth century and to have leveled off after 1900. Meanwhile, the number of workers in modern industry was rising rapidly in both periods. But in the 1910s, which include World War I, both traditional and modern sectors expanded rapidly while primary sector employment fell rapidly. This can be interpreted as the labor force movement among industries that accompanies urbanization. In the 1920s, growth in the modern sector was blunted but growth in the traditional sector did not wane. Population accumulated in the cities, and people looked for work in the traditional sector. This phenomenon occurred again after World War II. As one reason for these trends, in addition to urbanization, we can cite the rise in society's demand for secondary and particularly for tertiary products. In addition, however, we must also consider labor supply conditions. That is, the labor force that flowed into the cities seeking employment hoped to find job opportunities in the modern industries which were not

Table 1.18. Population Structure of Primary, Modern, and Traditional Industry

	Workers (thousands)					Rates of increase over previous period					Composition (A=100)			
	Number employed A	Primary total B	Nonprimary C=(A)-(B)	Modern industry D	Traditional industry E=(C)-(D)	A	B	C	D	E	B	C	D	E
1872–75	21,414	15,555	5,859	—	—	—	—	—	—	—	72.6	27.4	—	—
1876–80	21,730	15,624	6,106	—	—	1.5	0.4	4.0	—	—	71.9	28.1	—	—
1881–85	22,115	15,650	6,465	406	6,059	1.8	0.2	5.9	—	—	70.8	29.2	1.8	27.5
1886–90	22,683	15,625	7,059	468	5,591	2.6	-0.2	9.2	15.3	8.8	68.9	31.1	2.1	29.1
1891–95	23,458	15,509	7,949	681	7,268	3.4	-0.7	12.6	45.5	10.3	66.1	33.9	2.9	31.0
1896–1900	24,119	15,618	8,501	906	7,595	2.8	0.7	6.9	33.0	4.5	64.8	35.2	3.8	31.5
1901–05	24,752	15,843	8,909	1,165	7,744	2.6	1.4	4.8	28.6	2.0	64.0	36.0	4.7	31.3
1906–10	25,288	16,004	9,784	1,554	7,730	2.1	1.0	4.2	33.4	-0.2	63.3	36.7	6.1	30.6
1911–15	25,950	15,760	10,190	1,965	8,225	2.6	-1.5	9.8	26.4	6.4	60.7	39.3	7.6	31.7
1916–20	26,860	14,320	12,540	2,837	9,703	3.5	-9.1	23.1	44.4	18.0	53.3	46.7	10.6	36.1
1921–25	27,778	13,675	14,103	3,237	10,866	3.4	-4.5	12.5	14.1	12.0	49.2	50.8	11.7	39.1
1926–30	28,906	13,833	15,073	3,475	11,598	4.1	1.2	6.9	7.4	6.7	47.9	52.1	12.0	40.1
1931–35	30,548	14,185	16,364	3,696	12,668	5.7	2.5	8.6	6.4	9.2	46.4	53.6	12.1	41.5
1936–40	31,972	13,904	18,068	—	—	4.7	-2.0	10.4	—	—	43.5	56.5	—	—

Sources and Notes: Primary is agriculture and forestry only, with fisheries in nonprimary, traditional industry. The source for employed population in agriculture and forestry population is Umemura [167]. Modern industry employment is defined as the total number employed in factories with 5 or more workers in the following industries (sources given in parentheses): For mining, data for 1882–98 are linear interpolations based on a figure of 50,000 for 1882 (Nōshōmu Shō [98] and Shōkō Shō [136]). For education, data are from (Tōyō Keizai Shimpō Sha [154]); for civil service, from (Emi and Shionoya [22]); for private railroads and electricity, from (Minami [64]); for the maritime industry, from (Rōdō Undō Shiryō Hensan Kai [116]); for municipal and village government, from (Tōyō Keizai Shimpō Sha [154]). Data for 1882 are collected in Yamaguchi [171], for 1894–98 in Nōshōmu Shō [98], and thereafter Tsūshō Sangyō Shō [161]. Gaps are filled by linear interpolation.

in a period of stagnation. But workers often could not survive if unemployed, and, with no leeway to be choosy about working conditions, they had to take what jobs were available. Thus, the 1920s saw the emergence of the so-called dual structure.

In light of these conditions in the cities, why then did population flow off the farm? The basic reason was lack of space. The arable area in farm villages was small, and primary industry could support only a limited number of people. The limit can be thought of as the point where the income of those who had left the farm became equal to the average product of those who stayed behind. Thus, past this point, when demand for labor existed in nonprimary sectors, farm labor usually responded by leaving the farm. After the population outflow the average product in agriculture rose, equaling a substantial proportion of urban income. But after this, even if incomes in the cities fell, it was unthinkable for the population that had left farms to return on a large scale. This was because remaining farmers did not want their average product fall back. Farm population did rise somewhat during depressions but this was mostly due to natural increase. The emigrants had to stay in the cities. Table 1.19 shows the percentage change from the previous year of five-year moving averages of employed population in primary and nonprimary sectors. Despite the large outflows of farm population in the prosperous first half of the 1890s and last half of the 1920s, both were periods of depression. There were no large reverse migrations back to the farms.

JAPAN AND THE WORLD

External Trade and the Balance of Payments

Money supply is supposedly controlled by authorities through monetary policy, but the predominant true influence on the money supply in prewar Japan was that of gold (specie) reserves and, after 1931, foreign exchange reserves (especially the U.S. dollar). As seen in figure 1.3, the Japanese economy ran a slight deficit on international payments until the first Sino–Japanese War. Table 1.20 shows the yen chronically depreciating versus the U.S. dollar even from the start of the Meiji era. In 1876, at the time of the establishment of the abortive national banking system, the yen was fixed at 3.75 grams of gold but was not made convertible. With the establishment of the Bank of Japan in 1882, the nation went on a de facto silver standard, but the decline in the world price of silver relative to gold thereafter meant piecemeal devaluation of the yen versus gold. In 1897, after the first Sino–Japanese War, Japan went on the gold standard with the yen valued at 1.875 grams of gold. As

Table 1.19. Population and Labor Force Distribution and Growth (Year-to-year growth rate of five-year moving averages)

	Total population	Gainfully employed	Agriculture and forestry	Nonagriculture
1875	0.6	0.3	0.1	0.7
1876	0.7	0.3	0.1	0.9
1877	0.8	0.4	0.1	1.0
1878	0.8	0.4	0.1	1.1
1879	0.8	0.4	0.1	1.1
1880	0.8	0.3	0.1	0.8
1881	0.8	0.3	0.1	0.9
1882	0.8	0.4	0.0	1.3
1883	0.9	0.4	0.0	1.5
1884	0.9	0.4	0.0	1.5
1885	0.8	0.5	0.0	1.6
1886	0.8	0.5	0.0	1.7
1887	0.8	0.5	0.0	1.9
1888	0.8	0.6	0.0	2.0
1889	0.9	0.7	0.1	2.1
1890	0.9	0.7	0.1	2.3
1891	0.9	0.7	0.1	2.2
1892	0.9	0.6	0.1	1.9
1893	0.8	0.6	0.1	1.7
1894	0.9	0.6	0.1	1.5
1895	0.9	0.6	0.1	1.5
1896	1.0	0.6	0.2	1.4
1897	1.1	0.5	0.2	1.2
1898	1.1	0.5	0.2	1.2
1899	1.1	0.5	0.1	1.3
1900	1.2	0.5	0.2	1.2
1901	1.2	0.5	0.1	1.3
1902	1.3	0.5	0.0	1.5
1903	1.3	0.5	0.0	1.4
1904	1.2	0.5	0.3	0.7
1905	1.1	0.5	0.2	0.9
1906	1.0	0.4	0.2	1.0
1907	1.0	0.4	0.0	1.2
1908	1.1	0.4	−0.1	1.2
1909	1.1	0.0	−0.2	1.6
1910	1.3	0.5	−0.2	1.5
1911	1.3	0.5	−0.1	1.6
1912	1.4	0.6	0.0	1.5

Table 1.19 (*continued*)

	Total population	Gainfully employed	Agriculture and forestry	Nonagriculture
1913	1.4	0.6	−0.9	3.2
1914	1.4	1.1	−1.3	3.9
1915	1.4	0.8	−1.2	3.7
1916	1.3	0.7	−2.4	5.1
1917	1.1	0.6	−2.4	4.6
1918	1.0	0.6	−1.6	3.3
1919	1.0	0.7	−1.2	2.8
1920	1.1	0.6	−1.4	3.0
1921	1.1	0.7	−0.8	2.4
1922	1.2	0.6	−0.7	2.0
1923	1.3	0.7	−0.6	2.0
1924	1.3	0.7	−0.8	2.3
1925	1.4	0.6	0.6	1.8
1926	1.4	0.7	0.3	1.0
1927	1.5	0.9	0.3	1.5
1928	1.5	1.1	0.6	1.5
1929	1.5	1.0	0.8	1.2
1930	1.5	1.2	1.1	1.3
1931	1.5	1.2	0.6	1.6
1932	1.5	1.1	0.1	2.0
1933	1.4	1.0	−0.3	2.2
1934	1.9	1.1	−0.4	2.4
1935	1.2	0.9	−1.1	2.6
1936	1.0	0.8	−1.1	2.4
1937	0.9	0.9	−1.1	2.4
1938	0.8	1.9	−0.1	3.3

Source: Calculated from Umemura [167] or Ohkawa et al. [O], table A53.

a result of the developments up to 1897, exports expanded and virtual balance on the trade account was maintained.

However, after establishment of the gold standard in 1897 based on the ¥311 million (£32.9 million) indemnity from China following the first Sino–Japanese War, the.yen was fixed slightly weaker than ¥2/ U.S.$. Exports began to stagnate and a major deficit emerged in the balance of payments. The recession of 1900 was the first sign of this.

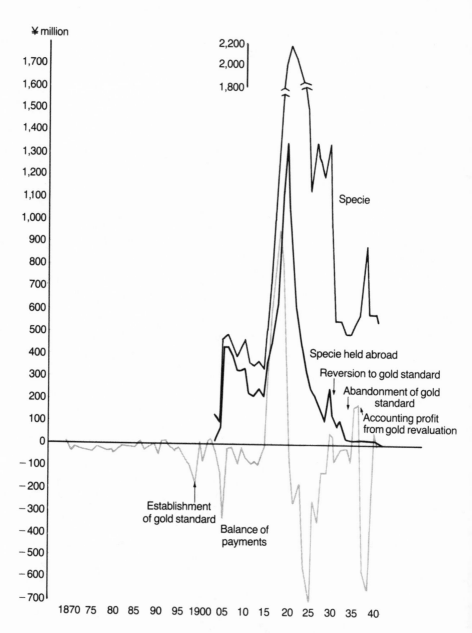

Figure 1.3. Balance of Payments and Specie Reserves.

Table 1.20. Value of the Yen vis-à-vis the Pound and the Dollar

	£/¥ 100			$/¥ 100		
	High	Low	Avg	High	Low	Avg
1874	21.3	20.4	20.9	103.0	100.0	101.5
1875	20.6	19.9	20.2	104.5	96.0	100.2
1876	21.1	18.8	19.9	101.5	90.0	95.6
1877	20.8	19.5	20.1	100.0	93.5	96.7
1878	19.5	17.8	18.6	95.0	86.5	90.7
1879	19.4	17.4	18.3	74.5	85.0	89.6
1880	19.4	18.3	18.8	95.3	89.3	92.2
1881	19.0	18.2	18.6	91.3	86.5	89.9
1882	19.1	18.0	18.5	93.0	88.0	90.5
1883	19.0	18.0	18.5	91.5	87.7	89.6
1884	18.7	17.7	18.2	90.7	86.5	88.6
1885	17.9	16.7	17.3	87.0	81.7	84.3
1886	16.9	14.9	15.9	81.7	72.7	77.1
1887	16.7	15.2	15.9	80.3	73.0	76.5
1888	15.8	14.9	15.3	76.3	72.5	74.4
1889	16.2	15.1	15.6	78.8	73.5	76.1
1890	19.2	15.3	17.1	93.0	74.7	83.4
1891	17.4	15.5	16.4	84.7	75.0	79.7
1892	15.5	13.4	14.4	75.0	65.5	70.1
1893	13.8	11.4	12.5	67.0	54.5	60.4
1894	11.5	5.7	8.1	55.0	47.3*	55.4
1895	11.2	9.6	10.4	54.5	46.7	50.5
1896	11.1	10.3	10.7	52.0	49.6	50.8
1897	10.6	9.9	10.3	51.5	48.1	49.8
1898	10.2	10.0	10.1	49.6	48.5	49.1
1899	10.3	10.1	10.2	50.0	49.0	49.6
1900	10.1	10.1	10.1	49.5	49.0	49.2
1901	10.2	10.1	10.1	49.6	49.1	49.4
1902	10.3	10.1	10.2	50.0	49.4	49.7
1903	10.3	10.1	10.2	50.9	49.0	49.5
1904	10.1	10.0	10.1	49.3	48.6	48.9
1905	10.3	10.1	10.2	49.9	49.1	49.5
1906	10.2	10.1	10.2	49.5	49.3	49.4
1907	10.2	10.2	10.2	49.6	49.3	49.4
1908	10.2	10.2	10.2	49.5	49.3	49.4
1909	10.2	10.2	10.2	49.6	49.4	49.5
1910	10.2	10.1	10.1	49.6	49.3	49.4

Table 1.20 (*continued*)

	£/¥ 100			$/¥ 100		
	High	Low	Avg	High	Low	Avg
1911	10.2	10.2	10.2	49.4	49.3	49.3
1912	10.2	10.2	10.2	49.6	49.3	49.4
1913	10.2	10.1	10.2	49.6	49.1	49.4
1914	10.2	10.0	10.1	49.5	49.0	49.2
1915	10.5	10.0	10.3	49.7	48.0	48.9
1916	10.6	10.5	10.5	50.4	49.7	50.1
1917	10.7	10.6	10.7	50.9	50.4	50.6
1918	11.0	10.7	10.8	52.1	50.9	51.5
1919	12.7	10.7	11.6	51.9	49.9	50.9
1920	14.3	11.5	12.8	50.6	47.7	49.2
1921	13.5	11.3	12.3	48.3	47.9	48.1
1922	11.4	11.2	11.3	48.5	47.5	48.0
1923	11.3	10.2	10.7	49.0	48.5	48.7
1924	11.3	8.1	9.6	48.3	38.5	43.1
1925	9.0	8.0	8.5	43.5	38.5	40.9
1926	10.1	9.0	9.5	48.7	43.5	46.1
1927	10.1	9.3	9.7	49.0	45.6	47.3
1928	9.8	9.2	9.5	48.0	44.7	46.3
1929	10.0	9.0	9.5	49.0	43.7	46.3
1930	10.2	10.1	10.1	49.4	49.0	49.2
1931	10.1	10.1	10.1	49.4	34.5	41.3
1932	10.7	6.1	8.1	37.3	19.7	27.2
1933	6.2	5.8	6.0	31.3	20.3	17.9
1934	5.9	5.8	5.9	30.4	28.5	29.4
1935	5.8	5.8	5.8	29.1	27.7	28.4
1936	5.8	5.8	5.8	29.5	28.5	29.0
1937	5.8	5.8	5.8	29.3	28.5	28.9
1938	5.8	5.8	5.8	29.3	27.0	28.1
1939	6.1	5.8	6.0	27.4	23.3	25.3
1940	7.4	5.8	6.6	23.4	23.4	23.4

Source: Nihon Ginkō Tōkei Kyoku [85].
*Source says 57.25 here but this would put the low for the year above the high.

And with the Russo–Japanese War requiring ¥2 billion in military expenses, ¥1 billion of which was borrowed in foreign currencies, the balance of payments thereafter was strained by repayments of principal and interest. In response, passive economic policies were adopted from 1910 to 1913, producing stagnation in the domestic economy.

But the outbreak of World War I changed the picture completely. Owing to strong exports and a surging price level, the trade balance showed a large surplus, credit extended to foreign countries rose, and specie reserves climbed to ¥2.2 billion. But when the war ended, the trade account reversed completely and specie reserves immediately began to dwindle. These were the developments that underlay the tight economic policies of the 1920s. The 1930 policy of removing the gold embargo attempted to restore the economy by returning to the gold standard and implementing strict austerity. (Japan had left the gold standard during World War I along with other major countries.) However, the effort failed with the onslaught of the Great Depression and the worldwide collapse of the gold standard late in 1931, and after this debacle a controlled foreign exchange system was instituted. The yen fell substantially when the nation went off the gold standard at the end of 1931, and exports grew well during the rest of the 1930s.

It of course goes without saying that trade and the expansion of demand in foreign markets were important in the development of domestic industry. Table 1.21 gives details. In early years all that could be exported were primary products such as silk thread, tea, and marine products, along with minerals such as coal and copper (not shown in table 1.21). But soon ceramics, matting, silk garments, and other traditional products were added to these. After the first Sino–Japanese War cotton thread, a modern industry product, was exported, and soon cotton fabric, silk thread, and silk textiles became the main export products.

The history of exports is very much the history of which industries were the star performers of their eras. The proportion of exports in GNE rose from 6% in 1885 to 20% by 1910, reflecting the strong growth of the industries that were the major exporters. Silk reeling and cotton textile products remained Japan's representative industries until the start of the Showa era (1926–), when they began to be displaced by emerging heavy and chemical industries. The power of exports to spur the entire economy was important. As can be understood from the theory of the export multiplier, export growth stimulates the entire economy. Like heavy and chemical industries in the postwar period, silk reeling and cotton textiles were the key industries of the prewar period.

Moreover, there is a common characteristic of prewar and postwar Japanese trade that should be pointed out: both eras' exports were based on processing trade. Silk reeling is the only exception to this. Raw materials were imported, processed, and exported with value added. Table 1.21 demonstrates this fact too, as seen in the structure of imports. To cite the extreme example of cotton spinning, the 1929 *Kōgyō Tōkei Hyō* (Census of Manufactures) shows that raw materials costs for the industry were 61% of total costs; this ratio rose later on, reaching 70% in the

Table 1.21. Major Components of Japanese Trade (Percentage of total trade)

	1870	1880	1890	1900	1910	1920	1930	1940
Exports (total = 100)								
Marine products	7.4	8.1	5.2	1.8	1.6	0.9	2.6	2.9
Tea	31.0	26.4	9.0	4.4	3.3	0.9	0.5	0.7
Cotton thread	—	—	0.0	10.3	9.8	7.8	1.0	1.6
Cotton textiles	0.0	0.1	0.3	2.8	4.5	17.2	18.5	10.9
Silk thread	29.4	30.3	19.8	21.8	28.4	19.6	28.4	12.2
Silk textiles	0.0	0.1	1.7	9.1	7.2	8.1	4.5	1.0
Synthetic fibers and textiles	—	—	—	—	—	—	2.4	3.6
Ceramics	0.2	1.7	1.8	1.2	1.2	1.6	1.8	1.7
Cement	—	—	—	0.1	0.3	0.5	0.7	0.4
Machinery	—	—	0.0	0.0	0.9	2.6	1.4	13.0
Ships	—	—	—	0.1	0.1	0.8	0.4	1.0
Steel	—	—	—	—	—	0.7	0.6	—
Imports (total = 100)								
Rice	43.3	1.2	15.1	3.1	1.9	0.7	1.3	5.7
Wheat	0.0	0.0	0.0	0.3	0.6	1.2	2.7	0.6
Sugar	9.0	9.7	10.3	7.0	5.8	2.6	1.7	0.0
Wool	—	—	0.5	1.4	3.0	5.2	4.8	3.0
Raw cotton	1.8	0.5	5.1	20.6	34.3	30.9	23.4	14.6
Coal	0.0	0.4	0.1	0.6	0.3	0.9	2.2	3.4
Crude oil	—	—	—	—	0.2	0.0	5.8	10.2
Iron ore	—	—	—	0.0	0.2	0.6	1.2	2.9
Scrap iron	—	—	—	—	—	0.2	0.1	5.2
Steel	0.7	4.6	2.7	7.6	7.0	11.3	6.1	—
Machinery	0.0	2.0	4.7	3.4	3.3	4.7	5.5	7.7

Sources: Calculated from Keizai Kikaku Chō Tōkei Ka [54], pp. 284–86, 292–94, and Tōyō Keizai Shimpō Sha [155].

1930s. Naturally imports had to rise if exports were to rise. In fact, the Japanese processing trade somewhat resembled that of England in that prewar Japan too was able to rely on some domestic resources such as coal. But there were differences as well, an advantageous one being that Japan could survive without food imports, and a disadvantageous one being that Japan had to export low value-added products at low prices.

It was Japan's deep ties with the world economy that made economic development possible; moreover, these ties to the international economy also helped determine the path economic development would take.

War, Colonies, and Imperialism
When Japan was opened to the world in the mid-nineteenth century, the Western powers were quite strong economically and militarily and were

expanding throughout the world both as traders and as colonists. This was the world of power politics. As a neophyte modern state, Japan had no choice but to resist the great powers, as expressed in the popular Meiji era slogan *fukoku kyōhei*, "a rich country and a strong army." The goal of being "a rich country" was not just for the benefit of the nation and the welfare of the people but also was essential for achieving the goal of "a strong army." It cannot be denied that the Meiji government strongly believed that railroads, communications facilities, and modern industry were all necessary for military strength. The Satsuma Rebellion of 1877 occasioned rapid construction of a communications network. The railroad trunk lines were built with military transport in mind— even to the extent of emphasizing the Chuo rail line through the middle of the nation over the Tokai line on the coast since the latter, according to General Headquarters, would be vulnerable to naval bombardment. Military circles rushed military preparations first against China and then against Russia. But the era cannot at all be seen as one ruled solely by the military. Fukoku kyōhei was in fact an element in a national consensus. Famous educator Yukichi Fukuzawa's slogan that Japan should "leave Asia and join the West" was merely another expression of the fukoku kyōhei consensus. And even the political parties of the early Diets that emphasized "building up of national resources" through cuts in military spending adopted this position as nothing but a political tool against the Satsuma and Chōshū factions in the government, and not as a denial of the goal of a strong army. The first Sino–Japanese War was precocious Japan's expression of its intention to "join the West," and the Russo–Japanese War, which ended the years of bitterness following the Tripartite Intervention, confirmed that intention. The two wars were the means by which Japan showed her will to walk the very same path as the Western powers.

The reason for developing this rather loose discussion of the international situation is to give a background for reexamination of the idea that Japanese capitalism had a very strongly military character. Military preparedness was absolutely essential to Japanese independence, and in order to join the ranks of Western powers it was necessary to employ the same policies of international power politics used by the Western nations. However, even if it is impossible to deny that this resulted in a hasty strengthening of the army at the expense of "enriching the country," it is still too arbitrary to say this was the essence of Japanese capitalism. Participation in international power politics made militarization unavoidable and forced unreasonable sacrifices on the economy.

Japan sent troops abroad more than ten times in the 50 years after 1895: for the first Sino–Japanese War, the Boxer Rebellion, the Russo–Japanese War, World War I, the Siberian Expedition, three times in connection with the Shantung Expedition, the Manchurian Incident, the

second Sino–Japanese War, and the Pacific War. The first Sino– Japanese War brought an indemnity of more than ¥300 million and possession of Taiwan; the Russo–Japanese War brought the southern half
of Sakhalin, and the Manchurian railway, along with the leased conces-
sions of Dairen and Port Arthur and annexation of Korea; World War I
brought trusteeship of South Pacific islands. The Manchurian Incident
established the puppet country, Manchukuo, while the second Sino-
–Japanese War and the Pacific War extended Japanese control through
north China, Burma, Indonesia, the Philippines, and the Solomon Islands, i.e., through the "Greater East Asia Co-Prosperity Sphere." At the
end of the Pacific War, however, all this was lost. Any discussion of the
economic development of prewar Japan must include a summary of the
economic effects of these wars.

First of all, in addition to direct war expenditures, preparatory armaments expenditures were needed. Table 1.22 gives data on military and
war expenses. As seen previously, the low growth period just after the
turn of the twentieth century was when military expenses were increasing, i.e., just after the first Sino–Japanese War and just before the Russo– Japanese War. This of course raised the tax burden but also brought
a rise in imports, deficits in the balance of payments, tight monetary
policy accompanied by the falling trend of real consumption growth
seen in table 1.7, and a slowdown in the overall rate of economic growth.
These circumstances were the basis for the opinion that the Japanese
domestic market was small and thus that foreign markets had to be
sought. Participation in World War I did little damage to the nation and
in fact occasioned a boom. Because of the wealth accumulated during
the war the "unwarranted" Siberian Expedition's continuation through
the early 1920s did not result in immediate economic disaster. Japan
participated in the Washington Conference of 1922 and in the disarmament that followed; this participation certainly lightened Japan's economic burdens during the international deflation of the 1920s.

But just when party governments seemed to have become the norm in
the years of Taisho democracy, the military began to reassert itself
against the background of the world depression and sparked the Manchurian Incident in 1931. As a general rule, of course, increased military
expenditures do not necessarily restrain economic growth. In times of
less than full employment such expenditures and their multiplier effects
promote recovery. The military expenditures of the early 1930s had this
effect. But the continued promotion of armaments expansion and then
actual entrance into war after reaching full employment, as happened in
the middle of 1930s, destroyed the welfare of the populace and even
squandered accumulated capital.

Japan's prewar expansionist policies that gambled on war can certainly

Table 1.22. Military Spending and the Tax Burden

	General account and temporary military expenses (A) ¥ million	Military spending and temporary military expenses (B) ¥ million	GNE (C) ¥ million	Composition*			Taxes		Tax burden*	
				$\frac{B}{A}$	$\frac{A}{C}$	$\frac{B}{C}$	Central government tax receipts (D) ¥ million	Total tax receipts (E) ¥ million	$\frac{D}{C}$	$\frac{E}{C}$
First six accounting periods	35.2	5.14	—	14.6	—	—	19.4	—	—	—
1873–77	65.1	10.59	—	16.3	—	—	60.1	—	—	—
78–82	65.9	10.93	—	16.6	—	—	58.3	88.1	—	—
83–87	76.7	16.3	808	21.3	9.5	2.0	63.6	94.8	7.8	11.7
88–92	80.7	23.6	1,028	29.3	7.9	2.3	66.8	97.1	6.5	9.4
93–97	217.3	137.4	1,542	63.2	14.1	8.9	77.5	119.0	5.0	7.7
98–1902	264.6	109.6	2,389	41.4	11.1	4.6	129.7	217.7	5.4	9.1
1903–07	927.8	620.7	3,171	66.9	29.3	19.5	218.3	334.9	7.5	10.9
08–12	583.5	196.2	4,142	33.6	14.1	4.7	330.7	503.1	8.0	12.2
13–17	831.4	413.7	5,896	49.8	14.1	7.0	361.0	559.3	6.1	9.5
18–22	2,067.9	1,352.1	14,729	65.4	14.0	9.2	770.9	1,291.2	5.2	8.8
23–27	1,894.7	756.4	15,807	39.9	12.0	4.8	871.1	1,507.9	5.5	9.5
28–32	1,707.2	519.2	14,886	30.4	11.5	3.5	815.2	1,417.2	5.5	9.5
33–37	2,977.3	1,686.7	18,552	56.7	16.0	9.1	1,000.3	1,624.1	5.4	8.8
38–42	19,345	11,957	31,392	61.8	61.6	38.1	3,804.7	4,617.5	12.1	14.7
43–45	39,758	20,906	69,415	52.6	57.3	30.1	9,946.8	10,892.8	14.3	15.7

Sources: Okura Shō [106], pp. 137, 163. On taxes, see Nihon Ginkō [85].
* In percent.

be called imperialism. But let us add a word on the idea that the root of imperialist policy is necessarily the search for profits by "monopoly capital." At least in Japan's case it is difficult to find instances of a resort to war for the expansion of economic markets or to obtain resources. The opening of the Pacific War in 1941 was a response to the U.S. embargo on oil exports to Japan, and the goal of the war was to secure oil from Southeast Asia. But this, too, can be seen as more a military than an economic motive. One school of thought says that the nature of a war corresponds to a nation's level of economic development, and thus the Russo–Japanese War would have to be called an imperialist one whereas the first Sino–Japanese War would be more a nationalistic one. Another school of thought contests this view but this author does not think such discussion important. In an international environment where imperialist expansion was the rule, it is not likely that a precocious late-developing country would have the leisure to heed to the desires of domestic firms. The financial circles that controlled the *zaibatsu* (financial cliques) and big business were timid about both the Russo–Japanese and Pacific wars and were usually skeptical when it came to matters of national power.

But this of course does not mean that there was no connection between the economy and imperialist expansion. Even when the acquisition of economic rights was not an issue when wars were begun, once actual inroads had been made into an area, firms always followed, pursued their interests, and established commercial rights. Firms attempt to maximize profits under the given conditions, and adapting to a changed environment and seeking profits is natural behavior. Faits accomplis were respected and the rights gained truly became the objects of national protection. The "Manchurian rights and privileges" redeemed with the blood of "100,000 souls" in the Russo–Japanese War are precisely of this character. Economics certainly cooperated with imperialism. But it is too dogmatic to analyze all wars as having economic motives as their basis.

Discussion of the economic meaning of prewar Japanese colonies is also difficult but the following points can be made. Japanese in control of colonies largely ignored local customs and carried out policies favoring the home country and home country nationals. Japanese capital usually took the lion's share of projects it participated in. The sugar industry on Taiwan is an example; in this case Japanese sugar growers got the better land, and local farmers had to become tenants of the sugar refiners. In Korea, the Japanese landownership system was introduced suddenly, and an important absentee landlord firm, the Tōyō Takushoku Company, was created and took possession of large amounts of unowned land. After such experiences, one can easily understand why even today disaffection toward Japanese remains. But from the Japanese point of view it cannot necessarily be said that the possession of colonies produced benefits for the Japanese economy as a whole, such as those produced by India for the British Empire. A thorough evaluation of Japanese colonies must await further research. (However, the interested reader may wish to consult Tadao Yanaihara's *Teikokushugi-ka no Taiwan* [176], which is the classic work. More recent efforts include *Chiang Ping-kun* [16], Tu Chiao-Yen [162], and Mizoguchi [67].)

PART ONE □ THE ERA OF BALANCED GROWTH FROM THE MEIJI RESTORATION TO WORLD WAR I

Two □ The Start of Economic Growth

ECONOMIC ACHIEVEMENTS OF THE EDO ERA

Population, Education, and Welfare

When considering what factors brought long-term economic growth after the Meiji Restoration, we must first evaluate the economic bequest of the Edo period (1600–1868). The popular image of the Edo period economy has been one of relative stagnation but this is not correct. There has been much progress recently in statistical analysis of the Edo period using techniques of quantitative economic history; as a representative work let us here use Akira Hayami's *Kinsei Nōson no Rekishi Jinkōgakuteki Kenkyū (Historical Demography of Early Modern Farm Villages* [35]), from which table 2.1 is constructed. The data analyze the Suwa district of Nagano prefecture, and from the data we can infer Edo period population trends and see how rapidly farm village society was changing.

Until recently it was accepted that the population of Japan at the start of the Edo period was about 18 million and then rose to about 32 million by the end of the period. This is derived from the estimate of grain production capacity at 18 million *koku* (1 koku = 4.96 bushels = 180 liters), with 1 koku assumed to be enough to support one person for a year. Hayami, however, says there is no basis for saying that 1 koku will support one person; rather, he takes surviving population data, calculates growth rates from them, and extrapolates backward, estimating a population of about 10 million at the start of the Edo period. Population growth for years after 1721 is known, due to contemporary government (*bakufu*) surveys; these data show almost no growth at all. Thus, between 1600 and 1720, the population increased roughly 2.5 times (this comes to an annual growth rate of 0.77%), which also implies that agricultural product had to grow enough to feed the added population. In other words, farm village development had to have proceeded at a rapid tempo in the first half of the Edo period.

Next let us look at fluctuations in the farm village population of Suwa. First, there is an obvious long-run downtrend to both birth and death

45

Table 2.1. Population Trends of the Suwa District

	1690–1700	1700–50	1750–1800	1800–50	1850–70
Birth rate	33.1	26.9	23.3	23.1	22.0
Death rate	24.5	23.8	20.6	21.2	18.4
Average scale of household	7.04	6.34	4.90	4.42	4.25
Proportion of households with two or more couples among all households with couples	0.421	0.413	0.302	0.259	0.195
Percentage of population 15 years old and younger	34.2	31.2	28.0	27.8	29.8
Percentage of population 61 years old and older (males)	6.7	9.1	11.6	13.3	9.5
Percentage of households with servants	13.1 (1690)	1.8 (1750)	0.1 (1790)	—	—

	1690–1700	1700–25	1725–50	1751–75	1775–1800	1800–25	1825–50
Child mortality rate (10 years old and younger)	408.7	333.3	301.1	213.8	101.9	105.6	155.0

Source: Hayami [35].

rates. Moreover, the average size of a household declined rapidly from 7 persons in early years to just over 4 persons at the end of the period. The decline was particularly rapid in the eighteenth century. This shows that the number of wealthy landlords who had used many field hands or tenants in the medieval period, was declining rapidly. The proportion of multihousehold families (those with two couples or more) fell as years passed. The eighteenth century saw the dissolution of the extended family system, and the change toward the modern, nuclear family with one couple as the unit. If population tripled over the 270 years of the Edo period, while the number of persons per household fell from 7 to 4.25, the number of households had to quintuple. This implies that in the Suwa district there was a large increase in cultivated area based on the opening of new fields, and that the number of farm households grew as offshoots of old families became new families. Moreover, the average age of the male population advanced gradually. Life expectancy rose, and we can infer that the living environment improved. Also, the improvements in living environment and nutrition are shown by the decline in the child (10 years and younger) death rate from 40% at the start of the period to 10% at the end.

Hayami's analysis was epoch making in that it proved that the characteristic population trends of modern societies were evident in Edo period farm villages. As a result, the economy of the Edo period must be seen in a new light.

However, the population of the nation ceased its rapid growth in the early eighteenth century and only began growing rapidly again in the last half of the nineteenth century. This was true not only of the Suwa district but also is symmetric with Morita's estimates that population growth began again in the Tempo era (1830–44). Table 2.2 shows Japanese population since the end of the Edo period, and according to the Morita estimate the birth rate was already 3% by the end of that period. With the death rate at about 2%, he concludes a population growth rate of just under 1%. The Suwa district was probably not atypical, so the conditions of nationwide population growth were similar. But why did population growth stop in the eighteenth century? The climate did turn colder, and the Tohoku (northeast) region waned as a result. Moreover, there was the end of an era of expansion of new fields, and so the nation's food supply ceased rising. But at the same time, there was also a trend among the populace to improve its standard of living rather than expand the number of children.

Table 2.2. Population Trends (10,000 persons)

1872	3,481
1880	3,665
1890	3,990
1900	4,385
1910	4,918
1920	5,539
1930	6,387
1940	7,140

Sources: For 1872–1910, estimate by Cabinet Statistics Office of Population as of Jan. 1; after 1920, national census data, as of Oct. 1. See Bank of Japan [85].

On top of these population trends, the dispersion of education was an important aspect of Edo period society, particularly from the start of the nineteenth century to the end of the period. Ronald Dore's *Education in Tokugawa Japan* [C] reveals that the level of education in Edo period Japan was high. He estimates that in 1868, 43% of the male population and 10% of the female population were literate, surprising numbers when seen in international comparison. In 1875, 54% of males and 19% of females had been through elementary school. Even in England in 1837, after the industrial revolution, only one in four or five had been to school. This was the level achieved by the Japanese commoner class by mere tradition during the Edo period. According to Dore, the meaning of early education is that, at the very least, it trains people to be trained. Thus, once the Meiji period began, the Japanese could vigorously introduce foreign technology and civilization.

Moreover, by the last part of the Edo period, there was wide dissemination of Confucian, Buddhist, and practical ethics. These are not to be thought of as merely reactions to accepted social mores. For example, Confucian ethics were predominant in the warrior-bureaucrat (*bushi*) class, and Dore says that these ethics contributed to the creation of intellectual curiosity and the desire to pursue learning, along with contributing to the improvement of intellectual power.

A domestic variety of stoicism was widely respected and practiced by many warrior-bureaucrats. Take the example of Toshiakira Kawaji, a leading government finance official at the end of the Edo period. Despite his elite post Kawaji kept a strictly Spartan diet, led his subordinates in rigorous martial arts drills at the end of each working day, and in the evening was an avid student of Confucian classics. When the bakufu fell in 1868 Kawaji committed ritual suicide. Yet his stoic existence had not made him a narrow-minded individual. Representing Japan in negotiations with the United States during the late 1850s, he impressed Townsend Harris with his unflagging interest in and ready comprehension of all aspects of American thought, civilization, and technology (see Sato [119]).

Most of the best bureaucrats of the late Edo period showed a similar flexibility. Even though elite bureaucrats of the bakufu such as Ryūhoku Narushima and Joun Kirimoto did not serve in the Meiji government, they learned foreign languages, started newspapers, wrote books and pamphlets, and helped introduce foreign culture. Yukichi Fukuzawa's "theory of starving endurance" (*yase gaman no setsu*) continued the same stoic philosophy.

The merchant class of the Edo period has been called overly conservative, with the progressive elements in post-Restoration business alleged to have come from warrior-bureaucrats turned businessmen (Hirschmeier [D]). But this does not seem to be perfectly true because, for example, merchants and landlords were large stockholders in spinning companies. This demonstrates that they had accumulated large amounts of wealth by the end of the Edo period and that they did have the spirit of entrepreneurship and an interest in new industries. Even Omi district merchants, alleged to have been the most conservative, had this spirit, as seen in Shigeru Tonomura's novel *Raft (Ikada)* [151], in which a merchant family correctly perceives planned policy in the Tempo Reform (1841–43) and actively participates in colonization and trade with Hokkaidō.

Thus, society at the end of the Edo period was not at all stagnant; indeed internal conditions for development were being prepared. It is not possible to see development in the Meiji era as caused solely by foreign pressure. Foreign pressure only encouraged, accelerated, and modified domestic changes already in progress.

Agriculture and Industry
Let us now consider agriculture. If we assume, along with James Nakamura [M], that output per *tan* (1 tan = 0.245 acres = 0.099 hectares) was 1.6 koku in the early Meiji period, then Japan's agricultural productivity would have exceeded that of Southeast Asian countries of today. At the time of the 1873 land tax reform, a government survey also found output per tan of 1.6 koku. Thus, productivity of Japanese land was probably quite high.

Next is the problem of landownership. During the Edo period the agricultural class was officially separated into two groups, freeholders and landless peasants. But in addition to this there was great progress in developing new fields, and many urban merchants provided funds for such development. There was a rather large growth in cultivated area, given development of new fields by the shogunate, provincial lords (*daimyo*), and the merchants. In the latter case the merchant was the de facto owner of the property, and provincial lords tacitly allowed collection of tenant fees. There are few samples from the late Edo years showing the proportion of tenant land in the total, but Tsutomu Ōuchi has made some estimates [115]. In advanced areas such as the Kinki region, the tenancy rate is estimated at 31%; moderately developed areas displayed some variation but were generally around 20%; in backward areas such as Tohoku the tenancy rate is estimated at about 11%. It must be noted that tenancy did not rise quickly after the beginning of the Meiji era.

And what were tenancy fees? According to Takeo Ono's interviews with people of the time, about 37% of product went to land taxes, with 20–28% going to the landlord, leaving 35–43% for the cultivator. The system of parasitic landlords taking a high proportion of product was thus well established by the end of the Edo period, and landlords seemed to have substantial power even before the Meiji era began.

At the same time, agricultural products were becoming tradable commodities. Of the rice shipped to Osaka, the chief city for rice exchange at the end of the Edo period, three-fourths is said to have been *Kuramai* (warehouse rice) sold by provincial lords, and one-fourth *nayamai* (shed rice) sold by farmers. During these years farmers could afford to start eating much preferred rice and even had some surplus. Most of the nayamai traded was apparently sold by landlords, and it is certain that there was large-scale trade in rice by farmers. Even in the Edo market the one-fifth of the total traded as nayamai was a substantial amount. Prices fluctuated substantially, as seen in table 2.3, and many fortunes were made and lost in rice speculation.

In addition to rice many other products circulated as commodities,

Table 2.3. Wholesale Price Index of Osaka City since the End of the Tokugawa Period (1874–75 = 100)

1757	12.0
1781	10.0
1787	14.9 peak
1806	10.3 trough
1809	12.1 peak
1820	9.6 trough
1826	12.5
1827	11.6
1835	13.4
1837	22.1 peak
1844	13.1 trough
1856	15.4
1860	22.8
1864	38.8
1865	57.6
1866	102.6
1867	123.3
1868	110.9
1869	156.0 peak
1872	85.9 trough
1874	108.3 peak
1876	88.7 trough
1881	153.0 peak
1886	100.6 trough

Source: Saito [117].

e.g., cotton, indigo, coleseed, tobacco, and sweet potatoes. The first three were wiped out by foreign trade after the Meiji era started but were important commodities before that. Furthermore, the agricultural population had left the self-sufficiency stage and was being absorbed into a money economy. The typical product on farms was fertilizer, primarily varieties made from sardines. Many landlords doubled as fertilizer merchants, especially in the advanced areas. National markets were already established in salt, cotton, and cloth; old clothing was even sent from cities to be sold on farms.

Kentarō Nomura has analyzed farmers' occupations during the last years of the Edo period[93]. He shows that during these years 20–25% of farmers also managed second businesses. Running small bars (*izakaya*) was the major side activity, with rapeseed oil selling next, along with lumber vending, eating house management, bean curd making, confection making, tobacco selling, and sundry shopkeeping. Also within this class were carpenters, plasterers, and others who were really industrial workers, but it is certain that a fair portion of the farm population was connected with commercial activity. The landlord class, besides being the lowest rung in the provincial lords' administrative systems, were fertilizer merchants, pawnbrokers, moneylenders, doctors, and dry goods merchants; but most often they were brewers of sake, soy sauce, and bean paste. And there were also many examples of merchants becoming landlords. The farm villages at the end of the Edo period were participants in a commodity economy, and division of labor among farmers had begun in earnest.

In manufacturing during the late Edo period the *tonya* (wholesaler) system was predominant. The system of urban merchants lending reeling machinery and looms to farmers was fairly widespread by the end of the period, and this system of farm village manufactures continued in existence until the start of the Showa era (1926–). Typical examples include the silk cloth made in Kiryu and Ashikaga and the splashed pattern cloth (*kasuri*) of Hachioji and Tokorozawa. Examples of areas producing cotton textiles at the end of the Edo period are given by Toshio Furushima (see table 2.4). In silk cloth producing areas there was usually a merchant called the "thread master" (*itoshi*), who bought the cocoons and organized the farm families to reel the silk and weave the thread, then sold the finished cloth to buyers and distributed the proceeds. Even medium-sized thread masters had 70 or more families in their networks.

Economic Policy and Inflation
The city of Edo was said to have had an economy primarily based on gold while that of western Japan was based on silver; at any rate, the

Table 2.4. Examples of Farm Village Cotton Manufacturing at the End of the Edo Period

1. Areas prosperous during the Bunka and Tempo eras that were wiped out after foreign trade started:

   Shimono, Maoka: More than 380,000 tan (1 tan ~ 10 yards) produced in the Tempo era (ca. 1840) but harmed by imports thereafter. By 1848 reduced to 120,000 tan; by 1872–73 to 50,000, and by 1881 to 10,400.

   Ise, Matsuzaka

   Hoki, Kurakichi: Sent more than 80,000 tan to Osaka in 1811 and more than 300,000 in 1835; disappeared thereafter.

   Hoki, Hamanome: At height produced more than 150,000 tan.

   Inaba, Aoya

2. Declined temporarily after foreign trade began, then recovered using imported thread:

   Musashi, Tsukagoshi

   Izumi, Hine district

	Bunka era 1804–18	Tempo era 1830–44	Keio era 1865–68	Meiji 10 1878	Meiji 16 1883
Amount produced (1,000 tan)	100	172	72	225	213
Weavers (establishments)	20	40	32	68	65
Numbers of looms	420	1,000	570	1,220	1,250

Source: Furushima [27].

amount of money in circulation rose substantially during the Edo period. According to Kazuo Yamaguchi, the total amount of silver and gold currency in the nation in 1736 was 14.55 million *ryō* (the ryō being the unit of currency) and rose to ₽33.69 million in 1818, to ₽46.86 million in 1832, to ₽52.75 million in 1854, and to ₽130.72 million in 1869. In the 80 years from the eighteenth century into the nineteenth, the supply of currency more than doubled, while in the next 50 years of the nineteenth century it almost quadrupled. During these years there were several recoinages, as the central government sought to rescue itself from fiscal difficulties by debasing the coinage. Moreover, the increases in issue of provincial paper currency were phenomenal. Thus, the total amount of money in circulation grew substantially. This of course contributed to the impoverishment of the finances of both the central and local governments, but the active, expansionary policies also in the final analysis stimulated the national economy and made the economy more active. This does not mean that there were Keynesian-style thinkers at the time, but there were several fights between active expansionists and passive moralists. The former wished to promote industrial development and thought inflation a method to achieve it. The latter thought that development of the commodity economy would drown men's souls in luxury. The last hurrah of the moralists was the Tempo Reform executed by Tadakuni Mizuno, who was prime minister of the bakufu, but after its failure the nation's fiscal situation deteriorated so much that the moralist position never again had a chance to be implemented. Many local provinces were also having fiscal crises. Those that overcame the crises were the southwestern provinces, Satsuma, Choshu, Tosa, Hizen, and others (Akimoto [2], Nishikawa and Akimoto [92]). Satsuma re-established itself by repudiating interest payments on its loans from Osaka merchants and by establishing monopolies on major local products, e.g., sugar and Oshima pongee fabric. The province's leading role in the restoration of 1868 was based on this fiscal recovery but it also stimulated economic growth in the entire southwest region.

The last years of the Edo period were marked by virulent inflation. The reasons for the inflation were the inflow of silver into the nation (in return for gold exports) after trade relations with foreign nations were established and the overissue of paper currency mentioned above. The silver/gold ratio of Edo period Japan was about 3 to 1, while that in foreign countries was about 15½ to one. Thus, the value of silver in Japan was about five times what it was abroad. By bringing silver to Japan and exchanging it for gold (or taking gold from Japan, exchanging it for silver, and bringing the silver back), tremendous profits could be realized. The silver/gold parity in Japan was brought to the world level only in 1868, so that throughout the end of the Edo period this disadvantageous exchange continued. With silver flowing into the country rapidly, the silver prices of goods naturally rose.

Let us give a recent estimate (by Osamu Saito) of the general price index for Osaka. Prices did decline after the surge during the Tempo famine, but after the nation opened up to trade, inflation accelerated and in the last half of the 1860s reached alarming proportions. Because wages only doubled, the real wage rate in the last half of the 1860s fell disastrously. This invited violent social upheaval. After the Meiji Restoration, the central government issued Dajōkan (cabinet) currency, but this circulated with all the old currency and thus only added to inflation. When the new central government reorganized the nation's provinces into prefectures, it assumed the burden of all provincial currency, and unification of the currency became a major topic of debate.

INTO THE MEIJI ERA: THE LANDLORD SYSTEM AND CAPITAL ACCUMULATION

Meaning of the Landlord System

Farm villages of the early Meiji era bore a double burden, the land tax and tenant rents. One hypothesis says that the land tax funded government capital accumulation and that tenant rents funded landlords' capital accumulation; thus, this hypothesis continues, farm villages were the basis of Meiji capital accumulation (Yamada [170]). This theory has some truth to it but is also a gross oversimplification. A further investigation of farm conditions in historical perspective shows why.

The Meiji government went to great lengths to destroy the economic barriers of the Tokugawa era. In 1868 the government disestablished road inspection stations (sekisho) and guardhouses (bansho) and terminated wholesalers' monopolies (tonyakabu); in 1868 it disestablished the four-tier class system (samurai–farmer–artisan–merchant [shi-nō-kō-shō]) and replaced it with an aristocracy and a commoner class; in 1871 it permitted the general public to sell rice and gave freedom of crop choice and permission for court nobles and former warrior-bureaucrat families to manage agricultural, industrial, and commercial businesses; in 1872 it no longer required villages to maintain and provide fresh mounts for passing samurai (tenma sukego), lifted the ban on permanent alienation of land, disestablished classes among farmers, and permitted farmers to engage in other trades.

The next question was the land tax. One contemporary, Takahira Kanda, proposed basing the land tax on the purchase price of land, i.e., free market determination. He also hoped that free sales of land would inevitably result in the progressive amalgamation of tracts (Kanda [49], pp. 301–03). Thus, the price of land would become an investment of capital at a specified interest rate: yield per unit of land times the price of rice minus loss to chaff, fertilizer expenses, and taxes (Kajinishi et al. [48], pp. 292–93). Parts of the Kanda plan were adopted in the government's land tax reform law of 1873. This new law ensured fiscal revenue, established title to all lands and rights to real property, made land grants, standardized taxes at 3% of the purchase price of land, and clarified the legal basis of landlord–tenant relations. In connection with the reforms mentioned above, it also helped introduce the commodity economy into rural areas and freed labor for urbanization. In short, the land tax reform created the framework for a liberal economic system suitable to early capitalism.

The Meiji government's land tax reform resulted in some expansion of tenancy but its effects were not revolutionary. Rather, the tax system helped reconstruct the traditional land system with higher farm rents.

Yoshitarō Hirano has estimated proportions of lands held by tenants and freeholders (Hirano [37], pp. 54–55, 78). He gives a tenancy rate of 30.6% for 1872, and Saburō Shimoyama has revised this to 28.9% (Shimoyama [125], p. 3). Shimoyama's estimate extrapolates backward averages of tenancy growth rates of 1883–87 and 1887–92. But tenancy grew quickly between 1883 and 1887, owing to the Matsukata deflation (see p. 61 below), so even diluting this rate by averaging it with the rate of the next few years yields a growth rate that is too high. Thus, Shimoyama underrepresents tenancy in earlier years. In fact tenancy at the time of the land tax reform was around 30% and probably slightly higher.

Kazuo Yamaguchi has calculated tenancy at 35.9% for 1883–84 in the nation excluding Hokkaido and five prefectures (Ishikawa, Nara, Tokushima, Kagawa, and Kochi). Table 2.5 presents rates for 1887, 1892, 1897, and 1903 from various sources, and from 1908 to 1940 from the government's Census of Agriculture (*Nōji Tōkei Hyō*). The percentage of land under tenancy rose slightly on trend, peaking in the early 1930s. Tenancy jumped most during depressions, as in the Matsukata deflation, twice at the start of the 1900s, and took a large jump in the early 1930s. Moreover, regions differed greatly in tenancy rates. The early rates are lower in Tohoku, Kanto, and Kyushu (relatively underdeveloped regions) but surpass the national average later on. In western and southern districts, e.g., San'in and Kinki, early rates were high but did not increase greatly. This was also true in Hokuriku. The Kinki and Chugoku rates peaked near the start of the century, then declined. Shikoku had no stable trend. Thus, the landlord system, centering on tenancy, developed most visibly in northeastern areas such as Tohoku and Kanto.

Some scholars have claimed that the landlord system took shape in the early Meiji years. But if the rate of tenancy at the time of the tax reform was already more than 30%, a mere 5% increase in tenancy would have created the system. Moreover, tenancy did not spread in advanced areas, such as the Kinki region, where the commodity economy was already progressing. Thus, tenancy was not the true essence of the landlord system; in fact it hardly expanded at all in the Meiji years and certainly was not new.

But something new did happen: land became an object for investment; people now profited from its alienation. A few late Tokugawa landlords had profited from opening new fields (*shinden*) but many more landlords opened many more new fields in the early Meiji years. Landlords also benefited from the Matsukata deflation by acquiring land in forced sales for nonpayment of taxes and in foreclosure of mortgages. Paul Mayet, a foreign adviser to the Meiji government in the field of

Table 2.5. Percentage of Cultivated Land under Tenancy by Region

	1883–84	1887	1892	1897	1903	1908	1912	1917	1922	1927	1932	1937	1940
Hokkaido	—	18.7	23.4	36.1	49.6	51.5	47.1	48.1	47.4	51.3	53.9	49.1	46.5
Tohoku	25.1	29.9	32.4	32.7	36.5	40.4	41.0	41.9	43.5	44.1	47.0	46.8	46.7
Kanto	35.2	36.8	38.4	39.3	42.2	44.1	44.7	46.5	46.7	46.5	48.5	49.0	49.1
Hokuriku	46.3	50.0	49.2	47.1	49.2	49.8	50.5	51.6	51.5	51.2	53.5	52.2	51.9
Tozan	36.5	40.8	41.5	42.9	45.1	46.9	46.8	47.7	46.4	43.6	43.9	43.1	42.1
Higashiyama													
Tokai	39.1	41.0	43.3	43.0	48.1	48.4	48.9	49.0	47.3	45.0	43.5	42.6	43.0
Kinki	40.2	44.8	44.4	48.2	49.0	49.5	50.1	50.5	50.8	48.7	47.5	46.3	45.1
Shikoku	41.9	46.8	42.9	42.0	41.9	45.0	42.2	40.7	42.2	41.1	45.2	44.0	43.5
Sanyo	34.4	39.3	40.9	42.4	46.9 }	47.4	47.9	46.8	46.3	44.7	44.4	43.5	42.8
San'in	47.9	50.9	51.4	52.3	53.5 }								
Kyushu	35.4	37.5	37.1	39.6	40.7	41.3	41.9	43.3	44.3	43.3	42.7	42.9	42.8
Total	—	39.5	40.0	41.2	43.9	45.4	45.4	46.2	46.4	46.1	47.5	46.8	45.9
Home islands	35.9	39.6	40.2	41.3	43.5	44.9	45.2	45.9	46.2	45.3	46.4	46.3	45.7

Sources and Notes: 1883–84: Yamaguchi [171], pp. 60–61. 1887, 1892, 1897, and 1903: Totals are summed from annual figures on area under cultivation and tenancy rates in prefectural statistics are given by Kayō [51]. However, some data are missing for various years and various prefectures. In such cases estimates obtained either by straight-line interpolations or by using figures for an adjacent year were substituted for the missing values. 1908–40: Kayō [51], pp. 94–95.

agrarian policy, said that the value of foreclosed lands in the three years from 1884 to 1886 was ¥203 million; thus, with total land value at ¥1.65 billion, "roughly one eighth of the entire arable acreage of Japan was given over to creditors in the space of but three years" (Mayet [60], p. 208). But this estimate is a bit exaggerated because in some cases land changed hands more than once.

Old landlords had usually tilled a few acres on their own but also employed and managed labor on a yearly basis. Ethnologist Kunio Yanagida has said that landlords, particularly in less developed regions, would give small parcels of land as tenant plots to workers who had finished their terms of employment and then rehire them on a daily basis when needed (Yanagida [175], pp. 231–33). But when city-dwelling merchants began investing in land, the old landlords found labor more difficult to hire. The landlords gave up cultivation to seek better profits in brewing, pawnbrokering, and moneylending and then accumulated lands through profits from these side trades. Next, the landlords rented newly acquired lands to tenants. Even old landlords ceased to till the soil and the phenomenon of the parasitic landlord emerged. Comprehensive parasitism is where Meiji landlords differed from their predecessors.

The high price of rice easily maintained profits for those who had already become landlords. But the profitability of buying land and becoming a landlord declined gradually during the middle Meiji years. Table 2.6 reveals that tenant rents changed very little in quantity from 1888 to 1913 but that the price of rice rose greatly. Thus, although landlord income grew rapidly, the price of land grew twice as fast. Land-

Table 2.6. Indexes of Landlords' Profitability

	Land price index	Index of tenant rents in kind	Index of tenant rents in money terms	Consumer price index	Industrial manufactures price index
1888	100	100	100	100	100
1898	210	102	132	153	159
1903	222	106	167	174	176
1908	312	103	195	201	218
1913	454	105	271	226	226

Sources: Land price index, index of tenant rent in kind (volume of unpolished rice), and index of tenant rent in money terms all calculated from Umemura [165], p. 220. Consumer price index and industrial manufactures price index calculated from Ohkawa [99], pp. 134, 192.

owning thus lost its allure as an investment, and later in the period those with enough capital to become landlords had better uses for their money. With fewer new landlords, tenancy grew slowly.

Moreover, not all tenants took on that status for reasons of poverty. Around 1900 development of technology and advantageous price changes combined to make freeholders want to expand production; thus, many farmers came to want tenant lands (Yanagida [175], p. 204). Until 1900 the share of tenant land held by those who were only tenants rose, but after 1900 the share held by those combining tenancy with freeholding rose.

Therefore, farming increasingly became an economic activity, not a subsistence one. Excess demand had arisen for the limited amount of land, and both landlord and tenant sought advantage from this relative scarcity. The landlord system was only rational economic behavior by both farmers and landlords, all questing for profit.

The Role of Agriculture in Capital Accumulation

The land tax was the major source of revenue for the early Meiji government. The old land tax had brought only ¥2 million in 1868; the reformed tax in 1873 brought ¥60.6 million, more than 90% of the tax revenue and about 70% of the fiscal revenue. In 1876 the government lowered the tax rate from 3 to 2.5%, but the burden of even this lower tax eased as a result of the inflation during the Satsuma Rebellion and the skyrocketing price of rice. Many people combined plots for high profits, and even large merchants and zaibatsu such as Fujita and Mitsubishi became land managers. Still, the land tax provided the largest share of government revenue. Not until after the Sino–Japanese War did the proportion of land tax in total tax revenue fall below 50%. Thus, tax revenue from agriculture clearly was the basis of the government's capital accumulation.

Parasitic landlords as well used tenant rents to accumulate capital for other industries. Yamaguchi gives the cotton spinning industry as an example. Data for 64 companies in the first business period (half fiscal year) of 1898 show that there were 866 stockholders in Japan holding a "relatively large number of shares" in their respective companies (i.e., 200 or more shares in large firms, 100–50 shares in medium-sized businesses, and 20–50 shares in small companies. Of these 866, 236 (27%) were directors of cotton spinning companies, 161 (19%) were clothing and dry goods merchants, 76 (9%) cotton-yarn dealers, 49 (6%) rice or fertilizer merchants, 103 (22%) other merchants, and large landlords only 21 (2%). But adding those who were landlords with side trades brings the figure to 63 (7%). Thus, says Yamaguchi, their significance "rose to a level which could not be ignored, particularly in local spinning companies.... [T]he largest stockholders of a firm in most cases were almost all residents of the same prefecture in which the firm was located ... [and] particularly the same city as the firm.... Thus, the spinning companies of this time were local enterprises which relied on local funds" (Yamaguchi [172], pp. 92–96). Landlords were indeed instrumental in some spinning firms.

Banking is another example. Farmers of the commoner class held only 3–4% of the stock of national banks between 1880 and 1896 (Asakura [13], p. 121). Even excluding the Fifteenth Bank (owned by court nobles) raises farmers' share to only 7–8%. But, many of the merchant stockholders, who held 15 to 22% of the total (over 30% excluding the Fifteenth Bank), were also landlords. Local railroads and sea transport companies were probably similar in stockholder composition.

Landlords were also active in traditional industry, as brewers, pawnbrokers, and village moneylenders. The number of sake brewers more than doubled from 14,445 in 1892 to 28,935 in 1898, and the number of soy sauce brewers increased from 10,368 in 1892 to 24,181 in 1899; most of them were also landlords. Thus, the landlords indeed played a key role in local capital accumulation, although not all their capital was agrarian in origin.

THE ESTABLISHMENT OF MODERN INDUSTRY

The *Shokusan Kōgyō* Policy
Japan faced two alternatives in the last half of the nineteenth century: (1) achieve the level of the West economically, politically, and militarily, or (2) settle for becoming a partial or complete colony of a European power. With only these two alternatives the Meiji government naturally chose economic reform and industrialization. Under the slogan *shokusan kōgyō* ("develop industry and promote enterprise") a wide range of modernization and industrialization activities was undertaken. First abolishing all traditional restrictions on the economy, the Meiji government affirmed freedom of employment and occupational choice, consolidated the central government's fiscal base by means of the land tax reform, and, under the shokusan kōgyō policy, made numerous efforts to transplant new industries into the country. But this was not a matter of government policy alone; private capital was also mobilized.

The shokusan kōgyō policies, first begun in the 1870s, comprised four main points: (1) the promotion of a national banking system; (2) building of railroad, postal, and telegraph networks; (3) establishment, and later selling, of public sector factories; and (4) lending and sale of equipment, and lending of funds to private firms. Public sector factories and their subsequent sales to the private sector were particularly important;

this was the method whereby many industries, including silk reeling, coal, copper, cement, and glass, were first introduced into Japan. By 1885 expenditures on shokusan kōgyō policies totaled ¥151 million; ¥16 million for the Ministry of Industry (Kōbushō); ¥51 million for industrial promotion encouragement expenditures, start-up loans, and subsidies (subsidies and loans to the private sector); ¥4 million for railroads (direct government investment), ¥51 million for public sector enterprises, and ¥22 million for colonial use, mainly in Hokkaido (Yukisawa [182], pp. 272–74). Naval and army arsenal expenses are a large portion of this, and these along with railroad, communications, and mining expenditures formed the major fiscal investments.

The shokusan kōgyō policies introduced much technology but hardly promoted growth of the entire economy. With GNP in the years around 1877 running at annual rates of between ¥400 and 800 million and fiscal expenditure at ¥60–100 million, the ¥150 million expenditures on the shokusan kōgyō policies over the course of 18 years cannot be considered all that large—leaving aside the question of the quality of the investments.

Shokusan kōgyō policies started afresh after the Sino–Japanese War. By 1896 the government was promoting the development of the shipbuilding industry (and of the machinery industry to back it up) by promulgating the Shipbuilding Promotion Law and the Navigation Promotion Law and by giving incentives for the establishment of ocean shipping lines and the construction of large, iron, ocean-going vessels. Moreover, government-operated steel works were set up at Yawata in Kyushu in an effort to establish a steel industry. It is undeniable that these policy measures on the part of the government were useful as a springboard for the development of heavy industry.

In sum, the shokusan kōgyō policies were helpful in transplanting the new industries into Japan and, in some cases, nurturing strategic industries, but they alone did not create modern industry in Japan.

The Sequence of Industrial Development

Although it might not have been necessarily intentional, Japan nevertheless introduced Western industries in a certain sequence. Banking and finance were first, and quickest to expand. This standardized the currency eventually and helped to create a goods distribution mechanism, integrate the national market, and channel savings into industry. Banking first grew in the 1870s and early 1880s due to government promotion of the national banking system on the American model, which accounts for the early development of financial institutions prior to other Western industries. The national banking system grew very quickly after 1876, when the government ceased requiring convertibility of bank notes to gold, and permitted the issue of bank notes backed by stipend commutation bonds. The government had commuted the stipends of warrior-bureaucrats, who were officials of the previous regime, into bonds. The bank notes backed by these bonds were not legal tender and did not aid government efforts at currency standardization. But the note-issuing privilege of banks did help the government raise funds to oppose the Satsuma Rebellion of 1877. The government hoped to change these bonds into financial capital.

However, the money supply expanded tremendously with these liberal note-issue rules; this, combined with high expenses in connection with the Satsuma Rebellion, worsened inflation considerably. After crushing the rebellion, the government tried to restore the pre-rebellion price level through a harsh deflation during the mid-1880s under Finance Minister Masayoshi Matsukata. The misery on farms brought on by the deflation was thus due in part to the overly liberal note-issue rules. But the experiment with the currency system and national banking did have beneficial aspects as well. It enlarged the area under the commodity economy and helped merchants (who had bought the cheap bank notes and stipend bonds) accumulate capital.

Liberal note issue ended in 1882 with the establishment of the Bank of Japan and the printing of Bank of Japan currency. National banks redeemed their own currency over the next decade or so and reorganized themselves into private banks. Banking now entered a new phase of development, and banks became conventional commercial banks. But problems still plagued this second era of banking. Two of the worst were "organ banks" (*kikan ginkō*), which lent heavily to firms managed by bank officials and speculated with deposits, and "arbitrage profiteering" (*sayatori*), in which banks unable to attract deposits instead borrowed from the Bank of Japan at low interest rates and then re-lent at much higher rates. A third problem was that banks did business only with the wealthier class of merchants and landlords. Small merchants, manufacturers, and farmers were forced to depend on usurious moneylenders or functionally identical "quasi-banks" (*ginkō ruiji kaisha*) (Asakura [13]). Nevertheless, from an early date the Japanese banking system did provide funds and contribute to the widespread development of many industries and was essential to industrial development.

Sea transportation and railroads developed next, after banks but before manufacturing. The Mitsubishi Group developed sea transport first and, with strong protection from the government, drove competitors such as the Pacific Ocean Company of England out of Japanese coastal shipping. With the change in government in 1881 the Mitsui Group's Kyōdō Shipping Company began receiving government backing, and the Mitsui and Mitsubishi shipping companies fought for supremacy.

After this fight these two companies merged and established Nihon Yūsen (NYK), the foundation of Japan's modern shipping industry.

Railroad construction began about 1880 and major trunk lines were completed by about 1900. The railroads were private in the early years, with few exceptions. Their prompt completion greatly speeded development of domestic industry and integration of national markets. For example, in silk reeling, railroads were a vital link among cocoon and mulberry leaf suppliers, reeling factories, and final markets. The case of the Suwa district of Nagano prefecture is telling. Between 1895 and 1904 the number of factories and boilers was stable and production rose only one-third, but in the eight years after the Chūō rail line was opened through Suwa in 1905, the number of factories and boilers doubled and production almost tripled.

Railroads helped develop coal mining as well. Production increased greatly in the Chikuho fields of Kyushu after completion in 1891 of the Moji–Kurume line and the Wakamatsu–Nogata line. Five years after their completion, production had risen 2.3 times, and after ten years, 5.4 times. (Coal production was about 940,000 tons in 1891.) Moreover, by 1895 the amount transported from these fields by rail surpassed that carried on even the important Ongagawa River route (Tetsudo-In [147], pp. 757–781, 878–81, 892–93).

Mining developed next after transportation. Coal was sold first as fuel for ships but gradually expanded into railroad and industrial markets. In the 1890s 50% of the coal produced was exported but this proportion fell to around 30% in the early 1900s. Thus, Japan developed coal not only for export but for domestic rail and sea transport as well. Large zaibatsu such as Mitsui, Mitsubishi, and Sumitomo founded their fortunes on coal, as did some smaller local zaibatsu (e.g., Yasukawa and Kaijima in Kyushu). The Miike and Takashima coal mines show the pattern; although they were once public, the government sold them to private interests after they had been developed through shokusan kōgyō policies.

Metal mining also developed. Although the metal mines were ancient in origin, as was the Besshi mine of Sumitomo, the Ministry of Industry nevertheless developed and managed them, later selling them to private interests. The Furukawa mines of Ashio, Innai, and Ani, the Mitsubishi mines of Sado and Ikuno, and the Fujita mine of Kosaka are all good examples. The metals from these mines were important exports; copper, for example, was Japan's fifth most important export in 1900.

The textile industry developed fourth after mining, and with relatively little protection from the government. Silk reeling and cotton spinning were especially representative of the industry. Favorable resource and labor conditions underlay the development of both these industries, which became the most important exporters in the manufacturing industries, though with different approaches. Silk reeling factories were small in scale and adapted foreign technology to rural conditions. Cotton spinning factories were large scale in both physical size and output per factory and were urban. But both were pivotal to Meiji industrialization.

Table 2.7 shows when each of these industries developed vis-à-vis the others. Each column uses different units of measurement, but data are expressed as rates of growth. This is sufficient for chronological comparison. The table suggests the following:

1877	Banking has its first growth rate peak. Almost all national banks are established.
1887	Railroads' first growth peak. Private lines boom, with full provision of important national trunk lines.
1896–99	Sea transportation and railroads have second growth peaks. (Sea transportation data before 1884 are scarce, but there must have been a peak in the late 1870s or early 1880s, since growth was negative in the late 1880s.) Ship production also peaks. These developments were due to the boom following first Sino–Japanese War.
1898–99	Expansion in the textile industry slows. Although not shown in table 2.7, there was a fall in growth of raw silk production.
1905	Pig iron production growth peaks.

Japan's sequence of industrial development was similar to czarist Russia's. In Russia railroads came first, followed by consumer goods such as sugar and cotton spinning; eventually heavy industrial products such as coal and pig iron were produced (Nakamura and Kumon [78]). It is dangerous to make hasty generalizations from the two examples of Japan and Russia, but at least one can say that sectors that developed first in early developers such as England (social capital, intermediate goods, capital goods, and consumption goods) were not initially the leading sectors in later developers like Japan and Russia. In such countries as these, finance, transportation, and communications developed first instead.

The Introduction of Systems of Social Organization
Adopting the corporate form for businesses was also of paramount importance to early Japanese growth. The government promulgated a new commerce law in 1890 but corporations had existed long before, even in the 1870s. Their legal status had not been clear but they accumulated capital by corporate methods and thus eased the introduction of modern industry. Early firms such as the Fifteenth National Bank, the Osaka Spinning Company, and the Japan Railways Company gathered capital

Table 2.7. Trends of Industrial Capacity Growth

	Railroads (kilometer of track in operation)	Textiles (net fixed capital stock)	Banking (paid-up capital)	Vessels owned (value of capital stock)	Pig iron (tons produced)	Ships produced (real value of production)
1875	24.9	—	—	—	—	—
1876	20.8	—	55.1	—	—	—
1877	11.9	—	55.3	—	18.2	—
1878	11.8	—	50.1	—	19.8	58.5
1879	9.8	—	36.2	—	8.8	42.1
1880	16.6	—	15.7	—	5.0	17.0
1881	20.6	—	10.4	—	−4.2	−5.8
1882	24.5	—	6.5	—	−17.6	−18.0
1883	27.0	28.1	3.4	—	−12.1	−27.0
1884	28.1	23.2	1.9	—	4.3	−23.4
1885	31.0	23.3	1.3	—	18.0	−13.0
1886	31.4	26.4	1.8	—	29.6	−4.5
1887	32.9	28.0	3.0	−5.3	37.1	4.6
1888	30.7	27.9	3.8	2.6	31.3	6.6
1889	27.3	25.8	4.0	1.3	14.0	6.2
1890	20.9	20.9	3.5	−1.3	3.2	−0.5
1891	14.7	14.8	3.8	−0.7	5.9	−1.5
1892	10.9	13.4	5.0	1.6	6.8	4.3
1893	8.8	16.4	8.8	7.2	8.6	1.8
1894	8.4	19.1	13.9	13.4	11.2	10.6
1895	10.0	19.4	18.0	18.9	5.3	29.4
1896	10.9	16.7	20.3	21.4	0.9	43.1
1897	10.3	12.8	19.5	18.9	−3.3	41.2
1898	9.1	7.9	16.3	15.1	6.1	42.7
1899	7.4	3.8	11.6	9.4	11.5	33.5
1900	5.5	1.9	7.6	5.3	10.7	17.9
1901	4.6	1.4	5.1	3.8	15.4	2.0
1902	5.0	2.0	3.3	3.9	24.3	1.8
1903	4.6	3.4	2.8	5.5	27.3	5.4
1904	4.1	5.3	3.5	7.0	24.5	3.8
1905	3.4	8.2	4.4	7.5	27.3	12.8
1906	2.8	11.4	5.2	7.4	26.4	9.8
1907	2.5	12.7	5.5	5.9	16.1	6.4
1908	2.6	11.9	5.7	5.4	7.9	1.7
1909	3.7	10.3	5.7	4.6	9.1	−0.5
1910	4.8	8.4	5.8	4.4	10.0	14.6

Table 2.7 *(continued)*

	Railroads (kilometer of track in operation)	Textiles (net fixed capital stock)	Banking (paid-up capital)	Vessels owned (value of capital stock)	Pig iron (tons produced)	Ships produced (real value of production)
1911	5.9	7.0	6.4	4.9	11.3	4.4
1912	6.6	5.8	7.0	4.7	11.0	11.3
1913	6.4	5.2	7.2	4.4	11.9	20.6
1914	5.8	4.9	7.5	4.1	13.0	28.8
1915	4.6	0.0	8.5	5.3	15.0	39.9
1916	3.4	4.0	11.9	10.0	15.7	42.4
1917	2.6	4.5	16.6	12.6	11.9	41.9
1918	2.6	6.2	20.8	14.1	7.3	19.3
1919	3.1	7.9	20.5	12.6	3.6	−2.3
1920	4.0	8.8	17.4	8.4	1.9	−27.2
1921	4.6	9.8	12.5	3.3	0.4	−37.4
1922	4.9	9.5	6.2	0.5	3.3	−33.8
1923	4.9	8.6	1.6	−0.3	7.6	−25.5
1924	4.6	6.8	−0.3	−1.6	10.1	−10.4
1925	4.2	4.9	−0.2	−0.6	11.4	−10.3
1926	4.0	3.2	−0.9	−0.8	11.8	−4.9
1927	4.0	3.0	−1.8	−0.8	11.8	0.0
1928	4.0	2.9	−2.5	−0.4	6.4	−6.0
1929	3.8	2.8	−2.8	−0.3	2.8	−8.4
1930	3.4	3.4	−3.4	−0.5	4.0	−9.8
1931	3.0	7.3	−2.4	−0.6	6.4	−1.5
1932	2.5	6.3	−2.3	−0.7	10.4	7.7
1933	2.1	8.3	−2.0	0.0	13.0	17.5
1934	1.9	10.3	−2.4	1.8	15.8	44.0
1935	1.8	10.9	−2.6	—	14.0	50.5
1936	1.4	—	−2.5	—	12.0	49.0
1937	0.9	—	−2.1	—	12.2	41.2

Sources: Railroads: Minami [64], pp. 204–05; textiles: Fujino and Ono [24], pp. 250–51; banking: Gotō [29], various pages (figure listed applies to sum of national, ordinary, savings, and five special banks [Yokohama Specie, Nihon Kangyō, Hokkaido Takushoku, Nihon Kōgyō, and Nōkō]); vessels owned: Ohkawa et al. [103], pp. 202–04; pig iron: Shinohara [126], pp. 228, 233; ships produced: Ohkawa et al. [103], pp. 202–04.

Note: Growth rates in the table represent the trend growth for the seven years surrounding the year for which the growth rate is listed; i.e., a regression of the form ln $y = a + gt$ is run, where ln y is the natural log of the series in question and $t = 1 \ldots 7$, and g is listed.

mostly from influential, upper-class investors, but soon the corporate form became popular with all classes. This popularity supported early expansion first of banking and then of railroad and mining industries. As is well known, the company system initially sunk its deepest roots in relatively underdeveloped countries such as Germany rather than in nations such as England, the mother country of capitalism. Japan adopted the company system at a very early stage.

Table 2.8 presents data on companies and paid-up capital. The composition by industry of corporate paid-up capital shows which industries were important when. Most capital in the 1890s was in banking and finance, land transport, cotton spinning, mining, and paper. These industries were significant in the 1900s too but electricity and gas grew as well. Between the Russo–Japanese War and World War I electricity and gas increased greatly in relative importance; mining and chemicals gained also. After World War I, electricity generating, heavy, and chemical industries grew even more. But still manufacturing did not take more than 30% of paid-up capital until 1934; until then the financial, electric, gas, and transportation industries were the giants. Late development of the corporate form in manufacturing is a distinctive feature of Japanese industrial development. In Germany in 1913, by contrast, mining and manufacturing took over half of corporate authorized capital while metal refining and machinery industries alone took one-third (Okura Shō Rizai-kyoku [108], pp. 300–02). Of course, Japan and Germany are not strictly comparable chronologically but the point still holds: The corporate form spread quickly in Japan in light and tertiary industries but relatively slowly in the manufacturing sector.

Thus, industrial development in Japan began with financial institutions, sea transportation, railroads, public sector infrastructure industries such as the postal service, telegraph, roads, and so forth. Next mining began, after sales of government mines to private interests. Textiles and heavy industry followed. This sequence of development differed from that of Europe; in Japan the government played an important role in establishing capitalism through the promotion of facilitating industries. Indeed, the facilitating sector was a precondition for the growth of other industry. In other words, when growth started, Japan's financial, communications, and transportation industries were underdeveloped compared to those of the West even when the latter were at a relatively early stage of development. Thus, even by the standards of the time, Meiji Japan was an underdeveloped nation.

Gerschenkron's idea of "borrowed technology" is generally applicable to Meiji Japan, but Japan borrowed not so much industrial technology as techniques of economic organization. The financial sector, the corporate form, and technology for facilitating industries are good examples. In

Table 2.8. Corporate Paid-up Capital and Number of Firms (Percentage of total number)

	1884	1887	1894	1899	1904	1909	1914	1919	1924	1929	1934	1939	1945
Agriculture, forestry, and fishing	0.4 (2.3)	0.7 (6.5)	0.4 (3.5)	0.3 (2.4)	0.3 (2.7)	0.9 (3.2)	1.2 (2.9)	1.3 (3.0)	1.5 (2.8)	1.7 (2.3)	1.6 (2.8)	1.5 (2.3)	1.5 (1.9)
Trade and commerce	0.8 (14.1)	3.9 (19.6)	2.7 (14.5)	4.9 (23.5)	4.7 (23.4)	5.5 (24.9)	7.4 (25.2)	9.8 (24.8)	12.4 (29.0)	11.5 (35.3)	12.2 (39.9)	12.0 (36.8)	6.8 (18.4)
Banking and finance	78.1 (60.7)	46.3 (38.6)	35.8 (40.1)	39.3 (27.9)	37.1 (29.6)	30.7 (24.8)	29.5 (23.6)	21.9 (13.9)	18.6 (9.5)	14.2 (5.5)	11.3 (3.6)	6.6 (2.7)	3.8 (1.4)
Insurance	— (—)	0.5 (0.3)	1.3 (1.7)	1.4 (1.0)	1.1 (0.6)	0.9 (0.4)	1.0 (0.4)	0.8 (0.3)	1.0 (0.2)	0.9 (0.2)	1.0 (0.1)	0.6 (0.1)	0.2 (0.1)
Family corporations	—	—	— (—)	—	—	— (—)	— (—)	— (—)	6.8 (1.0)	8.3 (1.4)	7.9 (1.0)	5.5 (1.1)	1.9 (1.2)
Other services	0.2 (2.0)	1.0 (3.6)	2.8 (7.8)	1.0 (5.7)	1.4 (6.2)	2.2 (6.5)	4.9 (6.3)	6.8 (8.3)	4.0 (7.3)	6.1 (8.3)	6.6 (8.7)	4.9 (8.2)	2.0 (18.4)
Manufacturing	2.0 (7.0)	9.0 (20.1)	11.4 (20.1)	14.6 (26.8)	13.8 (24.3)	20.5 (27.9)	19.3 (28.1)	28.8 (36.5)	26.3 (37.8)	25.2 (34.2)	28.5 (33.3)	39.1 (37.5)	60.3 (62.5)
Textiles	1.1 (2.4)	4.8 (8.6)	6.9 (8.2)	7.7 (8.5)	5.4 (7.0)	6.3 (7.5)	6.1 (6.4)	7.9 (7.9)	7.6 (7.9)	6.2 (5.8)	5.9 (5.4)	5.1 (4.9)	4.5 (5.4)
Heavy and chemical	0.6 (0.9)	3.5 (5.4)	2.7 (4.2)	4.0 (6.5)	5.6 (5.3)	8.8 (6.9)	8.5 (7.5)	15.6 (12.8)	12.2 (10.9)	13.0 (10.6)	15.4 (10.3)	29.0 (16.8)	48.6 (30.8)
Other	0.4 (3.1)	1.5 (5.4)	1.7 (7.8)	2.9 (11.8)	2.8 (12.0)	5.5 (13.6)	4.9 (14.2)	5.0 (15.8)	6.4 (19.0)	6.0 (18.1)	6.1 (17.6)	5.0 (15.7)	8.3 (26.2)
Electricity, gas, and water	—	0.5 (0.7)	0.8 (0.7)	1.1 (0.7)	2.0 (0.9)	5.5 (1.2)	12.4 (2.5)	8.7 (2.3)	11.1 (1.7)	14.8 (1.2)	14.7 (0.7)	12.6 (0.5)	12.0 (0.2)
Transportation	18.3 (13.7)	35.8 (7.4)	41.3 (6.5)	32.4 (7.8)	36.4 (7.8)	21.3 (7.1)	15.5 (7.0)	13.0 (7.0)	9.4 (7.4)	10.1 (8.8)	9.6 (7.3)	0.7 (7.5)	5.6 (4.3)
Warehouse	0.1 (—)	0.2 (0.5)	0.3 (1.2)	0.7 (2.0)	0.6 (2.7)	0.9 (2.2)	0.8 (2.3)	0.7 (1.9)	0.9 (1.5)	0.9 (0.9)	0.9 (0.6)	1.5 (0.5)	0.4 (0.7)
Construction	0.0 (0.0)	0.3 (1.7)	0.2 (0.6)	0.4 (0.8)	0.2 (0.5)	0.2 (0.5)	0.5 (0.6)	0.6 (0.8)	1.1 (1.1)	0.8 (1.5)	0.6 (1.5)	0.7 (1.8)	1.2 (3.1)
Mining	0.0 (—)	1.8 (1.0)	3.0 (8.4)	3.9 (1.5)	2.4 (1.4)	11.2 (1.3)	7.4 (1.0)	7.6 (1.2)	6.9 (0.6)	5.4 (0.5)	5.2 (0.4)	8.4 (1.0)	4.3 (0.9)
Total paid-up capital (¥1,000)	105,932	194,598	294,579	701,869	1,003,919	1,555,100	2,218,290	6,123,689	10,999,121	13,952,008	15,704,040	25,193,851	31,813,393
Number of companies	1,492	2,389	3,240	7,486	8,781	11,521	16,858	26,280	33,567	46,692	78,198	85,122	41,380

Source: Calculated by Shōzaburō Fujino [22a].

early developing nations such as England industrial development forced changes in firm organization and the means of transportation and communication; later developers such as Japan had to renovate firm organization, transportation, and communications first. In other words Japan introduced the framework of industrial society first and the content afterward.

THE CHANGING CHARACTER OF TECHNOLOGY INTRODUCTION

A Simple Schematic

Next we consider a schema to explain how an underdeveloped country borrows technology. Let us conceive of a simple model with two factors, capital and labor, and then construct curves depicting equal values of final product (isovalue curves). Because foreign technology generally requires fixed factor proportions, we shall exclude for the moment the possibility of factor substitution. Thus, each industry has a single, fixed capital/labor ratio. A country with factor endowments in the same ratio as needed for a certain industry's technology will maximize profit by specializing in that industry.

Figure 2.1 shows isovalue curves A_1 and A_2. Since there are only three industries for which factor combinations of K and L are possible in this model, the isovalue curves are actually kinked lines. Moreover, the points on line A_1 (or A_2) imply profits levels of A_1 yen (or A_2 yen) for the combinations of capital and labor. All nations will try to maximize profits with a limited amount of funds by purchasing capital goods and labor services and putting them to work. The question is which factors to use and in what proportions. If the nation is underdeveloped, labor services will be relatively cheaper than capital goods, i.e., the line depicting available factor combinations will slope as B_1B_1 does. The poor nation in which labor is relatively cheap will maximize value of output by specializing in labor-intensive industry number 1. For advanced nations, the opposite holds. Capital is relatively cheap, i.e., the factor availability line will slope as does B_2B_2. The advanced nation, where labor is costly, will maximize value of output by specializing in industry number 3, which economizes on labor.

This model is based on several restrictive assumptions, so restrictive that they are hard to fulfill in the real world; e.g., perfectly free international trade of all goods and services other than capital and labor services, no monopoly, and uniform world prices of all goods (except capital and labor). But the textile industry of Meiji Japan, which lacked the tariff autonomy that might have sheltered it from the rigors of free international trade, came relatively close to fulfilling these conditions.

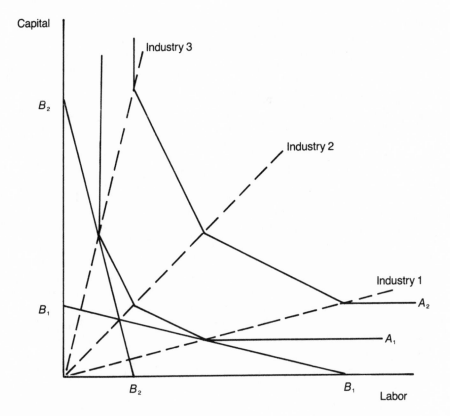

Figure 2.1. Industry Choice Model.

Thus, this simple schematic does help explain why textiles—an industry without government protection—developed so rapidly.

But let us bring the discussion closer to reality. Meiji Japan did specialize somewhat in textiles, but still the seeds of many other industries had been sown by the middle of the Meiji period, i.e., the 1890s. Thus we must revise the elementary schematic to take into consideration the following factors: (1) natural conditions prevailing with respect to resources and transportation, (2) adaptation of foreign technology to Japanese conditions, (3) stagnation of technology in certain modern industries, (4) monopoly, and (5) national economic policy.

The first point, on natural resources, has been well debated. Conditions for sericulture, for example, were excellent. This industry had been prosperous in Japan for centuries, and a silkworm blight in France and Italy in the 1870s made Japan's favorable endowments for silk even scarcer. Japan was similarly well endowed for other industries, such as cement, marine products, and tea, although comparative advantage in these industries was not so great as in raw silk. On the other hand, competition from abroad destroyed some industries completely, e.g., natural indigo, safflower, and raw cotton.

Let us now consider in detail some of the other factors listed above and revise our simple model.

Adaptation of Technology to Japanese Conditions

Borrowed technology includes not only methods adopted but also those adapted. In mechanical silk reeling two methods were introduced, one from France (as at the Tomioka silk reeling factory established by the government) and one from Italy (as at the Tokyo Tsukiji factory of the Ono-Gumi). The Japanese modified both methods to save capital. At the Tomioka plant, cost per boiler was ¥1,500 but the Rokku factory at Matsushiro in Nagamo prefecture improved the method and reduced the cost to ¥67. Then the Chuzan-sha of Suwa (Nagano prefecture) combined the improved French technique with the Italian and reduced the cost to ¥13.5. The foreign technology basically used steam to boil the cocoons and waterwheel power to spin the thread, although producers were those who had worked with hand-powered machines. Through these innovations mechanized silk reeling had an opportunity to develop.

Let me add a word about this process as seen by Hideko Wada, who worked at the Rokku plant: "The differences between the Tomioka plant and this one are like night and day. Copper, iron, and brass parts there are all wood here; for glass there is wire, and brick becomes earth. Even though the thread is spun by means of steam [power], it is still the hands of Japanese that have fashioned the process. It is an impressive accomplishment" ([170], p. 2).

The weaving industry was similar. The first Jacquard machines were introduced in 1872 but they were iron and quite expensive. Then Kohei Araki and others reconstructed the major parts in wood and created the wooden Jacquard. Unokichi Deguchi further improved the design, and it spread to Kiryu in Gumma prefecture, to Fukui prefecture, and to Yonezawa in Yamagata prefecture. The battan machine, introduced simultaneously, replaced older machines and increased productivity (Sampei [118], pp. 49–72).

Let us cite one other example, the match industry. This industry, introduced in 1875, adapted very quickly to become labor intensive. It relied on the labor of poor women and children in cities and avoided all mechanization for many years. Housewives folded and pasted together the boxes in spare moments. Applying chemicals to the matchhead and putting the matches in boxes were jobs done by hand until just before World War II (Komiyama [59], p. 158).

Japan's modern industries were often ruled by their borrowed technology. Capital was far more expensive than labor, but still most borrowed industries used relatively large amounts of capital. Highly capital intensive when introduced, many of the modern industries could not achieve high profit rates in the early years. This was true even in the cotton spinning industry. For example, the Jukki Spinning Company, a 2,000-spindle operation launched with government help under the shokusan kōgyō policies, was almost continuously in the red. Economies of scale were not enough; somehow the amount of labor used relative to the amount of capital still had to be raised. In spinning, all-night labor was the answer; it doubled the labor used per spinning machine. Following the installation of in-house electric power generating equipment, all-night labor was first introduced in 1882 at the Osaka Spinning Company, a 10,500-spindle mule-type factory. Significantly, this firm was the first Japanese textile firm to earn a profit. Only through all-night labor could the spinning industry achieve a return on investment at least not lower than those of other industries.

The spinning industry grew quickly after the introduction of all-night labor in the 1880s despite little technological progress in machinery. As seen in table 2.9, however, the capital/labor ratio grew quite slowly until just before the World War I period. And after 1900 increases in product per capita only followed the business cycle. Wages rose and the relative cost of spinning machines declined. In this process the spinning industry was able to establish its position as the most profitable industry in Japan.

Many industries adopted and adapted technology as spinning did. Examples include fabric weaving, flour milling, sugar refining, beer making, and cement mixing. All gradually transformed excessively capital-intensive foreign technology into forms better suited to contemporary domestic factor availability.

Monopoly and Economic Policy in the Early Years

In contrast to the examples cited above, some borrowed industries were highly monopolistic from the beginning. The classic example is the railroad industry. In this type of industry local monopoly was the rule, and entry by competitors was not easy. High prices and fares could be set to absorb high capital costs in the early years and then produce a profit. Sea transport, electricity, and gas were similar. Prices in these modern industries tended to be high (though there were exceptions, as when sea freight rates fell during the rate-cutting war between Mitsubishi and Mitsui). Table 2.10 illustrates how high prices were by comparing rail-

Table 2.9. Labor Intensity in Cotton Spinning

	Capital/labor I (¥ of real capital per person-day) (1)	Capital/labor II (¥ of real capital per person-day of female labor) (2)	Real value added per worker (3)	Real value added per female worker (4)
1890	4,133	5,817	—	—
1891	3,105	4,114	—	—
1892	2,603	3,489	—	—
1893	2,849	3,764	—	—
1894	2,411	3,153	—	—
1895	2,461	3,189	0.9	1.2
1896	3,343	4,445	0.9	1.2
1897	2,859	3,746	1.1	1.4
1898	2,561	3,343	0.7	0.9
1899	2,571	3,352	1.0	1.3
1900	2,734	3,508	1.1	1.4
1901	2,786	3,608	1.0	1.3
1902	2,511	3,240	1.1	1.4
1903	2,370	2,956	1.0	1.3
1904	3,331	4,099	0.3	0.4
1905	2,649	3,227	1.4	1.8
1906	2,656	3,291	1.5	1.8
1907	2,936	3,634	1.5	1.8
1908	4,052	5,087	0.8	1.1
1909	4,279	5,375	1.7	2.1
1910	3,881	4,830	1.3	1.6
1911	4,113	5,068	1.6	2.0
1912	3,946	4,838	1.6	2.0
1913	3,874	4,736	2.4	3.0
1914	4,051	5,073	0.8	1.0
1915	4,264	5,314	1.7	2.1
1916	3,559	4,422	1.7	2.1
1917	3,925	4,979	2.0	2.6
1918	4,359	5,604	2.3	3.0
1919	4,100	5,400	2.3	3.0
1920	4,247	5,567	1.8	2.4
1921	5,055	6,800	1.5	2.0
1922	4,274	5,619	1.8	2.4
1923	5,293	6,955	1.9	2.5
1924	6,192	8,123	2.7	3.5

Table 2.9 (continued)

	Capital/labor I (¥ of real capital per person-day) (1)	Capital/labor II (¥ of real capital per person-day of female labor) (2)	Real value added per worker (3)	Real value added per female worker (4)
1925	5,490	7,089	2.3	3.0
1926	5,408	6,943	1.7	2.2
1927	5,958	7,710	2.5	3.2
1928	6,392	8,324	2.7	3.5
1929	5,691	7,222	2.8	3.6
1930	8,294	10,583	2.0	2.5
1931	7,344	11,711	3.7	4.6
1932	9,105	10,860	2.9	3.5
1933	9,561	11,214	4.3	5.1
1934	9,554	11,007	4.1	4.7
1935	10,857	12,351	3.3	3.8
1936	12,683	14,387	3.4	3.9
1937	11,943	13,481	—	—

Sources: Column 1, Fujino and Ono [24], pp. 257, 250–51; 2, ibid., pp. 256, 250–51; 3, ibid., pp. 286–87 (for nominal value added and price index, p. 257); 4, ibid., with labor data from p. 256.

road fares to wholesale and retail prices. But the ratio of the two fell as time passed, a reason for which can be seen in table 2.11. Fixed equipment per worker on the national railroads declined in the first decade of the 1900s and remained steady thereafter. This adjustment was also partly due to nationalization of the railroads in 1906. In the background too was the fact that domestic production of engines, passenger cars, and freight cars became possible from about 1900.

The electricity industry developed differently. It began with small generation plants supplying electricity for electric lighting but prices were very high. For example, in 1887 a 10-candlepower lamp lit by the Tokyo Electric Light Company for one night cost 170 sen, (¥1.7)—at a time when 1 *shō* of rice (about 1.6 quarts) cost about 7 or 8 sen (Minami [64], p. 97). By 1910, however, technological progress had made feasible large-scale hydroelectric power generation and long-distance, high-voltage transmission. Fixed equipment per worker skyrocketed with the

Table 2.10. Relative Costs of Rail Transport (1934–36=100)

	Passenger fares Consumer prices	Freight rates Mfg. good prices		Passenger fares Consumer prices	Freight rates Mfg. good prices
1885	2,22	2.17	1913	1.00	0.83
1886	2.39	2.20	1914	1.13	0.88
1887	2.12	1.80	1915	1.17	0.81
1888	2.03	1.73	1916	1.09	0.64
1889	2.43	2.10	1917	0.88	0.52
1890	2.20	2.12	1918	0.77	0.47
			1919	0.65	0.43
1891	2.30	2.25	1920	0.77	0.43
1892	2.30	2.17			
1893	2.26	2.09	1921	0.88	0.70
1894	2.01	1.88	1922	0.89	0.69
1895	1.91	1.82	1923	0.88	0.67
1896	1.80	1.73	1924	0.87	0.67
1897	1.55	1.49	1925	0.85	0.70
1898	1.43	1.44	1926	0.89	0.80
1899	1.90	1.39	1927	0.90	0.86
1900	1.71	1.28	1928	0.93	0.86
			1929	0.96	0.89
1901	1.76	1.34	1930	1.04	1.06
1902	1.82	1.37			
1903	1.69	1.31	1931	1.18	1.27
1904	1.56	1.20	1932	1.14	1.15
1905	1.44	1.10	1933	1.11	0.99
1906	1.49	0.90	1934	1.05	1.01
1907	1.36	0.82	1935	0.99	1.01
1908	1.27	0.82	1936	0.97	0.99
1909	1.27	0.84	1937	0.89	0.74
1910	1.26	0.83	1938	0.81	0.69
			1939	0.76	0.62
1911	1.12	0.80	1940	0.68	0.53
1912	1.03	0.81			

Source: Minami [64], pp. 220–21.

installation of giant plants; power generation costs fell and power became easily available in many areas. But these economies of scale meant small local monopolies could no longer survive, so smaller firms merged, and by the end of World War I the Big Five power companies generated almost all Japan's electric power.

Table 2.11. Capital Intensity (Five-year moving averages)

	Railroads		Electricity		Railroads		Electricity
	(rail cars/ 1,000 workers)	(operating kilometers employee)	(kilowatts generated per worker)		(rail cars/ 1,000 workers)	(operating kilometers/ employee)	(kilowatts generated per worker)
1896	256	8.0	—	1921	382	17.2	21.5
1897	252	8.1	—	1922	377	17.0	24.0
1898	252	8.2	—	1923	375	16.5	26.4
1899	261	8.4	—	1924	375	16.1	29.9
1900	273	8.7	—	1925	376	15.6	33.6
				1926	379	15.3	37.4
1901	288	9.1	—	1927	384	14.8	39.7
1902	301	9.4	—	1928	391	14.2	44.0
1903	323	9.5	—	1929	395	13.6	47.6
1904	365	9.2	—	1930	399	13.7	51.7
1905	403	10.2	8.5				
1906	422	11.3	9.4	1931	401	13.8	54.1
1907	437	12.0	10.2	1932	401	14.1	57.4
1908	444	12.6	10.9	1933	397	14.5	60.8
1909	447	13.5	11.5	1934	394	15.0	64.4
1910	448	14.0	12.6	1935	385	15.4	66.5
				1936	376	15.6	69.6
1911	451	14.4	13.8	1937	364	15.6	74.1
1912	452	14.6	15.2	1938	353	15.3	74.5
1913	458	15.1	16.5	1939	338	14.7	76.0
1914	462	16.0	17.4	1940	328	14.3	76.5
1915	462	16.7	17.8				
1916	453	17.1	18.0				
1917	436	17.5	17.9				
1918	419	18.1	18.2				
1919	403	18.4	18.6				
1920	391	17.7	19.9				

Source: Minami [64], p. 209.

Capital-intensive industries such as the two examples cited above survived because they could charge high prices in semimonopolistic markets. But very few private industries could enjoy monopoly profits. Except for the electrochemical industry of the Showa era virtually all monopoly-prone industries were public utilities, as were railroads and electricity.

The industries discussed here received government protection, first under the shokusan kōgyō policies and then through tariffs and subsidies. But despite their modern technology most such industries—the state-protected ones in particular, such as the government's own Yawata Steel Works—were not competitive for many years. Neither shipbuilding nor steel caught up with the advanced nations technologically until the late 1920s or after. Of course, learning a technology is not tantamount to immediately becoming economically competitive.

Three □ Modern Industry and Traditional Industry

A STATISTICAL APPRAISAL

Modern industries progressed rapidly in Meiji Japan but their proportion of output was not great even at the end of the Meiji era—the eve of World War I. Their share of employed population was discussed in chapter 1 and documented in table 1.18, but let us add a few more pieces of evidence.

Japan's industrial production index expanded much more slowly than was once thought. Using different methods, Yasuba, Shionoya, and Shinohara have estimated growth rates for industrial production (Yasuba [178], Shionoya [135], Shinohara [126].) For 1874 to 1905, Shionoya gives a rate of 4.53% per year, and for 1905–35, 6.11%. Yasuba gives 6.42% for the latter period only. Shinohara gives 3.80% for the former and 6.7% for the latter. The great similarity of results born of different methods suggests confidence in them to be well placed. Although lower than originally thought and although "they are not head and shoulders above those of the rest of the world, they are among the higher rates. Particularly before World War I, only Sweden, America, Italy, and Germany had equal or higher rates of growth" (Shinoya [135]). (Shionoya's observation also implies that Japan's growth rate of industrial production was, along with that of the Soviet Union, high by international standards during the post-World War I period.)

The new estimates agree with the old on one point; industrial production grew much more quickly than GDP or agriculture. In the forty or so years before World War I (1879–1918) population grew 1.1% per year, agricultural production 1.7%, GDP 2.6%, and industrial production 4.8%. (See tables 3.1 and 3.2 for levels and rates of GDP growth.) Of course, industrialization is the essence of the path to capitalism, so such differential growth rates are to be expected.

But there is still a problem: What share of the industrial sector was modern and what share traditional? Increased industrial production

Table 3.1. Real GDP, Industrial and Agricultural Production (1934–36=100)

	GDP	Industrial production	Agricultural production		GNP	Industrial production	Agricultural production
1885	21.9	5.4	51.7	1911	45.6	24.0	79.5
1886	23.8	6.2	56.8	1912	47.3	25.9	79.3
1887	26.5	6.6	58.9	1913	48.0	28.9	80.5
1888	23.7	6.7	57.0	1914	46.6	29.6	88.2
1889	24.9	7.6	52.2	1915	50.9	34.5	87.5
1890	27.2	7.5	60.1	1916	58.8	39.8	95.7
				1917	60.8	41.7	93.2
1891	25.9	7.6	58.8	1918	61.4	44.0	90.2
1892	27.6	7.7	60.6	1919	67.7	44.1	97.7
1893	27.7	8.1	59.0	1920	63.4	41.2	97.0
1894	31.0	8.9	63.7				
1895	31.4	9.7	64.6	1921	70.4	43.6	87.6
1896	29.7	10.3	58.8	1922	70.2	48.0	89.7
1897	30.3	11.5	56.3	1923	70.3	46.4	87.2
1898	36.1	13.3	70.7	1924	72.3	47.7	90.1
1899	33.5	13.4	64.4	1925	75.2	49.7	98.1
1900	34.9	13.5	67.3	1926	75.9	53.2	90.9
				1927	77.0	56.0	97.3
1901	36.1	14.2	70.7	1928	83.3	62.0	95.5
1902	34.3	13.8	61.4	1929	85.9	70.9	97.0
1903	36.7	14.8	74.8	1930	79.6	71.3	101.8
1904	36.9	14.8	77.1				
1905	36.3	15.9	63.8	1931	80.3	75.9	89.8
1906	41.1	18.7	72.9	1932	87.1	75.2	100.2
1907	42.4	21.0	77.4	1933	95.6	82.7	110.5
1908	42.7	21.0	78.2	1934	95.8	91.2	94.0
1909	42.6	22.2	78.4	1935	98.4	101.5	99.3
1910	43.3	23.5	74.6	1936	105.6	107.3	106.7
				1937	110.6	109.5	109.3
				1938	118.0	137.9	106.2
				1939	136.6	163.1	114.4
				1940	140.6	177.6	111.2

Source: Ohkawa et al. [O], table A12.

Notes: GDP includes depreciation allowances for residences and riparian works. Agricultural production is sum of agriculture, forestry and fisheries; industrial production is mining and manufacturing.

Table 3.2. Real Growth Rates of Five-Year Averages, Year to Year

	GDP	Industrial production	Agricultural production		GDP	Industrial production	Agricultural production
1890	4.4	6.5	3.0	1916	5.5	11.1	3.9
				1917	5.4	10.0	3.2
1891	1.7	4.0	0.7	1918	5.1	8.7	2.2
1892	0.9	3.1	0.6	1919	7.6	7.6	2.1
1893	3.1	3.8	0.7	1920	4.2	3.3	2.0
1894	4.6	3.4	4.0				
1895	3.0	5.5	1.5	1921	3.7	1.8	−1.7
1896	2.6	6.4	0.0	1922	2.9	2.9	−0.8
1897	1.8	8.5	−1.4	1923	2.7	1.1	−0.6
1898	5.6	10.7	3.9	1924	1.3	1.6	−1.7
1899	1.6	8.4	0.2	1925	3.4	3.7	0.2
1900	2.2	6.5	0.9	1926	1.5	4.1	0.7
				1927	1.9	3.3	1.7
1901	3.9	6.3	3.7	1928	3.5	6.2	1.8
1902	2.3	3.5	1.5	1929	3.5	8.6	1.5
1903	0.3	2.2	1.2	1930	1.1	7.4	0.8
1904	1.9	2.0	3.8				
1905	0.8	3.4	−1.0	1931	1.1	7.2	−0.2
1906	2.8	6.1	0.6	1932	2.5	5.7	0.6
1907	4.4	9.2	4.6	1933	3.0	5.8	3.1
1908	3.1	7.3	0.9	1934	2.3	5.4	−0.6
1909	2.9	8.1	0.4	1935	4.3	7.6	−0.5
1910	3.4	7.7	2.9	1936	5.5	7.4	3.4
				1937	4.9	7.5	1.8
1911	2.1	5.0	1.7	1938	4.4	11.2	−0.8
1912	2.3	4.4	0.5	1939	7.7	13.1	4.0
1913	2.4	6.8	0.6	1940	7.4	12.3	2.2
1914	1.8	5.9	2.5				
1915	3.3	8.3	3.2				

Source: Calculated from table 3.1.

does not necessarily imply increased output at large, industrial factories. Cottage industry in Japan was too important to be ignored, even in later years. Even in 1930, according to the *Report on the National Income Survey of 1930 (Shōwa Go-nen Kokumin Shōtoku Chōsa Hōkoku)*, about one-third of net industrial income (¥893 million out of ¥2.97 billion) came from cottage industry. The continued widespread existence of cottage industry even in the 1930s is a major part of the issue of "dual structure," so let us determine how the position of cottage industry changed over the years.

Kazuo Yamaguchi's calculations of factory scale from analysis of pre-fectural statistics of 1884–92 and Shionoya's estimates of total industrial output give valuable clues to cottage industry studies. For the period after 1909 Shionoya's estimates can be compared to statistics in the *Census of Manufactures (Kōjō Tōkei Hyō)* for output of factories of five or more employees (see table 3.3). The growth of industrial production is steady, and the growth of factory output is particularly strong between 1892 and 1909. One reason for the latter is certainly that many factories were not included in early Meiji factory statistics. Thus, the true level of factory output is underrepresented in early years, and its share in total industrial output seems smaller than warranted. Thus, early figures are not strictly comparable with those after 1909. The ratio of factory output to total manufacturing output, calculated from the *Census of Manufactures* data, rose to more than half by 1914, an important symbolic turning point.

Table 3.3. Factory and Cottage Industry Production: Composition

	Manufacturing industry total production* (¥ million)	Factory production† (¥ million)	Cottage industry production (¥ million)	Cottage industry production in real terms 1935 prices (¥ million)	B/A	C/A
	(A)	(B)	(C) = (A) − (B)			
1884	220.9	(a) 6.5	214.4	664	2.9	97.1
		8.1	212.8	660	3.7	96.3
1892	443.6	(b) 16.7	426.9	1,280	3.8	96.2
		22.1	421.5	1,163	5.0	95.0
1909	1,800	881	919	1,237	48.9	51.1
1914	2,610	1,518	1,092	1,418	58.2	41.8
1920	10,212	6,544	3,668	1,744	64.1	35.9
1930	8,582	6,376	2,206	2,200	74.2	25.8

*Total manufacturing output according to Shionoya [135], appendix table 1.
†Figures for factory production for 1884 and 1892 are estimated by weighted averages from factory output data in tables 17 and 20 of chap. 5 of Yamaguchi [171]. These are thought to be lower than actual figures due to some factories' not being included in the survey. The opinion that these data are underrepresentations is based on the fact that even in 1892 only 69 rice mills in 18 prefectures, 23 silk weavers in 8 prefectures, and 70 cotton weavers in 10 prefectures are included. Factory production after 1909 includes estimated production of public enterprises.

The share of cottage industry production in total industrial output may well have been falling but its absolute level did not decline. Even if we correct for price changes, cottage industry output still increased over the prewar years, except for stability between 1892 and 1909.

Table 3.4 shows the proportion of factory output in total manufacturing output, combining data from Shionoya, Yamaguchi, and the *Census of Manufactures*. The table shows that "large" factories spread earliest in the textile industry and next in the ceramics, machinery, metals, and chemicals industries. The large proportion of factory production in the "other" column is a little odd; it reflects the manufacture of miscellaneous export products from the middle of the Meiji era. Factory production lagged in two of the largest industries, food and lumber. The former produced more than one-third of total industrial output until World War I, and the latter 20% at the start of the 1880s declining to 8% by the start of World War I. Thus, the expansion of factory production was far from uniform across industries.

The large share of traditional industries was not a phenomenon unique to manufacturing. Their share was large in total national income as well, even in very late stages of development. According to previous estimates by this author, even in 1952 the share of national income generated by "capitalist-type" (i.e., modern) enterprises was only about 60% (see table 3.5) (Arisawa and Nakamura [11], p. 112). The only industries in which capitalist production was in a commanding position were mining, electricity, gas, waterworks, communications, and transportation. In agriculture, forestry, fisheries, commerce, and services individual proprietorships were in the overwhelming majority. Thus, the proportion of farms, forests, commercial houses, and services managed according to capitalist methods was quite small even in 1952; after 90 years of development the only industries completely dominated by capitalist management methods were basic industries, primarily mining and manufacturing.

This creates a problem. It implies that industrialization was not so great a cause of rapid growth as once was thought. If firms managed under capitalist methods were late in dominating their industries, the traditional sector—which used noncapitalist methods—could not have been small. Thus, the economy's long-term rapid growth must have occurred in the traditional sector. A simple mathematical example will illustrate. The shares of output in the capitalist and the traditional sectors are labeled a and $1 - a$, respectively, and the overall growth rate is g. The growth rate of the capitalist sector is labeled g_k and that of the traditional sector g_i. Overall growth is of course the sum of the growth rates of the two sectors weighted by their respective shares of output. In algebraic terms:

Table 3.4. Factory Output in Total Manufacturing Output (Percent)

	Food products	Textiles	Lumber and lumber products	Chemicals	Ceramics	Metals	Machinery	Other	Total
1884	0.3	10.5	—	3.2	8.2	6.4	5.5	7.5	—
1892	1.7	9.4	—	8.5	13.4	9.1	3.4	18.5	—
1909	24.3	74.3	13.9	52.0	55.4	31.2	44.5	42.4	44.2
1914	30.2	84.1	19.4	59.4	69.1	29.0	57.8	53.5	52.6
1920	36.2	83.8	26.9	65.8	65.7	59.2	60.5	50.8	67.4
1925	45.0	89.4	31.1	70.0	59.3	75.6	69.4	50.2	65.1
1930	47.3	83.1	42.0	79.4	70.3	72.9	80.5	56.2	69.1
1935	52.9	80.9	48.1	82.8	74.4	104.1	79.4	55.0	77.5
1940	68.8	74.3	52.1	80.1	84.6	107.8	96.7	44.5	77.1

Sources: Data for 1884 and 1892 divide Yamaguchi [171] figures by those of Shionoya [135]. Data for 1909–40 divide figures of Tsūshō Sangyō Shō [161] by those of Shionoya [135].

$$g = ag_k + (1 - a)g_i$$

and thus,

$$g_i = \frac{(g - ag_k)}{(1-a)}.$$

Thus, if we know g, a, and g_k, we can calculate g_i.

In two hypothetical cases growth rates of 2% per year for the traditional sector are obtained. First, for the Meiji years, using known sector weights and a hypothetical overall growth rate of 3%, the growth rate of the traditional sector would be about 2%. Second, for the Taisho and early Showa years, with hypothetical weights of 30 and 70% for capitalist and traditional sectors, respectively, and an overall growth rate of 4%, the traditional sector again would have had to grow about 2% per year.

This then is the essential question: How was it possible for the traditional sectors, i.e., agriculture and noncapitalist manufacturing and services, to grow so fast? What relationship did the modern sector have with the traditional sector? To answer these questions, a few hypotheses are needed and also an overview of the general facts of the sectoral relationship.

INTERDEPENDENCE OF MODERN AND TRADITIONAL INDUSTRIES

Many scholars have held that the progress of capitalism requires the oppression and ruin of traditional small- and medium-scale enterprises. For example, the number of farm households in England began to decline in the 1830s; however, this phenomenon actually did not occur in.

Table 3.5. National Income by Sector in 1952 (¥100 million)

	Capitalist system production (A)	Total production (B)	A/B (%)
Agriculture, forestry, and fisheries	1,289	12,446	10.4
Mining, manufacturing, construction, electricity, gas, and water	16,253	17,110	95.0
Transportation and communications	3,296	3,486	94.5
Commerce, services, finance, and real estate	8,403	16,212	51.8
Total	29,241	49,254	59.4

Source: Arisawa and Nakamura [11], p. 112.

Table 3.6. Scale in Manufacturing: Number of Establishments and Employees (For establishments having five or more workers)

	Total		Factories of 100 or fewer employees		Percentage of small factories in the total C/A	Percentage of workers in small factories D/B
	A Factories	B Employees (thousands)	C Factories	D Employees (thousands)		
1909	32,032	821	30,985	476	97.6	58.0
1914	31,458	1,009	30,108	530	95.7	52.6
1919	43,723	1,808	41,492	817	95.0	45.2
1920	45,576	1,758	43,486	812	95.5	46.3
1921	49,252	1,817	47,090	868	95.5	47.9
1922	46,184	1,871	44,022	781	95.5	41.7
1923	47,491	1,939	45,146	791	95.0	40.6
1924	48,097	1,968	45,663	802	94.8	40.8
1925	48,850	1,996	46,370	810	94.9	40.2
1926	51,513	2,062	48,958	846	94.9	41.1

1927	53,286	2,083	50,559	858	94.9	41.2
1928	55,503	2,133	52,697	901	95.1	42.3
1929	59,436	2,056	56,783	920	95.6	44.8
1930	61,768	1,875	59,189	917	95.8	48.9
1931	63,938	1,842	61,394	902	96.0	48.9
1932	66,810	1,921	64,228	858	96.1	44.7
1933	71,384	2,102	68,628	1,035	96.4	49.3
1934	79,759	2,392	76,752	1,162	96.2	48.6
1935	84,625	2,620	81,356	1,253	96.0	47.9
1936	90,032	2,864	86,534	1,351	96.2	47.2
1937	105,349	3,253	101,529	1,466	96.4	45.1
1938	111,663	3,590	107,400	1,543	96.3	43.1
1939	137,079	4,354	132,547	2,000	96.6	46.0
1940	137,142	4,486	132,643	2,016	96.6	44.9
1941	135,754	4,505	131,500	2,044	97.0	45.4
1942	125,680	4,736	121,431	1,937	96.7	41.0

Source: Tsūshō Sangyō Shō [161].

continental Europe until the 1920s. In Japan's case traditional industries not only survived but in fact prospered. In some cases, such as silk reeling and matches, Japan even turned modern industries introduced from abroad into traditional ones. Moreover, as seen in table 3.6, the absolute numbers of small and medium firms in industry almost never declined but rather increased steadily. There are several reasons for this failure of the relative share of agriculture and of small- and medium-sized enterprises to decline, which conflicts with the prediction of traditional theories. The problem can be considered from two angles: from the standpoint of the traditional industries' position and function in the commodities markets, and from the standpoint of their position and function in the capital and funds markets.

Functional Division in the Commodities Market

First let us consider the commodities market. According to Ohkawa and Rosovsky [104], even in 1955, about 48% of Japanese consumption consisted of traditional items (78% of food consumption was of traditional items, 13% of clothing, 35% of heat and lighting, 77% of residential repairs, 42% of furniture and housewares, and 10% of miscellaneous expenditures). We can surmise that during the Meiji, Taisho, and early Showa periods the share of traditional goods in total consumption was overwhelming. Table 3.7 presents figures for two farm village areas, both around 1910. We can compute that almost 97% of farm area expenditures went for traditional goods. Consumption patterns change during the course of modernization but with long lags. For example, Japanese city dwellers began wearing Western style clothes in large quantities only in the 1920s, whereas in rural areas this change took place only in the latter part of the 1950s.

Besides consumption goods, traditional industry produced a major portion of exports. As seen in table 1.21, the composition of exports of Meiji Japan shifted quickly, especially between 1890 and 1900. In 1868 exports were overwhelmingly agricultural, 40.2% silk thread, 21.8% silkworm egg cards, and 21.5% green tea, a total of almost 84% among only these three. In fact traditional industries first expanded through strong export demand. Silk thread exports were high through the entire Meiji and Taisho periods, while silk and cotton fabric and match exports grew steadily. In 1900 straw plait, matting, ceramics, brushes, Western umbrellas, cotton towels, and buttons were all among the 30 most exported products. Thus, the expansion of Japan's exports was largely sustained by exports of miscellaneous goods.

But strong export demand did not necessarily induce technological progress. Even when such progress came, it came in a form that did not appreciably raise the amount of expensive capital goods used. An example is the establishment by silk wholesalers and cooperatives of common cutting and packing stations with inspection and quality control to improve international competitiveness. Traditional industries could not always compete with modern ones in the intermediate goods market. Cotton imports completely crushed the indigenous cotton industry, and synthetic dyes wiped out indigo and safflower production. Another example is cotton thread; it could be produced in quantity only after the establishment of large cotton spinning companies, which introduced mechanical looms. And these large spinning companies could produce only wide cotton fabric for export. On the other hand the large companies did not produce narrow fabric for domestic use. Diversity of preferences for patterns and coloring of the narrow breadth cloth used in the home market necessitated small-scale production. It was in this market that the small local producers were able to survive and prosper.

Between these extremes was an interdependence of traditional and modern industries. In general, modern industries were suppliers of intermediate goods, and many industries were created solely for this purpose. Supply by modern firms of cheap, uniform thread spurred the development of small-scale local weavers. For example, Kijirō Kunitake, manufacturer of home-market-oriented *kurume-kasuri* cloth, founded the Kurume Spinning Company specifically as a supplier of thread for kurume-kasuri (Kinugawa [55], pp. 362–78). Flour milling and sugar refining gave rise to many small businesses while shipbuilding and rolling stock construction fostered the modern industries of motor and electric machinery manufacturing. The lumber industry grew in response to the furniture industry and other traditional industries. Thus, although there were traditional industries unable to compete with the emerging modern industries in the developing capitalist economy, there were many other industries where the traditional sector grew stronger as the economy developed. Indeed, from the Meiji period onward, the traditional industries consolidated their position, and their interdependence with the modern sector became both possible and necessary. Herein lies the reason for the balanced growth between the two sectors.

An Abstract Example
Let us now try a simple mathematical simulation of interdependence, using a two-sector input–output model. The variables are as follows:

x_i output of the ith sector

a_{ij} an input coefficient, the value of good from the ith industry used in making an amount of good from the jth industry with value 1.

f_j the rate of value added in the jth industry; i.e., the proportion of value left over in good j after the values of all inputs have been subtracted,

Table 3.7. Consumption in Farm Villages

Aomori prefecture, Minami Tsugaru district (1908) (¥1,000)

	Total	Amount spent on modern consumption	Products
Food	3,526	23	Sugar, tobacco, canned goods, beer and foreign liquor, ice, and lemonade
Clothing	104	40	Woolens, flannel, serge, blankets, knit goods, cotton yarn
Furnishings	217	10	Rickshas, baby carriages, wagons, bicycles, books
Other supplies	268	60	Matches, foreign paper, shoes, petroleum, medicine
Total of the above	4,115	133	

Source: Aomori Prefecture, Minami Tsugaru District, *Gunze* (The Objectives of This District) (1911).

Niigata prefecture, Naka-kubiki district (ca. 1916) (¥1,000)

	Total	Purchases outside the district	Amount spent on modern consumption	Products
Food	5,883	457	32	Beer, lemonade, cider and other beverages, meat, milk, canned goods
Clothing	1,137	1,133	37	Western clothing, Japanese socks, blankets, other Western garments
Furnishings	279	89	4	Shoes
Other supplies	630	311	189	Notebooks, pencils, vehicles, bicycles, books, newspapers, magazines, clocks, medicines, lamps, petroleum, electric lanterns
Total of the above	7,929	1,990	262	

Source: Niigata prefecture, Naka-kubiki district, *Gunze* (The Objectives of This District) (1916).

$= (1 - \sum_{i=1}^{n} a_{ij})$. Thus the total value added of industry j is

$f_j X_j = (1 - \sum_{i=1}^{n} a_{ij}) X_j$, that is, the rate of value added multiplied by the amount produced.

α the propensity to consume; thus, total consumption would be

$\alpha \sum_{i=1}^{n} f_i X_i$

c_i share of ith good in total consumption

$(\sum_{i=1}^{n} c_i = 1)$

d final demand other than consumption (a column vector)
x a vector of x_is (column)
c a vector of c_is (column)
f' a vector of f_is (row) ($f'x$ is total income)
A a matrix of a_{ij}s (square) showing the state of technology and implicitly the degree of interdependence among sectors.

The only difference between this and the normal input–output model is that this model makes consumption endogenous. With these definitions, the following equation, comprising elements for intermediate, consumption, and other final demand, can be formed:

$Ax + \alpha c f'x + d = x.$

Solving for x, we get

$x = (I - A - \alpha c f')^{-1} d,$

where I is the identity matrix.

To simplify matters, I will limit this model to two sectors, a modern sector (sector 1) and a traditional (sector 2). To show the varying degrees of interdependence of sectors, table 3.8 gives the technology matrix (A) in five possible versions. The matrix in case I shows the modern sector's output of intermediate goods to be low even for its own use; in this case the traditional sector provides most intermediate output although even the rate of supply by the traditional sector to the modern is not high. This is a case of low interdependence. Case V is the opposite, one of high interdependence. Both sectors in this case supply more intermediate goods although the modern sector has developed more relative to case I than the traditional has. Cases II–IV are possible matrices between the

Table 3.8. Permutations of Technology Matrix *A* and Value-Added Vector *f*

	Input from	Output of Modern sector	Traditional sector
Case I. Heavily weighted traditional sector	M	$\begin{bmatrix} .1 \\ .2 \end{bmatrix}$	.1
as in early stages of growth	T		.2
Value-added vector		(.7	.7)
Case II. Increased trade within the modern	M	$\begin{bmatrix} .2 \\ .2 \end{bmatrix}$	.1
sector and increased trade between sectors	T		.2
Value-added vector		(.6	.7)
Case III. Further increased trade within the	M	$\begin{bmatrix} .3 \\ .3 \end{bmatrix}$	.2
modern sector and increased trade	T		.2
between sectors			
Value-added vector		(.4	.6)
Case IV. Increased inputs from modern	M	$\begin{bmatrix} .3 \\ .3 \end{bmatrix}$	.4
sector into traditional sector	T		.2
Value-added vector		(.4	.4)
Case V. Still further increase in trade within	M	$\begin{bmatrix} .4 \\ .3 \end{bmatrix}$	.4
the modern sector	T		.2
Value-added vector		(.3	.4)

Note: M, modern sector; T, traditional sector.

extremes. For the sake of convenience, α is fixed at 0.8. For the consumption pattern vector two cases are used, the first with great dependence on the traditional sector [0.1 0.9], and the second with decreased but still high dependence on it [0.3 0.7]. Exogenous demand is assumed to total 1, with three cases considered, heavy dependence on the traditional sector [0.1 0.9], equal dependence on both [0.5 0.5], and heavy dependence on the modern sector [0.9 0.1].

Thus we have five possibilities for A, two for c, and three for d. In all there are 30 permutations. For each of these the basic equation can be solved, and outputs and total values added can be derived for both the modern sector (x_1 and f_1) and the traditional sector (x_2 and f_2). However, we must be careful of the assumption that the elements of d sum to unity. In normal economic circumstances this value would grow. But for our present purposes it will suffice to focus on the relative sizes of the outputs and values added of the two sectors. Thus, we can set the sum of elements in the exogenous demand vector equal to unity without harming the results. Moreover, with α fixed at 0.8, the value of d must be 0.2 of total value added; then, with the value of d set to one, total national income (total value added) is set at five.

Table 3.9. Simulation Model

Case	Technology matrices A	Implied value-added vectors f	Consumption patterns c	Final demand d
I	$\begin{bmatrix} .1 & .1 \\ .2 & .2 \end{bmatrix}$	$\begin{bmatrix} .7 \\ .7 \end{bmatrix}$	Case (a) $\begin{bmatrix} .1 \\ .9 \end{bmatrix}$	Case (i) $\begin{bmatrix} .1 \\ .9 \end{bmatrix}$
II	$\begin{bmatrix} .2 & .1 \\ .2 & .2 \end{bmatrix}$	$\begin{bmatrix} .6 \\ .7 \end{bmatrix}$		(ii) $\begin{bmatrix} .5 \\ .5 \end{bmatrix}$
III	$\begin{bmatrix} .3 & .2 \\ .3 & .2 \end{bmatrix}$	$\begin{bmatrix} .4 \\ .6 \end{bmatrix}$	(b) $\begin{bmatrix} .3 \\ .7 \end{bmatrix}$	(iii) $\begin{bmatrix} .9 \\ .1 \end{bmatrix}$
IV	$\begin{bmatrix} .3 & .4 \\ .3 & .2 \end{bmatrix}$	$\begin{bmatrix} .4 \\ .4 \end{bmatrix}$		
V	$\begin{bmatrix} .4 & .4 \\ .3 & .2 \end{bmatrix}$	$\begin{bmatrix} .3 \\ .4 \end{bmatrix}$		

Value of gross output

		I	II	III	IV	V
(a)	i					
	M	1.21	1.37	2.60	5.00	6.11
	T	5.93	5.96	6.60	7.50	7.92
	ii					
	M	1.61	1.83	3.08	5.37	6.56
	T	5.53	5.58	6.28	7.14	7.59
	iii					
	M	2.01	1.37	3.56	5.73	7.00
	T	4.33	5.96	5.96	6.77	7.25
(b)	i					
	M	2.01	2.27	3.56	5.73	7.00
	T	5.13	5.19	5.96	6.77	7.25
	ii					
	M	2.41	2.73	4.04	6.10	7.45
	T	4.73	4.81	5.64	6.41	6.92
	iii					
	M	2.81	3.18	4.52	6.46	7.89
	T	4.33	4.42	5.32	6.04	6.58

Share of value added in traditional sector

		I	II	III	IV	V
(a)	i	.83	.84	.79	.60	.63
	ii	.83	.78	.75	.57	.61
	iii	.68	.74	.72	.54	.58
(b)	i	.72	.73	.72	.54	.58
	ii	.66	.67	.68	.51	.55
	iii	.61	.62	.64	.48	.53

Source: Calculation by the author.

Note: Vector of modern and traditional gross output is

$$\begin{bmatrix} M \\ T \end{bmatrix} = (I - A - \alpha c f')^{-1} d,$$

where α is marginal propensity to consume, set constant at .8.

The results of size of output x_i and its composition are presented in table 3.9 for the various permutations. The different cases of interdependence are denoted by upper case roman numerals, with lower case roman numerals for the different cases of final demand. Lower case (a) and (b) denote different consumption patterns. The simulation yields the following results:

1. As interdependence grows (i.e., as one goes from case I to case V), both sectors expand output but the expansion is greatest for the modern sector.
2. When interdependence is low, growth of output is due chiefly to changes in the composition of consumption (c) and of exogenous demand (d). However, when interdependence is high, growth of output is most dependent on the structure of interdependence.
3. A similar trend is seen for value added but changes are not so great as in the case of output. Even for case V and combination (b) and combination iii (i.e., high interdependence, consumption structure skewed toward the modern sector, and exogenous demand skewed toward the modern sector), the share of value added of the traditional sector is still greater than 50%.
4. Thus, even though input structure, consumption patterns, and exogenous demand may change greatly, traditional industries still provide the major share of output. Moreover, since employment per unit of output or of value added is greater for the traditional sector, that sector's share of total employment will be even greater than its share of value added.

Calculating actual input–output coefficients (i.e., degree of interdependence) for the Meiji and Taisho periods is not yet possible, so we cannot specify which permutation is closest to Japan's actual experience. But the simulation does provide some excellent clues for the analysis of the process of Japanese economic development. Japanese traditional industry was not only a supplier of consumption goods but of intermediate goods as well. It was only slowly replaced by modern industry. Input–output analysis reveals one of the mechanisms accounting for the traditional sector's stubborn persistence in the process of capitalist industrialization.

The Function of Price

Price increases for traditional goods also helped the traditional sector survive and expand despite low productivity growth and small-scale operations. No rapid technological progress occurred in traditional industry and capital did not flow in from other sectors; moreover, agriculture was also constrained by the limited availability of arable land. It is a general phenomenon in economic growth for agricultural products to increase in price; this occurred in many countries before World War I. A similar trend occurred in prices of manufactured goods of small-scale firms. Two numerical series demonstrate this. The first, seen in table 3.10, shows price indexes of agricultural and industrial goods (seven-year moving averages) and a ratio of the two. Both price indexes rose after 1886 (when the Matsukata deflation hit bottom) and continued rising until after World War I. The relative position of agricultural prices worsened considerably during the Matsukata deflation, especially when compared to manufactured goods prices. Relative agricultural prices improved greatly thereafter until 1895 but worsened again from that time until the middle of World War I. Overall, the agricultural terms of trade remained relatively stable between 1890 and 1920.

To look at modern versus traditional prices within the industrial sector, we shall compare the food products industry, the strongest of the traditional manufacturing industries, with three representative modern industries: textiles, machinery, and metals. Table 3.11 shows the ratios of the food products price index to the indexes of the other three industries. Food product prices relative to manufactured goods prices rose steadily from early Meiji years until World War I, except during violent fluctuations about 1885. Thus, at least until World War I, price increases compensated for low productivity growth in the traditional sector and kept it profitable.

The Financial Side

As noted above, one of the first modern industries to develop was the financial industry, whose development helped traditional industries in many ways. For example, the 1886 deposit and loan statistics of national banks (see table 3.12) indicate that nearly 60% of both deposits and loans came from or went to merchants. Next in importance came aristocrats and former officials who had converted bonds granted in lieu of stipends into capital. Certainly this "merchant" class included landlords or landlord-merchant-industrialists, but just as certainly it included traditional industrialists as well as debtors and creditors in the general economy. For example, the most important financial sponsors of the silk reeling industry were raw silk wholesalers in Yokohama and in rural areas. In the case of cotton spinning, the cotton yarn merchants and even raw cotton merchants played a significant financial role at least until the 1890s (see Yamaguchi [172], [173]). These merchants borrowed money on their own account from financial institutions and then provided funds to producers. This new financial institution—the bank—thus played an extremely important role both for merchant houses and for the manufacturing industry that these houses in turn supported.

Table 3.10. Agricultural Terms of Trade (Seven-year averages centered on year listed)

	Agric. goods price index (1)	Refrig. goods price index (2)	Agric. terms of trade (3) =(2/1)×100
1888	25.5	35.5	72
1889	26.0	35.9	72
1890	27.0	36.6	74
1891	28.7	37.3	77
1892	30.6	38.5	79
1893	32.4	39.8	81
1894	34.1	41.8	82
1895	37.5	44.8	84
1896	39.8	47.9	83
1897	42.3	57.2	83
1898	43.8	54.0	81
1889	45.8	56.3	81
1900	48.4	58.7	82
1901	49.7	60.6	82
1902	50.0	62.9	79
1903	51.7	65.2	79
1904	54.1	67.9	80
1905	56.4	70.4	80
1906	57.2	72.6	79
1907	57.1	74.4	77
1908	59.2	76.2	78
1909	62.8	77.5	81
1910	65.8	78.2	84
1911	64.7	77.5	83
1912	63.6	78.0	82
1913	64.5	81.7	79
1914	68.8	89.4	77
1915	78.1	101.3	77
1916	92.8	116.2	80
1917	102.3	132.7	77
1918	114.7	143.3	80
1919	125.3	153.3	82
1920	136.5	161.1	85
1921	145.5	164.8	88
1922	147.8	162.9	91
1923	140.9	155.0	91

Table 3.10 (*continued*)

	Agric. goods price index (1)	Refrig. goods price index (2)	Agric. terms of trade (3) =(2/1)×100
1924	136.9	144.7	95
1925	132.0	140.9	94
1926	131.0	136.3	96
1927	122.0	128.1	95
1928	110.7	117.3	94
1929	100.5	108.7	92
1930	93.6	104.7	89
1931	90.0	101.4	89
1932	87.9	97.9	90
1933	86.9	95.2	91
1934	93.0	100.2	93
1935	101.2	108.8	93
1936	114.6	118.0	97
1937	129.5	127.2	102

Source: Ohkawa et al. [O], table A50.

The next nationwide statistics after 1886 on depositors and borrowers do not appear until the last half of the 1920s. But a process similar to the following is most likely to have occurred. Until the end of World War I the most important customers of financial institutions were indeed local traditional industries. This situation changed visibly only in the 1920s after small- and medium-sized banks in local areas began to have management problems and after the Panic of 1927 and enactment of the Banking Law had started the process of merger of these small banks into larger banks. This is seen in the loan statistics of table 3.13.

As further evidence in favor of this contention, we can cite the degree of concentration of banks. The total paid-up capital of banks increased markedly in three major periods of pre-1920 banking growth: (1) the National Bank era (1876–85), (2) the period of change from National Banking to an "ordinary bank" (*futsū ginkō*) system (1895–1900), and (3) the period of World War I. But even in these periods the shares of paid-up capital, deposits, and loans held by the large city banks did not increase significantly. The position of local banks in financial statistics weakened only slightly, except during World War I. Moreover, data on

Table 3.11. Relative Prices

	Textiles/ agriculture	Machinery/ agriculture	Metals/ agriculture
1874	2.45	3.62	2.29
1875	2.04	3.05	2.06
1876	2.81	3.28	2.32
1877	2.17	2.58	1.90
1878	2.07	2.24	1.74
1879	1.81	1.82	1.49
1880	1.78	1.54	1.66
1881	1.98	1.41	1.72
1882	2.21	1.61	1.86
1883	2.15	2.01	1.96
1884	2.22	1.95	1.65
1885	2.12	1.68	1.40
1886	2.10	1.53	1.25
1887	2.28	1.96	1.41
1888	2.43	2.42	1.96
1889	2.29	2.03	1.53
1890	1.76	1.67	1.23
1891	1.74	1.73	1.28
1892	1.91	1.61	1.21
1893	2.07	1.60	1.27
1894	1.81	1.44	1.32
1895	1.94	1.57	1.39
1896	1.74	1.57	1.31
1897	1.61	1.45	1.31
1898	1.48	1.26	1.11
1899	1.91	1.60	1.60
1900	1.76	1.56	1.64
1901	1.77	1.58	1.54
1902	1.67	1.44	1.27
1903	1.53	1.28	1.16
1904	1.64	1.45	1.27
1905	1.73	1.49	1.34
1906	1.70	1.42	1.34
1907	1.68	1.36	1.31
1908	1.52	1.29	1.12
1909	1.67	1.31	1.15
1910	1.70	1.33	1.14
1911	1.50	1.11	0.96
1912	1.28	1.11	1.01

Table 3.11 (*continued*)

	Textiles/ agriculture	Machinery/ agriculture	Metals/ agriculture
1913	1.29	1.08	0.97
1914	1.58	1.36	1.20
1915	1.60	1.80	1.81
1916	1.83	2.00	2.25
1917	1.81	1.94	2.18
1918	1.61	1.41	1.61
1919	1.61	0.84	0.86
1920	1.85	1.10	1.00
1921	1.32	1.00	0.70
1922	1.54	1.08	0.77
1923	1.51	1.02	0.78
1924	1.43	0.93	0.71
1925	1.42	0.77	0.72
1926	1.26	0.79	0.72
1927	1.26	0.80	0.77
1928	1.29	0.91	0.86
1929	1.29	0.94	0.68
1930	1.34	1.24	1.07
1931	1.16	1.21	0.89
1932	1.14	1.16	0.98
1933	1.22	1.21	1.21
1934	1.08	1.11	1.12
1935	0.97	0.97	0.95
1936	0.96	0.93	0.93
1937	1.00	1.24	1.61
1938	0.97	1.19	1.57
1939	0.89	0.85	0.99
1940	0.90	0.77	0.93

Source: Calculated from Ohkawa [99], pp. 166, 192.

borrowers from local banks show that ties between local banks and traditional industry were strong. The major portion of banks' money went to local, traditional industry. The data are from the late 1920s and the 1930s after the process of bank concentration had begun. But outside cities, where old practices persisted, the proportion of loans to farmers and merchants was high nevertheless. Of course, not all merchants were traditional ones in the 1930s, but outside the six metropolitan areas most

Table 3.12. National Banks in 1886: Composition of Depositors and Borrowers (Percent)

		Aristocrats	Agriculture	Industry	Commerce	Enterprises	Misc.	Total	Total amount (¥1,000)
Nationwide	Depositors	16.56	3.35	1.14	57.11	14.81	7.03	100.00	19,167
	Borrowers	17.78	10.59	0.70	57.94	8.34	4.65	100.00	35,063
Tokyo	Depositors	21.75	0.03	1.18	52.04	19.40	5.61	100.00	6,735
	Borrowers	39.44	2.00	0.44	41.24	14.81	3.07	100.00	8,717
Non-Tokyo	Depositors	13.75	5.15	1.12	59.87	12.33	7.80	100.00	12,431
	Borrowers	10.94	13.43	0.79	63.47	6.19	5.17	100.00	26,345

Source: Fujino [24], pp. 561–65, bases estimates on Ministry of Finance, *Ninth Annual Report of the Banking Bureau* (Ginkō Kyoku Daikuji Hōkoku).

Table 3.13. Bank Loans by Occupation of Borrower (Percent)

Percentage of nationwide total	June 1928			June 1933			
	Merchants and industrialists	Agriculturalists	Other	Merchants	Industrialists	Agriculturalists	Other
Ordinary banks Six largest cities	81.2	0.4	18.4	44.0	26.2	0.6	29.2
Other cities	67.0	5.9	27.1	42.0	17.7	5.0	35.2
Nonurban areas	57.2	22.3	20.4	35.9	16.1	33.1	25.0
Total	71.8	7.4	20.8	42.0	22.4	5.8	27.7
Savings banks Six largest cities	75.4	0.6	24.0	56.3	10.7	0.5	32.5
Other cities	65.7	6.7	27.6	54.2	10.7	5.3	29.8
Nonurban areas	61.9	19.0	19.0	—	—	—	—
Total	71.1	4.0	24.9	54.9	10.7	3.1	31.5

Source: Ministry of Finance, *Nationwide Survey of Ordinary and Savings Banks' Loans by Amount and by Occupation,* quoted in Gotō [29], pp. 136–37, 140–41.

Table 3.14. Bank Loans by Industry: Developed vs. Less Developed Areas (Percent)

A. Major banks in Aichi, Gifu, and Mie prefectures

	Year-end, 1936	Year-end, 1941
Manufacturing	23.6	44.0
Textiles	12.4	9.5
Machinery and steel	1.4	24.3
Chemicals	—	1.6
Ceramics	1.9	3.0
Lumber	4.5	4.0
Other	3.4	1.6
Commerce	32.3	21.8
Textiles	18.1	13.1
Machinery and metals	4.0	2.7
Other	10.2	6.0
Agriculture, forestry, and fisheries	2.9	1.5
Public enterprise	6.4	3.5
Financial and stockbrokerage	11.8	4.6
Public bodies and industrial associations	0.9	3.5
Real estate	4.9	2.9
Other	17.2	18.2
Total	100.0	100.0

B. All banks in Akita prefecture

	Year-end, 1937
Agriculture	31.9
Lumber products	11.3
Finance	9.5
Public bodies	7.8
Sake brewery	5.3
General merchants	5.1
Clothing merchants	4.3
Mining	2.2
Marine products and fertilizer merchants	1.6
Shipping and warehousing	1.4
Miso and soy sauce	1.1
Electricity and gas	0.0
Other	18.5
Total	100.0

Sources: For Aichi, Gifu, and Mie prefectures, Tōkai Ginkō [148], p. 121. For Akita prefecture, Akita Ginkō [3], p. 405.

probably were. Local statistics for the three prefectures of the Tokai region (Aichi, Gifu, and Mie) and for Akita prefecture are even later, but still show high proportions of loans to local industries. (See tables 3.13 and 3.14.) The three Tokai prefectures had large amounts of loans to textile-related industry and commerce as well as to ceramics while Akita prefecture's loans were concentrated in the lumber and brewing industries.

At first this may seem to be only normal banking but beneath the surface lie significant facts. On one hand banking, which was a modern industry borrowed from abroad, played a vital role in supporting traditional industry; on the other hand the traditional wholesaler's system helped create certain modern industries. The relationship between the two types of industry, modern and traditional, not only in input–output relations but in financial matters as well, was one of interdependence. Thus, it took more than 50 years from the time of the Meiji Restoration for the interdependent relationship between the traditional and modern sectors to change so that the modern sector clearly dominated. This domination of the modern sector dates from the 1920s. Both in Japan and in the European countries except England several trends were evident: Agricultural and small merchant or industrialist classes were dissolving even though the traditional sector of the economy, which consisted of these same classes, was expanding and the relative prices of its products were increasing. The latter two tendencies substantially slowed the dissolution of these classes. These trends are common to all the industrialized nations with the exception of England.

APPENDIX TO CHAPTER 3: □ THE FORMATION OF MANAGERIAL AND CAPITALIST CLASSES

THE FLOW OF TRADITIONAL INDUSTRY CAPITAL INTO MODERN INDUSTRY

Japan is said to have adopted capitalism from the top down, and this notion is indeed partly valid. As seen before, the government promoted shokusan kōgyō policies and encouraged investment in new industries by opening trade fairs, directing regional officials to solicit the financial support of locally powerful people, and enlisting high central government officials who themselves sounded the call for industrialization. One cannot forget economic leaders linked to the government such as Eiichi Shibusawa, Tomoatsu Godai of Osaka, Masaka Okuda of the Nagoya area, and Masana Maeda, who spent a lifetime promoting industry in farm villages. Politically connected businessmen (*seishō*) and financial cliques (zaibatsu) like Mitsui, Mitsubishi, Sumitomo, Yasuda, Furukawa, Asano, Kawasaki, and Okura and smaller concerns like Takada or Akaboshi had ties with the government that are well known. This aspect of Japanese growth was certainly "capitalism from the top."

But capitalism cannot succeed if adopted only at the top. The "bottom" must also adopt it, and to do so it must have economic and intellectual ability as well as adaptable social values. We must consider the followers, not just the leaders. For example, dissemination of education in the late Tokugawa and particularly the Meiji periods was critical to developing a managerial class, as were the effects of traditional Confucianism and Buddhism.

Three issues are most important in studying the managerial class. First, who accumulated the capital for modern enterprises, and how was the capital procured by the firms? Second, what were the attitudes of managers, or what characterized their "entrepreneurial spirit?" Third, assuming that a qualitative change in the managerial class did occur, when and how did it occur?

First, let us summarize previous scholarship on these issues. Takao Tsuchiya has conducted an analysis of origins and class rank (*shusshin mibun*) of prominent business leaders. This deals essentially with issue number two above. "Most notable," he says, "is the preponderance of businessmen from the former warrior-bureaucrat (*bushi*) class. Next come those of agrarian origin. Conversely, old-style merchants are very few and craftsmen extremely rare. Of those left, a fair number come from medical families." In a sample of 27 representative businessmen, 10 were from warrior-bureaucrat backgrounds, 10 agrarian (particularly rich farmers), and the rest were from sake brewing or medical families. There was only one merchant among them. Tsuchiya concludes that the old merchant class "had but little modern learning, modern sensibility, or innovative spirit." On the other hand, he continues, the warrior-bureaucrat class was quick to absorb the new knowledge and took the lead in introducing new organizational forms. (See Tsuchiya [159], pp. 170, 182.)

Johannes Hirschmeier has taken 50 businessmen as representatives of the Meiji era and collected data on their origins and education. Among these 50, 23 were of warrior-bureaucrat families, 13 from farm families, 12 from merchant families, and two unknown. Thirty received training in commerce, 11 as teachers, and nine in other professions. Hirschmeier criticizes the view that merchants held first rank among business leaders throughout the Meiji era. This viewpoint, he says, does not take account of the difference between "revolutionary business methods and customary business methods." Moreover, he emphasized that the merchants as a group were the latest group to enter modern business. But for industrialists class origin was not a decisive factor. Regardless of class origin these men severed the ties of their previous economic lives and started fresh. These businessmen with no class ties were the revolutionary entrepreneurs (see Hirschmeier [D], pp. 216–19).

The two works cited above have one point in common. They both deal only with men such as Shibusawa and Godai, who helped start many industries aided by the central government, or with men such as Takeo Yamabe, who developed one industry (cotton spinning) thoroughly. That is, both works deal only with top leaders. While these men may have been the crème de la crème of Meiji capitalism, they were but a small elite. They probably are not representative of the myriad of nonelite entrepreneurs. Moreover, even though the elite may have accumulated much wealth, many began life empty-handed. An investigation into the finances of these firms speaks directly to the general issue of the class origins of Meiji entrepreneurs, as will be demonstrated below.

Thus, banking once again takes center stage. According to Asakura, the first few national banks were established by merchants and landlords, e.g., the First, Second, Fourth, and Fifth National Banks. After 1874 and the commutation of stipend bonds, the court nobles and warrior-bureaucrats acquired power in the banking system but within a few years their importance waned. Particularly after the 1883 revision of the national banking regulations the national banking system was supported and managed by merchants, not by those of warrior-bureaucrat origin. Thus, bond commutation caused temporary upheaval in the national banking system, but in the final analysis national banks were built by, and eventually returned to, merchant hands.

Yukio Chō [17] has classified founders of banks into five categories: (1) merchants with political connections from the Tokugawa period, (2) former moneylenders and money changers, (3) former aristocrats, (4) former warrior-bureaucrats, and (5) former merchants. But which were most important? In Asakura's words, "Merchants were the moving force. This includes the giant commercial houses, moneychangers, and traders who dated from the Tokugawa period, along with moneychangers, traders, and wholesalers who arose in the Meiji era. There were many types, but they were all merchants or landlords" (see Asakura [13], p. 134). The meanings of *merchant* and *landlord* in this quotation are not quite clear, but it is clear that capitalists of traditional industry scattered throughout the various regions had large financial savings and played a major role as suppliers of funds for the establishment of industry.

Table 3.15 gives statistics on the origins of managers and suppliers of funds for 74 spinning companies. There were indeed many former warrior-bureaucrats among the company founders and funds suppliers of the Jukki Spinning Company in the earlier period, but many other firms were started by rich farmers or by combinations of merchants and landlords. After 1885 there was not a single case of funds being supplied solely by a former warrior-bureaucrat. As can be seen from the data virtually all money came from merchants or from combinations of merchants, landlords, and warrior-bureaucrats.

Warrior-bureaucrats did function in intellectual capacities as administrators and technicians. Examples include Takeo Yamabe of Osaka Spinning (later Tōyō Spinning) and Kyōzō Kikuchi, who was chief engineer for three companies, Hirano Spinning, Settsu Spinning, and Amagasaki Spinning. But in most cases the upper level of management of the spinning companies, especially of the large spinning companies, was controlled by the merchants who supplied the money. The names of merchants such as Heizaemon Hibiya, Jiemon Takeo, Nihei Kanazawa, Heibei Hirano, Ichirōbei Abe, and Fusazō Taniguchi are of great importance in the beginnings of cotton spinning companies in Tokyo and Osaka. The use of aristocratic money by Eiichi Shibusawa in founding Osaka Spinning was a pioneering and significant move, but it did not reflect normal practice for spinning companies of the era.

Isao Denda has said that the leaders of the cotton spinning industry in the 1880s were not merely "local notables" but rather were a group that had achieved "a certain level of education and critical ability." He views them as "more than the founders of local spinning concerns." They contributed to other enterprises, involved themselves in the founding of local banks, and took leading positions in agriculture and local politics. (See Denda ([19], p. 295.) Particularly considering the reorganization of

Table 3.15. Financiers and Managers of Spinning Companies Established by 1897

		Merchants and industrialists	Landlords	Ex-warrior bureaucrats	Merchant–landlord joint ventures	Ex-warrior bureaucrats	Others	Total
Those established before 1885	Financiers	6	1	6	4	2	—	19
	Managers	6	2	9	2	—	—	19
	Successors to management positions	4	—	—	1	—	—	5
Those established between 1885 and 1896	Financiers	32	1	—	7	10	5	55
	Managers	34	2	11	4	—	5	55
	Successors to management positions	6	—	—	—	—	—	6

Source: Kinugawa [55], vol. 7.

the cotton spinning industry in the 1890s in corporate form by the Osaka-centered merchants who were its financiers, Denda points out that "the industry needed from its earliest days the skills of the merchants, especially in buying raw materials [as well as in sales]." This phenomenon was not unique to the cotton spinning industry; it occurred as well in the flour milling and noodle industries. (See Denda [19], pp. 312, 354.)

Thus, the merchants of the early Meiji years provided a great deal of capital from personal funds, established new industries, and managed them. Quantitative analysis is not yet possible, but landlords in rural localities and merchants in cities certainly accumulated capital in substantial amounts and created a relatively large class of capitalist industries. In analyzing Japan's relatively rapid industrialization, one should not overlook the role played by small and local capitalists and their financial accumulation.

But even in the spinning industry, financial and enterprise management could not be left to the merchant entrepreneurs forever. With the evolution of giant firms, the power of large stockholders must inevitably weaken and later control must slip completely from their hands. But at the earliest this transformation took place during the interim between the Russo–Japanese War (1904–05) and World War I even for the spinning firms, which boasted the greatest capital accumulating ability. Be it in banking or spinning, the real power over company management was wielded for the most part by merchants and landlords.

Numerous examples have been given by Asakura, Denda, Kinugawa, and others. The following cases may also be cited. The families of Kimpei Jinnō, Kinnosuke Jinnō, and Jūsuke Tomita were landlords and village leaders in a farm village on the outskirts of Nagoya at the end of the Tokugawa era. During these years they established themselves in Nagoya in the Momijiya, a house dealing in Western merchandise. They acquired wealth through sales of foreign woolens and after the restoration lent their funds at high interest. In the words of a biographer, "Once they had made a profit, then they lent it out again. What they first lent out on a deed, they later lent as mortgage on property. By foreclosing on unpaid mortgages, they entered the land management business, then progressed to forestry and eventually into opening new agricultural lands" (Hottā, [38], p. 51). The Jinnō family became large-scale landlords with the development of 1,100 chō (about 2,700 acres) of new farmland on Atsumi Bay but later funded and managed Dai Nippon Crucible, the Tōkai Steamship Company, the Meiji Bank, the Atsuta (later Meiji) Savings Bank, the Bishu Agricultural and Industrial Bank, Fukuju Life Insurance, Fukuju Fire Insurance, the Nagoya Electric Railroad, and Chōsen Industries (a farming development near Pusan).

Moreover, they had interests in Tōyō Spinning and in Nagoya Electric. The Jinnō family followed the path of landlord to merchant to moneylender, back to landlord, and formed ties with many firms. But they always combined being landlords and industrialists.

Another example is the Taki family of Befu in Hyogo prefecture. Katsuichiro Taki began as a landlord-freeholder in the Tokugawa era with 5 chō and 2 tan (about 13 acres) of land, but soon started to brew soy sauce and vinegar and to sell fish fertilizer. After extending an* official loan to the lord of Himeji province, he even won the right to bear arms. But with the Meiji Restoration and the revision of the land tax law, Taki acquired large-scale wealth through land purchase. His eldest son Katsubei managed a raw silk trading house in Tokyo, while the next son Toyoji and the fourth son Senkichi started with a fan belt manufacturing concern in Osaka and succeeded as well with the Osaka Leather Factory. The third son Kumejirō later started the Taki Fertilizer Company but for many years carried on the brewing and fish fertilizer merchandising concerns. Kumejirō also founded the Befu Light Railway, the Banyō Bank, and the Sanyō Railroad, as well as participating in trust and life insurance concerns and providing a fair amount of capital to mining concerns. Around the time of World War I he took over 570 chō (about 1,400 acres) of farmland and later another 2,700 chō (about 6,600 acres) (see Aritake [12]).

Fusazō Taniguchi of Osaka provides another interesting example. Beginning as a merchant of cotton cloth, he was selected in 1893 as a member of an "internal investigation committee" for the troubled management of the Meiji Spinning Company. Soon he became a board member and later executive director. As various Osaka area spinning companies went bankrupt, he merged them all into the Osaka Gōdō Spinning Company with himself as president and thus ascended into the ranks of the capitalist class.

In summary many enterprises were started under the shokusan kōgyō policies, but the leaders of these firms were either bureaucrats of upper class origin who had learned the new sciences from abroad or businessmen closely connected with the government. Kaoru Inoue and Eiichi Shibusawa, two representatives of this class, were pioneers who had dispensed completely with traditional merchant and landlord activities.

But these elite leaders alone neither supplied the funds for nor managed all industry. City merchants and rural landlords funded and managed new industries in banking, railroads, silk reeling, and cotton spinning. Most did not devote their time solely to the new businesses. Without breaking ties with their traditional callings, they took on two or more activities and invested their total income where most beneficial to themselves. At times they even funded and managed enterprises in the modern sector the better to carry on traditional businesses. Cold calculations of rates of return and of risk led to the diversification and dispersion of capital. Naturally, these small capitalists did not indulge in objective assessments of the contribution that the resulting new industries would make to economic growth. They just followed the path to wealth.

The early introduction of a means for the accumulation of capital in the form of the joint stock company created conditions that were most beneficial to the profit-maximizing behavior of landlords and merchants that is described above. With limited liability they could invest a portion of their family wealth in equities. Not only were they able to diversify their personal holdings but also, as stockholders, they were able to participate in planning and management. The corporate form certainly did speed capital accumulation but just as certainly it worked to the advantage of traditional landlords and merchants.

THE FORMATION OF A MODERN MANAGERIAL CLASS

Decision making on the everyday affairs of a firm cannot, of course, be left to the "capitalist-class" directors who meet only infrequently. Full-time managers must emerge as well. Among the examples above, Taki and Taniguchi eventually devoted their time solely to their respective enterprises. There were many other cases in which the founders, whose primary occupation was merchant or landlord, were only intermittently involved as company executives. Their heirs later became full-time enterprise managers after inheriting equity and positions as directors. Examples include Magosaburō Ohara of Kurashiki Spinning and Fusajirō Abe first of Kanakin Spinning and later of Tōyō Spinning. However, there was a gradual rise in the number of directors from administrative or technical posts. With the last half of the 1890s the trend became apparent; Takeo Yamabe became a director of Osaka Spinning in 1895, Kyōzō Kikuchi of Settsu Spinning in 1897, and Jūemon Tashiro of Amagasaki Spinning in 1901. The former two came from technical backgrounds while Tashiro was in sales but all pioneered in rising from supervisory posts to directorships. Other examples include Toyoji Wada, who left Kanegafuchi Spinning to become executive director of Fuji Spinning in 1901, and Sanji Mutō, who rose from manager to executive director of Kanegafuchi Spinning in 1908. Both men were graduates of Keio University.

Other industries were similar. In the paper industry, Oji Paper had been founded by Eiichi Shibusawa and progressed under the technical expertise of Heizaburō Ohkawa. But with the capital increase of 1896, Raita Fujiyama of Mitsui became executive director, replacing Ohkawa and Shibusawa. In 1902, however, Fujiyama quit the company, and Umishirō Suzuki and Hisakichi Maeyama took over as directors. They in turn were replaced by Ginjirō Fujiwara in 1911. In the meantime technical genius Ohkawa had become president of Fuji Paper, chief rival to his old firm Oji. (See Morikawa [69].)

But even the professional managers who ascended through the ranks were quite different from today's directors. Almost without exception the directors who came from the ranks of professional managers used their high director's bonuses and other income to buy stock in their own companies and thus become large stockholders and capitalists in their own right. Yamabe, Kikuchi, Mutō, and Wada of the spinning industry were all of this type. The clear separation of ownership and management was to come only in the distant future.

Thus, the process of gradually establishing management as a proper function only began late in the Meiji period. There were several reasons for this. (1) The need emerged for managers with full-time responsibility for their firms. (2) Talented professional managers emerged from inside firms, and with wealth from director's bonuses and other sources they became large stockholders. (3) The firms themselves succeeded in accumulating capital and reduced their financial dependence on wholesalers and others. (4) The capital base of enterprises enlarged, gradually decreasing the share of stock controlled by related merchants. (5) Over the longrun, men who at one time were large stockholders but who had their original trades to tend sold their stock in side concerns when their principal business was doing poorly. For these reasons the real power over management eventually shifted into the hands of professional managers. However, this shift had barely begun in the Meiji era. The Meiji period was an era of individual capitalists with deep roots in traditional industry.

Four □ The Structure of Employment and Wages

THE FARM VILLAGE AS SOURCE OF LABOR SUPPLY

Early Meiji Japan has been said to have had a population that was 80% agricultural. But in view of the fact that the commodity economy had largely penetrated farm villages, one may well wonder if this percentage is not exaggerated. In fact an 1880s census of Yamanashi prefecture (Tōkei-In [149]) reveals many farmers to have had side occupations, as pointed out by Umemura. In mining and manufacturing (including carpentry and plastering), transportation and communications, and services there were often more secondary participants than primary (see table 4.1). Yamanashi was of course an advanced area for the times due to silk reeling and weaving, but the data still show how secondary and tertiary industries developed as side occupations in farm villages. Indeed, early Meiji farm villages were in the process of transition from self-sufficiency to various industrial activities. This implies that, even during the Tokugawa era, the differentiation of the agricultural class into rich farmers and tenant laborers was in progress (see Ōuchi [115], chap. 2).

Though second occupations were always common among farmers, the characteristics of the second occupations evolved with the level of progress of capitalist production. For example, as capitalism rises, so does the number of small concerns and the amount of wage labor and quasi-wage labor. Demand for labor from the capitalist sector was as broad and deep as was its supply from the farms from which labor migrated. But the labor market was not built in a day; first regional markets formed, then these regional markets merged into larger blocks, and finally the national market formed. With fairly abstract models in mind let us consider the movements of employed population and the labor market.

Two contradictory views of the Japanese labor market have been standard. In one, generally low wages are attributed to a relative surplus of labor, which in turn is attributed to a plethora of second and third sons

112

Table 4.1. Occupation Structure in Yamanashi Prefecture in 1879

	All industries	Agriculture, forestry, and fisheries	Mining, manufacturing, and transport & communications	Services
Percentage of those with main occupation as shown above having secondary occupation				
1879 Yamanashi Male	31.8	35.6	5.2	9.7
Female	33.4	29.8	47.4	10.5
Total	32.5	33.1	37.1	9.9
1920 Yamanashi Male	30.5	49.5	11.6	13.9
Female	27.7	40.0	7.6	6.7
Total	29.4	45.3	10.5	11.3
1920 Nation Male	54.5	73.3	22.4	22.0
Female	37.5	51.2	17.9	8.1
Total	46.8	63.3	20.0	17.1
Ratio of secondary labor force to main occupation labor force in occupations shown				
1879 Yamanashi Male	31.8	14.8	162.2	121.1
Female	33.4	17.4	89.4	17.7
Total	32.5	15.9	107.1	100.0
1920 Yamanashi Male	30.6	40.9	22.1	19.1
Female	38.0	31.9	38.3	7.6
Total	29.6	37.0	26.3	11.3
1920 Nation Male	54.5	69.0	31.9	25.7
Female	37.7	55.3	7.7	12.5
Total	46.9	62.8	19.2	20.9

Source: Umemura [166].

on farms and excessively intensive farming technology. The second view contradicts this sharply, saying that capitalist enterprises often faced labor shortages. Particularly in silk reeling, cotton spinning, and coal mining this gave rise to coercive labor policies such as the recruiting and company-dormitory systems. In the heavy industries the shortage of skilled labor continued even into the 1930s. As has already been demonstrated, this shortage was one reason that the need arose for measures to retain skilled labor, e.g., the seniority wage system.

The contrast between overall labor surplus and simultaneous labor shortage in certain areas is explained convincingly by models such as that of Arthur Lewis. It is their view that the wage level in underdeveloped countries is not set in the labor market of the modern industrial sector. Instead industrial wages are determined by exogenous factors (e.g., farm conditions), which in turn determine the level of employment. Thus, the farm villages had "excess labor" but this was only an excess relative to industry. If the income that labor received in industry had been higher than that received in agriculture, there would have been a nominal "surplus" and an outflow from farms should have occurred. If agriculture were more advantageous, labor would have stayed in agriculture. This would be especially true for female workers with potential jobs in silk reeling. Although contemporary journalists decried factory work conditions for young women, the decision to abandon the farm for the factory involved a comparison of work conditions in the two sectors, and life in the farm villages could be difficult as well. The natural result was a limited outflow of labor from the villages and a competitive struggle for female operatives among the firms. One cannot necessarily conclude that wage and other labor conditions for these workers were worse in industry than on the farms. Female working conditions were certainly pathetic from an objective viewpoint, but most of the labor that flowed out of farm villages did indeed choose that path as better than remaining in villages. Shortages occurred in the midst of surplus because industrial working conditions were not sufficiently attractive. Modern industries, in the Meiji years, were no more than isolated islands floating on a sea of premodern industries. However, once the modern sector attained a certain scale, the above explanation is no longer applicable. With the increasing visibility of this sector, wage differentials between agriculture and industry became more apparent to those in the labor market. Herein may lie a primary reason for formation of the "dual structure." However, these differentials had not become widely apparent in the Meiji era.

THE EMPLOYMENT STRUCTURE IN FARM VILLAGES

The Meiji era labor market had two overriding traits, continued existence of secondary occupations and regional divisions of the labor market. Japan was not, of course, alone in this; rather, these elements are general characteristics of underdeveloped countries.

No quick judgment is possible on whether secondary labor in the mining, manufacturing, and service sectors fell as a proportion of the total during the Meiji and Taisho eras. Here, the dynamics of the composition of secondary and dual employment in agriculture, manufacturing, and commerce become problematical. A person with "dual" employment will hereafter mean one with a main occupation but engaged in another as well, while a person with "secondary" employment shall be one with a main occupation but *managing* another on the side.

First let us look at the movements of those with only one occupation and those with dual occupations, and the ratio of the populations of the two classes (see table 4.2). The data cover most areas of the country between the 1890s and 1910s. Regional variations are noteworthy. For the 1890s the following facts emerge. Comparing regions in the sole occupation column (the table is presented by prefecture from north to south), we see that the ratio of those whose sole occupation was commerce, relative to those in agriculture, gradually increases toward the south. For example, Iwate prefecture has the lowest percentage in commerce while Chiba and Niigata have a bit less than 20%; Gifu, Wakayama, and Kochi have a bit more than 20%, and Fukuoka surpasses even these. This can be taken as one measure of the development of a commodity economy.

The dual occupation column yields similar results. Excluding as exceptions the extremely high figures for dual occupation labor in Niigata and Yamanashi prefectures, we see the ratio of dual occupation labor to sole occupation labor to be low in Tohoku (the northeast area), to rise substantially in Fukushima, to reach the 50% level in the Kinki (including Osaka and Kyoto) region and in Shikoku, and then to fall again in Kyushu. This configuration is typical of the regional differentials often cited during the process of the differentiation within the agricultural class. However, dual occupation among merchants shows a different trend, being high in Iwate (in the Tohoku region), Chiba, and Tokushima prefectures. The ratio is fairly high in Wakayama (in Kinki) and other advanced areas, but in areas of only moderate advancement where the ratio of population engaged solely in merchant activity is not high, we can hypothesize that merchants evolved out of the agrarian class along with the progress of the commodity economy. Thus, we see a high proportion of dual occupation labor where merchants had not yet specialized in a single occupation. Where the commodity economy was most advanced, dual occupation merchants gradually gave way to sole occupation merchants. This is probably what happened in Wakayama. But despite specialization in commerce the merchants did not cut themselves off completely from agriculture but instead kept it as a second type of dual occupation, as will be seen below.

Next let us look at the chronology of population movements and the ratio of dual occupation labor. First, although no definite movements of agricultural population can be seen in table 4.3, long-term, prefectural series on the number of farm households are presented. With these we can estimate the overall picture. On the basis of these prefectural time series on farm households, three facts emerge: (1) that until the Taisho era the number of households *increased* in less developed regions such as Tohoku, northern Kanto, and southern Kyushu; (2) that the number of households *declined* in advanced areas such as Kinki, Sanyo, areas bordering the Inland Sea, and northern Kyushu; and (3) that in southern

Table 4.2. Population with Single and Dual Occupations

Prefecture		Single occupations (thousands)			Dual occupations (thousands)			Ratio of dual to single (percent)			Ratio to agricultural population, single occupation	
		Agricultural	Industrial	Commercial	Agricultural	Industrial	Commercial	Agricultural	Industrial	Commercial	Industrial	Commercial
Aomori	1883	274.0	—	50.3	50.0	—	21.9	18.2	—	43.5	—	18.4
	1897	333.1	—	—	66.2	—	—	19.8	—	—	—	—
	1908	265.2	—	48.5	—	—	17.5	—	—	36.1	—	18.3
Iwate	1886	270.2	—	—	111.9	—	—	40.5	—	—	—	—
	1898	—	—	29.0	—	—	21.3	—	—	73.5	—	—
	1900	414.2	—	28.9	63.0	—	23.9	15.2	—	82.6	—	7.0
	1904	378.9	—	23.9	57.4	—	20.4	15.2	—	85.4	—	6.3
Fukushima	1896	530.2	—	—	132.2	—	—	24.9	—	—	—	—
	1910	498.5	—	—	121.6	—	—	24.4	—	—	—	—
	1913	422.4	21.7	74.7	156.5	8.0	24.2	37.1	36.8	34.4	5.1	17.7
	1920	465.2	30.9	88.3	111.3	12.4	41.3	24.5	40.2	27.7	6.5	19.0
	1925	448.2	49.4	91.7	117.0	14.9	31.5	26.1	30.2	34.4	11.0	20.4
Chiba	1895	565.7	18.8	87.2	266.3	58.3	174.8	47.1	311.0	200.0	3.3	15.4
	1901	510.5	21.6	86.9	221.7	55.4	142.1	43.4	255.0	159.0	4.2	17.0
Niigata	1899	970.8	48.9	170.0	150.5	60.0	95.1	155.1	122.9	55.9	5.0	17.5
	1909	915.0	62.3	160.3	199.1	81.4	117.2	218.0	130.6	72.2	6.8	17.5

Yamanashi	1915	77.5	23.3	12.3	171.8	17.2	6.7	222.0	73.8	54.5	30.1	15.9
	1925	61.4	22.8	19.7	188.4	18.0	12.8	291.0	79.0	65.0	32.4	32.1
Gifu	1947	724.9	81.4	149.7	118.1	57.9	75.3	16.3	71.1	50.6	11.2	20.7
Tottori	1899	—	—	33.1	—	—	27.5	—	—	83.3	—	—
	1909	—	—	44.4	—	—	40.0	—	—	90.2	—	—
Wakayama	1899	255.0	18.6	45.7	131.9	13.1	38.6	54.5	70.6	84.4	7.3	17.9
	1908	243.4	19.5	54.1	142.7	17.0	37.3	58.7	87.3	69.1	8.0	22.2
	1900	265.6	6.7	27.0	126.1	7.6	35.7	47.5	106.2	132.0	2.5	10.2
Tokushima	1909	265.8	9.0	37.4	109.3	10.5	42.0	40.5	116.6	112.6	3.6	14.0
	1909	367.0	31.1	67.8	149.4	18.7	22.3	40.7	60.2	30.4	8.5	18.5
Kagawa	1899	201.4	19.7	40.7	77.1	19.2	23.6	38.3	96.8	58.0	9.8	20.2
Kōchi	1901	260.7	21.6	46.4	60.7	15.9	20.6	23.3	73.6	44.4	8.3	17.8
Fukuoka	1893	568.9	68.1	126.0	151.1	40.8	62.7	26.5	60.0	49.7	12.0	22.2
	1962	697.4	97.7	192.1	203.2	54.1	94.5	33.7	54.9	49.1	12.1	31.7
	1969	570.9	120.5	207.1	265.7	67.2	126.3	46.5	55.7	61.1	21.1	36.3
Saga	1885	254.8	—	—	79.2	—	—	31.1	—	—	—	—
	1896	237.8	7.0	—	108.9	3.4	—	45.9	48.6	—	2.9	—
	1909	207.1	21.0	—	89.6	20.0	—	43.3	95.2	—	10.1	—
Kumamoto	1885	595.4	—	—	141.8	—	—	24.8	—	—	—	—
	1896	556.0	13.3	38.7	164.5	8.0	21.7	29.6	60.2	56.1	2.4	7.0
	1905	432.3	17.9	47.2	151.9	11.5	22.6	36.7	64.3	47.9	4.1	10.9

Source: From Naikaku Tōkei Kyoku [71] and various prefectures' statistical publications.

Table 4.3. Types of Changes in Number of Agricultural Households between 1870 and 1920 (By prefectures)

Increase	Hokkaidō, Aomori, Iwate, Miyagi, Akita, Yamagata, Tochigi, Gunma, Tokyo, Yamanashi, Nagano, Shizuoka, Tottori, Miyazaki, Kagoshima
Decrease	Fukui, Aichi, Shiga, Osaka, Hyōgo, Shimane, Okayama, Hiroshima, Kagawa, Ehime, Fukuoka, Saga, Nagasaki, Kumamoto, Oita
Small decrease	Kanagawa, Toyama, Ishikawa, Gifu, Tokushima
No change	Chiba, Niigata
Decrease, then increase	Fukushima, Ibaraki, Saitama, Nara
Increase, then decrease	Kyōto, Wakayama, Yamaguchi, Kōchi

Sources and Notes: Drawn up from "Fu-ken-betsu Ruinen Kihon Tōkei" (Basic Prefectural Annual Statistics), and Nōrin Suisangyō Seisansei Kōjō Kaigi, as given in Kayō [51]. The basic data are from various prefectural statistics and, after 1908, the *Nōji Tōkei* (Agricultural Statistics). A virtually identical table appears in Umemura [163].

Kanto, Tokai, and southern Shikoku the number vacillated irregularly. Overall, the number of households grew in areas from Kanto north and declined in Kinki and areas to the south.

With this in mind, let us reconsider table 4.2. The changes in agricultural population in table 4.2 do not always agree with the household data of table 4.3; where discrepancies arise, the latter are more reliable. But for industrial and commercial population movements, table 4.2 is superior. Both show a steady growth of population except in special areas such as Niigata prefecture. In areas such as Yamanashi and Tokushima, where a low proportion of the population was engaged in commerce, the commercial sector showed a striking expansion. Similarly, in areas such as Niigata, Fukushima, and Saga, where a low percentage of the population was in manufacturing, that sector grew most conspicuously. Moreover, although the Chiba area is an exception, the dual occupation ratio in commerce increased with time in San'in and eastern Japan, but in the Kinki and Inland Sea regions it remained stable. The ratio for industrial occupations grew in general for all regions except Chiba, Kochi, and Fukuoka.

Using data from four prefectures, we now turn to the structure of dual employment. Figures for the numbers of dual workers in the various industries are presented for Miyagi prefecture (Tohoku region) in 1913 and 1920, Wakayama prefecture (Kinki region) in 1911, Ehime prefecture (Shikoku–Inland Sea region) in 1919, and Yamanashi prefecture (Chubu region) in 1879, 1915, and 1925 (see tables 4.4 and 4.5).

Somewhat exceptional is the particularly high proportion of mining and manufacturing conducted by those engaging in such activity as a secondary occupation as seen in table 4.1's data for Yamanashi in 1879. But tables 4.4 and 4.5 show that this figure was heavily influenced by the development of the putting out system (especially in cottage industries like raw silk production and silk weaving) as a secondary occupation for agriculturalists. Yamanashi's figures for 1915 and 1925 (table 4.5) do illustrate clearly the upward progress of dual occupation labor. But the decline in the absolute number of those engaged in manufacturing was due to the decrease in those who were in manufacturing as a secondary occupation.

These facts show the progress of dual occupation among farmers during the late Meiji and Taisho eras. However, this does not necessarily imply the dissolution of the agricultural class because those occupying its lower strata become wage workers. Rather, in virtually all areas the dual activity of farm households was cottage industry production based on orders from wholesalers, day labor, commerce, or other nonagricultural traditional industry. For example, in relatively backward Miyagi prefecture the overall number of those with dual occupations was relatively small, and there was practically no change in the occupation structure until after World War I. About one-third of Miyagi farm households were engaged in dual occupations, and of these more than one-third as laborers (mostly day labor) and the rest in commerce or manufacturing. Those with commerce or manufacturing as their main occupation increased only slightly, and one-third of the manufacturers and one-fourth of the merchants had farming as a secondary occupation. In comparatively advanced Wakayama and Ehime prefectures the overall rate of dual occupation was high but almost all farmers and fishermen had secondary occupations in commerce or industry. The proportion of merchants and manufacturers with secondary occupations in agriculture far exceeded that in Miyagi prefecture. In short the now more numerous merchants and manufacturers continued farming as a secondary endeavor and became a second type of dual occupation farmer.

To summarize, the development of the commodity economy is generally said to have hastened the dissolution of the agricultural class. In fact, backward areas such as Tohoku, San'in, and southern Kyushu saw agricultural population increase. In contrast, developed areas like Kinki and

Table 4.4. Composition of Population by Industry and by Single or Dual Occupation

1. Miyagi prefecture, 1913 (thousands of households)

		Agriculture and forestry	Fisheries	Mining and manufacturing	Commerce	Day labor	Other	Total
Sole occupation		72.9	5.5	9.8	20.7	19.1	16.4	144.4
Dual occupation		26.2	3.9	4.7	7.5	8.3	3.2	53.8
Within	Agriculture	—	2.9	2.9	5.2	6.0	2.1	19.1
dual	Fisheries	4.4	—	0.3	0.4	0.6	0.3	6.0
occupation	Manufacturing	4.1	0.1	—	0.4	0.5	0.1	5.2
	Commerce	5.5	0.5	0.8	—	0.7	0.4	7.9
	Day labor	9.2	0.3	0.5	0.7	—	0.3	11.0
	Other	3.0	0.1	0.2	0.8	0.5	—	4.6
Total		99.1	9.4	14.5	28.2	27.4	19.6	198.2

2. Miyagi prefecture, 1920 (thousands of households)

		Agriculture	Fisheries	Manufacturing	Commerce	Labor	Other	Total
Sole occupation		75.6	6.1	10.7	21.6	20.3	17.2	151.2
Dual occupation		27.0	5.2	4.9	7.2	8.2	3.5	56.0
Within dual occupation	Agriculture	—	4.1	3.2	5.0	6.5	2.1	20.9
	Fisheries	5.2	—	0.2	0.4	0.4	0.1	6.3
	Manufacturing	3.8	0.1	—	0.6	0.4	0.9	5.8
	Commerce	4.7	0.4	0.7	—	0.5	0.3	6.6
	Day labor	10.4	0.5	0.6	0.6	—	0.1	12.2
	Other	2.9	0.1	0.2	0.6	0.4	—	4.2
Total		102.6	11.3	15.6	28.8	28.5	20.7	207.5

3. Wakayama prefecture, 1911 (thousands of persons)

		Agriculture	Fisheries	Manufacturing	Commerce	Other	Total
Sole occupation		220.0	27.0	33.0	60.8	80.3	421.1
Dual occupation		115.1	22.7	37.8	54.2	60.7	291.2
Within dual occupations	Agriculture	—	15.7	13.4	26.1	36.2	91.4
	Fisheries	19.4	—	0.7	2.1	6.4	28.6
	Manufacturing	18.7	0.4	—	7.0	5.9	32.0
	Commerce	29.0	4.8	9.6	—	12.2	55.6
	Other	48.7	1.8	14.1	19.0	—	83.6
Total		335.1	49.7	70.8	115.0	141.0	712.3

Table 4.4 (*continued*)

4. *Ehime prefecture, 1919 (thousands of persons)*

		Agriculture	Fisheries	Manufacturing	Commerce	Other	Total
Sole occupation		312.2	5.7	64.7	52.4	52.9	487.9
Dual occupation		113.2	14.6	19.3	25.6	19.2	191.9
Within	Agriculture	—	11.1	13.1	17.3	12.3	53.8
dual	Fisheries	18.2	—	0.3	1.0	0.6	20.1
occupations	Manufacturing	30.9	1.1	—	5.6	2.8	40.4
	Commerce	32.5	2.3	5.6	—	3.5	43.9
	Other	31.6	0.1	0.3	1.7	—	33.7
Total		425.4	20.3	83.0	78.0	72.1	689.8

Sources: 1 and 2, *Tōkei-In* [149]; 3 and 4, prefectural statistics.

Notes: The industries shown across the top of each table represent sole or principal occupations. Those listed on the left-hand side are dual occupations, with figures given at the right for the total number of households or persons so engaged. Reading a row's secondary occupation, e.g., fisheries, from the left-hand side and moving across the table to the right, one may determine how many pursuing this given secondary occupation were principally occupied in each of the industries for which a column is shown.

Table 4.5. Population Movements by Industry in Yamanashi Prefecture (Thousands)

Industry	1879			1915			1925			Annual totals		
	Sole	Dual	Secondary	Sole	Dual	Secondary	Sole	Dual	Secondary	1879	1915	1925
Total	172.6	85.3	85.3	122.6	196.9	225.2	117.5	224.0	257.7	204.9	440.9	460.4
Agriculture	120.1	74.3	10.1	77.5	171.8	191.6	61.4	188.4	210.6	110.4	64.2	66.2
Manufacturing	39.2	10.2	61.0	23.3	16.8	24.1	22.8	18.0	25.4	16.6	27.1	43.7
Commerce	7.3	0.6	8.7	12.3	6.7	8.1	19.7	12.8	17.0	11.7	12.5	23.1
Other	6.0	0.2	5.5	9.5	1.6	1.4	13.6	4.8	4.7	—	—	—

Source: Yamanashi Prefecture [174], various years.

the Inland Sea districts saw both the number of households and the population in agriculture decline. However, the development of the commodity economy also meant increased employment opportunity, especially for poorer farmers. These opportunities were not just as day laborers or for pieceworkers under the putting out system but also as commercial brokers, food products middlemen, and in various other small trades. For the commodity economy to extend into the farm villages the merchants had to come from somewhere. An economy based on trade meant not only that merchants had to exist but also that farmers had to become both merchants and consumers in order to create employment opportunities. The actual manufacturing activities of the farm villages were quite diverse; the data from the Mishima district of Niigata prefecture, given in table 4.6, will suffice here. This district had no ties with textile manufacturing except pattern lace production wholesalers. Even granting that this area thus engaged in manufacturing, it is

Table 4.6. Workers in Mishima Gun of Niigata Prefecture (Year-end 1914)

	Main occup. households	Sec. occup. households	Main occup. population	Sec. occup. population
Saw makers	221	0	55	9
Cutlers	46	1	231	1
Oil field workers	242	255	26	31
Carpenters	578	664	122	145
Plasterers	63	11	76	16
Sawyers	213	68	237	72
Silk reelers	15	64	15	89
Dyers	135	156	53	62
Roofers	135	53	156	62
Pattern lace makers	0	451	0	524
Tobacco workers	63	213	63	221
Straw bag makers	—	450	—	739
Sandal makers	52	12	62	14
Writing implement makers	30	10	150	49
Brewers	29	41	181	198
Coopers	105	25	132	28
Bakers of sweets	59	10	100	13
Rice malt makers	42	8	49	12
Bean curd makers	36	36	54	54
Total (including other)	2,299	1,883	3,165	2,394

Source: Niigata Ken, Mishima Gun, [90].
Note: Occupations involving 50 or more workers are the only ones included.

nevertheless important to remember that the reality of "industry" in these farm villages involved "operatives" who were utterly different from today's disciplined urban workers.

The high rate of dual occupation seen above in advanced regions depended upon a diversity of alternatives. In advanced regions manufacturing under contract to wholesalers was widespread. Although income for workers was relatively high and although the system did bring workers in villages into the capitalist mode of production, the wholesalers' system also slowed the transformation of the workers into wage laborers. However, in the less advanced regions opportunities for dual employment were few. This is why the agricultural population grew. To put it another way, the more backward the region, the larger the outflow of population interested in other work. The advance of the commodity economy into farm villages meant the spreading of dual occupation among farmers. Becoming a wageworker was but one option among many for a dual occupation; although the choice had decisive long-run implications, the question was settled by determining which possibility offered the greatest short-run advantage. Joining a wholesalers' system was yet another alternative.

To rephrase the point, the direct procurement of labor by the capitalist production system was small during the Meiji and early Taisho periods. Farmers were looking for profitable secondary occupations to practice in addition to farming. A considerable portion gradually left farming altogether to specialize in regional commerce and industry while others migrated to the cities.

URBANIZATION AND EMPLOYMENT STRUCTURE

As seen in the introductory chapter, population flowed into the cities continuously from the middle of the Meiji era onward. The flow became most visible in the middle of World War I but it had been building since Meiji times. We now turn to the question of what type of employment existed in the cities.

The *Tokyo Census Survey* for 1908 and that for 1920 (Tokyo-shi [150]) are valuable clues in the investigation of urban employment in the Meiji and Taisho eras. In the twelve years between 1908 and 1920 the employed population of Tokyo grew about 300,000, to 1.01 million. Two tables based on the *Survey* are presented. Table 4.7 shows workers by industry, sex, and independents vs. employees and family workers. Table 4.8 shows occupational structure by workers' area of origin. Let us first consider the interesting points in table 4.7. First is the high proportion of workers in mining and manufacturing. According to the Census of Manufactures [161] of 1909, the number of workers in Tokyo facto-

Table 4.7. Changes in Employment Structure in City of Tokyo, 1908–20 (Thousands)

		1908			1920			Rise or fall			Composition (%)	
		Independents	Employees and family workers	Total	Independents	Employees and family workers	Total	Independents	Employees and family workers	Total	1908	1920
Agriculture, forestry, and fisheries	Male	5.5	2.7	8.2	4.0	4.7	8.7	-1.5	2.0	0.5	1.2	0.9
	Female	0.3	0.2	0.5	0.4	0.9	1.3	0.1	0.7	0.8	0.1	0.1
Mining and manufacturing	Male	86.8	147.9	234.7	82.3	259.2	341.6	-4.5	111.3	106.9	33.0	33.6
	Female	19.2	35.3	54.5	8.2	31.2	39.4	-11.0	-4.1	-15.1	7.7	3.9
Commerce	Male	79.4	92.0	171.3	99.8	156.8	256.6	20.4	64.8	85.3	24.1	25.7
	Female	18.4	27.3	45.7	20.1	33.9	54.0	1.7	6.6	8.3	6.4	5.3
Communications and transportation	Male	37.4	33.5	70.8	10.3	48.3	58.6	-27.1	14.8	-12.2	9.9	5.8
	Female	0.1	2.5	2.6	0.1	5.4	5.5	0	2.9	2.9	0.4	0.5
Public and self-employed	Male	22.7	52.7	67.3	16.6	73.0	89.6	-6.1	20.3	22.3	9.4	8.8
	Female	14.6	7.2	15.2	6.1	22.7	28.8	-8.6	15.5	13.6	2.1	2.8
Day labor	Male	12.2	3.1	15.3	0.8	12.6	13.4	-11.4	9.5	-1.9	2.2	1.3
	Female	6.6	0.3	6.9	2.2	5.6	7.9	-4.4	5.3	1.0	1.0	0.8
Total (including other)	Male	248.9	332.0	580.9	266.1	556.8	822.9	17.2	224.8	242.0	81.5	81.2
	Female	58.5	72.8	131.3	90.5	100.3	190.8	32.0	27.5	59.8	18.5	18.8
		307.4	404.8	712.2	356.6	657.1	1,013.7	49.2	252.3	301.5	100	100
Addendum: servants	Male	—	—	7.6	—	—	4.2	—	—	-3.4	—	—
	Female	—	—	59.3	—	—	71.6	—	—	12.3	—	—

Source: Calculated from Tokyo Shi [150].

Table 4.8. Employment in City of Tokyo by Area of Origin, 1908 (Thousands)

	Tokyo	Kanto	Koshin-etsu	Tohoku	Hokuriku	Tokai	Kinki	Chugoku	Shikoku	Kyushu	Hokkaido	National total
Total employed population	253.5	206.4	67.6	22.6	35.9	57.3	25.4	11.7	7.4	8.1	1.7	708.5
Independents and public officials	138.0	93.4	29.0	10.3	16.9	30.0	13.8	5.2	3.2	2.1	0.6	347.0
Male laborers	89.3	92.7	33.0	15.2	15.9	22.9	10.2	5.8	3.8	5.9	0.9	296.2
Male mining and manufacturing	48.9	44.2	16.6	6.8	6.2	9.6	3.5	1.6	0.9	1.3	1.0	142.3
Other males	40.4	48.5	16.4	8.4	9.7	13.3	6.7	4.2	2.9	4.6	?	153.9
Female laborers	26.2	20.3	5.6	4.1	3.1	4.4	1.4	0.7	0.4	0.4	0.2	65.3
Female mining and manufacturing	13.2	9.5	3.4	3.0	1.9	2.1	0.6	0.3	0.1	0.1	0.1	34.1
Other females	13.0	10.8	2.2	1.1	1.2	2.3	0.8	0.4	0.3	0.3	0.1	31.2
Addendum: (female servants)	16.6	25.6	4.9	2.5	3.4	3.2	1.3	0.7	0.4	0.6	0.1	59.2

Source: Tabulated from Tokyo Shi [150].

ries having 5 or more employees was only 86,219. The difference of about 200,000 workers between this and the 1908 figure of 290,000 (which would exceed 300,000 if neighboring districts were included) could come from three sources, those workers in factories of fewer than 5 employees, apprentices and helpers, and those engaged in cottage industry. A similar gap exists with the industrial statistics of 1920. However, employment had risen by about 100,000 workers by this time. Commercial sector data manifest the same problem as the data for industry. More than 100,000 people were employed in commerce, most in the traditional labor-management hierarchy of shop boys or clerks under chief clerks (*bantō*). Employment in commerce also rose by 90,000 over the twelve years. The expansion of traditional industry certainly contributed to the expansion of employment.

The population in the transportation and communication industries was larger in 1908 than in 1920, reflecting a large number of ricksha, carriage, and wagon drivers in the earlier period. The decline demonstrates the changes occurring in the transportation industry. Another group that shrank was the classic lumpen proletariat, the day laborers. This testifies to the large oversupply of labor power in the late Meiji years. Finally, the large number of servants is notable. Moreover, a tremendous element of labor demand that absorbed more female workers than any other industry, that for domestic maidservants, is not even included in these employment data.

Sources of labor supply are shown in table 4.8. Native Tokyoites are only 35%, or 250,000. Those from the various sections of the Kanto region number 200,000, followed by the Koshin-etsu region, (Yamanashi, Nagano, and Niigata prefectures), Tokai, Hokuriku, and Tohoku. Among these, the number of laborers is large, particularly among those from Koshin-etsu and the latter two areas. Among female servants, the Kanto region has the largest share. This, then, is how Tokyo grew, by filling demand for labor with migrants (*dekasegi*) from other regions.

And what type of city was Tokyo at this time? Many small shops stood side by side and all the various occupations existed in each district of the city. In fact the number of workers in modern enterprises was small. Rather, Tokyo was a city of small merchants and manufacturers with the bulk of employees being traditional workers, merchants, apprentices, and clerks.

However, modern industry did expand quickly and employment therein took three specific forms. The first was in large manufacturing enterprises, represented by the spinning industry. The main labor force was unskilled temporary female migrants, and rapid turnover was anticipated by firms. After leaving the spinning factories, the women became—and almost necessarily so—wives of urban workers. The second form of labor was that found in the manufacture of modern goods in small cottage-like industries, in home production, or in a wholesaler subcontracting system. Matches, bookbinding, Western umbrellas, and knitted goods industries are good examples. The third form was that of industries using imported technology that required craftsmen raised in an apprenticeship system such as carpenters or plasterers. Machinists and printers are good examples, along with tinsmiths and shoemakers. The biography of Hōsui Shigemune (founder of Meidensha, a large electric machinery factory) tells of an episode of his being called "master" (*danna*) by the "craftsmen" (*skokunin*). This testifies to the fact that the relationship between master craftsmen and apprentices was being copied to a certain extent from labor management relations in the merchant houses. Even at arsenals, the most skilled workers became foremen (*oyakata*), controlling the operatives subordinate to them, and underlings often had to pay kickbacks from their earnings. In this sense, then, there were really very few modern wageworkers, even in the cities. Rather, for the most part, the attempt was to produce modern products under traditional labor management conditions.

Thus, labor power flowed from farm villages to cities but few opportunities existed for migrants to become modern wage laborers. The young men mostly became apprentices and shop boys, small merchants, minor craftsmen, ricksha drivers, and day laborers. It is unquestionably true that this situation changed slowly through the Meiji era. Wage labor did emerge but the market for it was quite small. For women, the main demand was for jobs as operatives (e.g., in spinning and silk reeling) or as domestic servants. Cities grew, absorbing the labor power that migrated from the countryside at first temporarily but later permanently, but this did not necessarily imply an increase in modern wage laborers. Only World War I gave rise to true wage labor on a large scale. But before describing this change, let us speak a bit more of the mechanism of the labor market.

THE LABOR MARKET MECHANISM AND WAGE DIFFERENTIALS

We now turn to the labor market mechanisms that helped to create the occupational structure described above. The occupational structure in local areas continued to change, as division of labor progressed with the increasing incidence of dual occupations. Except for those who migrated outright to the cities, labor was continuously tied to the farm with choice of dual activity limited to nearby areas. A labor market usually consisted of one village, one district, or a group of districts. Let us hypothesize three districts, A, B, and C, in a row. Part of the population of B can go either to A or to C, but movement between A and C is virtually impossible. In such a case wage differentials can exist between A and C. Even in 1967, for example, the wage of a junior high school graduate in Kanazawa was ¥12,000 but only ¥8,000 in Wajima, although both cities are in Ishikawa prefecture. Even when migrant labor flows are high, those who for some reason cannot move must accept wage differentials. If this was still true even in recent years, how much more true must it have been during the Meiji era. Thus, the population of B is freely mobile and can choose where to work but the populations in A and C have no such geographical choice.

With this example in mind we can conceive of the labor market at the end of the Meiji era as a multiplicity of small units. The sizes of the intraprefectural wage differentials that will be seen below are evidence supporting this viewpoint. It is true that the recruiting by large firms among the mutually isolated labor markets provided for some interchange among them with the resulting labor outflow. However, this interchange was on a very small scale. For example, the large spinning companies were first established in the Osaka–Kobe area and gradually diffused through the country. They did this, however, by taking advantage of the regionalized character of labor markets, seeking to locate new operations in areas where wages were low.

Let us now turn to the economic environment surrounding occupational choice within isolated labor markets. The foremost element was rapid growth of labor productivity in agriculture during the twenty-five years from around 1900 until after World War I. Productivity growth was stimulated by improvements in rice varieties and cultivation techniques and was accompanied by larger inputs of labor and fertilizer. Second, the price of rice was on the upswing. Farm household income rose steadily and determined the changes in various other wages in rural villages. Region-by-region proof of this point is not available. However, nationwide averages show daily agricultural wages as well as female operative wages in weaving and silk reeling to have increased in concert with agricultural productivity, while the relative levels of wages for the various types of work, both male and female, hardly changed at all (see table 4.9).

These movements imply that choices within agriculture changed little; nonagricultural wages were the ones that adapted to farm conditions. There were, of course, many occupational opportunities for farm workers that, though they offered only low income, could not be totally passed by. Earthworks construction during the off season and straw goods production are two examples. However, if the renumeration had been too low compared to other occupations, even these occupations would have been passed by.

Table 4.9. Movements of Wages in Agricultural-Related Industries (¥ 1/100)

	Male			Female			
	Agric. day labor	Silkworm cultivation	Loom work	Agric. day labor	Silkworm cultivation	Loom work	Silk reeling
1900	30	31	33	19	19	20	20
1901	32	33	29	20	20	19	20
1902	32	32	33	19	20	20	20
1903	31	32	34	19	19	19	20
1904	33	39	35	20	18	17	21
1905	32	29	34	20	23	13	22
1906	34	34	42	21	22	21	23
1907	36	42	42	22	27	21	27
1908	39	42	44	23	27	24	25
1909	38	43	44	23	27	26	27
1910	39	43	49	24	27	27	31
1911	42	45	43	25	28	25	30
1912	44	44	43	27	28	27	31
1913	46	50	45	29	28	28	33
1914	47	50	46	30	28	29	35

Source: Shōkō Shō [137].

Along with the rise of agricultural productivity, choice of secondary occupations by farmers influenced external labor markets. Owing to narrow labor markets, areas of low productivity would have low wages for all types of labor, the lowest being agricultural day wages. To large firms seeking to use idle agricultural labor power, possibilities existed for intensive recruiting and even locating factories in these low wage areas. Thus the multiplicity of regional labor markets had special meaning, i.e., that differentials could persist due to labor immobility. Nationwide examples reflect these labor market conditions. Table 4.10 shows that the regional wage differentials were indeed large. Until the end of the Meiji era even carpenters' wages were twice as high in Tokyo as in Niigata. Moreover, the large gap across regions in female silk-reeling workers' wages demonstrates the isolation of the different labor markets.

The second point of importance on regional differentials is that they shrank around 1920 but reexpanded during the ensuing economic slump. The narrowing of the gap that occurred up until World War I was due to integration of the labor market through expansion of mod-

Table 4.10. Day Wages by Occupation and by Region (¥ 1/100)

	Tokyo	Nagoya	Hiroshima	Kanazawa	Niigata	Kōchi	Sendai
1. Female silk reeling operatives							
1900	—	10	23	12	20	24	30
1907	—	22	25	25	—	28	19
1914	—	27	—	35	—	56	25
1920	103	113	—	93	45	93	81
1926	88	79	92	110	—	82	80
1929	103	72	92	105	—	80	78
2. Female servants							
1900	133	200	87	300	80	250	300
1907	300	248	190	200	200	225	200
1914	313	325	250	240	400	300	250
1920	1,138	1,150	900	988	700	588	1,000
1926	1,500	1,800	1,317	1,317	1,000	500	1,000
1929	1,405	1,500	1,263	958	1,000	800	883
3. Metalworkers							
1900	65	50	60	42	33	40	35
1907	81	65	57	45	58	58	58
1914	73	58	73	75	93	70	70

1920	182	225	265	175	203	264	241
1926	203	305	244	220	178	235	210
1929	247	347	268	220	179	200	210

4. *Carpenters*

1900	81	58	56	50	40	70	55
1907	100	70	65	60	53	75	58
1914	115	88	75	81	80	80	78
1920	296	259	250	230	224	208	250
1926	350	300	252	250	256	225	250
1929	221	293	257	250	243	197	263

5. *Day laborers*

1900	45	40	36	33	31	—	33
1907	48	54	48	40	40	55	40
1914	62	70	50	68	50	63	56
1920	211	166	223	170	165	185	188
1926	195	240	180	174	194	168	200
1929	201	228	180	194	180	147	197

Source: Monthly wage for female servants boarding with employer (Shōkō Shō [137]).

ern industries during the boom—or at least some increase in the limited amount of intermarket exchange. Expansion of employment in large firms of the manufacturing sector, particularly transport, communications, and mining, definitely contributed to rapid movements of labor. A symbolic example can be seen in the previous jobs of job applicants in Ehime prefecture (see table 4.11). Labor started moving out of agriculture and fishing with the beginning of the war boom, and most who changed occupation left the prefecture. However, at the peak of the boom there was great labor mobility within the industrial sector, and demand from within the prefecture was strong. These movements naturally raised wages and foreshadowed equalization of wages with other prefectures. Moreover, the strength of intraprefectural labor demand forced wage increases by large firms outside the prefecture that sought Ehime labor. Then, firms at home had no choice but to follow suit. Thus, labor market integration nearly eliminated regional differentials for a time. This situation was not seen again until the 1960s.

Third, we must ask why the differentials expanded again after World War I. One reason was the need for large firms, particularly in heavy and chemical industries, to stabilize and retain their skilled labor force. This need arose not only from the shortage of skilled labor but also because the firms wanted to insulate their own labor forces from the burgeoning labor movement. The lifetime employment and seniority wage systems also stem from these same needs. After the boom, demand for new labor fell quickly. The fall in demand derived not only from the lifetime employment system but also because heavy and chemical industries now beset with overstaffing problems were limiting hiring and trying out labor-saving technology.

Thus, after the boom, wages in large enterprises either increased or remained stable while farm villages faced a labor surplus. That is, external demand slackened, so internal employment fell through dismissals and other means. According to the *Census of Manufactures,* the number of factory workers in Ehime in 1922 was 37,084 but fell in 1923 to 34,685 (Tsūshō Sangyō Shō [161]). Some of them returned to farming but the large majority remained in the city or sought temporary industrial employment elsewhere. The swift increases in population in the tertiary sector and small-scale manufacturing after World War I reflect this shift in labor demand. Wages had to fall. A national labor market was created for a time but then the strength of transmission effects among sectors in this market declined. Thereupon, a multiplicity of labor markets reemerged.

Thus, the post-World War I wage differentials arose from differences of scale of enterprises and from weakened transmission effects among regions. One cannot view prewar differentials in the same way as post-

Table 4.11. Previous Employment of Job Applicants in Ehime Prefecture, 1917–19 (Persons)

| | | Prerecruitment job | | | | | | | | | | Total | | |
| | Manufacturing | | Agriculture | | Commerce | | Fisheries | | Other | | | | | |
	Male	Female	Male	Female	Male	Female	Male	Female	Male	Female	Male	Female	Total
1917 Within Ehime	44	81	278	1,590	40	77	72	364	102	543	536	2,655	3,191
Outside Ehime	3	46	108	661	1	37	13	138	36	308	161	1,190	1,351
Total	47	127	386	2,251	41	114	85	502	138	851	697	3,845	4,542
1918 Within Ehime	161	912	395	2,380	72	200	139	459	108	716	875	4,667	5,542
Outside Ehime	9	13	163	423	9	24	18	56	79	229	278	745	1,023
Total	170	925	558	2,803	81	224	157	515	187	945	1,153	5,412	6,565
1919 Within Ehime	2,346	6,768	1,474	8,344	242	607	159	451	753	2,995	4,974	19,165	24,139
Outside Ehime	222	519	67	953	14	58	3	56	40	211	346	1,797	2,143
Total	2,568	7,287	1,541	9,297	256	665	162	507	793	3,206	5,320	20,962	26,282

Source: Ehime Ken [20] (1919).
Note: Data record only recruitments made in accordance with the employee recruitment control laws of the prefecture.

war ones. Of course the labor market was not integrated at a single stroke by World War I; the path to market integration was zigzagged. But the postwar differentials affected a labor market that had already become nationwide. It is precisely because wage differentials reemerged after establishment of a national market that dual structure becomes a problem.

PART TWO □ THE ERA OF UNBALANCED GROWTH FROM WORLD WAR I TO THE PACIFIC WAR

Five □ The Character of Interwar Economic Growth

THE CHANGING INTERNATIONAL ENVIRONMENT

In the six years from the beginning of World War I in 1914 to the Panic of March 1920, the economies of both Japan and of the world were transformed. The war did not simply throw the global economy's inter-relationships of production into temporary confusion. Rather, entire economic mechanisms, both domestic and international, of many nations went through a structural upheaval. The notion that the prewar period was "normal," as symbolized by President Harding's call for a "return to normalcy," dominated economic policy in the postwar years. It took the chronic postwar stagnation and a world depression to prove this notion a fantasy. A further change, from Japan's perspective, was that the influence of world economic trends on the Japanese economy expanded considerably beyond their prewar levels. I will treat this in depth later but for now let me list a few major reasons why it came to be.

First, the gold standard was no longer able to function well. Trade patterns changed considerably, as seen in table 5.1, and this caused changes in the mechanism of classical imperialism, as suggested by table 5.2. From 1870 to World War I England consistently ran a trade deficit but the service and remittance accounts were continuously in surplus; the latter dominated, and England's current account balance was in the black. But because overall receipts and payments of the entire world must by definition balance, one nation's current surplus means others must have current deficits. Deficits have to be offset by capital flows if currency parities vis-à-vis gold are to be maintained. And indeed, England did invest almost all her current account surplus abroad, spreading gold through the world, keeping other nations' overall payments in balance, and supporting the gold standard. Table 5.2 shows unequivocally that the net increase in England's foreign investment almost exactly equaled her surplus on current account. England not only created the

Table 5.1. Trends of World Trade

Value of exports (f.o.b., in $U.S. million)						
	1880	1913	1924	1929	1932	1938
North America	932	2,801	5,518	6,298	2,006	3,887
Western Europe	3,542	9,224	11,724	13,249	5,341	9,082
Third countries	2,007	6,376	10,353	13,199	5,210	9,521
World	6,481	18,401	27,595	32,746	12,557	22,490
Volume index of exports (f.o.b., 1913=100)						
United States	32.7	100	123.6	161.2	84.2	127.9
Western Europe	39.6	100	82.2	110.3	70.1	83.2
Third countries	27.8	100	134.9	172.8	162.4	186.2
World	34.5	100	107.4	141.5	103.6	128.2

Source: Maddison [H], pp. 181, 185, 187.

gold standard system but also preserved and protected it through foreign investment.

In a political sense though, the main characteristic of economic "imperialism" is the creation or control of backward areas through capital export. Thus, the capital exports that supported the gold standard were also the basis of imperialism. The maintenance of the international gold standard, which ensured free capital flows and stable currency prices, was closely tied to the world order of imperialism. Moreover, this imperialism became self-reinforcing because, as England continued to invest abroad, investment income remittances kept rising (they were 10% of national income by about 1913) and most of this income was in turn reinvested abroad, bringing in yet more investment income. On the other hand the strength of English foreign investment lowered domestic investment, and this just when the relatively underdeveloped United States and Germany were investing in heavy and chemical industries. Hence, England lagged in heavy industry. British foreign investment really implied lack of investment opportunities at home.

But World War I destroyed this international economic mechanism. England's foreign assets fell by one-quarter, as did investment income. The United States, which had changed from a debtor nation to a creditor nation because of the war, then became the focus of reestablishment of the gold standard. But America, instead of investing enough of its surpluses abroad to support a reconstructed gold standard, chose rather to accumulate a good deal of gold domestically, following a policy of "neutralizing" it. Then France, after returning to the gold standard in

Table 5.2. Britain's Overseas Investment and Balance of Payments (Five-year averages; £ million)

| | Outstanding foreign loans* | Net increase during period | Current account | | | | |
			Merchandise trade balance	Investment income	Other nontrade payments	Gold, silver bullion, and specie	Current account balance
1851–55	263.9	7.6	−27.4	+11.7	+29.5	−5.4	+8.4
1856–60	388.0	24.8	−32.9	+16.5	+43.4	−0.8	+26.2
1861–65	503.0	23.0	−56.1	+21.8	+59.3	−2.9	+22.1
1866–70	699.5	39.3	−56.9	+30.8	+74.8	−8.2	+40.5
1871–75	1.069.3	74.0	−59.7	+50.0	+88.7	−4.3	+74.7
1876–80	1.187.5	$23.6	−122.8	+56.3	+92.2	−0.7	+25.0
1881–85	1.495.7	61.6	−100.2	+64.8	+96.1	+0.7	+61.4
1886–90	1.927.8	86.4	−87.0	+84.2	+92.5	−2.0	+87.7
1891–95	2.192.2	52.9	−126.7	+94.0	+91.6	−7.2	+51.7
1896–1900	2.394.3	40.4	−156.3	+100.2	+99.1	−3.3	+39.7
1901–05	2.627.5	46.6	−173.6	+112.9	+112.8	−3.4	+48.7
1906–10	3.351.8	124.9	−141.1	+151.4	+138.2	−2.9	+145.6
1911–13**	3.915.0	207.7	−132.2	+187.7	+157.9	−7.5	+205.9
...							
1920–24	—	—	−299	+199	+221	+21	—
1925–29	—	—	−395	+250	+213	+1	—
1930–34	—	—	−324	+174	+127	−67	—
1935–38***	—	—	−360	+199	+133	−77	—

Sources: For foreign investment Imlah [E], pp. 234–39. For current account Mitchell [I], pp. 333–35.
*Figures for end of period.
**Three-year average.
***Four-year average.

1928, pursued a similar policy of converting her surpluses, including money from increased investment income from foreign nations, to gold. Between 1925 and August 1931, U.S. gold reserves rose $650 million, and French gold reserves $1.59 billion, for a total of $2.24 billion, an amount almost equal to the world's production of gold during these years. (For details, see Cassel [A].) As a result, with the exception of the Netherlands, Switzerland, and Belgium, gold reserves of all other nations decreased. Funds went from the United States to Germany as loans, from Germany to France and Britain as reparations payments, and then from Britain and France back to the United States as repayment of war debts. One factor that heightened the severity of the world depression of the 1930s was that once this complicated international flow of funds centering on the United States had come into being, these flows were disrupted when America, the largest holder of gold reserves, was hit by the Great Depression. The resulting stoppage in the international flows of funds destroyed the financial mechanisms of other nations. This in turn occasioned the shift from the gold standard to an administered currency system.

Another aspect of the attempt to return to normalcy at the beginning of the 1920s was tight monetary policy and falling prices in many nations. The Genoa Conference of 1922 had approved the reduction of currency parities versus gold to below prewar levels and/or the adoption of a gold-exchange standard instead of a strict gold standard. Germany, France, and Italy, where the inflation had been worst, did indeed return to gold at new parities. But the United States, England, and others returned at the old, prewar parities, and this required that the latter group force domestic prices down. Table 5.3 shows this through wholesale price index comparisons. Japan is commonly believed by economic historians to have experienced "chronic depression" in the 1920s but in fact its prices fell the least of all nations that returned to gold at the old parities. Severe deflation, rollback of wartime and postwar inflation, was needed to return to normalcy.

Moreover, the idea that deflation was unavoidable created several other problems for the international monetary system. The first was agricultural crisis. In the 1920s, particularly the latter half, the supply of agricultural commodities grew while deflation was already suppressing aggregate demand. Not only did agricultural prices fall relative to industrial goods prices, but the absolute level of agricultural prices also fell. Farmers responded to lower prices by expanding production, trying to make up for lower prices with higher volume, and thus invited further price declines. This phenomenon occurred in wheat, barley, oats, rice, cotton, rubber, sugar cane, and coffee. (See League of Nations [58].) Farm income fell, and debts rose.

Table 5.3. International Comparison of Various Prices

	Wholesale price index				Price index of agricultural products		Consumer's price index		
	United States	England	France	Japan	United States	Japan	United States	England	Japan
1917	168	206	253	147	180	104	129	107	114
1920	221	313	488	260	211	193	202	152	263
1925	149	163	529	203	154	187	177	107	196
1929	134	139	588	166	147	147	173	100	173
1931	102	107	435	116	91	93	154	90	137
1933	95	104	365	147	72	105	131	85	143
1935	104	108	329	154	110	132	138	87	149

Source: For United States, U.S. Department of Commerce [B], for Japan, Ohkawa [99], and for other countries, Mitchell [J].

Second, deflation aimed at returning to the gold standard raised world unemployment. Europe in the 1920s suffered high rates of joblessness, while England and the United States, even in prosperous 1928, had unemployment rates close to 10%, much higher than before the war.

Thus, economic growth slowed considerably during the postwar years and world trade stagnated. Under such conditions it is not at all unreasonable for Stalin to have formulated the "general crisis" of the capitalist system.

Furthermore, the nature of imperialism changed the postwar years. The Soviet Union was established, and many new nations were born in Central Europe and the Middle East under the banners of self-determination and democracy. In Asia, Chinese and Indian nationalist movements emerged, a representative example of which was the May Fourth movement in China (1919). Meanwhile, Japan faced the March 1 Incident in Korea (also 1919), the Musha Incident in Taiwan (1930), and the Japanese expulsion movement in Manchuria. These movements indicated a political environment quite different from the prewar system characterized by the partitioning of colonial areas and control by the old empires. The Washington Conference of 1922, and the resulting Washington Treaty, symbolized these changes. Japan gave up Tsingtao, withdrew troops from Siberia, and supported conference diplomacy by reduction of naval armaments. This trend continued through the Kellogg–Briand Pact of 1928 and the London Conference of 1930.

But changing conditions for imperialism did not mean it was destroyed. Organized outbreaks of nationalism in colonies and semicolonies meant that, although adopting conciliatory policies to the extent possible, the colonial powers had to be prepared to take coercive measures, including their trump card, the use of military force. Overall, this destabilized the political atmosphere. And economic stagnation only worsened the situation.

In the midst of the world depression in 1931 Japan's conservative Minseito cabinet fell and the successor Seiyukai cabinet led by Tsuyoshi Inukai took Japan off the gold standard permanently. The fiscal and monetary policies adopted at this time aimed for domestic recovery, a devalued exchange rate for the yen, and increased domestic fiscal expenditures to stimulate economic recovery. The results, both good and bad, were very important. On one hand the door was opened to economic growth such as occurred in the post-World War II period. But on the other, given the political climate of the time, the new policies were modified under pressure from the military and hence also helped open the path to war.

The name *interwar period* symbolizes a period in which the old order—both in politics and in economics—teetered on the verge of collapse while the new order had not yet taken shape. This then was the environment Japan faced as World War I began to affect the economy.

WORLD WAR I AND THE POSTWAR PANIC

And what did World War I bring to Japan? Let us look at several statistical indicators. First was a rise in production. As seen in table 5.4 (which gives the Yasuba estimates of production), industrial production grew 9.3% per year during World War I, a rate much higher than either before or after the hostilities. This is only natural considering the prosperity brought by the war but several interesting points are contained within the data. First, ranking industries by growth rates for the 1915–20 period produces the following order: machinery and tools, metals, chemicals, food products, clay and ceramics, tobacco, lumber and lumber products, textiles, and other industries. While only natural in a wartime era of low imports it is still revealing to note that heavy and chemical industries boomed. Second, and this is often overlooked, the differentials among growth rates were tremendous, with growth rates ranging from 28% for machinery and tools to 2% for other industries. For all light industries except food products, the growth rates of the 1920–25 period—which was one of overall stagnation—were actually higher than during the war. Growth of consumption goods output during World War I was quite low. Although growth of consumption goods

Table 5.4. Five-Year Average Growth Rates, 1905–35 (Percent)

	1905–10	1910–15	1915–20	1920–25	1925–30	1930–35
All manufacturing	5.2	4.8	9.3	3.9	6.2	8.8
Spinning	6.1	7.3	4.1	4.9	6.3	7.8
Metals	8.7	9.2	10.7	5.4	10 1	12.5
Machinery and tools	2.1	15.3	28.1	0.2	9.1	11.7
Ceramics	13.3	4.8	5.7	10.8	3.0	9.0
Chemicals	8.1	10.0	8.8	8.0	10.9	12.6
Lumber and wood products	8.5	2.9	4.6	12.6	5.8	−0.8
Food products	3.8	1.2	7.9	2.2	0.4	1.5
Tobacco	1.9	0.7	5.3	0.2	1.3	0.1
Other manufacturing	4.6	−3.5	2.2	3.5	3.1	5.7
Electricity (amount generated)	31.1*	17.8	17.6	14.4	11.7	9.3
Coal production	6.3	5.5	7.8	1.5	−0.1	3.9
Railroad freight (ton-kilometers)	9.8	9.4	12.0	2.1	−0.5	5.0

Sources: For manufacturing, Yasuba [178], pp. 282–83; for electricity and railroads, Minami [64], pp. 194, 196; for coal, calculated from p. 99 of Nihon Ginkō Tōkei Kyoku [85].
*1905–07 three-year average.

output naturally lags during booms, the lag was exceptional in this case. Moreover, because consumption goods output was low and export production high during the war, real consumption in some areas of the domestic economy actually dropped.

The war also affected income distribution and consumption. Data problems for income statistics restrict coverage to city employees and farmers but table 5.5 gives the general trend of the period. Real wages and farm income had not increased by 1918 and in fact even receded a bit. Individual proprietors such as merchants and industrialists as well as corporations saw large increases in income, and many individuals became millionaires overnight. Corporate profit rates passed 20% and dividends reached 35%. But within this boom vast disparities in wealth emerged. Income equality, as estimated by Saburō Shiomi, declined sharply. Even in these good times the real income of low-paid workers and farmers fell, and merchants', landlords', and industrialists' incomes rose sharply. The degree of inequality ballooned, as latent dissatisfaction

Table 5.5. Income Distribution Indicators

	(1) Real wages in manufacturing		(2) Index of real per capita income in agriculture	(3) Annual rate of return on corporate paid-up capital (%)	(4) Dividend rate (%)	(5) Pareto coefficient
	Male	Female				
1914	100	100	100	16.4–13.4	10.9– 9.8	1.89
1915	106	106	101	18.6–17.8	11.2– 9.8	1.89
1916	103	94	106	28.7–33.8	13.7–14.2	1.78
1917	94	88	101	42.1–44.4	20.9–21.7	1.58
1918	88	79	99	44.3–46.6	26.2–24.4	1.55
1919	105	91	106	47.0–50.7	26.1–25.5	1.62
1920	121	124	110	60.0–30.6	35.3–23.0	1.85
1921	140	142	100	22.5–23.8	16.6–16.0	1.74
1922	143	145	106	22.4–26.4	15.1–14.7	1.75
1923	148	142	96	21.7–17.8	14.4–12.2	1.72
1924	154	145	100	19.1–14.0	12.4–12.5	1.76
1925	148	142	108	18.5–17.9	12.6–12.7	1.71
1926	154	151	100	16.9–15.1	12.5–11.8	1.72
1927	152	148	109	14.8–14.8	11.8–10.9	1.68
1928	158	155	107	15.3–14.2	10.8–10.7	1.67
1929	161	161	107	12.8–	10.7–10.3	1.66
1930	164	157	119	—	8.7–	1.65
1931	176	155	101	—	—	1.70
1932	173	136	110	—	—	1.59
1933	170	130	129	—	—	1.60

Sources and Notes: (1) Averaged from 20 occupations included in Chamber of Commerce survey (see Umemura [163], pp. 193–94), deflated by Ueda's cost of living index (see Nihon Tōkei Kenkyū Sho [89]). (2) Real value added as given by Umemura [164], p. 182, divided by the number of employed persons, also from Umemura, p. 218. (3), (4). Left is first half of fiscal year, and right is second half (Nihon Ginkō Tōkei Kyoku [85], p. 355). (5) Shiomi Saburō [133], pp. 332–33.

accumulated, and eventually resulted in the Rice Riots of 1918. Shiomi has also measured income inequality in two regions, Tohoku (Akita, Aomori, Yamagata, Miyagi, Iwate, and Fukushima prefectures) and Kinki (Kyoto, Shiga, Fukui, Ishikawa, Toyama, Osaka, Hyogo, and Wakayama prefectures). With 1 equivalent to complete inequality and higher numbers indicating more equality Tohoku's coefficient in 1914 was 1.94 and Kinki's 1.92. By 1917 Tohoku's was still 1.90 but Kinki's had fallen to 1.40. (See Shiomi [75], pp. 88–89) The two regions showed almost identical income distribution before the war, but in only three years the degree of income inequality in Kinki (which was economically advanced and hence more closely tied to national trends) increased tremendously.

On the other hand the third major trait of the interwar economy was increased employment. As is well known, no national census was conducted between the Household Survey (*Kokō Chōsa*) of the early Meiji period and the census of 1920, and even in these, data on the service sector is weak. Still, the following facts can be inferred from table 5.6. Between 1915 and 1920, employment in the secondary sector rose by 1.4 million people. The sector with the largest absolute increase was the textile industry but the rate of increase was highest for heavy and chemical industries, with an absolute rise of about 300,000.

To find support for these estimates of employment, let us look at statistics for one or two prefectures to convey the general idea. Data on changes in population by industry are available for Ibaraki, Okayama, and Hyogo (see table 5.7). Commercial population also rose a good deal during the war but not so much as that of industry. Moreover, in at least two of the prefectures the number of day laborers and workers climbed dramatically. In all these prefectures agricultural population decreased. Assuming that these trends were general, we may draw the following conclusions. The industries that grew fastest during World War I were secondary industries while tertiary industry, including the service sector, lagged. Volume of business and demand for services increased but labor was absorbed first by the secondary sector. A labor shortage naturally developed, and in the harder times after the war the decline in demand for labor in the secondary sector was one reason for the sudden rise in the number of people engaged in tertiary industry.

These employment trends also had political implications. We have seen above that farm population dropped by about 2 million during the boom and that urban population rose rapidly. This urban population was given much stronger weight in policy decisions after the Rice Riots. Government leaders came to feel the importance of social legislation, low rice prices, and finally general elections. Conversely, agrocentric economic policy became untenable.

Table 5.6. Changes in the Structure of Employment by Industry (Thousands of persons)

	Annual figures					Net increase			
	1910	1915	1920	1925	1930	1910–15	1915–20	1920–25	1925–30
Total employed population	25,475	26,305	27,125	28,105	29,619	830	820	980	1,514
Primary industry	16,383	15,615	14,344	14,056	14,648	−768	−1,271	−288	592
Secondary industry	4,131	4,940	6,315	6,404	6,273	809	1,375	89	−131
Metals, machinery, and chemicals	556	727	1,053	1,126	1,216	171	326	73	90
Textiles	1,146	1,251	1,822	1,673	1,422	105	571	−149	−251
Tertiary industry	3,901	4,445	5,230	6,352	7,209	544	785	1,122	857
Commerce	2,631	3,093	3,378	4,260	4,902	462	285	882	642
Transportation and communications	693	756	1,067	1,153	1,174	63	311	86	21

Source: Umemura [167].
Notes: Census of Manufactures (see Tsūshō Sangyō Shō [161]) gives the following data for factories of five or more operatives.

	1914	1919	1924	1929
All manufacturing	942	1,716	1,901	1,955
Metals, machinery, and chemicals	152	414	484	456
Spinning and weaving	583	955	1,002	1,081

Table 5.7. Changes in Population by Industry around World War I (Main occupations, with dual occupations in parentheses) (Thousands)

1. Ibaraki prefecture (population)

	1910	1913	1916	1920	Rate of increase 1913–20 (%)	Net gain 1913–20
Agriculture	572.5	607.3	626.2	562.0	−7.4	−45.3
	(215.4)	(234.0)	(258.0)	(257.8)	(10.2)	(23.8)
Manufacturing	34.6	33.1	38.7	50.0	51.1	16.9
	(15.2)	(17.6)	(19.5)	(20.2)	(14.8)	(2.6)
Commerce	80.4	78.2	89.2	90.7	16.1	12.5
	(33.5)	(31.1)	(33.1)	(32.8)	(5.6)	(1.7)
Transportation and communications	7.2	6.9	8.6	9.6	43.2	2.7
	(3.6)	(5.7)	(6.1)	(5.9)	(3.6)	(0.2)
Civil service and the professions	11.9	14.8	16.2	17.2	16.3	2.4
	(2.9)	(1.2)	(0.6)	(0.9)	(−25.0)	(−0.3)
Other	12.4	15.0	9.2	9.2	−38.6	−5.8
	(4.2)	(3.9)	(1.8)	(2.5)	(−35.8)	(−1.4)
Total	719.0	755.3	788.3	738.8	−2.3	−16.5
	(274.9)	(293.4)	(319.1)	(320.1)	(9.3)	(27.5)

Source: Ibaraki Ken [40], pp. 44–47.

2. Okayama prefecture (population)

	1914	1918	Rate of increase (%)	Net gain
Agriculture	622.3	610.8	−1.8	−11.5
	(215.5)	(209.2)	(−2.9)	(−6.3)
Fisheries	20.4	18.2	−10.8	−2.2
	(20.9)	(17.1)	(−14.8)	(−2.9)
Manufacturing	40.7	78.2	92.1	37.5
	(45.1)	(44.1)	(−2.2)	(−1.0)
Commerce and transportation and communications	111.6	135.9	4.8	24.3
	(90.5)	(61.4)	(−32.2)	(−29.1)

Table 5.7 (*continued*)

Civil service and the professions	66.3	54.7	17.5	−11.6
	(32.6)	(16.5)	(49.4)	(−16.1)
Total	861.3	897.8	4.2	36.5
	(403.7)	(348.3)	(−13.7)	(−55.4)

Source: Okayama Ken [105], pp. 74–75.

3. Kagawa prefecture (employed population)

	1915	1919	1925
Agriculture	284.9	272.3	246.9
	(52.9)	(47.3)	(52.4)
Fisheries and salt production	32.1	34.4	31.7
	(41.9)	(71.4)	(44.9)
Manufacturing	69.4	60.3	54.5
	(24.2)	(23.9)	(23.6)
Commerce and transportation and communications	11.6	15.6	15.4
	(5.3)	(5.2)	(5.9)
Civil service and the professions	18.1	15.7	14.4
	(5.3)	(4.3)	(6.4)
Total	416.1	398.3	362.9
	(129.6)	(152.1)	(132.9)

Source: Kagawa Ken [47], 198, pp. 74–77, 125, 21.

4. Gifu prefecture (population)

	1913	1920
Agriculture and fisheries	724.4	718.3
	(1,047.4)	(1,012.7)
Manufacturing	120.0	141.5
	(99.3)	(105.1)
Commerce	131.2	141.2
	(75.9)	(80.5)
Communications and transportation	28.0	28.6
	(38.2)	(34.9)
Civil service and the professions	30.8	36.1
	(7.4)	(7.1)
Day and other laborers	32.3	39.6
	(26.7)	(35.6)

Table 5.7 (*continued*)

Household servants	3.7	5.1
	(1.8)	(1.2)
Other	7.8	6.2
	(3.0)	(1.4)
Total	1,078.1	1,116.6
	(1,299.7)	(1,278.5)

Source: Gifu Ken [28], 1913, pp. 26–27; 1921, pp. 6–7.

5. *Changes in numbers of Hyogo prefecture households by occupations (thousands of households)*

	1910	1914	1918	1922
Agriculture and fisheries	186.4	181.3	178.2	177.5
Manufacturing	66.3	70.7	91.7	103.9
Commerce	88.7	93.7	102.5	115.2
Communications and transportation	9.7	11.1	16.1	17.1
Day and other laborers	15.7	19.8	31.6	33.9
Sundry occupations	4.7	4.8	3.5	4.3
Household servants	2.6	3.0	4.2	3.9
Civil service and the professions	14.8	18.0	26.7	29.9
Total	388.9	402.4	454.5	485.7

Source: Hyogo Ken [39], 1922, pp. 48–49; 1929, pp. 78–79.

A fourth new element in Japan's economy in the war years was the spread of heavy and chemical industries along with the spread of electric power. Looking at industrial output composition data from the *Census of Manufactures,* we see that the share of heavy and chemical industries in industrial output grew from 21.2% in 1909 to 26.7% in 1914, to 30.3% in 1919, and to 32.8% in 1920. The share declined after 1920, hitting bottom in 1925 at 25.8% but went up again after that. This prosperity during and just after the war was due to interruption of imports, and the decline was due to postwar reopening of trade.

But the heavy and chemical industries had several problems even during the war. First was their low technological level. In the production of intermediate goods such as iron and steel, the basic fields such as forging and casting saw tight bottlenecks, as did precision machinery. Besides, skilled labor was in short supply, and import blockages made plant and equipment capacity expansion difficult. Heavy and chemical industrialization had to proceed almost entirely with existing equipment and a hastily assembled labor force.

Fifth, we must point out the change brought by the war in Japan's foreign exchange position, exports of capital, and development as an imperialist power. During the war Japan sacrificed internal demand to increase exports as rapidly as possible, and the results were remarkable. In the words of Junnosuke Inoue, governor of the Bank of Japan from 1918 to 1923 and finance minister during the period of the return to the gold standard (1930–31), "In 1914 Japan was a debtor nation of ¥1.1 billion, but by 1920 had become a creditor of ¥2.7 billion, a reversal of ¥3.8 billion." The data behind Inoue's statement are seen in table 5.8. Owing to the large increase in exports and invisible receipts, foreign investment jumped from ¥460 million to ¥2.2 billion. Figures for year-end 1923 indicate the composition of foreign assets. (See Inoue [42], pp. 272–73.) Of the total outstanding of ¥1.8 billion, ¥1.3 billion was in China (in Manchuria ¥630 million in corporate paid-up capital and individual proprietorships, ¥160 million in other equity categories, with loans of ¥430 million to the central government, ¥20 million to local governments, and ¥140 million to individuals), ¥130 million in Malaya, India, the Dutch Indies, and the Philippines, and finally ¥290 million in Russia. Investment in China expanded particularly during this period with the Nishihara loans, extended by the Terauchi cabinet (1917–19) to support the government in Peking, alone comprising ¥145 million. However, the quality of some of these assets seems doubtful. Loans to the governments of China and Russia were virtually uncollectable. To boot, these figures do not include loans made to Kolchak and Semyonoff of the White Army in Russia, reputed to have been worth ¥300 to ¥400 million. Nishihara defended such policy-oriented loans, saying "conditions in fact seemed good for using these areas as outlets to put the idle funds to work" (Nishihara [91], p. 179). But actually almost half the foreign reserves built up during the war at the expense of domestic welfare were wasted on imperialistic ambitions and on political and military expansion overseas.

But there were also economically effective investments, such as the Manchurian railroad, investments of the Okura group, and spinning companies in China proper. Moreover, investments expanded from this time on in Korea and Taiwan. Table 5.9 gives a few indicators to elucidate the situation. During the war large increases occurred in employment and paid-up capital in the home islands, but these stagnated after the war; in Taiwan and Korea, however, increases continued into the 1920s. The wave of industrialization and incorporation brought by World War I was also the beginning of industrialization in the hitherto suppressed colonies.

These five trends—the increase of production, the relative (and sometimes absolute) decline of consumption and worsening of income distribution, the rise of employment and particularly a working class in

Table 5.8. Japan's Overseas Loans (¥100 million)

Japanese overseas liabilities			Japanese overseas claims		
	1914	1920		1914	1920
Bonds floated abroad	19.0	16.0	Foreign investment	4.6	22.0
Other debts outstanding	−10.9	27.7	Specie reserves	1.3	11.1
			Specie held abroad	2.2	10.6
Total	8.1	43.7		8.1	43.7

Source: Inoue [42], pp. 272–73.

secondary industry, heavy and chemical industrialization with electrification that changed the character of traditional industry, and the evolution of imperialism—brought by the war were not foreseeable. But they were the deciding factors in determining the direction of the Japanese economy in these years. The mechanism can be described as follows. The war came to Japan unexpectedly, the greatest shock being the virtually limitless expansion of foreign markets. As a result exports soared but production elsewhere could not keep pace. Even mobilizing all labor and productive capacity could not raise production enough to keep pace with exports. Domestic income also rose, along with consumption demand. The supply/demand gap that naturally resulted just as naturally raised prices, and exogenous inflation reinforced this domestic inflation. With rising prices corporate profits swelled suddenly but wages did not rise proportionally. The result was a boom distorted in favor of capital income, which found an outlet in investment in heavy and chemical industry.

The boom continued in 1919 but ended abruptly in the Panic of 1920. The panic will not be discussed in detail here but a few indicators can be given. Table 5.10 shows how great the shock was. General wholesale prices fell 41% during the year-long panic while silk and cotton yarn prices fell 65 and 73%, respectively. The cotton, silk, and steel industries sustained heavy blows. Bankruptcies were rampant and industries feverishly formed cartels in self-defense.

Japan was not alone in this panic. In the United States's panic, from spring 1920 to summer 1921, general wholesale prices fell 44%, agricultural prices 53%, raw materials prices 51%, general industrial production 33%, durables production 55%, and nondurables production 36% (see U.S. Department of Commerce [B]). These declines were worse than Japan's, but at least the United States recovered after a year and a half. In Japan the business dislocation and upheaval continued.

Postwar Japan continued to suffer recessions: the Ishii Panic of 1922 (a speculator's bankruptcy that induced a chain of bankruptcies of relat-

Table 5.9. Indicators for Colonial Areas and China Spinning Company

	Taiwan		Korea		China Spinning Company		Home Islands	
	Workers in factories (thousands)	Corporate paid-up capital (¥ million)	Workers in factories (thousands)	Corporate paid-up capital (¥ million)	Spindles (thousands)	Workers in factories (thousands)	Corporate paid-up capital (¥ million)	Spindles (thousands)
1913	—	74	21	34	233	—	2,013	2,414
1914	—	77	22	39	307	1,085	2,137	2,657
1915	—	80	25	39	307	—	2,231	2,807
1916	19	87	29	44	307	—	2,468	2,875
1917	28	104	42	48	397	—	3,333	3,060
1918	40	136	47	70	424	—	4,606	3,227
1919	41	210	49	108	456	1,778	6,457	3,488
1920	48	313	55	183	541	1,743	8,418	3,813
1921	45	324	49	205	903	1,820	9,505	4,161
1922	41	349	55	219	1,268	1,691	6,963	4,517

1923	42	357	69	279	1,405	1,765	10,789	4,436
1924	45	363	73	259	1,553	1,790	11,893	5,125
1925	50	351	80	221	1,636	1,808	11,664	5,447
1926	54	346	83	216	1,636	1,875	12,189	5,679
1927	56	341	89	239	1,636	1,899	12,548	5,929
1928	61	321	100	248	1,675	1,936	13,031	6,467
1929	63	313	78	311	1,675	2,095	13,644	6,836
1930	58	297	84	328	1,675	1,805	13,763	7,214
1931	58	295	86	360	—	1,807	13,966	7,535
1932	60	294	90	375	—	1,880	14,075	7,964
1933	65	311	97	431	—	2,057	14,389	8,643
1934	67	316	113	432	—	2,333	15,576	9,530
1935	69	342	136	591	—	2,469	16,392	10,649
1936	82	422	149	723	—	2,692	17,387	12,139

Source: Figures for Taiwan, Korea, and the Home Islands from Nihon Tōkei Kenkyū Sho [89], pp. 355, 359. China Spinning Company data are in Fong *Cotton Industry in China* (Tientsin, 1932), pp. 8, 10.

Table 5.10. Effects of the Panic of 1920

	Prepanic peak		Postpanic trough		Change (%)
Tokyo wholesale price index	338.2	(1920.3)	199.7	(1921.4)	−41
Rice	462	(1919.12)	219	(1921.3)	−53
Sugar	695	(1920.5)	286	(1921.5)	−59
Silk thread	520	(1920.1)	184	(1921.8)	−65
Cotton thread	747	(1919.11)	201	(1921.3)	−73
Lumber materials	451	(1920.3)	309	(1921.7)	−32
Foreign steel	394	(1920.3)	145	(1921.8)	−63

Source: Tokyo Wholesale Price Index, 1900 = 100 (Nihon Ginkō Tōkei Kyoku [85]).

ed firms), the great Kanto earthquake and debt moratorium of 1923, the Hamaguchi deflation of 1925, the Financial Panic of 1927, and finally the Gold Standard Reversion Panic of 1930–31. Until the present, the dominant view has been that the era's special traits were only these panics and the advance of monopoly. But, as seen above, investment and industrial structure changes also started in the middle of the war and continued in its aftermath. These developments were not isolated from the rest of the economy. Although extremely curious, it is true that the Japanese economy was actually growing fast by international standards, quite contrary to the general impression of overall recession. As seen in the introductory chapter Japan's growth rate until World War I was higher than average, although not amazingly so, but after the war Japan's growth rate joined the Soviet Union's and Norway's as one of the highest in the world, while growth in the other sections of the world fell precipitously.

The reasons for this change in relative position must, of course, be sought in the changes of the wartime and postwar years. The first problem is how growth could occur in the midst of these panics, and we shall consider the problem primarily from the aspects of investment and fiscal policies. Second, we shall look at the implications of several changes that occurred during World War I, e.g., electrification, heavy and chemical industrialization, monopolization, urbanization, and the expansion of tertiary industry. Third, we shall consider the problems produced by economic stagnation in the areas of agriculture, small enterprises, and surplus population, i.e., the dual structure. And after these, we shall turn to the post-1932 period and an analysis of the policies of Finance Minister Korekiyo Takahashi along with the launching of the wartime controlled economy under pressure from the army.

Six □ Construction, Investment, and Heavy Chemical Industrialization

URBANIZATION AND PUBLIC INVESTMENT

Some of Japan's most important economic characteristics of the interwar period are shown in table 6.1. The table shows growth rates of gross national expenditure (both nominal and real), and plant and equipment investment as a percentage of GNE. First, we see that both nominal and real growth were slow in the 1920s. Although growth rates were indeed above those of the United States and European nations, the era was still one of recession for Japan. But the rate of plant and equipment investment was not at all low; on the contrary, it was 10.7% in the first half of the decade and 7.4% in the second. And the share of investment in GNE computed from real data is even greater than that computed from nominal data. Relative prices of investment goods had fallen greatly in these years, and thus a relatively large-scale investment could be had for relatively little money.

But the above facts, that the growth rate (G) was low and that the investment rate (equaling the savings rate s) was high, taken together mean that the marginal capital coefficient (C) must have been rising. By Harrod's formula $G(C) = s$, the marginal capital coefficients would have been as shown in the final column of table 6.1. Thus, Japan's marginal capital coefficient for most of the interwar years was high. In very general terms we can say that in international comparison, interwar Japan was characterized by high growth and high investment, but in domestic terms it was also deficient in effective demand. This partly reflects worldwide economic stagnation but also reflects the large part of investment of the period that was construction. To clarify this, let us look at the trends in construction investment in these years.

First, in table 6.2 we shall look at the composition and changes in fixed capital investment, using the nominal amounts in order to better see the demand side. The table, using five-year moving averages, shows the

Table 6.1. Growth Indicators for the Interwar Period

	(1) Nominal GNE growth %	(2) Real GNE growth %	(3) Producer's durable equipment (including military, as share of GNE) (nominal) %	(4) Producer's durable equipment (including military, as share of GNE) (real) %	(5) Government fixed capital formation (nonmilitary, as share of GNE) (nominal) %	(6) Government fixed capital formation (nonmilitary, as share of GNE) (real) %	(7) Capital coefficient 4 ÷ 2
1910–15	4.9	0.5	7.9	6.2	4.5	4.2	12.4
1915–20	29.2	7.0	12.1	9.1	2.7	2.4	1.3
1920–25	−0.3	0.3	8.2	10.7	5.1	4.4	35.7
1925–30	0.3	3.1	5.9	7.4	6.0	5.8	2.2
1930–35	4.3	4.6	6.9	7.7	5.4	5.3	1.7
1935–40	13.8	4.7	18.1	15.4	3.8	3.9	3.3

Sources: Ohkawa et al. [O], tables A1–A4, A38.

Notes: Data for growth rates, cols. (1) and (2), represent growth rates based on five-year moving trend growth. Columns (3)–(6) are ratio for five-year averages.

Table 6.2. Fixed Capital Formation (Excluding military) (¥ million)

	Total	Machinery	Government	Private	Nonres. const.
1887	108.6	29.4	14.2	94.4	22.8
1888	119.6	34.2	14.6	105.2	25.6
1889	130.8	40.4	17.4	113.6	29.2
1890	141.0	43.4	19.4	122.0	31.8
1891	147.2	45.6	21.2	126.4	33.4
1892	159.4	53.4	23.0	136.6	55.2
1893	175.8	61.4	24.6	151.4	37.6
1894	202.6	73.4	27.6	175.2	42.2
1895	243.2	90.0	34.8	208.6	55.6
1896	284.2	103.8	42.6	241.6	69.6
1897	307.4	105.2	51.6	256.0	80.8
1898	328.2	108.0	63.0	265.2	92.4
1899	338.0	103.6	72.8	265.2	102.0
1900	329.2	92.4	78.4	250.6	102.2
1901	323.2	83.6	84.2	238.8	104.4
1902	321.8	90.4	84.0	237.6	102.0
1903	343.4	111.6	82.4	260.8	102.0
1904	371.6	132.2	81.2	290.4	108.6
1905	423.4	162.2	90.6	333.2	124.0
1906	473.4	191.6	107.2	366.8	141.2
1907	578.8	204.6	126.2	393.6	163.0
1908	556.0	205.2	147.2	410.2	193.6
1909	617.4	220.2	174.4	444.4	235.4
1910	660.0	244.4	190.2	471.2	250.4
1911	699.4	268.2	197.8	503.0	258.6
1912	737.0	293.4	205.0	533.2	268.0
1913	755.8	316.2	204.8	551.8	258.2
1914	791.2	367.4	195.2	596.8	234.0
1915	971.2	509.6	197.2	774.6	238.6
1916	1,310.2	760.6	212.8	1,098.0	297.8
1917	1,695.6	993.6	257.8	1,438.4	402.6
1918	2,195.6	1,245.2	353.8	1,843.6	586.6
1919	2,491.4	1,258.6	466.8	2,027.4	752.8
1920	2,679.8	1,221.2	586.6	2,097.4	940.4
1921	2,636.6	1,042.6	697.2	1,944.4	1,035.2
1922	2,654.6	907.4	786.6	1,874.2	1,165.2
1923	2,503.0	729.2	830.0	1,679.4	1,196.0
1924	2,547.8	751.4	875.4	1,679.6	1,283.2

Table 6.2 (*continued*)

	Total	Machinery	Government	Private	Nonres. const.
1925	2,562.0	724.2	913.2	1,656.8	1,350.2
1926	2,614.8	738.6	947.6	1,677.4	1,413.2
1927	2,573.0	753.6	977.8	1,627.0	1,398.0
1928	2,530.6	761.4	979.0	1,574.4	1,360.2
1929	2,352.0	722.4	922.4	1,444.2	1,249.6
1930	2,158.2	688.2	877.0	1,300.4	1,109.8
1931	2,075.6	696.8	842.0	1,257.6	1,035.0
1932	2,049.2	750.6	799.4	1,276.6	972.8
1933	2,195.4	864.6	809.4	1,412.0	998.0
1934	2,462.2	1,058.4	846.0	1,642.2	1,056.6
1935	2,928.8	1,385.0	864.2	2,087.0	1,175.2
1936	3,470.8	1,846.8	873.6	2,614.4	1,241.0
1937	4,212.6	2,462.8	899.8	3,328.2	1,326.8
1938	5,137.2	3,189.8	957.0	4,200.4	1,453.6

Source: Ohkawa et al. [O], table A38.

Note: Figures listed are five-year moving averages in nominal amounts centered on the year listed.

following basic trends in investment in machinery and construction and in private and public investment:

1. Total fixed capital investment boomed between 1916 and 1920. Although prices also rose, this increase was nevertheless exceeded by the rise in fixed capital investment. For the rest of the unstable 1920s the gross level was more or less maintained, but it fell with the gold standard reversion and the world depression, only to rise rapidly again in the 1930s.
2. Plant and equipment investment peaked in 1921 but fell sharply by 1925, then recovered in the 1930s. Construction investment continued rising after 1921, peaked in 1925, and then dropped. It hit bottom in 1932. Thus, one factor that retarded output during the world depression was actually the same factor that had supported it before, construction investment.
3. Private investment declined throughout the 1920s and recovered in the 1930s. Government investment was stable through the 1920s and rose in the 1930s.

Thus, to summarize, construction investment supported the level of total investment in the 1920s (except in recession periods) while government investment also helped. Indeed, Miyohei Shinohara has said that interwar Japan saw a complete Kuznets cycle (Shinohara [132], pp. 46–47). Shōzaburō Fujino has tried to confirm this pattern with the following hypothesis. A Kuznets cycle is composed of two investment cycles. The first is a great peak led by plant and equipment investment, and the second a less striking one centering on construction investment. (See Fujino [24], pp. 20–21, 525–28.) As an example of this phenomenon we may present, as in table 6.3, seven-year moving averages of central and local government total expenditure and of military expenditure. From this point of view the 1920s were the continuation of the Kuznets cycle begun by the plant and equipment investment boom of World War I; i.e., the 1920s were the period of construction investment. As seen above, the government was a major contributor to investment in the 1920s.

But to see the actual elements at work here, we must take a more detailed look at the composition of investment. Government construction is seen in table 6.4. From a level of ¥150 million in 1915 it rose continuously, reaching ¥800 million in the middle of the 1920s. Reconstruction after the Kanto earthquake was one factor but, even discounting this, growth was quite high. However, central government construction investment leveled off about 1920 while local government construction investment continued to grow. Moreover, when examined by use of funds, the greatest increases were in public utilities, i.e., social overhead capital such as roads, bridges, ports, and waterworks. These areas saw increased activity during panics. Thus, the main element of government construction investment in the 1920s—and the pillar of government support of investment—was public works.

As seen in table 6.5, private investment expanded steadily until the middle of the 1920s. But the fall in the last half of the 1920s was steep. Within private investment, electric power-related construction was a particularly large component, and private railroads also took a major share. Factory and store construction were stable through the 1920s and did not fall during panics. Putting these two factors together, we can conclude that electric power was the sector responsible for the waves in construction in the 1920s, supporting the level sustained in the first half of the decade but also contributing to the decline in the last half.

Let us add a word on plant and equipment investment (see table 6.6). Government plant and equipment investment was stable throughout the 1920s and then rose quickly in the 1930s. But within this category military investment including weapons and warships as investment) declined in the 1920s and rose in the 1930s. But nonmilitary investment increased gradually in the 1920s and was another factor supporting investment. On the other hand, private plant and equipment investment fell until

Table 6.3. Government Expenditure (Seven-year moving averages; ¥ million)

	Gross central government expenditure	Military expenditure	Gross local government expenditure
1878	61.8	16.8	—
1879	62.0	16.9	—
1880	65.5	14.9	—
1881	69.3	13.8	—
1882	69.6	15.0	32.5
1883	72.8	16.3	34.2
1884	75.2	17.7	35.0
1885	76.6	19.3	35.1
1886	77.5	20.9	35.2
1887	78.8	21.0	36.0
1888	80.9	21.6	37.3
1889	84.2	22.4	39.9
1890	85.6	23.1	42.2
1891	87.3	38.2	45.0
1892	90.1	51.7	48.3
1893	104.9	58.9	52.7
1894	127.5	71.7	59.3
1895	150.5	84.4	66.7
1896	178.1	97.3	76.0
1897	211.8	112.9	87.7
1898	242.5	109.8	102.2
1899	272.8	105.4	116.6
1900	288.6	116.6	130.2
1901	303.5	196.9	136.4
1902	345.9	285.2	141.9
1903	386.7	323.0	150.3
1904	446.4	334.7	160.8
1905	517.3	349.9	172.3
1906	577.3	363.0	188.2
1907	604.4	367.9	205.8
1908	673.4	301.2	243.6
1909	720.4	255.5	272.4
1910	761.6	198.8	294.5
1911	788.5	199.8	311.7
1912	798.0	203.5	323.3
1913	829.4	217.1	332.6
1914	930.5	246.4	346.9
1915	1,055.6	308.6	362.2
1916	1,243.5	420.1	408.8

Table 6.3 (*continued*)

	Gross central government expenditure	Military expenditure	Gross local government expenditure
1917	1,469.6	526.8	499.6
1918	1,689.2	615.4	608.9
1919	1,924.8	680.1	750.5
1920	2,162.4	716.7	884.8
1921	2,382.7	730.5	1,019.1
1922	2,511.2	703.0	1,151.2
1923	2,583.3	625.2	1,287.8
1924	2,664.0	561.6	1,436.1
1925	2,753.4	515.4	1,535.0
1926	2,831.2	487.4	1,616.3
1927	2,838.8	475.2	1,687.7
1928	2,799.6	471.6	1,733.2
1929	2,852.5	508.2	1,812.1
1930	2,970.3	572.4	1,961.7
1931	3,057.9	637.9	2,024.5
1932	3,153.9	712.8	2,089.3
1933	3,277.6	797.5	2,267.7
1934	3,584.4	1,205.3	2,345.9
1935	4,120.3	1,981.3	2,458.0
1936	4,840.3	2,808.5	2,555.7
1937	5,763.9	3,781.4	2,621.3

Source: Emi and Shionoya [22], pp. 168–70, 186–88.

1925, was stable thereafter, but did not fall with the panics of the late 1920s and early 1930s. Indeed, private plant and equipment investment increased despite the panics.

Let us summarize the above:

1. Government sector investment was stable during the 1920s, supported by local and especially urban public works investments and by nonmilitary plant and equipment investment. Thus, local fiscal and financial policies played an extremely important role during the era. At the same time pressure from military investment was small.

2. Increases in private sector construction investment in electric power and private railroads partially compensated for the lack of industrial investment. Although construction and railroad investment fell in the

Table 6.4. Government Construction (Five-year moving
averages including military; ¥ million)

1887	13.0	1911	156.6
1888	13.6	1912	157.6
1889	16.0	1913	153.6
1890	17.6	1914	140.6
		1915	138.4
1891	19.0	1916	143.6
1892	20.8	1917	172.8
1893	21.8	1918	248.2
1894	25.0	1919	337.8
1895	33.2	1920	437.4
1896	41.0		
1897	49.4	1921	529.4
1898	60.6	1922	598.8
1899	68.4	1923	625.0
1900	70.6	1924	648.8
		1925	664.4
1901	73.0	1926	685.2
1902	70.0	1927	706.8
1903	65.4	1928	696.2
1904	62.0	1929	658.2
1905	70.2	1930	617.8
1906	88.4		
1907	106.2	1931	583.2
1908	123.8	1932	546.6
1909	146.8	1933	556.0
1910	156.8	1934	585.4
		1935	598.0
		1936	597.8
		1937	606.6
		1938	593.4

Source: Calculated from Ohkawa et al. [O], table A38.

last half of the 1920s, industrial and commercial investment stayed
level, so the overall level of private investment did not plunge.

3. These trends show that the investment of the 1920s did not so much
directly increase productivity as increase social capital, railroads, and
electric power. Thus, we can see why the capital coefficient moved as
it did. However, these infrastructure investments were still important
because they corrected a previously skewed distribution of
investment.

Next let us look at some data on fiscal conditions, the major source of

Table 6.5. Private Construction (Five-year moving averages;
¥ million)

1887	11.2	1921	536.6
1888	13.4	1922	594.8
1889	14.6	1923	593.8
1890	15.6	1924	653.4
		1925	705.6
1891	15.8	1926	750.0
1892	16.0	1927	715.8
1893	17.2	1928	691.4
1894	19.4	1929	619.8
1895	27.0	1930	524.2
1896	35.2		
1897	39.6	1931	489.6
1898	42.6	1932	469.8
1899	45.6	1933	488.6
1900	42.6	1934	523.2
		1935	632.6
1901	41.0	1936	703.4
1902	40.6	1937	792.2
1903	43.0	1938	905.2
1904	51.6		
1905	60.2		
1906	64.6		
1907	71.4		
1908	85.8		
1909	105.6		
1910	110.4		

Source: Ohkawa et al. [O], table A38.

infrastructure investment. First we must consider data on central and local government expenditure.

A peculiarity of the post World War I period, seen in tables 6.7 and 6.8, was the slowing of growth of central government expenditure, contrasted with the rapid rise of local expenditure. There were several reasons for this. One was progress in disarmament between the Washington Conference of 1922 and the London Conference of 1930. Withdrawal of troops from Siberia lowered the burden of military expenditure from ¥990 million in 1920 to about ¥500 million in 1923. Notable is the increase of subsidies and grants to local governments and communities under the Seiyukai cabinets of Kei Hara (1917–20) and Giichi Tanaka (1927–29). In these years expenditure on education and on interest and principal payments on public bonds rose along with expen-

Table 6.6. Capital Formation of Producers' Durable Equipment (Five-year moving averages including military; ¥ million)

	Total	Government		Private
		Total	Nonmilitary	
1887	33.8	7.2	2.4	26.6
1888	38.6	7.0	2.6	31.6
1889	45.2	7.8	3.0	37.4
1890	48.8	8.6	3.4	40.2
1891	51.0	9.0	3.8	42.0
1892	62.6	13.0	3.8	49.6
1893	74.0	16.8	4.2	57.2
1894	87.8	19.2	4.8	68.6
1895	111.0	27.4	6.2	83.6
1896	134.2	38.8	8.2	95.4
1897	141.4	47.0	10.4	94.4
1898	149.0	54.6	13.2	94.4
1899	148.0	61.2	16.4	86.8
1900	133.6	60.2	18.8	73.4
1901	120.2	57.6	21.0	62.6
1902	127.4	59.4	22.6	68.0
1903	154.4	65.8	23.2	88.6
1904	180.4	71.8	23.8	108.6
1905	217.2	80.8	26.0	136.4
1906	250.6	88.6	29.6	162.0
1907	262.0	91.0	33.6	171.0
1908	258.6	91.8	37.8	166.8
1909	275.4	99.0	43.2	176.4
1910	301.8	107.0	49.0	194.8
1911	329.4	115.0	53.2	214.4
1912	360.6	125.5	57.4	235.4
1913	386.0	131.2	61.4	254.8
1914	436.8	134.0	64.6	302.8
1915	591.2	150.0	68.4	441.2
1916	870.8	189.6	79.4	681.2
1917	1,140.6	246.4	99.2	894.2
1918	1,446.6	327.2	125.6	1,119.4
1919	1,580.2	421.4	153.6	1,158.8
1920	1,584.2	484.6	175.4	1,099.6

Source: Ohkawa et al. [O], table A39.

Table 6.7. Changes in Scale of Central and Local Government Fiscal Spending (Five-year moving averages; ¥ million)

	Total central and local government	Central	Local	Prefectures	Cities	Villages
1895–99	275.7	190.3	85.4	27.3	10.3	37.8
1900–04	421.0	275.0	146.0	53.3	23.9	64.4
1905–09	735.4	531.3	204.1	63.0	47.1	84.6
1910–14	929.3	594.0	335.3	86.7	101.6	120.8
1915–19	1,261.1	819.6	441.5	128.1	122.8	168.5
1920–24	2,626.2	1,485.1	1,141.1	361.0	351.4	380.7
1925–29	3,426.2	1,684.1	1,742.1	466.4	733.1	516.7
1930–34	4,038.4	1,880.5	2,158.0	721.0	891.2	523.5
1935–39	5,561.8	2,995.9	2,565.9	933.3	1,040.0	582.1
Composition of the above (%)						
1895–99	100	69.0	31.0	13.5	3.7	13.7
1900–04	100	65.3	34.7	12.7	5.7	15.3
1905–09	100	72.2	27.8	8.6	6.4	11.5
1910–14	100	63.9	36.1	10.4	10.9	13.0
1915–19	100	65.0	35.0	10.2	9.7	13.4
1920–24	100	56.5	43.5	13.7	13.3	14.5
1925–29	100	49.2	50.8	13.6	21.4	15.1
1930–34	100	46.6	53.4	17.9	22.1	13.0
1935–39	100	53.9	46.2	16.8	18.7	10.5

Source: Calculated from Emi and Shionoya [22], pp. 164–68.

diture on social capital investment in public works. Moreover, prefectures did not spend as much as cities, and among cities, the big six (Tokyo, Osaka, Nagoya, Yokohama, Kyoto, and Kobe) spent the largest share. The trend to urbanization made this only natural, particularly with the recovery of Tokyo and Yokohama after the great earthquake of 1923. Funds for swollen local fiscal expenditures had to be provided by localities themselves through local bond flotations, of which municipals took by far the largest share (see tables 6.9 and 6.10). The amount outstanding between 1920 and 1930 increased ¥1.86 billion, of which ¥1.19 billion was municipal bonds. And as public debt expanded, the amount of local revenue devoted to interest and principal payments of course rose. Thus, even though central government fiscal policy was austere, local governments' fiscal policies were expansionary.

Two prime ministers, Tomosaburō Katō and Takaaki Katō, tried to hold down local expenditure as part of an economic policy aimed at

Table 6.8. Trends in Net Government Expenditure (Five-year moving averages; ¥ million)

	Central	Local	Total A	All government net spending B	General government net spending C	GNE	Proportion of GNE (%) A	B	C
1910–14 Average	594	326	899	1,315	941	4,583	19.6	28.9	20.5
15–19	820	415	1,199	1,848	1,131	9,401	12.8	19.7	12.0
20–24	1,487	1,101	2,466	4,461	3,163	15,371	16.0	29.0	20.6
25–29	1,684	1,630	3,106	5,058	3,482	16,265	19.1	31.1	21.4
30–34	1,881	1,936	3,522	6,316	4,600	14,791	23.8	42.7	31.1
35–39	2,996	2,324	4,942	11,947	8,636	23,614	20.9	50.6	36.6

Source: Calculated from Emi and Shionoya [22], pp. 168–71.

Table 6.9. Local Bonds Outstanding (¥ million)

A. By issuer

	Total	Prefectures	Cities	Districts (*gun*)	Villages	Associations
1915	337	51	260	2	12	9
1920	510	111	356	4	29	10
1925	1,268	282	840	—	116	30
1930	2,374	534	1,541	—	256	43
1935	3,373	976	2,005	—	391	—
1940	4,121	1,315	2,358	—	448	—

Source: Nihon Tōkei Kenkyujo [89], p. 250.

B. By uses of funds

	Education	Public works (roads, bridges, flood control, etc.)	Sanitation (sewers and waterworks included)	Industrial promotion	Public welfare services	Other	Electricity and gas enterprises	Total (excluding electricity and gas)
1914	11	104	55	16	—	5	192	134
1920	30	155	83	3	22	18	312	198
1922	63	225	148	34	46	29	545	243
1924	94	324	138	25	90	75	746	373
1926	135	411	180	35	114	166	1,041	473
1928	172	478	272	76	134	363	1,496	554

Source: Moulton [L], appendix statistics.

Table 6.10. Revenue and Bond Floatations of the Big Six Cities (¥ million)

	Tokyo		Yokohama		Osaka		Kobe	
	Surplus or shortfall of revenue	Proceeds of bond floatations	Surplus or shortfall of revenue	Proceeds of bond floatations	Surplus or shortfall of revenue	Proceeds of bond floatations	Surplus or shortfall of revenue	Proceeds of bond floatations
1914	−5	6	0	0	−3	1	0	2
1921	−15	17	−5	3	−19	32	−11	12
1922	−35	51	−2	1	−23	16	−9	6
1923	−49	47	2	1	−27	36	−6	7
1924	−41	75	−4	12	−26	29	−5	2
1925	−45	28	−12	24	−37	50	−29	29
1926	−88	110	−39	47	−50	51	−20	20
1927	−140	168	−37	21	−196	171	−16	20
1928	−129	127	−16	9	−52	28	−12	9
1929	−124	122	−6	4	−49	28	−12	10

	Kyoto		Nagoya		Total	
	Surplus or shortfall of revenue	Proceeds of bond floatations	Surplus or shortfall of revenue	Proceeds of bond floatations	Surplus or shortfall of revenue	Proceeds of bond floatations
1914	−1	0	−1	1	−10	10
1921	0	3	−2	3	−52	68
1922	2	3	−16	18	−83	95
1923	−2	5	−6	6	−88	102
1924	−4	1	−4	1	−84	120
1925	−5	4	−8	8	−136	143
1926	−2	2	−21	21	−220	251
1927	−3	4	−50	47	−442	431
1928	−8	4	−7	7	−224	184
1929	−8	6	−8	7	−207	177

Source: Moulton [L].

returning to the gold standard but neither was successful. On one hand, since the world trend in the 1920s was toward a return to the gold standard, Japan was partly compelled to follow suit and so Japanese leaders pushed austere economic policies. But in the domestic economy, on the other hand, the expansion of local fiscal expenditures was unavoidable due to the need to respond to drastic increases in urban populations.

Thus, in general terms the de facto fiscal policy of high public investment while the gold standard was suspended required deficit spending. In this sense the fiscal policy of the 1920s was similar to the fiscal policy

Table 6.11. Changes in Specie Reserves (¥ million)

	Total specie held	Amount held abroad	Amount held at home
1914	341	213	129
1915	516	379	137
1916	714	487	228
1917	1,105	643	461
1918	1,588	1,135	453
1919	2,045	1,343	702
1920	2,179	1,062	1,116
1921	2,080	855	1,225
1922	1,830	615	1,215
1923	1,653	444	1,208
1924	1,501	326	1,175
1925	1,413	257	1,155
1926	1,357	280	1,127
1927	1,273	186	1,087
1928	1,199	114	1,085
1929	1,343	255	1,088
1930	960	134	826
1931	557	88	470
1932	554	112	443
1933	495	38	457
1934	495	28	466
1935	531	28	504
1936	576	28	548
1937	890	28	862
1938	583	23	559
1939	586	27	559
1940	593	26	567

Source: Okura Shō [106], p. 223.

that Korekiyo Takahashi pursued as finance minister in the 1930s, in that even the policy of the 1920s entailed spending to support aggregate demand. There were, of course, contradictions within the policy. With exports weak, such domestic demand support increased imports and worsened the balance of payments. Moreover, imports rose particularly quickly after the 1923 earthquake. Japan was able to pursue this domestic expansion only by drawing down the stock of specie that had been accumulated during the war.

But the demand support policy could not continue indefinitely, because specie reserves were decreasing. Table 6.11 shows the figures. Specie held abroad fell from ¥1.0 billion in 1920 to less than ¥200 million in 1927—a fall of over 80%. It is reasonable theoretically to support domestic demand while awaiting recovery abroad. But to be consistent, either reversion to the gold standard should have been postponed or reversion should have been made at the market rate of the time, i.e., reversion at a new parity. If the government was determined to return to gold at the old parity, spending should have been suppressed early on, regardless of recession. Of course this last alternative was not attractive compared to the earlier ones but certainly would have been better than returning at the old parity in 1930.

Economic policy decisions had to be difficult given the panics on one hand and the balance of payments deficits on the other. During the years of indecision the preconditions were unconsciously set for the fiscal course taken by Takahashi in the first half of the 1930s. However, as will be seen below, the Takahashi policies differed from the 1920s demand support policies on three points: spending was consciously pursued by the central government, the yen exchange rate was deliberately allowed to fall, and the objects of expenditure shifted from urban public works to military expenditure and farm village relief.

ELECTRIFICATION AND CHEMICAL AND HEAVY INDUSTRIALIZATION

World War I may have begun electrification and chemical and heavy industrialization but the process was far from completed during the war. In fact, because of the war boom, too much time elapsed between the initiation of plant and equipment investments and their completion. Plans for new plant expansion followed in rapid succession in the 1915–16 boom but were realized as productive capacity only much later (see table 6.12). Despite the peak of paid-in capital growth in 1920 the growth of durables production was relatively smooth. The large increase in productive capacity occurred only after the war, when equipment imports were again possible. But a more detailed look reveals that the

Table 6.12. Capital Formation

	Net increase in paid-up capital (¥ million)	Real durable goods production (¥ million)
1901	—	32
1902	—	33
1903	—	36
1904	38	31
1905	10	28
1906	69	32
1907	42	40
1908	133	56
1909	114	60
1910	175	64
1911	98	74
1912	212	80
1913	211	80
1914	114	83
1915	94	72
1916	237	63
1917	865	55
1918	1,273	65
1919	1,851	109
1920	1,961	130
1921	1,087	167
1922	−2,542	159
1923	3,826	202
1924	1,104	210
1925	−229	223
1926	525	278
1927	359	287
1928	483	272
1929	613	280
1930	119	282
1931	203	290
1932	109	313
1933	314	295
1934	1,187	276
1935	816	292
1936	995	313
1937	1,987	272
1938	2,285	272

Sources and Notes: Net increase in paid-up capital from Nihon Ginkō [85], p. 330, for total corporate sector. Real durable goods production from Ohkawa et al. [O], table A39, column for all sectors, excluding military equipment, in 1934–36 prices.

process of chemical and heavy industrialization that characterized Japan's postwar economy was different from that during the war. Both electrification and heavy and chemical industrialization had different roles from the ones they had had during the war.

Long-range transmission of electricity was possible before the war; in 1907 the Komabashi generating plant was completed and sent 55 kilovolts of power 75 kilometers. In 1914 the Inawashiro generating plant was completed and sent 115 kilovolts of power 200 kilometers. The cost was half that of steam-generated power, an estimate based on the Komabashi plant's cost of 1 sen (1/100 yen) per kilowatt. (For details, see Arisawa [7], p. 110.) There followed an explosive boom in power generating firms. Growth rates of paid-up capital were near 30% per year for several years. And demand for power also grew rapidly. Thus, the basis of the electric power industry was formed before the outbreak of the war.

However, during the hostilities the rate of increase of paid-up capital in the electric power industry temporarily slowed, as did the growth rate of capacity. Money for paid-up capital concentrated in other, booming industries, and the rate of return in them was stable. Although growth in electric power was strong, boom conditions did not exist, and the rate of increase of supply capacity was constrained by the breakoff of imports. Still, demand for electricity grew apace during the war (see table 6.13). Demand growth weakened, though only temporarily, in the first half of the 1920s. This is somewhat ironic since this was precisely when the import restraints were lifted and when construction and capital increases began again. But it was also inevitable because prices had to be raised to cover construction costs (see table 6.14). In spite of these problems and some others mentioned below, the electric power industry did progress on the basis of technological change and demand growth.

In contrast to electric power, the machinery and steel industries were lagging before the war. Outstanding is the example of the protected shipbuilding industry, which was subsidized by the government. But other machinery industries as well had firms that, although pioneers in Japan, clearly lagged behind foreign competitors. Even the steel industry, led by the Yawata Steel Works, could not produce well enough to contend with imports. And the chemical industry was not really competitive. All this changed entirely with the outbreak of the war. Despite import interruption internal demand became strong and shortages abroad meant that even exports of these products rose. But as seen in table 6.12, owing to the import cutoff and the export orientation of policy, the level of real investment in fact fell.

Thus, plants planned during the war were completed only at the end of the war or after. With peace, imports were possible again, and so investment plans could be realized; however, it was precisely at this time

Table 6.13. Electricity

	Power generated (million kw) (1)	Light consumed (million kw) (2)	(2)/(1)
1907	277	95	.34
1908	376	135	.36
1909	440	174	.40
1910	621	227	.37
1911	786	322	.41
1912	1,144	460	.40
1913	1,489	617	.41
1914	1,791	756	.42
1915	2,217	800	.36
1916	2,575	941	.37
1917	3,084	1,053	.34
1918	3,648	1,190	.33
1919	4,193	1,387	.33
1920	4,669	1,548	.33
1921	5,113	1,701	.33
1922	5,586	1,884	.34
1923	6,103	1,948	.32
1924	7,835	2,144	.27
1925	7,093	2,341	.26
1926	10,553	2,524	.24
1927	12,089	2,637	.22
1928	13,680	2,699	.20
1929	15,123	2,781	.18
1930	15,773	2,780	.18
1931	16,027	2,815	.18
1932	17,440	2,800	.16
1933	19,522	2,610	.13
1934	21,774	2,680	.12
1935	24,698	2,800	.11
1936	27,135	2,830	.10
1937	30,245	2,950	.10
1938	32,424	3,000	.09
1939	34,144	3,000	.09
1940	34,566	2,900	.08

Source: Minami [64], pp. 196, 198.

Table 6.14. Energy Prices (Coal price/electric power price)

	Coal prices 1934–36 = 100 (1)	Electric power prices 1934–36 = 100 (2)	Relative price (2)/(1)
1907	44.3	65.6	1.48
1908	46.0	61.4	1.33
1909	43.7	96.8	2.22
1910	42.0	97.4	2.32
1911	41.7	101.0	2.42
1912	43.0	80.5	1.87
1913	44.7	105.2	2.35
1914	48.0	123.7	2.58
1915	43.7	97.4	2.23
1916	48.3	107.5	2.23
1917	94.3	110.1	1.17
1918	129.0	132.2	1.02
1919	140.3	177.0	1.70
1920	140.3	215.3	1.53
1921	105.7	214.0	2.02
1922	104.3	223.7	2.14
1923	103.7	224.7	2.17
1924	111.3	177.6	1.60
1925	100.0	180.5	1.81
1926	96.0	168.5	1.76
1927	103.0	150.3	1.46
1928	99.0	133.8	1.35
1929	96.0	135.1	1.41
1930	86.3	123.4	1.43
1931	79.0	120.5	1.53
1932	75.1	108.1	1.44
1933	88.5	105.9	1.20
1934	97.6	102.9	1.05
1935	100.2	95.5	.95
1936	102.2	101.6	.99
1937	117.8	102.6	.87
1938	149.4	95.1	.64
1939	145.2	108.8	.75
1940	147.8	122.1	.83

Source: Column (1): Ohkawa [99], pp. 192–93; col. (2): ibid., p. 210.

that demand fell, so the new capacity was excessive. As a result heavy industries entered a recession. For the steel industry we can compare plans and capacity during and after the boom. Pig iron production in 1918 was 600,000 tons but capacity planned as of January 1919 was a gigantic 1,610,000 tons. This was about 400,000 greater than the actual capacity of 1,234,000 tons achieved three years later in 1922. Moreover, actual production in 1922 was only 687,000 tons. (See Imaizumi [41], pp. 452–53, 759.) Thus, a major portion of the plans made during the war were never realized. But even with many plans left unrealized, capacity still climbed 100% while domestic production rose by less than 15%; imports also rose (46%). A similar story can be seen in shipbuilding by comparing 1913, 1918, and 1924. Firms capable of producing iron ships of over 1,000 tons numbered 5, 41, and 16 in these years, respectively; shipyards numbered 6, 45, and 23, and stocks numbered 17, 135, and 83—solid testimony to overexpansion and subsequent contraction. (For details, see Kōgaku Kai [57], pp. 717, 734.) In response to these structural recessions heavy industry sought protective tariffs on one hand and pursued cartelization and mergers on the other.

Despite all these problems Japan's industrial structure changed its composition through the upheavals of the war, as seen in table 6.15). The table shows the rank of heavy industry in total manufacturing. From 1920 to 1932 employment in heavy industry was stable at 25% of that in light industry. But clear fluctuations can be seen in its proportion of value of output. Heavy industry's share in value of output grew from the middle of the war to a peak of 33% in 1920, fell to 26% in 1925, and then rose again to 37% in 1930, after which it continued rising in the quasi-wartime economy. In gross amounts the increment in the value of output during the 1920s hit ¥11 million. In contrast the growth of light industry was much smaller. Thus, we can see the most important feature of heavy and chemical industries in the 1920s: Output grew but employment did not. Per capita product soared from ¥3,200 in 1922 to a peak of ¥5,500 in 1929. In light industry both employment and product increased little, and per capita product went from a trough of ¥2,900 in 1921 to a peak of only ¥3,500 in 1929. Thus, per capita output in heavy and chemical industries expanded rapidly in the 1920s and the first effects of industrial rationalization were felt in these years. In other words productivity did not rise much in light industry, in contrast to the large gains in heavy industry.

The above analysis uses nominal data because real data are unavailable due to lack of sectoral price indexes. This is unfortunate for purposes of this analysis since prices were in a long-term decline during this period. But as a substitute for real value data, let us analyze the growth rates of indexes of production volume by industry (see table 5.4, based on estimates by Yasuba). The growth rate of the textile industry was above average in the 1920s, but the rate for food products was uncommonly low and that for heavy and chemical industries higher than average. This helps show that the output of heavy and chemical industries was growing at a high rate. Of course one cannot deny that the absolute level of their output in these years was not high. But production was not stagnant; rather it was expanding apace. Although employment expanded but little, heavy and chemical industrialization was progressing step by step. The biggest markets were for fertilizers in farm villages, and for cement and steel products used in construction.

And what were the implications of heavy and chemical industry development? As seen in table 6.16, these new activities transformed the nation's structure of production as exemplified by supply–demand conditions in the steel industry. The table shows long-term data on domestic demand for steel products. In the 1920s domestic production of steel products quadrupled. Furthermore, steel product imports began falling sharply with the beginning of the world depression. Despite the economic slumps in the 1920s (e.g., the price of steel fell by two-thirds between 1920 and 1930), production continued to rise and at the same time domestic demand rose to twice what it had been during the war. Thus, the domestic steel sector established itself as provider of a basic construction input, and dependence on imports eventually lessened.

Simultaneously, the intensity of use of steel in the domestic economy was expanding. In light of the growth of the steel sector we can see more clearly the significance of increases in public works and construction investment. Figures on the share of construction in the structure of domestic demand adequately substantiate this point (table 6.17). In the last half of the 1920s private industrial demand, beginning with that in the machinery (including steel) industries, constituted a low proportion of overall domestic demand, while the relatively high proportion attributable to civil engineering construction and railroads changed very little, in contrast to the large business fluctuations experienced elsewhere in the economy. Hence, it was public works and railroad construction that supported steel demand.

The progress—despite all the troubles—of the heavy and chemical industries as exemplified by steel gives proof that the production structure of the Japanese economy was transformed in these years. Development of these industries during an era of disarmament shows that plant and equipment investments made during World War I had begun to bear fruit. No such sector of basic materials industries had hitherto been established in relatively underdeveloped Japan. The import stoppages during the war hastened establishment of the new industries. Then, resuming competition with foreign goods after the war these industries

Table 6.15. Process of Chemical and Heavy Industrialization

	Employees (thousands) (A)		Production (¥ million) (B)		Product per employee (B/A)		Share of heavy industry in total (%)		Product-per-employee ratio heavy/light industries
	Light industry	Heavy industry	Light industry	Heavy industry	Light industry	Heavy industry	A	B	D/C
1909	229	98	626	168	2.74	1.72	32.7	21.2	0.63
1914	267	149	1,005	367	3.77	2.46	35.8	26.7	0.63
1919	1,288	428	4,782	2,106	3.71	4.91	25.0	30.3	1.32
1920	1,241	424	3,970	1,942	3.19	4.58	25.4	32.8	1.44
1921	1,386	414	4,014	1,540	2.90	3.72	23.6	27.7	1.28
1922	1,309	491	4,068	1,576	3.11	3.20	27.3	28.0	1.03
1923	1,397	477	4,292	1,588	3.07	3.34	25.4	27.1	1.09

1924	1,403	497	4,812	1,705	3.43	3.43	26.1	26.2	1.00
1925	1,449	477	5,143	1,781	3.54	3.74	24.3	25.8	1.06
1926	1,486	508	4,940	1,994	3.32	3.92	25.5	28.8	1.18
1927	1,480	536	4,656	2,090	3.18	3.90	26.8	31.1	1.23
1928	1,499	563	4,897	2,309	3.26	4.10	27.1	31.6	1.25
1929	1,482	471	5,134	2,604	3.46	5.54	24.1	33.7	1.60
1930	1,368	435	3,760	2,176	2.75	5.00	24.1	36.6	1.82
1931	1,350	430	3,334	1,825	2.49	4.26	24.1	36.1	1.71
1932	1,359	496	3,754	2,215	2.78	4.46	26.7	39.8	1.60
1933	1,420	616	4,701	3,162	3.31	5.14	30.3	40.3	1.55
1934	1,536	783	5,121	4,247	3.33	5.43	33.8	45.4	1.63
1935	1,627	917	5,536	5,278	3.40	5.75	36.0	48.7	1.69
1936	1,685	809	6,193	7,167	3.66	7.98	34.8	53.6	2.18
1937	1,774	1,386	7,224	10,102	4.07	7.30	43.7	58.3	1.80

Source: Calculated from Tsūshō Sangyō Shō [161].

Note: Heavy industry: chemicals, metals, machinery, cement, and lime industries; light industry: total of all others.

Table 6.16. Fluctuations in Steel Demand

	Production	Export	Import	Net domestic demand	Price of steel bar #4 per ton (¥)
1914	283	30	483	736	75
1915	343	26	303	620	144
1916	328	24	568	872	211
1917	459	63	860	1,256	339
1918	456	74	814	1,196	390
1919	479	131	922	1,270	230
1920	453	100	1,316	1,669	215
1921	495	89	797	1,203	131
1922	599	87	1,388	1,900	127
1923	702	108	1,013	1,607	136
1924	785	103	1,416	2,128	115
1925	982	126	674	1,530	111
1926	1,190	120	1,188	2,258	97
1927	1,347	145	1,110	2,312	89
1928	1,646	200	1,128	2,575	107
1929	1,947	229	1,167	2,885	97
1930	1,855	226	626	2,255	71
1931	1,616	250	396	1,762	—
1932	2,038	311	327	2,054	—
1933	2,666	426	648	2,888	—
1934	3,172	680	653	3,145	—
1935	3,806	984	768	3,590	—
1936	4,349	1,120	710	3,938	—
1937	4,829	848	1,459	5,440	—
1938	5,128	908	758	4,978	—

Source: Compiled from appendix in Arisawa [7]. Prices are from same publication, p. 41.

Table 6.17. Demand for Ordinary Steel and Steel Products (Thousands of tons)

	Railways	Public works and construction	Shipbuilding	Machinery	Oil, gas, waterworks, and electricity	Mining	Military government, and other	Total
1926	245	253	90	264	22	25	149	1,048
1927	275	239	107	262	17	29	226	1,156
1928	337	400	165	476	28	31	177	1,613
1929	331	697	219	541	56	40	352	2,236
1930	251	619	117	313	52	36	225	1,613
1931	172	488	111	344	49	39	289	1,493
1932	232	621	159	662	60	38	413	2,185
1933	212	730	275	1,009	132	65	266	2,690
1934	319	792	330	1,003	70	130	404	3,048
1935	255	846	321	1,090	81	71	482	3,145
1936	281	1,198	567	886	187	96	545	3,761
Composition								
1926–31 average	17.6	29.4	8.9	24.1	2.4	2.2	15.5	(1,526,000 tons) 100
1932–36 average	8.7	28.1	11.1	31.2	3.5	2.7	14.8	(2,965,000 tons) 100

Source: Calculated from Tōyō Keizai Shimpō Sha [157], p. 140.

finally were able to become independent and usher in the development of the 1930s. The 1920s were thus the era in which heavy and chemical industries sank roots.

Let us touch on two or three general by-products of heavy and chemical industrialization. First, there was a close relationship between the electric power industry and the development of the chemical and lighting equipment industries. Excess power from hydroelectric generating stations was used in electrochemical, electric furnace steel, and special steel plants and thus was a prime force behind heavy and chemical industrialization. Even in the interior of the country excess power was available for the extraordinarily low price of 5 to 8 *rin* (1 rin equals 1/1,000 yen). (For details, see Yokomizo [180].) As a result the chemical fertilizer industry, beginning with ammonium sulfate, was established in these years. Moreover, it was in this era that the most clearly imperialistic capital exports were promoted: the Japan Nitrogen (Nippon Chissō) venture in Korea and the Boo-Jeon River Development.

A second by-product of heavy and chemical industrialization was the formation of industrial belts. As seen in table 6.18, the formation of metals and machinery industrial belts in the Tokyo–Yokohama, Osaka–Kobe, and north Kyushu areas accelerated during the 1920s. Industry in general did not centralize geographically during these years but the fact that the metals and machinery industries had done so meant that core areas for later heavy industrial belts were established. It also meant the formation of conditions favorable to united action among laborers and the creation in major industrial areas of a proletariat with no links to farming to fall back on. In turn these changes meant the birth of paternalistic policies, such as seniority wages and lifetime employment, so firms could attract and keep labor.

But chemical industry development actually fostered regional dispersion due to dependence on dispersed sources for the hydroelectric power used in industrial parks. Examples of dispersed development include electrochemicals, paper, and synthetic fiber factories such as in Hokkaido (Oji Paper), in Toyama (paper and fertilizer), and in Miyazaki (Asahi Chemical). The following passage on the formation of the Tokyo–Yokohama industrial belt eloquently describes this phenomenon (see Yokohama Shiritsu Daigaku Keizai Kenkyū Sho [179], pp. 95–96):

> The Yokohama Sugar Co. was established in 1897 to use the convenient water transport to the west of the railroad station, while behind Kawasaki station Nippon Electric stood with the present-day Columbia of Japan on the Tama River. The core of the industrial belt was formed when Nippon Kōkan (Japan Steel Tube) Co., now the largest firm in the belt, located here to have easy use of barges to transport raw materials. Between 1913 and 1929, in these 17 years, a factory belt approximately 4.6 kilometers long and 1.5 wide—with an

actual area of 578 hectares or 1428 acres—was formed through the work of Sōichirō Asano's Tsurumi Reclamation and Construction Co., later known as Tokyo Harbor Reclamation and Construction. It stretched from the mouth of the Tsurumi River to Kawasaki–Oshima. Even within the city of Kawasaki a 978-acre factory district was completed. Ocean-going ships could pass along the Tokyo-Yokohama canal, and wharfs, moorings, and landings were built one after another. Between 1915 and 1919, Asahi Glass, Asano Shipyard, and Asano Steel were built. In Kawasaki, the Ajinomoto Co., Daiichi (formerly Asano) Cement, and Japan Electric Wire (Nippon Densen) were founded. Nippon Kōkan built a blast furnace, and Tokyo Electric combined with G.E. of America to build Mazuda Lightbulb (the present-day Toshiba-Horikawa plant). Yokohama Sugar evolved into Meiji Seika, a bakery of western-style cakes and sweets, while Columbia of Japan, Japan Truss Concrete, and Fuji Electric (broken off from the Furukawa group in a joint venture with Siemens) both developed.... On June 1, 1926, the Tsurumi Railroad began operations. By the end of the Taisho period, Tokyo Electric's Tsurumi Shioda Plant, Nisshin Flour, the Kawasaki and Ogimachi plants of Nippon Kōkan, Tōyō Wharf and Warehouse, Mitsubishi Oil Company, and Showa Oil Company had all been established. As the Showa period began, factory locations became even more numerous, with the founding or relocation into the belt of Fuji Electric Machinery Company, Japan Casting, Tokunaga Glass, Showa Electric Wire and Cable, Sanki Engineering Company, Tokyo Machinery, Isuzu Motors, Nippon Yakin (Japan Metallurgy), and Tokushu Seikō (Specialty Steels).

But in addition to such by-products, electrification and chemical and heavy industrialization had extremely important direct effects. First was transformation of the structure of even traditional industry and second was rationalization, i.e., upgrading productivity.

The changes in industrial structure due to the dissemination of electricity were as follows. Owing to cost declines resulting from the perfection of long distance power transmission and the resulting possibility of lower electricity rates and also owing to the end of limitations on the hours of electricity supply, electricity was able to shift quickly from use merely as a source of light to use as a prime mover. Both the relative drop in electric rates and increasing reliance on domestically produced electric motors were essential in expanding the use of electricity. As seen in table 6.19, in 1909 the saturation rate for any kind of prime mover in workplaces defined as "factories" was only 28.2%, and in factories employing nine or fewer persons, only 14.4%. Moreover, even among these the proportion of electric prime movers was extremely low. But twenty years later the electric motors were used in 87% of all factories.

The dissemination of electric motors significantly changed the production processes of traditional industries. Traditional processes simply could no longer fulfill consumption demand, so the advent of electricity

Table 6.18. Concentration of Production in Major Industrial Areas (¥ million)

	1914		1920		1930	
	Rank order of prefectures	Amount produced	Rank order of prefectures	Amount produced	Rank order of prefectures	Amount produced
All industries						
	1. Osaka	252	1. Osaka	995	1. Osaka	996
	2. Tokyo	193	2. Tokyo	831	2. Tokyo	818
	3. Hyogo	173	3. Hyogo	695	3. Hyogo	629
	4. Aichi	82	4. Aichi	374	4. Aichi	448
	5. Nagasaki	54	5. Kanagawa	310	5. Kanagawa	295
	6. Fukuoka	47	6. Fukuoka	216	6. Fukuoka	229
	7. Okayama	44	7. Shizuoka	175	7. Shizuoka	173
	8. Kyoto	39	8. Kyoto	173	8. Hokkaido	172
	9. Kanagawa	39	9. Hokkaido	159	9. Kyoto	169
	10. Shizuoka	32	10. Nagano	150	10. Okayama	107
Total for top 5		754 (54.9)		3,205 (54.2)		3,086 (51.7)
Total for the 10		955 (69.6)		4,028 (68.2)		3,936 (66.1)
Nationwide total		1,372 (100)		5,912 (100)		5,955 (100)
Metal and machinery industries						
	1. Osaka	442	1. Osaka	2,256	1. Osaka	2,836
	2. Tokyo	421	2. Tokyo	2,182	2. Tokyo	2,577
	3. Hyogo	357	3. Hyogo	1,869	3. Hyogo	1,640
	4. Nagasaki	115	4. Kanagawa	1,381	4. Kanagawa	1,446
	5. Tochigi	75	5. Nagasaki	650	5. Ibaraki	984

	(1)		(2)		(3)
6. Hokkaido	56	6. Hokkaido	424	6. Nagano	554
7. Fukuoka	55	7. Hiroshima	388	7. Aichi	436
8. Kanagawa	51	8. Aichi	341	8. Fukuoka	382
9. Aichi	46	9. Kyoto	279	9. Tochigi	369
10. Kyoto	39	10. Fukuoka	256	10. Hokkaido	350
Total for top 5	1,410		8,338		9,483
	(76.5)		(73.2)		(80.1)
Total for the 10	1,657		10,026		11,574
	(89.8)		(88.1)		(98.0)
Nationwide total	1,846		11,387		11,883
	(100)		(100)		(100)
Chemical industries					
1. Tokyo	43	1. Tokyo	189	1. Tokyo	193
2. Osaka	43	2. Osaka	175	2. Osaka	165
3. Hyogo	41	3. Hyogo	126	3. Hyogo	114
4. Niigata	12	4. Fukuoka	61	4. Hokkaido	47
5. Hokkaido	10	5. Kanagawa	46	5. Fukuoka	41
6. Aichi	8	6. Shizuoka	43	6. Yamaguchi	35
7. Fukuoka	8	7. Aichi	41	7. Niigata	34
8. Kanagawa	7	8. Kumamoto	29	8. Shizuoka	34
9. Shizuoka	7	9. Yamaguchi	14	9. Toyama	32
10. Kumamoto	4	10. Toyama	13	10. Miyazaki	29
Total for top 5	149		597		560
	(68.8)		(63.8)		(60.6)
Total for the 10	183		737		724
	(84.5)		(78.6)		(78.3)
Nationwide total	217		937		925
	(100)		(100)		(100)

Source: Calculated from Tsūshō Sangyō Shō [161].

Note: Figures in parentheses are percentages.

Table 6.19. Percentage of Factories Having Prime Movers (A) and Percentage of Total Prime Mover Horsepower from Electric Prime Movers (B)

		Total	Spinning and weaving	Metals	Machinery and tools	Chemicals	Persons 5–9	10–29	30–49	50–99	100–199	200–499	500–999	1,000 or more
1909	A	28.2	31.5	42.0	49.8	28.6	14.4	30.2	63.8	78.1		87.3	95.2	100.0
	B	13.0	8.6	15.6	40.0	9.0	10.6	9.8	7.0	9.9		13.2	9.7	18.2
1914	A	45.6	51.9	57.6	64.4	52.4	28.6	48.9	76.1	87.7		92.9	96.7	97.5
	B	30.1	22.2	46.9	61.8	27.4	27.3	26.1	20.5	23.8		24.3	33.7	36.8
1919	A	61.2	63.3	80.8	78.9	66.1	46.0	65.1	85.8	92.7		97.2	100.0	99.4
	B	58.6	54.6	74.1	67.8	54.9	56.9	58.6	55.1	59.8		59.4	69.0	55.6
1930	A	82.5	89.6	92.3	89.3	82.9	76.6	84.1	90.2	93.8	97.5	99.2	100.0	100.0
	B	86.8	85.0	92.3	91.8	92.1	84.5	86.2	83.0	88.0	82.6	89.7	95.6	80.6

Source: Calculated from Minami [64], pp. 228–40.

provided the opportunity for basic change in the production methods of traditional industry. Typical of these changes were the shifts from hand-operated to power-driven looms and from hand-turned to power lathes. These changes so transformed manufacturing processes that consumer goods production for the masses could no longer be adequately handled by cottage industries. The major locus of production shifted to real factories. Based on the supply of cheap electricity and the spread of electric motors, machinery that had been invented earlier was introduced from abroad. The industrial revolution in advanced nations was caused by the very invention of machinery to produce consumer goods, but in Japan it was the dissemination of electricity that brought industrial transformation to methods of consumer goods production. Japan's case is characteristic of industrialization in latecomer countries.

The second result of electrification was the mushrooming of industries that use electricity as a primary input. The best examples are electrochemical industries and electric-based refining industries. In the chemical industry the soda, carbide, and ammonium sulfate industries grew explosively. Very often problems of excess power arose where hydroelectric power stations were built. So it was desirable to relieve the excess by attracting industries that consume much electricity. Moreover, owing to stoppage of imports of chemical industry products during the war, one after another new firms were established in these fields. Many of these faced retrenchment after the war but those that survived formed a new chemical industry. Representative soda firms include Hodogaya Soda, Japan Soda, Osaka Soda, Asahi Denka (Electrochemical), Kanto Sanso, and Mitsui Mining's soda venture. In the ammonium sulfate industry Jun Noguchi's Japan Nitrogen, which had been using the hydro power of Sogi Electric produced in the Minamata and Kagami districts of Kumamoto prefecture (Kyushu), soon began using power from the Gokase River at Nobeoka in Miyazaki prefecture to make ammonium sulfate while Japan Synthetic Fertilizer used power from the Kurobe River in Toyama prefecture and Showa Fertilizer in Kawasaki prefecture used excess power from Tokyo Power and Light. Noguchi later built a dam on the Boo Jeon River in Korea to use waterpower for electricity generation and built a chemical complex at Hungnam. In the carbide industry—where 30% of cost was electricity even in 1955—Noguchi's Japan Nitrogen, Joichi Fujiyama's Mitsui-related firm, Ginjiro Fujiwara's Electrochemical Limited (using power of the Omi and Kurobe rivers), Tekkō Limited (Power from Sakata) and others built new factories as new electricity sources were developed. In electrometallurgy the same period of years witnessed development of Daidō Steel (connected with Daidō Power) in Nagoya, Hirota Steel in Fukushima, and others. Demand also rose for the products of ancillary industries, e.g., electric machinery and transmission wire. Thus, in the ten years after the war electric power was a leading industry.

But heavy industry was not able to lead development. Machinery and steel imports rose rapidly after the war, pressing domestic products and hurting domestic firms. The inverse relationship between imports and domestic production is clear in table 6.20. Heavy industry was competitively weak, bankruptcies were rampant, and under these conditions rationalization proceeded apace. As seen before, plant and equipment expansion of firms was a postwar phenomenon, even in recessions. Introduction of new equipment led to great improvements, as seen in data on real output per worker by industry. Most notable is the high produc-

Table 6.20. Production and Imports of Machinery (¥ million)

	Prime movers		Electric machinery		Machine tools	
	Production	Imports	Production	Imports	Production	Imports
1909	3.5	2.2	3.0	1.8	0.1	2.8
1910	—	1.8	—	1.2	—	1.3
1911	—	3.5	—	3.1	—	1.9
1912	—	3.2	—	4.1	—	4.0
1913	—	3.0	—	4.3	—	3.3
1914	28.5	1.9	10.5	2.8	0.0	2.5
1915	—	0.9	—	0.8	—	0.9
1916	—	1.9	—	0.8	—	1.8
1917	—	3.7	—	1.7	—	3.5
1918	—	8.9	—	3.6	—	6.6
1919	39.6	11.0	43.1	6.0	6.4	10.6
1920	20.0	14.3	86.5	6.8	11.3	13.7
1921	19.9	12.9	71.0	10.3	9.4	11.0
1922	31.5	10.9	60.1	12.8	7.3	6.5
1923	16.9	7.0	64.5	11.4	4.7	3.8
1924	16.3	14.0	74.2	21.3	8.9	7.8
1925	17.8	13.6	92.9	12.9	6.4	5.7
1926	22.7	12.7	93.5	11.4	7.0	3.0
1927	25.6	9.6	107.6	8.2	8.3	5.0
1928	26.8	16.7	112.8	7.8	7.7	4.4
1929	39.6	21.6	95.3	8.8	5.6	5.6
1930	42.7	18.8	78.0	5.0	4.4	4.8
1931	28.6	14.1	62.2	2.3	3.9	3.1
1932	38.5	13.9	66.6	1.8	8.2	5.8
1933	69.3	18.1	109.5	1.9	15.4	16.2

Source: Tsūshō Sangyō Shō [161], pp. 195, 199, 202.

tivity growth in metals and machinery with the highest growth in the last half of the 1920s.

The rationalization of industry attracted attention as a government-instigated movement, but this was only after 1929 in reaction to the world depression. But prior to that, the Taylor system of management and Ford's mass production system had been introduced, promoting the standardization of methods and products. The fact is that the rationalization of the heavy and chemical industries had begun quietly long before the government rationalization policies.

As also mentioned above, employment in heavy industry increased very little during the 1920s while production rose considerably. But owing to declining prices profitability lagged. To defend themselves against retrenchments, firms had no choice but to increase production and lower costs by rationalizing their operations.

"Rationalization" has been used in a broad sense here. But to be a bit more specific, one important type was, of course, technological improvement, and indeed during the 1920s there was a spate of tie-ups with foreign firms and of patent buying. Examples include Mitsubishi Electric Machinery's tie-up with Westinghouse and Fuji Electric's birth from the tie-up between Furukawa and Siemens. (Toshiba had formed a partnership with General Electric earlier.) Production rights for diesel ship engines were purchased by Mitsubishi's Nagasaki shipyards. Similar rights to produce Garvey boilers and Shelley steam turbines were also acquired, and Hitachi purchased the patent rights on a boiler and a turbine. The level of technology was raised with the assimilation of such methods brought into the country through patent purchases abroad. Substitution of domestically produced machines for imported machinery was nearly completed in the electric machinery sector around 1930. This was also a time of standardization in the machinery industry, and high-powered plant and equipment built with postwar machinery imports had come on line. Thus, one reason for the growth in productivity was certainly these improvements in technology.

At the same time rationalization meant saving labor. Labor power in secondary industry rose precipitously during the war but hardly at all during periods of stagnation and panics. Hiring stopped, and so did movement of labor among firms. Length of employment thus increased and with it the degree of skill of workers. With cutbacks in the use of labor power, all that was demanded of labor was the technical proficiency to operate the newly built plant and equipment. This gave rise to an overall labor surplus while at the same time a small force of skilled laborers was accumulated. This core of skilled labor is an important factor in explaining the resumption of economic growth after 1932.

For a more detailed look at the stagnation of employment and the

Table 6.21. Growth Industries and Nongrowth Industries

	Industries in which both product and employment declined in the mid-1920s	Industries in which both product and employment continued growing in the mid-1920s	Industries that stagnated or fluctuated irregularly in the mid-1920s
Metals industries	Iron refining, bolts, nuts, rivets, construction-use metal shapes, metal plate	Cast pig iron products, plating, electric wire, steel cable	
Machinery industries	Prime movers, machine tools, mining equipment, iron ships, scientific instruments, optical equipment, weapons	Electric machinery, batteries, light bulbs, spinning and weaving machinery, agricultural and construction machinery, pump compression machinery, cranes, automobiles, measuring instruments, gages, clocks, acoustical equipment, aircraft	Railway cars
Textile industries	Hemp spinning, wool spinning, silk weaving, hemp weaving, wool weaving, rope making, cotton products	Silk spinning, yarn making, dyeing and bleaching, hosiery, woven goods, hats, clothing and other sewn goods	Silk reeling, cotton spinning, and hemp plait
Chemical industries	Industrial chemicals, dyes, celluloid, animal oils, and fats, wax making, paint, cosmetics, gunpowder, pulp, leather and pelts	Chemical fertilizers, chemical fibers, vegetable oils, soap, medical drugs, paper, mineral oils, rubber products	

Source: Constructed from Tsūshō Sangyō Shō [161].

growth of production in these years, let us examine table 6.21, which presents, using industry-by-industry data, changes in output and employment in four types of industries. During these years of supposed depression many new industries grew steadily although not remarkably. Examples include electric wire, electric machinery, light bulbs, and batteries in the electric-related fields; spinning and weaving machinery, agricultural and construction machinery, pump compression machinery, and cranes in the industrial machinery field; woven and knitted goods and machine-sewn goods; and the new chemical industries. These fields had been lagging in technology but finally established themselves in the 1920s. But more significantly these were either industries toward which consumer tastes had shifted (e.g., manufactured textile products) or new technology industries like chemicals. While existing industries were being forced to rationalize by poor business conditions, the new industries were developing inconspicuously.

Seven □ Concentration, Cartels, and Conglomerates

CONCENTRATION AND CARTELS

The period after World War I is often called an era of monopoly and strengthening of zaibatsu (financial cliques or conglomerates). However, can this assertion be substantiated? Let us look at some of the data.

Using the *Census of Industries (Kōgyō Tōkei Hyō*, included in Tsūshō Sangyō Shō [161]), let us look at degrees of concentration in production and employment. Data on concentration of production are available only after 1929, so let us begin with concentration of employment. Table 7.1 shows the degree of concentration of employment to have risen considerably between the middle of the war and the mid-1920s but to have started to decrease after 1926. On the other hand it also shows concentration of *production* to have increased between 1929 and 1934, a result, as will be shown later, of heavy and chemical industrialization. Thus, except for a few years after the war, concentration did not increase greatly.

But looking at aggregate figures obfuscates the problem in some ways. For example, suppose we have two classes of industry, low concentration (A) and high concentration (B). If employment in class B were to rise relatively, the degree of concentration of the aggregate would also rise. Thus, even if the rates of concentration in the two classes do not change, a shift in the industrial structure could make the aggregate rate of concentration change. If we assume that concentration is greater for heavy and chemical industries than for light industries, the expansion of the former would make the overall rate of concentration increase. Thus, we also need to examine the degree of concentration in employment of various industries over time. But data problems remain. Even industry data are still relatively aggregated. If the structure within an industry changes quickly, the same problem as described for the overall rate may occur. For example, the development of the electrochemical industries rapidly transformed the class of chemical industries that had hitherto

Table 7.1. Concentration Rates of Large Firms in Manufacturing (Percent)

		Factories		Employees		Production	
		1,000 or more workers	500–999 workers	1,000 or more workers	500–999 workers	1,000 or more workers	500–999 workers
Manufacturing	1914	0.3	0.4	16.7	8.5	—	—
	1920	0.3	0.5	21.7	10.6	—	—
	1925	0.5	0.6	26.8	10.8	—	—
	1929	0.3	0.5	20.1	11.3	19.9	11.5
	1934	0.3	0.4	18.7	10.6	26.2	12.1
Spinning and	1914	0.5	0.6	20.7	10.5	—	—
weaving	1920	0.6	0.8	24.0	13.8	—	—
	1925	0.9	1.1	30.9	13.7	—	—
	1929	0.7	1.0	25.3	15.3	32.5	14.6
	1934	0.4	0.8	18.8	14.5	32.6	17.2
Chemicals	1914	0.0	0.5	0.0	10.2	—	—
	1920	0.2	0.3	9.9	5.8	—	—
	1925	0.3	0.7	11.0	10.8	—	—
	1929	0.3	0.6	12.6	10.8	7.3	11.6
	1934	0.5	0.6	25.6	10.2	16.6	12.0
Metals	1914	0.1	0.3	7.6	8.0	—	—
	1920	0.3	0.4	24.9	10.8	—	—
	1925	0.2	0.4	31.8	7.3	—	—
	1929	0.1	0.3	11.8	9.3	14.8	13.6
	1934	0.2	0.5	25.0	10.0	46.0	11.2
Machinery	1914	0.6	0.5	43.1	8.4	—	—
	1920	0.6	0.9	47.1	11.0	—	—
	1925	0.8	0.8	46.7	10.1	—	—
	1929	0.5	0.5	37.0	8.4	35.5	9.0
	1934	0.5	0.4	34.0	9.2	35.7	10.8

Source: Calculated from Tsūshō Sangyō Shō [161].

chiefly consisted of the drug, rubber, and leather goods industries. We can easily imagine that the degree of concentration of the chemical industries as a class appeared to change. So, with this reservation in mind let us examine and compare the composition of employment by scale of factory for the four industries, metals, machinery, chemicals, and textiles (see table 7.1).

Most notable is the fact that only chemicals continued to become more concentrated throughout the period from 1914 to 1934. The others, and the aggregate as well, became more concentrated until 1925, then less so. The rise in concentration in the metals industry between 1929 and 1934 is due to inclusion of the Japan Steel Company, theretofore excluded, in the 1934 census, which means adding the data for the Yawata Steel works. Thus, a simple comparison is meaningless. In short, even after an industry-by-industry examination we cannot say that overall concentration increased between the wars but rather that it even declined beginning with the Showa period.

Moreover, a declining trend was seen for absolute numbers of factories of more than 1,000 workers from the mid-1920s in textiles and metals. The number of such large factories in the machinery industry fell from 40 in 1928 to 19 in 1931 and surpassed 40 again only after 1934. As measured by scale of employment it is an incontrovertible fact that concentration decreased.

Let us now look at two or three industries a bit more closely. The steel industry displayed distinctive fluctuations in degree of concentration, as seen in table 7.2. Until 1923 the share produced by the Yawata works increased but thereafter declined steadily. In pig iron the share of Kyomip'o (in Korea), Anshan, and Penhsihu (both in Manchuria) advanced quickly, and in steel the weight of the top five firms rose. But the total amount of steel produced by all firms soared.

In the spinning industry the share of the big six (Kanebō, Tōyōbō, Dai Nippon-bō, Osaka Gōdōbō—which merged with Tōyōbō in the last half of 1931—Fujibō, and Nisshin-bō) in both capacity and production declined on trend (see table 7.3). After the war the big six temporarily had expanded capacity, and their share of output did grow until 1922. But after that, their attitude toward plant expansion was passive, and their share of both output and total industry plant and equipment dropped. Although their management was smooth and although they did invest in China, the data reveal little movement toward oligopoly and even some strengthening of competition. Despite control by the Spinning Federation (*Bōseki Renmei*), a classic cartel, one cannot deny the gradual strengthening of competition within the industry.

The above paragraphs discuss only the steel and textile industries by firm whereas all other analysis was by factory size. Thus, the objection may remain that this discussion does not correctly treat the problem of concentration as usually approached, i.e., by firm. Although the data are indeed limited, the limitations do not condemn the results. On the production side the progress of concentration was temporarily stopped and in fact competition became more intense.

One can find several reasons for the reduction in concentration. First is progress in rationalization. In times of declining profitability firms have no choice but to restrict production, use existing facilities more

Table 7.2. Production Concentration in Steel

| | Pig iron | | | | Steel | | |
| | Share of Yawata Works in domestic production (%) | Share of total production of Japanese-capitalized steelworks (including those in Manchuria and China) | | | Share of domestic production | | |
		Yawata Works (%)	Kyomipo, Anshan, and Penhsihu (%)	Total product (thousand tons)	Yawata Works (%)	Next top four firms (%)	Total product (thousand tons)
1923	82.0	57.0	24.7	797	64.4	29.0	959
1924	72.5	59.3	28.5	820	61.1	31.0	1,100
1925	66.6	60.4	25.7	921	63.9	28.6	1,300
1926	65.8	56.8	26.0	1,123	62.6	28.6	1,506
1927	67.2	47.5	29.4	1,269	62.5	29.5	1,685
1928	76.5	55.0	28.3	1,523	57.4	33.5	1,910
1929	74.4	52.1	30.2	1,662	53.5	33.8	2,294
1930	70.0	45.7	34.9	1,407	52.5	36.1	2,389
1931	72.5	47.5	34.5	1,541	45.7	41.9	1,883
1932	77.7	54.8	29.2	2,031	47.6	38.9	2,398
1933	—	48.7	28.5	2,415	44.7	38.4	3,190
1934	—	—	—	—	40.6	35.0	3,844
1935	—	—	—	—	38.7	34.2	4,703

Notes and Sources: The four top firms after Yawata are Nippon Kōkan, Kawasaki Shipbuilding, Kobe Steel, and Sumitomo Metals. Calculated from *Seitetsu-gyō Sankō Shiryō* [120]. For 1917–22 the percentage share of the Yawata Works in total domestic pig iron production was as follows:

1917	1918	1919	1920	1921	1922
67.4	46.9	50.7	53.2	65.0	73.0

Table 7.3. Production Concentration Rates among the Big Six Spinning
Companies

		Spindles		Bales produced	
		Total spindles (thousands)	Big six share (%)	Total product (thousands)	Big six share (%)
1921	1st H	3,489	60.5	992	54.3
	2nd H	4,161	60.1	825	67.8
1922	1st H	4,518	65.0	1,125	56.9
	2nd H	4,528	58.7	930	63.9
1923	1st H	4,667	58.6	1,131	63.6
	2nd H	4,437	51.8	1,040	57.1
1924	1st H	4,850	53.5	1,024	57.5
	2nd H	5,126	56.6	1,049	58.8
1925	1st H	5,292	55.0	1,129	59.6
	2nd H	5,447	55.0	1,244	55.2
1926	1st H	5,585	54.2	1,316	51.0
	2nd H	5,680	54.4	1,392	54.2
1927	1st H	5,930	53.8	1,314	54.0
	2nd H	6,079	53.4	1,217	54.1
1928	1st H	6,272	52.2	1,187	52.8
	2nd H	6,426	52.2	1,265	50.2
1929	1st H	6,488	52.4	1,348	49.3
	2nd H	6,796	51.3	1,445	49.3
1930	1st H	7,048	49.9	1,358	48.7
	2nd H	7,172	49.1	1,167	47.3
1931	1st H	7,269	49.0	1,227	43.4
	2nd H	7,339	49.2	1,341	45.3
1932	1st H	7,762	47.4	1,406	43.6
	2nd H	7,930	46.8	1,404	43.2
1933	1st H	8,174	46.8	1,508	42.9
	2nd H	8,608	47.0	1,591	43.2
1934	1st H	9,125	45.3	1,661	43.6

Source: Dai-Nippon Bōseki Rengō Kai [18].
Note: *1st H* and *2nd H* mean first and second halves of corporate fiscal year,
i.e., April–September and October–March, respectively.

intensively, hold down employment, raise productivity, and cut costs.
The rate of profit in heavy industries was indeed falling, as was capacity
utilization, so the large firms had no choice but to pursue the above
policies. Second, we must consider the large firms in the context of the
international fashion of a "return to normalcy." We have seen how gold

standard reversion policies brought a declining trend to prices. A drop in firms' profitability naturally followed, and, faced with weak demand growth, firms had no choice but to adopt policies of extreme caution. Because borrowing becomes more burdensome as prices fall, it was preferable that any expansion of plant be made with internal funds. Hence, the old, venerated principle of "sound finance", i.e., avoiding borrowing, was once again revived by large firms. Accumulated capital might well be used for domestic financial investments or for foreign expansion, but plant and equipment investment was certainly to be avoided. The objective of management was not to increase the market share but instead to be "sound."

Given these factors, the lack of concentration in these years is not surprising. But there are two elements about concentration that deserve comment. First was the concentration of financial capital, which facilitated zaibatsu acquisition of equity or of management control of other firms by pressure on the distribution system or on corporate finance. This is the most important way in which oligopoly advanced during these years, and zaibatsu were at the core of this movement. The second problem was oligopolization through cartels and mergers. Both trends changed direction after the start of the world depression but were most influential in the 1920s. Thus, let us point out some of the more salient features of capital concentration in these years.

First we may see the buildup and concentration of the corporate capital base. Table 7.4 shows the total capital base and number of firms by industry and year. Let us examine the data under the following set of assumptions. An oligopoly industry is one in which the number of firms is declining (or at least not rising) and the capital per firm is rising, here called type a. In some industries such a trend was seen during only certain years. Industries where oligopolization proceeded only between 1919 and 1924 will be called type b, and those where it occurred between 1924 and 1929 type c. Industries that became more competitive, i.e., where the number of firms rises but capital per firm does not increase, are called type d. Industries with no clear trend are called type e.

Using the above categories, we can divide industries into classes and, as seen in table 7.4 derive the following results:

Type a	Electricity, banking, and finance
Type b	Cotton spinning, metals
Type c	Silk reeling, paper, warehousing
Type b/c mix	Ceramics, food products (trading firms)
Type d	Food products, chemicals, machinery, printing and publishing; others (all these manufacturing firms only): textiles, metals and machinery, fuels, printing

Table 7.4. Capital per Firm and Number of Firms

	1914		1919		1924		1929		1934		Type
	A	B	A	B	A	B	A	B	A	B	
Manufacturing											
Food products	5.5	1,350	17.1	851	17.4	1,835	25.9	1,751	26.7	1,861	d
Textiles	11.9	1,112	44.0	1,052	52.5	1,506	66.1	1,227	66.1	1,321	c
Cotton spinning	257.9	30	239.5	88	538.0	51	605.3	56	639.0	58	b
Silk reeling	1.8	321	18.5	213	27.3	392	38.0	320	—	—	c
Chemicals	9.1	405	32.2	628	39.7	696	51.7	794	72.6	968	d
Metals	5.9	168	81.6	257	82.1	217	93.1	243	194.4	344	b
Machinery	13.6	323	55.6	485	74.6	534	87.9	589	77.1	836	d
Ceramics	10.5	200	26.9	315	43.4	298	76.6	231	98.7	232	b–c
Paper	38.0	71	61.9	138	109.8	149	136.8	119	133.6	146	c
Printing and publishing	2.7	177	7.7	132	9.8	258	10.2	280	10.7	298	d
Lumber products	2.9	270	7.6	294	10.9	533	12.4	418	10.8	385	c
Other	7.5	427	16.0	350	37.1	430	14.4	479	14.0	564	d

	A	B	A	B	A	B	A	B	A	B	
Mining	84.0	197	114.0	301	219.3	278	264.3	291	214.5	381	c
Electric power	59.7	344	88.0	528	221.2	505	397.4	468	457.3	453	a
Gas	83.3	83	114.3	60	159.1	62	272.0	74	239.1	96	d
Waterworks	—	—	—	—	126.6	3	122.6	8	87.0	16	b–c
Commerce											
Food products	1.3	1,294	7.0	458	10.5	396	13.1	386	19.4	650	d
Textiles	3.9	806	26.9	237	43.3	352	43.8	418	27.5	617	d
Metals and machinery	1.7	163	34.6	100	21.1	211	16.4	349	16.7	512	d
Fuels	1.7	181	14.9	161	14.6	165	14.2	176	10.8	243	d
Printing and publishing	3.7	175	10.2	115	16.8	164	21.4	247	24.9	309	d
Foreign trade	12.7	132	54.7	211	61.1	230	87.8	313	87.6	363	a
Banking and finance	17.3	4,100	50.3	2,671	86.3	2,580	114.9	2,021	122.2	1,853	c
Warehousing	4.6	391	10.9	372	23.7	407	36.0	355	36.9	358	d
Construction	9.4	123	47.9	55	77.6	127	46.7	175	24.4	214	d
Transportation	19.8	1,178	61.3	1,138	56.5	1,752	52.8	2,739	52.9	2,739	d

Source: Calculated from Nōshōmu Shō [98].
Note: A: ¥ 10,000, B: number of firms.

and publishing, foreign trade (all these trading firms), gas, waterworks, civil engineering and transportation

Type e   Lumber, mining

By this measure there were only two industries of type a displaying a clear trend to capital concentration in this period: electric power, in which the economies of scale were most clearly evident, and banking and finance, which had been shaken by legal reorganization and panics and which became strategically important bases for industrial control by the zaibatsu. It is mainly due to concentration in these two industries that the interwar period has been characterized as one of monopolization. The only others that began to be monopolized in these years were type b/c borderline cases of food product commerce and ceramics. Monopolization in silk reeling and paper began only in the late 1920s. Metals did concentrate later due to the establishment of the Japan Steel Company, and cotton-weaving did likewise with its integration into the ten big spinning companies. But in the mid- and late 1920s, even these industries saw rather stronger competition.

Almost all other industries were of type d, those tending to more competition. This fact presents a different image from the usual one that Japan was becoming more oligopolistic during the 1920s. Chapter 6 showed that output was expanding, heavy and chemical industrialization proceeding, firms rationalizing internally, and growth continuing. Thus, under such conditions one would conclude that the failure of the trend toward concentration to develop further was quite natural. This is a feature of the economy of this period that has been largely ignored.

Another aspect of concentration that is said to have proceeded rapidly during the intense competition of the era was cartelization. Kamekichi Takahashi has shown that of the major cartels extant in 1932, only 7 existed before 1914, 12 were formed between 1914 and 1926, 12 more between 1927 and 1929, while the years 1930–32 saw the formation of 48 (with 4 unknown) (see Takahashi [144], p. 127). These data reveal that the real age of cartelization was not the 1920s but rather after 1930 during the world depression. During the latter years the government promoted cartelization as a means of rationalization and also promulgated the Key Industries Control Law. Of course some cartelization did occur after World War I but its pace was slow. Cartels tend to be effective as a defense against short-term business cycle fluctuations and to maintain themselves only in periods of low growth and low profitability. But cartels are ineffective in deep, chronic recessions, and firms have no choice but concentration and merger. Moreover, cartels usually have only a limited effective life. Post-World War I cartels in Japan were formed against a background of fierce competition just after the war. They expanded even though markets were slack and were able to increase production only as new demand was discovered. Thus, they came to be instruments to protect members against growth recessions. On top of this, cartels were easy to form in rapidly growing industries such as steel, petroleum, cement, and chemicals, where scale was large and firms were few. But despite all these factors the 1920s did not see cartelization on the scale of the early 1930s.

FINANCIAL CAPITAL AND THE ZAIBATSU

Having surveyed the limitations of the power of cartels, we can now turn our attention to concentration in the financial sector, which was the core of oligopoly in this era and which strengthened its power over a broad range of industries. Bank concentration proceeded slowly after the Panic of 1920 but progressed quickly after the Panic of 1927 and the revision of the banking law (see below). There were many bankruptcies among small urban and rural banks, giving large banks targets for takeovers. A Bank of Japan report described the problems of the banking sector as follows: "Bank directors had direct links with outside firms, and speculated on their own account. Banks became financial organs for speculation by bank directors, or for firms with links to these directors. Reckless lending, favoritism in loans to individuals and their related firms, loans collateralized by real estate or other difficult-to-convert assets, and loans on credit alone were widespread" (Nihon Ginkō [82], p. 548). These practices invited banking crises and reflected the "organ bank" character of many banks of the period. A surprisingly large number of small banks, most of which were overloaned, continued in existence even after the 1927 crisis. Table 7.5 gives data on the structure of ordinary banks classified by paid-up capital.

Authorities in charge of financial policy recognized these problems even during the war and after the armistice promoted merger and amalgamation when bankruptcies occurred. For example, in 1923 the eleven banks related to the Yasuda zaibatsu merged into the bigger Yasuda Bank. In 1926, the year before the big panic, the Financial System Research Committee (*Kinyū Seido Chōsa Kai*) was formed, with the goals of "planning for a filling out of the financial base of banks, fostering sound management, hoping to implement meticulous supervision, preventing unfair competition, and planning the progress of adjustment among banks." Based on the report of the committee calling for minimum bank capital of ¥1 million (and in large city regions ¥2 million), encouragement of local bank mergers, reduction of loans collateralized by real estate, and restrictions on outside connections of directors, a new bank-

Table 7.5. Number of Ordinary Banks Classified by Amounts of Authorized Capital

	Less than ¥100,000	¥100,000–500,000	¥500,000–1.0 million	¥1.0–2.0 million	¥2.0–5.0 million	¥5.0–10.0 million	¥10.0–50.0 million	More than ¥50.0 million	Total
1919	404	545	206	99	40	25	26	7	1,345
1923*	232	525	442	281	126	53	38	9	1,706
1927	140	350	327	251	112	48	47	8	1,283
1928	99	250	267	217	103	46	41	8	1,031
1929	70	176	235	209	99	43	41	8	881
1930	51	138	212	192	98	43	41	7	782
1931	32	89	189	196	92	39	39	7	683
1932†	0	0	147	214	94	38	38	7	538
1935	0	0	129	183	83	30	35	6	466
1938	0	0	80	135	69	24	32	6	346
1941	0	0	27	51	49	21	32	6	186

Source: Gotō [29], pp. 78–79.

Notes: "Ordinary bank" is a legal classification. The activities of ordinary banks in Japan are similar to those of commercial banks in the United States.

*The rise in the number of banks between 1919 and 1923 was due mostly to the conversion of bank charters from the savings bank class to the ordinary bank class.

†The new banking law put into effect in 1928 required banks with head offices in cities of fewer than 10,000 people to have minimum capital of ¥500,000, those in cities of more than 10,000 population to have minimum capital of ¥1.0 million, and those in Tokyo or Osaka to have minimum capital of ¥2.0 million. The period of grace ended in 1932, which accounts for the extinction of small banks after that year.

ing law was promulgated in March 1927. The new law promoted bank concentration through legal means, and, given the concentration of deposits in large banks resulting from the 1927 panic, the law played a basic role in establishing the hegemony of large banks.

A major result of the trend to bank amalgamation was the concentration of bank financing in large firms. Between the end of the war and 1925 monetary policy was tight but after the Panic of 1927 money became easy. The decline of interest rates shows this (see table 7.6).

The concentration of deposits in the five large banks (see table 7.7) meant that the environment of funds supply changed substantially. The ratio of loans to deposits was low for large banks; they made few loans to small, medium, or local firms, and even the loans they made to large firms were restricted to specific firms in specific industries. These tendencies intensified when banking was concentrated. Weak industries or firms had difficulty taking advantage of easy monetary conditions and thus were faced with hard times. On the other hand, under such conditions the big banks held an advantageous position over industry and used their clout to pull selected firms into their respective orbits. Moreover, management of zaibatsu-related firms was stable, as seen in the case of the Mitsui group, where deposits by the Mitsui-related firms in the Mitsui Bank were greater than the bank's loans to the firms. This gave banks the opportunity to use the idle funds from within the group to enlarge the group's network of control. (See Mitsui Bank [65], pp. 386, 423.)

The electric power industry provides an excellent example of fund demand in the industrial world. On one hand, concentration was progressing due to technological advances mentioned earlier; on the other hand severe competition for markets, particularly among the Big Five power firms, impelled even further plant and equipment investment. As a result of the heavy investment the profitability and capital structure of power companies deteriorated precipitously. Tokyo Power and Light, Tōhō Power, and Ujigawa Electric were in especially bad shape, and Mitsui Bank along with other banks troubled by frozen loans helped float foreign bonds for the power firms. The banks also intervened in the selection of power company directors, and in 1932, with advisers representing the five largest banks, a plan was worked out for forming the Electric Power Federation (*Denryoku Renmei*). The federation would acknowledge, in the words of Shigeaki Ikeda, that the electric power industry would "be controlled according to the principles of men of the financial industry." This was partly a means for protecting the health of bank assets but at the same time was a way of forcing surrender of the Fukuzawa and Matsunaga zaibatsu of Nagoya and the Kōshū zaibatsu to rivals Mitsui, Mitsubishi, and Sumitomo.

Table 7.6. Interest Rates (Percent per year)

	Loans aver. rate (1)	Discounts aver. rate (2)	Call rate	
			Peak (3)	Trough (4)
1919	8.1	7.6	12.0	2.2
1920	10.1	10.4	12.0	2.2
1921	9.9	9.0	11.7	1.8
1922	9.7	9.3	11.0	3.7
1923	9.7	9.5	11.3	4.0
1924	9.7	9.6	9.9	4.0
1925	9.6	9.2	8.6	4.2
1926	9.5	8.9	7.7	5.7
1927	9.3	8.4	5.8	2.6
1928	8.8	7.6	6.2	1.8
1929	8.4	6.9	5.8	1.8
1930	8.0	6.7	5.8	1.8
1931	7.8	6.6	9.1	1.5
1932	8.1	7.1	8.0	2.0
1933	7.8	6.2	3.7	2.4
1934	7.4	5.6	4.0	2.5
1935	7.0	5.3	4.4	2.5
1936	6.7	5.1	4.0	2.5
1937	6.5	4.9	3.3	2.5

Sources: Cols. (1) and (2): Gotō [29], p. 273; cols. (3) and (4): Okura Shō Rizaikyoku Kinyū Jikō Sankō Sho, 1939, pp. 26–27.

One can find many examples of bank influence in industries. For example, the failure of Suzuki Shōten, a major trading company to which Mitsui had lent large sums, led to Mitsui control of Ensuiko Sugar, the Fuji–Minobu Railroad, Gōdō Woolens, Japan Match, and others because the Mitsui Bank, either alone or with other zaibatsu providers of funds, took "absolute right of control" of subsidiaries of the failed firm (see "History of Mitsui" cited in Shibagaki [122], pp. 244–45). The absorption into the Mistui group of Japan Flour, Dai Nippon Coal, and Japan Camphor is thought to have been aided by the financial power of the Mitsui Bank. At the same time, Mitsui bought Meiji Sugar (of the Mitsubishi Group) and two Tōyō Sugar factories (Suzuki group) while the rest of the firms formed Dai Nippon Sugar (weakly related to Mitsubishi). The Mitsui Bank also provided the money for Oji Paper's pur-

Table 7.7. Banking Concentration

	Loans		Deposits		Paid-up capital	
	Total (¥ million)	Share of Big 5 (%)	Total (¥ million)	Share of Big 5 (%)	Total (¥ million)	Share of Big 5 (%)
1901	635	12.0	450	20.7	252	5.6
1902	698	13.0	538	20.3	258	5.4
1903	725	13.7	566	20.7	253	5.5
1904	733	15.4	605	23.1	249	5.6
1905	796	15.7	693	21.9	253	5.9
1906	1,112	16.1	1,034	19.6	257	6.2
1907	1,113	17.0	944	21.3	286	5.9
1908	1,098	16.8	938	22.4	296	7.4
1909	1,123	17.9	1,054	22.6	311	11.9
1910	1,250	17.2	1,180	21.5	315	11.7
1911	1,393	16.8	1,256	20.3	327	11.3
1912	1,523	17.5	1,357	20.6	369	13.6
1913	1,671	17.9	1,444	20.6	392	13.5
1914	1,727	18.3	1,520	22.5	401	13.2
1915	1,729	20.5	1,700	23.9	358	14.8
1916	2,233	22.6	2,257	25.9	374	16.3
1917	2,979	23.7	3,234	26.6	437	15.6
1918	4,147	24.8	4,639	27.0	513	16.2
1919	5,660	27.4	5,744	25.7	717	21.9
1920	5,703	20.9	5,827	26.9	964	18.5
1921	6,242	20.4	6,445	24.5	1,045	18.6
1922	7,848	15.5	7,801	19.4	1,450	13.9
1923	8,059	20.1	7,805	25.4	1,491	18.5
1924	8,289	18.9	8,093	24.8	1,508	18.8
1925	8,843	18.4	8,727	24.1	1,501	18.9
1926	8,635	20.7	9,179	24.3	1,497	19.1
1927	7,974	24.3	2,028	31.2	1,481	19.6
1928	7,545	25.6	9,331	33.5	1,379	21.1
1929	7,246	27.8	9,292	34.5	1,381	23.4
1930	6,815	29.5	8,737	36.5	1,297	24.9
1931	6,815	30.3	8,268	38.3	1,249	25.9
1932	6,591	31.4	8,318	41.2	1,218	26.5
1933	6,280	33.0	8,815	42.0	1,186	27.2
1934	6,084	34.3	9,438	42.4	1,162	27.8
1935	5,933	38.7	9,950	42.5	1,134	28.5
1936	6,192	44.1	11,007	41.7	1,099	29.4
1937	6,763	50.0	12,433	42.1	1,047	30.9
1938	7,792	50.1	15,190	42.6	1,019	31.7
1939	8,847	57.7	17,965	63.5	1,000	32.3
1940	11,349	57.1	24,670	41.8	980	33.0

Source: Gotō [29], pp. 90–92, 108, and calculation by author.

chase of the Anamizu family's stock in Fuji Paper so that Oji could take over management of Fuji.

Zaibatsu banks also helped underwrite the debentures of Tōhō Power, Tokyo Power and Light, and Osaka municipal bonds. The Mitsui Bank was particularly generous in such flotations, floating record amounts of such securities, with aid from Mitsui Trust. In addition to profits from premiums and fees, the flotations meant transformation of the bank's frozen loans into bond form, which eased the liquidity position of the bank. This is why Mitsui made such an all-out effort to take advantage of its own reputation to float the foreign bonds of Tokyo Power and Light. The Mitsubishi and Yasuda banks also carried on similar business, though not to the same extent as the Mitsui Bank.

A second effect of bank concentration was to allow idle funds of large firms to be used for extension of zaibatsu power. If control by financial power is the tentacle for extending concentration, expansion of certain firms based on the internal accumulations of other, large firms, which were mostly tied to zaibatsu, was the basis of horizontal and vertical integration. After the war the Mitsui, Mitsubishi, and somewhat smaller Sumitomo zaibatsu all expanded into directly related firms. These expansions were sudden; in the case of Mitsubishi the mining, coal, and banking divisions were set up as operations independent of the parent company in 1917. Between 1917 and 1921, nine related firms were formed: Mitsubishi Shipbuilding (¥50 million in capital), Mitsubishi Steel (¥30 million), Mitsubishi Warehouse (¥10 million), Mitsubishi Trading (¥150 million), Mitsubishi Mining (¥50 million), Mitsubishi Fire and Marine Insurance (¥5 million), Mitsubishi Bank, (¥50 million), Mitsubishi Internal Combustion Engine (later Mitsubishi Aircraft, ¥5 million), and Mitsubishi Electric Machinery (¥150 million). Even more firms were added later, e.g., Mitsubishi Trust (¥30 million, 1927), Mitsubishi Petroleum (¥5 million, 1931), and Mitsubishi Synthetics (¥5 million, 1934). Added to the long-standing affiliated firms Tokio Marine and Fire, Meiji Life Insurance, and Asahi Glass, these firms only heightened the prestige of the group. The Mitsui group founded Mitsui Trust, Mitsui Life Insurance, Tōyō Rayon, Tōyō Kōatsu Chemicals, and, as a subsidiary to Mitsui Trading, Tōyō Cotton. The importance of these zaibatsu-related firms became very great. According to Kamekichi Takahashi's estimates for 1928, seen in table 7.8, their shares of the nation's total paid-up social capital were as follows: Mitsui 6.5%, Mitsubishi 4.5%, Sumitomo 1.4%, and Yasuda 2.8% for an aggregate share for the four of 15.2%. Comparing these figures with comparable ones from other years suggests 1928 to have been the peak. There are of course problems of defining which firms were actually members of a group. Firms directly under control of the main company through stock ownership or execu-

Table 7.8. Capital Controlled by the Big Four Zaibatsu

		Mitsui	Mitsubishi	Sumitomo	Yasuda	Total
Direct control	Number of firms (A)	6	10	13	12	41
	Paid-up capital (B [¥ million])	242	225	132	159	758
Related firms	A	11	11	5	18	45
	B	204	181	47	67	499
Subsidiaries of directly controlled firms	A	34	14	6	12	66
	B	179	84	8	18	289
Subsidiaries of related firms	A	24	12	0	3	39
	B	170	41	0	4	215
Subtotal	A	75	47	24	45	191
	B	795	531	187	248	1,761
Quasi-controlled firms	A	21	13	3	—	—
	B	54	57	1	113	225
Total	A	96	60	27	—	—
	B	849	588	188	361	1,936

Source: Tabulated from Takahashi [145].

tive placement obviously belonged to a particular group. But there were also subsidiary firms (e.g., for Mitsui, the Kanebō and Mitsukoshi Department Store) with no clear lines of control from the head company. While there is doubt as to whether the subsidiaries of subsidiaries should also be included in a zaibatsu group, there were other firms under close financial control (e.g., for Mitsui, Tokyo Power and Light) that were not included in Takahashi's count. Still, Takahashi's data do give a rough measure of the weight of zaibatsu in the economy. But it is noteworthy that directly held companies, with the exception of Mitsubishi's heavy industrial firms, were mostly in finance and distribution, with relatively few engaged in direct production. This tertiary orientation was a special quality of Japanese zaibatsu.

Third, bank concentration had implications for control extended over firms through the distribution system. Zaibatsu-related firms had powers of control that exceeded their share of financial capital. Despite the fact that real assets and sales of zaibatsu firms greatly surpassed those of regular companies, not all zaibatsu firms could boast of high earning power. Looking at the structure of dividends received from stock by head firms (*honsha*) of zaibatsu we see for example the case of Mitsui, where Mitsui Trading, Mitsui Mining, and the Mitsui Bank contributed over 85%, far more than all the rest. In the Mitsubishi group Mitsubishi Mining, the Mitsubishi Bank, and Mitsubishi Heavy Industries contributed 66% (see *Mochikabu Gaisha Seiri Iinkai* [68]). That the source of profits was skewed to particular firms in the case of Mitsui, i.e., to those in commerce, mining, and finance but not to those in direct manufacturing, is a most telling characteristic of the Mitsui group. Even for Mitsubishi, if we exclude Mitsubishi Heavy Industries (shipbuilding and aircraft), nonmanufacturing provided the larger share of profits.

It is of course jumping to conclusions to say that zaibatsu viewed manufacturing lightly. Indeed, Mitsui Trading and Mitsui Mining themselves created small concerns and pulled under their own influence others such as for Mitsui Trading, Tōyō Cotton, Tōyō Rayon, Japan Flour, and Sanki Industries. Of course, both Mitsui Trading and Mitsui Mining as well as others such as Mitsubishi Trading formed exclusive buying and selling agreements with firms in their own groups and sometimes even with firms in other groups or with cartels to which the latter belonged. Zaibatsu structure indeed meant that the groups had a hand in the profits of manufacturing firms (see table 7.9). But the main emphasis of zaibatsu management was on mining, commerce, and financial sectors, all of which had relatively high profit rates and all of which were stable. These sectors were the origins of high zaibatsu profits and were the base from which they could exercise their tremendous power over the economy. But tertiary concentration was also the reason that zaibatsu

Table 7.9. Dividends Received by Mitsui and Mitsubishi Holding Companies, 1932–36 Total

	Mitsui			Mitsubishi	
	¥ 1,000	Composition (%)		¥ 1,000	Composition (%)
Mitsui and Company (Bussan)	49,667	43.5	Mitsubishi Mining	17,024	28.7
Mitsui Mining	33,789	29.6	Mitsubishi Bank	13,048	22.0
Mitsui Bank	13,313	11.7	Mitsubishi Heavy Industries	9,128	15.4
Oji Paper	4,198	3.7	Tokio and Marine Fire	5,544	9.4
Denki Kagaku Kōgyō			Mitsubishi Corporation (trading)	4,431	7.5
(electrochemical)	2,680	2.3	Mitsubishi Electric	3,812	6.4
Hokkaidō Colliery and	2,588	2.3	Mitsubishi Paper	3,640	6.1
Steamship			Mitsubishi Trust	1,980	3.3
Kanebō (spinning)	2,301	2.0	Mitsubishi Warehouse	239	0.4
Shibaura Engineering	2,141	1.9	Nippon Yūsen (shipping)	230	0.4
Dai Nippon Celluloid	1,101	1.0	Meiji Life	144	0.2
Mitsui Trust	998	0.9			
Japan Steel Works	566	0.5			
Onoda Cement	371	0.3			
Mitsui Life	268	0.2			
Tropical Industries	161	0.1			
Total	114,148	100.00	Total	59,220	100.0

Source: Mochikabu Gaisha Seiri Iinkai [68], pp. 42, 45.

power weakened with the advance of heavy and chemical industry. It was in this way that Japanese zaibatsu differed from the classic industrial groups of Germany.

Thus, monopolization did proceed after World War I. But the degree of industrial concentration did not rise and there was a limit to the control to be had through cartelization. Thus competition actually stiffened. What did restrict competition was the power of large aggregates of capital, beginning with zaibatsu, that participated in management through stock acquisition, financial pressure, and monopolization of distribution channels. As seen previously, conditions after the war made such a form of control most advantageous, and the second-class zaibatsu who tried to oppose the giants during the depression lost power or were destroyed. This is how zaibatsu power got as far as it did. It was the most advantageous—low risk, high profit—formula and was better than direct control of production. But, as we shall see later, this method of control was not able to continue in the changed environment of the next era. Prewar monopoly control based on zaibatsu power achieved its peak in the 1920s and early 1930s but declined thereafter.

Eight □ Formation of the Dual Structure

THE AGRICULTURAL CRISIS

Japanese agriculture entered a severe recession after World War I, with agricultural production, gross value added, and productivity all becoming increasingly stagnant. Prices continued to fall from the peak level of the war years until the late 1920s, with a total decline of one-third from the peak. After the Rice Riots of 1918 the home islands were not self-sufficient in rice, and a policy of increasing production and importing colonial rice was adopted. The riots were the immediate cause of a shift in basic government policy away from favoring protection of farmers and the military as the foundation of political power. Instead, emphasis shifted to letting only the Ministry of Agriculture protect farmers; then more policy emphasis was placed on aiding urban working classes to prevent organized labor and socialism from emerging. Moreover, the development of agricultural technology slowed in the 1920s and productivity growth slackened, as seen in table 8.1. These conditions combined to create a chronic farm crisis. Japanese agriculture, which had been developing so steadily since the early Meiji years, now faced an era of hardship due to internal difficulties of domestic agriculture, shifting agricultural policy, and worldwide agricultural depression.

Domestic agriculture was transformed during these years. Until the 1920s production of cultivated crops such as rice, barley, vegetables, potatoes, and beans grew along with that of new crops such as fruits, silkworms, and livestock. But after the war, production of staple crops stagnated and only cocoon, fruit, and livestock production rose. This structural shift in output was greatly abetted by the aforementioned policy shift.

But policy changes were not the only reason. Consumption patterns also shifted in these years due to effects of urbanization, and Western-style eating habits spread gradually while growth of demand for traditional products was slow. Moreover, prices of cocoons, fruit, and livestock fell relatively less than those of other crops, so the former crops

213

Table 8.1. Agricultural Indicators

	Absolute levels				Average annual rates of growth (%)		
	1907	1917	1927	1937	1917–1907	1927–1917	1937–1927
A. Amount produced	2,304	2,880	3,090	3,360	2.2	0.7	0.8
B. Gross value added	1,953	2,411	2,498	2,646	2.1	0.4	0.6
C. Agricultural productivity	81.66	97.24	101.52	104.46	1.7	0.4	0.3

Source: Umemura [165], pp. 164, 226, 227.

Notes: Absolute levels are 7-year moving averages. A and B (¥ million) at 1934–36 prices, C as index with 1934–36 = 100.

were still more or less profitable. Thus, agriculture was eventually forced to change in ways that were not immediately obvious.

The stagnation of farm income after World War I takes on a special meaning when compared to the trends of income in other industries (see tables 8.2 and 8.3). Indexes of farm income rose temporarily in the mid-1920s but by 1931 fell one-third from this peak level, a reflection of the world agricultural depression. The drop in agricultural income had started in 1927–28, several years before the world depression, but thereafter the decline was much more rapid than that of industrial wages, particularly for male wages, which until then had followed a pattern similar to that of agricultural wages. Farm wages, both male and female, fell together with farm income, but not so rapidly.

But most interesting is that female industrial wages fell from the time of the world depression and recovered only very slowly thereafter. The reasons were that turnover among female laborers in industry was very high and that most such female labor came from farms. Thus, their industrial wages reflected closely the changes in farm income and farm wage levels. Male industrial wage movements departed from farm income because, as will be seen later, male labor's rates of stability and length of employment were rising and because the number of new entrants was declining. Thus, the male labor market was breaking its ties with farming, or at least loosening them, quite contrary to the female labor market. This, then, was how the relative decline of farm income affected the labor market.

As agricultural stagnation proceeded, its effects were not only dramatic ones such as increasing tenancy disputes, tragedies of starving children, and the selling of daughters. A more widespread effect was expansion of small and traditional industries in cities to sop up excess farm

Table 8.2. Farm Prices

	All farm goods	All but livestock, poultry, and cocoons	Livestock and poultry	Cocoons
1907	63.8	57.4	101.6	129.6
1908	60.9	56.4	101.9	93.2
1909	54.3	49.9	83.2	93.2
1910	55.3	51.2	80.4	88.7
1911	68.0	64.3	80.1	93.2
1912	79.3	76.2	82.0	93.2
1913	78.8	74.9	84.8	104.6
1914	56.5	51.7	83.7	102.3
1915	53.3	49.3	82.2	84.1
1916	60.5	54.8	86.1	122.8
1917	85.5	77.7	96.5	178.4
1918	132.7	124.7	129.6	205.5
1919	182.0	170.9	170.6	284.1
1920	145.6	140.5	201.3	153.5
1921	143.3	136.3	191.4	171.9
1922	127.8	109.2	183.5	251.6
1923	138.5	122.4	176.6	252.6
1924	148.5	140.8	173.5	198.8
1925	148.8	134.3	170.2	258.5
1926	134.1	123.3	171.9	202.9
1927	117.3	110.4	165.5	145.5
1928	115.6	107.9	156.1	156.3
1929	114.3	105.7	142.2	170.6
1930	75.3	71.8	122.3	76.0
1931	69.3	66.4	98.7	75.5
1932	77.8	76.4	80.5	88.1
1933	85.6	79.8	91.6	131.5
1934	92.2	95.4	95.8	62.2
1935	101.0	97.7	98.8	113.7
1936	106.8	104.9	105.4	124.1
1937	118.0	117.0	114.1	129.8
1938	126.8	126.5	138.4	122.3

Source: Ohkawa et al. [O] tables A50, A52.

labor. Japan was found to face labor problems in these years of re-establishment of the gold standard, of urbanization, and of heavy and chemical industrialization. But the problem of overall excess labor was unavoidably shifted to the rural villages, where it was most strikingly revealed.

Table 8.3. Wages and Agricultural Prices (1934–36 = 100 for cols. 1–5)

	Agricultural prices (1)	Male wages Agric. (2)	Male wages Mfg. (3)	Female wages Agric. (4)	Female wages Mfg. (5)	(2)/(1)	(3)/(1)	(4)/(1)	(5)/(1)
1901	44.8	41.6	18.7	43.2	27.4	.93	.42	.96	.61
1902	48.8	46.1	18.2	44.1	27.4	.94	.37	.90	.56
1903	55.4	48.4	18.7	49.4	29.0	.87	.34	.89	.52
1904	53.6	44.0	20.7	46.4	29.0	.82	.39	.87	.54
1905	54.4	44.2	20.7	45.9	29.0	.81	.38	.84	.53
1906	57.7	47.4	20.7	48.4	30.6	.82	.36	.84	.53
1907	63.8	51.1	24.2	54.5	33.9	.80	.38	.85	.53
1908	60.9	51.9	25.2	55.3	37.1	.85	.38	.85	.53
1909	54.3	48.2	24.2	51.9	38.7	.87	.41	.91	.61
1910	55.3	49.0	24.2	52.5	38.7	.89	.45	.96	.71
1911	68.0	58.8	26.2	58.2	38.7	.86	.39	.86	.57
1912	79.3	65.8	27.2	65.2	41.9	.83	.34	.82	.53
1913	78.8	68.8	27.7	70.6	43.5	.87	.35	.90	.55
1914	56.5	59.2	27.2	56.2	43.5	1.05	.48	.99	.77
1915	53.3	56.7	27.7	53.1	41.9	1.06	.52	1.00	.79
1916	60.5	60.9	29.2	60.0	45.2	1.01	.48	.99	.75
1917	85.5	75.4	38.8	77.6	54.8	.88	.45	.91	.64
1918	132.7	117.8	51.4	114.0	79.0	.89	.39	.86	.60
1919	182.0	190.7	87.7	172.7	135.5	1.05	.48	.95	.74
1920	145.6	191.1	91.3	177.4	137.1	1.31	.63	1.22	.94

Year									
1921	143.3	183.3	106.9	179.1	156.5	1.28	.75	1.25	1.09
1922	127.8	176.3	107.4	180.6	150.0	1.38	.84	1.41	1.17
1923	138.5	171.6	103.4	177.6	158.2	1.24	.75	1.28	1.11
1924	148.5	165.8	105.9	173.0	143.5	1.12	.71	1.16	.97
1925	148.8	168.1	104.4	176.0	143.5	1.13	.70	1.18	.96
1926	134.1	158.8	106.9	163.8	146.8	1.18	.80	1.22	1.09
1927	117.3	166.9	108.4	183.7	140.3	1.42	.92	1.57	1.20
1928	115.6	162.3	110.4	163.8	137.1	1.40	.96	1.42	1.19
1929	114.3	152.9	109.9	160.7	132.3	1.34	.96	1.41	1.16
1930	75.3	130.7	103.4	128.6	114.5	1.74	1.37	1.71	1.52
1931	69.3	103.9	96.3	101.0	103.2	1.50	1.39	1.46	1.49
1932	77.8	91.1	97.8	85.7	98.4	1.17	1.26	1.10	1.26
1933	85.6	94.6	100.3	91.8	98.4	1.11	1.17	1.07	1.15
1934	92.2	94.6	101.8	96.4	98.4	1.03	1.10	1.05	1.⁄
1935	101.0	100.4	99.8	99.5	100.0	.99	.99	.99	.99
1936	106.8	105.1	98.3	104.1	101.6	.98	.92	.97	.95
1937	118.0	117.9	102.9	125.5	109.7	1.00	.87	1.06	.93
1938	126.8	141.2	109.4	151.5	114.5	1.11	.86	1.19	.90
1939	171.8	186.8	117.0	197.4	125.8	1.09	.68	1.15	.73
1940	190.2	221.8	n.a.*	231.1	n.a.	1.17	n.a.	1.22	n.a.

Source: Ohkawa et al. [O], tables A50, A52.
*Not available.

EXPLOSIVE GROWTH OF TRADITIONAL INDUSTRY

Let us look a bit more closely at the labor market during these years. As seen in tables 1.9, 1.13, and 1.16, the labor force kept growing after World War I but employment in the modern sector did not. The result was rising employment in the traditional sector. What form, then, did employment take in the traditional sector? Neither farming nor large-scale industry had the ability to absorb labor, owing to relatively lower income on farms and to rationalization and labor saving in large firms to increase productivity. But complete unemployment and idleness were not possible, so labor had no choice but tertiary and traditional industries in the cities.

Tadao Ishizaki's estimates of occupational composition by industry are presented in table 8.4. The occupational structure of the ten years after the war evolved as follows. First, the class of employed persons that expanded most was hired workers; industries with the greatest increases in numbers of employees were wholesale and retail sales, and services. By class of employment within industries the greatest expansion was in wholesale and retail sales, where the numbers of hired workers, individual proprietors, and family employees all increased. In the service industries hired workers increased most, while in construction and manufacturing, the number of proprietors and family employees expanded. In transportation and communications the hired worker category grew most quickly. On the other hand in mining and construction the number of hired workers declined, as did proprietors in finance and insurance and both proprietors and family employees in transportation and communications.

Thus, these years saw rapid expansion of tertiary industry in general but with two internal trends. One was expansion of traditional fields, represented by wholesale, retail, and service sectors. In these fields there was an increase in the number of hired workers, proprietors, and family employees, many of whom had no regular employment. Rather they turned to these industries, despite the low pay, as an alternative to unemployment. The second trend within the tertiary sector was an increase in transport, communications, and public utilities, which reflected the expansion of large firms such as electric power and railroads during this period. This trend was only normal, as changes in postwar industrial structure ran their course through the economy.

In the midst of these two trends there was an increase in the number of hired workers in the commerce and service industries, where on the one hand, hard-pressed labor was seeking work even at low wages while at the same time demand in the commercial and service industries increased. The situation is indicated clearly by the industries that expanded; commodity sales, particularly food and beverages, along with

Table 8.4. Occupational Structure by Industry and by Class of Employment

	1920			1930			10-Year increase or decrease			10-Year change (%)		
	A Hired workers	B Individual proprietors	C Family employees	A Hired workers	B Individual proprietors	C Family employees	A Hired workers	B Individual proprietors	C Family employees	A Hired workers	B Individual proprietors	C Family employees
All industries	7,842	8,855	9,843	9,478	9,578	10,246	1,636	724	403	20.8	8.2	4.1
Agriculture	392	5,011	8,322	437	4,871	8,434	45	−140	112	11.5	−2.2	1.4
Forestry	82	65	41	83	64	39	1	−1	−2	1.2	−1.5	−4.9
All nonagriculture and nonforestry	7,367	3,779	1,479	8,957	4,643	1,774	1,590	864	295	21.6	22.9	19.9
Fisheries	183	200	143	190	229	141	7	29	2	3.8	14.5	−1.4
Mining	405	12	3	301	10	3	−104	−2	0	−25.7	−16.7	0.0
Construction	539	155	23	471	428	65	−68	277	42	−12.6	176.7	182.6
Manufacturing	2,781	1,121	536	2,841	1,218	642	60	97	106	2.2	8.7	19.8
Wholesale and retail	641	1,455	566	1,289	2,100	735	648	645	169	101.1	44.3	29.9
Finance and insurance	99	30	1	164	18	1	65	−12	0	65.7	−40.0	0.0
Transport, Communications, and other public utilities	797	261	75	1,078	167	44	281	−94	−31	35.3	−36.0	−41.3
Services	1,310	492	130	1,855	473	143	545	−19	13	41.6	3.9	10.0
Civil service	544	35	—	733	—	—	189	—	—	34.7	—	—
Other	68	17	—	34	—	—	−34	—	—	−50.0	—	—

Source: Compiled from Ishizaki [44], pp. 690–94.
Note: Totals are not exact due to rounding.

food stalls, itinerant peddling, street vending, barbershops, inns, public baths, laundry and dyeing, household service, education, medicine, and nursing. The modernization of the structure of employment that had been proceeding since the Meiji years thus came to a standstill.

The formation of a dual structure labor market was a natural result. Large wage differentials by scale and industry did not exist during the Meiji years, as is well known (Umemura [164], p. 257). It has been said that such differentials emerged gradually after World War I. Table 8.5 gives data on differentials by industry, along with data on the gap between highest and lowest. The data confirm that differentials widened after 1929 although they are based on establishments of five or more workers. Table 8.6 is more indicative of conditions in smaller scale establishments of traditional industry workers, artisans, day laborers, unskilled workers, and household servants. Wages for relatively highly paid traditional artisans rose after 1914 at about the same tempo as those of manufacturing workers but fell sharply after 1924. But for semiartisans such a foundry workers, male laborers at Japanese-style paper factories, tailors, shoemakers, and tatami makers, wages advanced only a small amount but still dropped after 1924. Day labor wages rose the least but then fell sharply while servants' wages rose steeply but fell just as steeply. Industrial wages kept increasing until 1929 but traditional occupation wages peaked in 1924 and then declined sharply. Thus, wage differentials between modern and traditional industry broadened rapidly after 1924; the supply–demand gap in the labor market was reflected in wage differentials by scale, industry, and occupation.

LABOR POLICY IN LARGE FIRMS

There were three reasons that wages did not fall in factory industries, where the relative importance of heavy and chemical industry was growing and where large firms were dominant. First, large firms were economizing on the use of labor through rationalization policies, hiring slowdowns, and retention of skilled labor. When overall employee levels were cut in business slumps, the first to go were workers with less seniority. Moreover, firms treated senior workers well in order to isolate them from the newly emerging labor movement. Table 8.7 gives examples of male labor force composition by years of experience. (This is not, however, a perfect proxy for seniority as workers could have moved among similar factories.) The first point is that the level of experience was rising, not only in heavy and chemical industry as expected but in all industries even down to spinning and silk reeling. It is especially striking that this happened in such fields as metal refining, Western-style paper making, and cement production. The lifetime employment system long established in shipbuilding and some other industries spread, and the

Table 8.5. Wage Differentials

I. By standard industrial classification (total average: 100)

Rank	1914	1919	1930	Classification no.	
1	199 (37)	154 (37)	226 (37)	20	Food
2	174 (35)	152 (35)	209 (29)	22	Textiles
3	172 (38)	148 (25)	198 (33)	23	Clothing and accessories
4	171 (33)	146 (31)	187 (36)	24	Wood and wood products
5	163 (31)	141 (33)	184 (38)	25	Furniture
6	146 (25)	139 (38)	180 (31)	26	Paper and related products
7	144 (36)	130 (24)	172 (35)	27	Printing and publishing
8	136 (29)	126 (32)	143 (34)	28	Chemicals
9	135 (34)	124 (34)	142 (28)	29	Coal and oil products
10	125 (28)	123 (27)	140 (27)	30	Rubber products
11	124 (32)	116 (29)	136 (25)	31	Leather products
12	124 (24)	115 (20)	130 (26)	32	Glass and ceramic products
13	122 (20)	112 (28)	123 (32)	33	Ferrous and nonferrous metals
14	117 (30)	108 (36)	123 (30)	34	Metal products
15	115 (27)	98 (26)	110 (24)	35	Machinery
16	111 (21)	98 (30)	92 (23)	36	Transportation machinery
17	110 (26)	98 (39)	85 (20)	37	Electric machinery
18	93 (39)	94 (23)	85 (39)	38	Precision instruments
19	79 (22)	79 (22)	69 (22)	39	Miscellaneous

Number in parentheses shows number of firms in industry.

II. Index of differentials

(A: Ratio between Maximum and Minimum Industry, B: Coefficient of Variation %)

	1909	1914	1919	1920	1921	1922	1923	1924	1925	1926	
A	2.21	2.28	1.89	2.06	2.03	2.22	2.25	2.18	2.17	2.25	
B	22.3	22.8	17.5	19.4	20.7	22.4	22.1	21.4	21.4	22.0	

	1927	1928	1929	1930	1931	1932	1933	1934	1935	1936	1937
A	2.23	2.26	2.57	2.86	2.79	3.18	3.24	3.10	2.87	2.81	2.70
B	21.9	22.5	30.4	31.9	32.5	33.8	35.6	33.6	33.6	33.0	31.4

Source: Shōwa Dōjin Kai [138], pp. 460–70.
Note: Original data depend on manufacturing census.

Table 8.6. Wages (Daily) and Wage Indexes by Occupation

	Average for manufacturing	Foundry workers	Male Japanese paper workers	Sake brewers	Soy sauce brewers	Male baking workers	Western clothing tailors	Leather workers	Lumberjacks and sawyers	Cabinetmakers	Tatami makers	Carpenters	Plasterers	Male day laborers	Male servants	Female servants
Amount (sen*)																
1914	47	74	45	69	44	46	84	72	84	80	78	86	89	105	18	12
1919	144	169	106	140	99	97	157	157	190	180	159	184	191	227	39	26
1924	163	221	150	215	170	171	276	244	248	278	259	309	332	216	85	75
1929	176	235	151	193	185	153	244	228	222	232	256	278	307	193	65	49
1934	150	249	148	151	147	146	183	177	155	172	179	192	213	131	49**	39**
Index (1914=100)																
1919	307	229	236	203	225	211	187	218	226	225	204	214	214	216	217	217
1924	354	299	333	297	387	372	328	339	295	347	332	390	373	206	474	626
1929	375	318	336	279	421	333	291	317	264	290	327	321	345	184	361	410
1934	320	337	329	219	335	318	218	246	185	215	224	224	239	125	273**	326**

Source: Rōdō Undō Shiryō Hensan Kai [116], except for all industries average, which is from Tsūshō Sangyō Shō [161].

Note: Average 25-day month for all industries (entire period), and for sake brewing, soy sauce brewing (through 1919), and male and female servants (entire period).

*1 sen = 1/100 yen.

**1933 figures.

Table 8.7. Composition of Males Employed in Manufacturing by Length of Employment (Percent)

	1924				1933			
	Number of workers	Less than 3 years	3 to 10 years	10 years or more	Number of workers	Less than 3 years	3 to 10 years	10 years or more
Shipbuilding	53,044	3.9	46.9	47.9	79,846	20.2	20.2	59.0
Weapons	42,262	14.3	46.0	39.0	16,736	26.7	21.8	48.8
Metal refining	32,981	28.7	43.5	27.2	52,284	24.2	33.2	43.6
Western-style paper	13,212	34.8	39.6	25.0	15,165	18.4	38.0	43.4
Cement	9,216	43.8	32.7	23.1	9,168	15.1	43.1	41.5
Lumber	14,344	39.5	37.7	22.2	14,738	25.2	38.0	36.5
Beer	3,756	47.0	34.0	18.3	2,558	6.1	37.9	56.0
Spinning	59,025	46.5	36.4	15.2	39,466	21.6	45.2	32.2
Silk reeling	22,195	44.4	39.4	16.5	19,582	36.2	37.2	26.2

Source: Naikaku Tōkei Kyoku [73], 1924, 1933.

Note: Except for number of workers, figures represent percentages of actual number of workers.

labor market for workers in large firms could not help but reflect this trend.

Second, differentials by years of experience (seniority) began to appear around this time in heavy industry, as seen in table 8.8. That is, for male workers in heavy industry, wages fell a bit but differentials remained the same. For female textile workers wages declined considerably and differentials increased. One element of this difference is certainly that heavy industry was less tied to trends in the labor market whereas textile industries were very sensitive to them. At the same time there were fundamental reasons for the dissimilarity, i.e., that the big firms in the heavy industries tended to have skilled laborers with many years of experience and seniority who were accordingly highly paid while textile companies and small firms had unskilled workers of short tenure with low pay. Moreover, the wages of unskilled laborers in modern industry and of labor in traditional industry were closely related.

A third reason for the maintenance of high wages for a small core of manufacturing workers was the ready availability of extra workers when they were needed. Large firms' policies of economizing on unskilled labor and retaining skilled labor could work only when labor markets were in surplus so that firms could mobilize extra labor at any time. Thus a class of temporary workers was born. Temporary workers who were "used under contract for relatively short-term employment" to make up for workers who had left their jobs appeared about 1921, and employing them had become general practice "nationwide" by about 1927 (see Sumiya [40], p. 240). Temporary workers became a national issue only in 1933–34, when their numbers were growing rapidly and when poor labor conditions had become a social problem, but in fact a long tradition lay behind the institution of temporary workers.

The spread of subcontracting to small firms at this time also reflected labor conditions. Subcontracting began at the start of the Showa era and spread quickly after 1931. The subcontracting system was universal by 1934, e.g., in the machinery industry 78% of factories with more than 30 operatives ordered final products from outside, accounting for about 12% of total product (see Komiyama [59], pp. 44–45). It is not clear whether subcontracting at this time followed the lines of the financial groups and already extended to the management of everyday affairs, but the reasons big firms could use subcontracting to fill orders were the same reasons that made their labor policies possible.

MONOPOLY AND THE FORMATION OF THE DUAL STRUCTURE

We have looked at dual structure so far in terms of excess supply in the labor market but other reasons can be listed. For example, Miyohei

Table 8.8. Wages in Various Manufacturing Industries by Length of Employment (Sen)

	Less than 1 year	1 to 3 years	3 to 5 years	5 to 10 years	10 to 15 years	15 to 20 years	20 to 25 years	25 to 30 years
All male workers	128	146	188	221	266	286	300	319
	113	124	153	190	240	266	287	303
All female workers	63	83	95	102	105	107	113	107
	45	56	64	72	83	92	97	91
Metal rolling	189	213	226	277	352	392	386	429
(males)	153	195	261	264	302	362	378	367
Shipbuilding	142	139	177	231	265	286	299	322
(males)	161	175	189	220	263	286	299	322
Silk reeling	36	60	73	84	88	88	89	87
(females)	23	38	44	48	48	46	47	45
Cotton spinning	69	93	112	128	139	143	144	146
(females)	42	57	71	80	89	92	94	94

Source: Naikaku Tōkei Kyoku [73], 1927, 1933.
Notes: For each category, first row is for 1927, second for 1933. One sen = 1/100 yen.

Shinohara stresses "capital concentration" [129], while Mitsuharu Itō
stresses "oligopoly power in the commodities market" [45]. The core of
Shinohara's theory is that large firms were able to accumulate capital so
that differentials in capital intensity emerged between themselves and
small firms and thus in the per capita value added and productivity of
labor. Large firms were thus able to pay higher wages (although whether
they did pay more is a separate question). Government policy since the
start of the Meiji era had been both protective and stimulating through
subsidies and financing, and ties of big firms with financial institutions
had been close. Thus, the tendency for capital concentration in large
firms was already strong but it became especially so after World War I.
In addition to labor market conditions stronger ties between big firms
and financial institutions along with the financial advantages big firms
enjoyed caused a widening of the technological gap between large and
small. Thus, the big firms were able to become even more capital intensive while small ones remained labor intensive, and per capita labor
productivity differentials (measured either in goods or in value) only
increased. This then caused the wage differentials to enlarge. This is
Shinohara's theory.

In contrast Itō stresses that a few firms may be able to raise physical
productivity through technological progress, and thus may even gain
excess profits temporarily through a rise in value added per worker, but
under perfect competition new entrants will soon bring profits down to a
normal level. However, if an industry is oligopolistic or cartelized, entry
is difficult and high value added and profits are possible for extended
periods; these excess profits then become a possible source for wage
differentials. However, without excess labor and a fluid labor market,
labor will flow in from low wage sectors to the extent that differentials
exist. In order to maintain production, the industries that lose labor will
become more capital intensive, raising productivity and wages and
thereby shrinking wage differentials. If low-wage industries are cartelized and raise relative prices vis-à-vis high wage sectors, wage differentials will narrow. But in a market with excess labor and no such cartels
in traditional industries, such narrowing will not occur because relative
price changes cannot have an effect on wage differentials. (This combination of circumstances did, however, occur in the high growth period
of the 1960s, as relative prices did shift and wage differentials nar-
rowed.)

Shinohara has responded to this criticism by postulating imperfections
in the labor market that, combined with capital concentration and imperfections in the commodities market, produced wage differentials. "In
fact," he says, "wage differentials expanded after the middle Taisho
years, originating in capital concentration, the seniority wage system,

lifetime employment, relative price maladjustment due to monopolies, exploitation of small firms by the large through subcontracting, etc.; i.e., in all aspects of capital, labor, and commodities markets." Still, Shinohara gives prime importance to the role of capital concentration. (See Shinohara [132], p. 100.)

Further description of the course of debate is not needed here. Instead we shall consider the meaning of the term *dual structure*. The problem of dual structure had its origins, as described in chapter 4, neither in the takeoff of capitalism prior to the integration of the national market, i.e., when large wage and income differentials by industry and region were common, nor in the low wage and income levels of farmers and laborers later on. In the former it is only natural that differentials exist during the integration and formation of a single market in any country. In the latter case it is only natural for farmers and workers to have low wages when the economy as a whole is at a low level of production. Neither of these cases justifies a label of "dual structure."

But in the interwar period the differentials of income by scale and by industry arose and became fixed over a long period of time well after regional barriers were broken, after integration was proceeding, and after a good measure of development had been achieved. With the spread to small enterprises of the subcontracting system, which indirectly took advantage of low paid labor in such firms, the textile industry used subcontracting interchangeably with young, female labor from farm villages and adopted the policy of cutting wages in accordance with the level of agricultural income. Thus the large firms' policies of exploiting such wage differentials became systematized. The basic reason behind formation of the dual structure must be sought in excess supply in the labor market, but it is also important to view the labor market from the perspective of strengthening monopoly.

Thus, let us reexamine the formation of the dual structure from the perspective of the interwar economy as presented in previous chapters. The first point to be made is that there was a contrast between the relatively unfluctuating path of steady growth of the 1890–1910 period and the many booms and busts of the interwar years. The interwar period as a whole was not one of low growth; despite the violent fluctuations an overall growth rate of 4.0% (1915–40) was achieved, as related in chapter 1. But the interwar years also saw formation of the dual structure. If we consider only the 1920s, we see continuing depression, low growth, stagnant agricultural production, tremendous differentials among industries, particularly between secondary industry on one hand and primary and tertiary on the other, and intense agricultural poverty. Small commercial and manufacturing firms grew in number while oligopolies such as in the financial and electric power industries also progressed, as did industrial control by zaibatsu. In commodities markets, even after the weeding out of fly-by-night companies set up during the war, the number of firms remained high and the share of production coming from large firms fell. The competitive environment intensified and cartels flourished.

A second factor in the background of formation of the dual structure is the combination of the progress of urbanization and the labor movement's emergence. Government policies responded to urban labor with some laws for the protection of labor and the safeguarding of their rights and with price decreases for daily necessities, especially rice. A revision of the factory law was drafted for the first time in the twentieth century. Part of the revision went into effect in 1916 and part, prohibition of night labor and mine labor for females and children, in 1929. The Kenseikai party proposed a labor union law and an unemployment insurance law in 1920 and 1922, respectively. An employment agency law was passed in 1921 and a health insurance law in 1926. In 1931 the Home Ministry's labor union bill was tabled only in the Upper House. Along with the general election law of 1925 these laws show that the focus of national policy was gradually moving toward urban labor. Despite the Peace Preservation Law and other movements to suppress the left, the change in emphasis was undeniable. This then was the background against which the dual structure was formed.

But for monopolistic economic behavior to strengthen, several conditions over and above these background factors were indispensable. First was the further development of the electricity, metals, and chemical industries, which had begun during the war and which had been oligopolistic from the start. In these industries investment per unit of output was quite large, so the number of firms was necessarily limited. Moreover, because many firms in the new industries went bankrupt after the war, the tendency to oligopoly in them strengthened. Moreover, firms were pessimistic about the future due to the uneven growth and deflationary trend of the 1920s. In general, firms expecting future growth do not want to place restrictions on themselves through monopolistic organizations such as cartels even when business conditions are poor. To desire such cartelization, and even to agree to merger and interference of financial institutions in management, is behavior seen only when firms completely lose the power to manage. With the coming of the Great Depression, following as it did the brief periods of prosperity and long recessions of the 1920s, cartelization and trust formation proceeded and the control of financial capital was indeed strengthened. This in turn was a factor in the expansion of differentials between large and small firms both in the commodities market and in the capital market. The reasons for the rise of these differentials were also important reasons in the formation of the dual structure.

Unfortunately, measuring the impact of these many factors is far from simple. We can only scratch the surface here but let us quickly look at one or two examples. First is a comparison of cartel prices with noncartel prices. As seen in table 8.9, cartel prices were rather high at the time of the gold standard reversion panic, compared to noncartel prices, but the two had largely equalized by 1934. A second indicator is the financial position of farm villages and small firms. For example, as a result of the bank mergers, "small commercial and industrial firms had always had the financial convenience of relying on small banks in their own areas of activity, but along with the progress of the [bank] merger movement came the rapid destruction of large numbers of these banks. The small banks that survived fell into severe financial difficulties due to withdrawals of deposits. Since the [degree of] participation by the head offices of the large banks in the small-scale finance demanded by these small commercial houses and manufactures had been comparatively insignificant until that time, these businessmen lost their sources of finance [through the small local banks] and experienced extreme hardships in management" (Kinyū Kenkyū Kai [56], p. 670). Concrete examples are given in table 8.10. In the five years between 1928 and 1933 the number of small loans declined sharply as did their weight in the total. In contrast the decline in large loans of ¥ 100,000 or or more was not so steep, and their share of the total by both value and number of cases rose.

Both Shinohara and Itō view the strengthening of monopoly as harmful to farmers and small enterprise and thus say it promoted formation

Table 8.9. Cartel and Noncartel Prices (Jan. 1913 = 100)

		Cartel price index	Noncartel price index
1931	Mar.	146.6	123.5
	Sept.	134.5	115.4
1932	Mar.	145.5	126.5
	Sept.	153.7	141.9
1933	Mar.	173.0	149.2
	Sept.	177.2	160.5
1934	Mar.	168.2	159.3
	Sept.	174.1	174.1

Source: Nihon Ginkō Chōsa Kyoku [84], p. 89.

Table 8.10. Number of Loans Outstanding at Ordinary Banks by Size of Loan

	Less than ¥500	¥500–1,000	¥1,000–5,000	¥5,000–10,000	¥10,000–50,000	¥50,000–100,000	¥100,000 and more	Total
30 June 1928								
Commerce and manufacturing	394,290	197,959	331,280	56,984	49,657	6,864	6,892	1,043,908
Agriculture	442,247	100,785	96,467	9,022	5,621	367	157	654,666
Other	123,323	43,830	75,925	15,845	16,076	2,378	2,264	279,641
Total number	959,860	342,574	503,672	81,851	71,354	9,591	9,313	1,978,215
Percentage of all loans	48.5	17.3	25.5	4.1	3.6	0.5	0.5	100.0
Amount (¥ million)	198.2	235.4	1,053.0	548.1	1,399.8	627.9	3,296.3	7,358.8
Percentage of total amount of all loans	2.7	3.2	14.3	7.4	19.0	8.5	44.9	100.0
30 June 1933								
Commerce	267,439	110,240	169,560	29,579	26,483	3,589	3,698	609,988
Manufacturing	49,862	23,031	39,449	8,392	9,547	1,723	1,939	133,943
Subtotal of 2 above	317,001	133,271	209,009	37,971	35,730	5,312	5,637	743,931
Agriculture	308,246	64,629	57,467	5,215	3,430	250	132	439,069
Other	108,745	35,491	62,786	13,525	14,476	2,479	2,683	239,885
Total number	733,992	233,391	328,962	56,711	53,636	7,741	8,542	1,422,885
Percentage of all loans	51.6	16.4	23.1	4.0	3.8	0.5	0.6	100.0
Amount (¥ million)	146.0	162.0	692.0	382.3	1,054.8	500.5	3,187.8	6,425.3
Percentage of total amount of all loans	2.4	2.6	11.3	6.2	17.2	8.2	52.4	100.0

Sources: Okura Shō, "Zenkoku Futsū Ginkō Sho Kashidashi-kin Shokygyō-betsu narabi Kingaku-betsu Shirabe" (National Survey of Ordinary Bank Loans by Industry and by Amount), quoted in Gotō [29], pp. 136–37, 140–41.

of the dual structure. But in fact the strengthening of monopoly was itself but a result of more basic factors. The more basic reasons for monopoly lie in the wartime boom and the depth of the recessions that followed. Excess labor also was a result both of the boom and of the flow of population into the cities. Population increase in the cities during the 1920s was not so much due to demand for labor; rather, labor was pushed off the farms by income that was low relative to other industries. Both monopoly formation and bank concentration were born of recessions of the 1920s, and it is only natural to see them as causes of the dual structure.

But it was the boom and subsequent recessions that had destroyed the quality of balance that had characterized Japan's previous economic growth. Moreover, the post-World War II reestablishment of the dual structure reflected conditions similar to those of the interwar period. Economic activity declined severely after the war while excess labor surfaced (and on a scale far greater than after World War I). Meanwhile, recovery policy was promoting development of heavy and chemical industries along with electric power. During these years imbalance existed between these favored sectors and all others. In this sense the post-World War II reestablishment of the dual structure can be understood as a recurrence of interwar conditions on a far larger scale.

Nine □ Economic Mechanisms in the Era of Emergency

THE SHIFT TO A CONTROLLED MONETARY SYSTEM

The 1930s were years of political upheaval beginning with the March Incident, an aborted coup plot, of 1931 and the Manchurian Incident of September 1931, in which a skirmish at Mukden was used as a pretext for the Japanese army to occupy southern Manchuria. Terror continued with the October Incident of 1931, an aborted plot to bomb a cabinet meeting, the bloody Ketsumeidan Incidents of early 1932, in which former Finance Minister Junnosuke Inoue and Mitsui's general manager, Takuma Dan, were assassinated, and the May 15 Incident of 1932, in which Prime Minister Tsuyoshi Inukai was assassinated. After Inukai's death, political parties no longer formed cabinets, and the military's role in politics grew. The army assumed political hegemony after the February 26 Incident of 1936, a full-scale revolt by elements within the army in which Finance Minister Korekiyo Takahashi was murdered and from which Prime Minister Okada barely escaped. Finally came war in China in July 1937 and the Pacific War in December 1941. Army propaganda pamphlets of the time spoke constantly of an "era of emergency" of crises in Manchuria and Mongolia, and of the crisis of 1935–36.

The economy of this era of emergency has been perceived in two ways, either as an era of economic militarization with social dumping and inflation or as one of success in the Keynesian experiment of Finance Minister Takahashi. Each of these views portrays one aspect of the era, and both aspects are presented here in an integrated way. Another major point discussed here is how the economic system established during the early 1930s prepared for the postwar economic growth mechanism.

The decisive element in this period's economics was the abandonment of the gold standard and adoption of a control-based monetary system, including exchange controls. The latter allowed fiscal expansion at home through easy money, isolated the domestic economy from the international in certain respects, protected the nation from the world depression, allowed domestic fiscal expenditure without fear of excess imports, and promoted exports through depreciation of the yen. This system of foreign exchange controls was not limited to Japan but was also adopted, albeit later, in the United States, England, and Germany. In this sense Takahashi was a pioneer in international economic policy.

As seen in chapter 5, this type of monetary system rose from the ashes of the gold standard, which had been sustained for about a hundred years by England. This new system did not revive the integrated functioning of the international economy until the establishment of the Bretton Woods system and the International Monetary Fund after World War II. Conditions for this were not yet ripe in the 1930s. But looking back from today, we must view Takahashi's policies as the starting point of the postwar economic system under fixed exchange rates. However, political leadership during this period gradually shifted into the hands of the army, making control of the "controlled monetary system" impossible. Therein lay the turning point toward the wartime economic controls.

The chief policy objective during the tenure of Takahashi's predecessor as finance minister, Junnosuke Inoue (1929–31), had been to return to the gold standard at the pre-World War I parity. But first prices had to fall, and to accomplish this deflation, Inoue used tight money and low demand. We have already seen how the years of Inoue's tenure were depressed to start with. The third part of Inoue's plan was to "clean up the business world" by integrating and rationalizing. Moreover, we might say his most serious mistake was miscalculation of the depth and scale of the world depression that had broken out in 1929. This does not mean that Inoue's policy direction was right or that he failed only due to unforeseen events along the way. There is still much discussion of his basic theories and even now opinion is divided (see Ōuchi [114], pp. 113–28; Suzuki [141], pp. 202–03; Chō [17], pp. 163–68; Emi [21], pp. 199–201; and Nakamura [74], pp. 198–204).

TAKAHASHI'S EXPERIMENT

With the fall of the second Wakatsuki cabinet in December 1931 and Inoue's consequent retirement, Takahashi shifted policy 180 degrees. In addition to abandoning the gold standard and devaluing the yen, he lowered domestic interest rates and stimulated the economy through deficit financing of bonds underwritten by the Bank of Japan. Evaluations of Takahashi's policies, just as of Inoue's, still differ. Thus, we shall now look at the roles played by these two contrasting policies and their various effects.

Table 9.1. Changes in Aggregate Demand (¥ million)

	Personal consumption	Private fixed capital formation	Government fixed capital formation	Military investment	Government consumption	Exports	Imports	Total demand	Gross national product
1929	11,782	1,605	1,210	(187)	1,612	3,300	3,223	19,509	16,286
1930	10,850	1,312	1,010	(173)	1,452	2,486	2,439	17,110	14,671
1931	9,754	1,043	902	(176)	1,685	2,029	2,105	15,414	13,309
1932	9,804	937	1,093	(260)	1,839	2,466	2,479	16,139	13,660
1933	10,850	1,270	1,194	(356)	2,046	3,092	3,107	18,454	15,347
1934	12,097	1,686	1,237	(427)	2,005	3,580	3,639	20,605	16,966
1935	12,668	1,992	1,354	(466)	2,117	4,158	3,991	22,289	18,298
1936	13,328	2,195	1,427	(518)	2,183	4,580	4,389	23,713	19,324

Amount of change

1929–30	−932	−293	−200	(−14)	−160	−814	−784	−2,399	−1,615
1930–31	−1,096	−269	−108	(3)	233	−457	−334	−1,696	−1,362
1931–32	50	−106	191	(84)	154	437	374	725	351
1932–33	1,046	333	101	(96)	207	626	628	2,315	1,687
1933–34	1,247	416	43	(71)	−41	488	532	2,151	1,619
1934–35	571	306	117	(39)	112	578	352	1,684	1,332
1935–36	660	203	73	(52)	66	422	398	1,424	1,026

Contribution to rise or fall in total demand (%)

1929–30	−57.7	−18.1	−12.4	(−0.9)	−9.9	−50.4	48.5	−100	
1930–31	−80.5	−19.8	7.9	(0.2)	17.1	−33.6	24.5	−100	
1931–32	14.3	−30.2	54.4	(23.9)	43.9	124.5	−106.6	100	
1932–33	62.0	19.8	6.0	(5.7)	12.3	37.1	−37.2	100	
1933–34	77.0	25.7	2.7	(4.4)	−2.5	30.1	−32.9	100	
1934–35	42.9	23.0	8.8	(2.9)	8.4	44.0	−26.4	100	
1935–36	64.3	19.8	7.1	(5.1)	6.4	41.1	−38.8	100	

Source: Ohkawa et al. [O], tables A1, A38.

Notes: Military investment is a component of government fixed capital formation and hence is listed in parentheses. Total demand is GNP plus imports.

First, let us look at real economic conditions, beginning with demand. As seen in table 9.1, the basic sources of deflation of aggregate demand in 1930 were declines in fiscal expenditure and exports. By 1931 the drop in consumption played a larger role, and the reduction of private investment was also large, reflecting the effects of the depression. Aggregate demand fell about ¥3.00 billion (18%) between 1929 and 1931. Leaving aside private consumption and private investment for the moment, we see that the largest decline in value was that of exports, the effects of which only added to those of fiscal restraint. Export volume fell only a few percent between 1929 and 1931, so the decline in export value was due mostly to the 40% fall in export prices. Thus, Japan's depression was not solely domestically induced by the return to the gold standard but also had part of its origin in the world depression.

If both fiscal restraint and export stagnation had negative multiplier effects during Inoue's tenure, the reversal of policy and export recovery under Takahashi brought positive multiplier effects. In 1932 the sum of government purchases and investment rose about ¥600 million, so the rise of ¥400 million in exports brought a total increase in effective demand from these sources to about ¥1.0 billion. The effects of this were not immediately felt elsewhere, because private consumption and investment remained extremely weak in 1932. But in 1933 and after, both consumption and investment rose substantially. GNP climbed about ¥1.7 billion per year between 1932 and 1935, the nominal growth rate being 10.3%. This expansion was supported by high fiscal expenditure, at home under Takahashi's policies and abroad by higher exports. Looking first at the domestic sector, we see a textbook case of demand expansion. After the large-scale increase in government investment and purchases in 1931–32, government investment ceased rising, purchasing stagnated, and government spending in general was gradually restrained. But then private investment suddenly stepped up, and multiplier effects from this temporarily increased national income. However, subsequent investments of the same magnitude would have had progressively weaker effects, and national income would have approached a new equilibrium level—just as described in textbooks on national income determination. Takahashi's policies involved such one shot impact effects.

The main expenditure increases in Takahashi's budgets were for the military and for farm village relief. Comparing, as does table 9.2, the expenditures in the general account of the budget from 1929 to 1937, we see that after Takahashi took office the amounts for categories other than military, farm relief, and bond costs remained stable, or even declined, despite the yearly expansions of the budget. The relief expenditures as far as the central government was concerned were not so large,

Table 9.2. Composition of General Account Expenditures

	General account expenditure	Military spending	Emergency relief expenditures	National bond costs	Other
1929	1,736	495	—	280	961
1930	1,588	443	—	273	872
1931	1,477	455	—	214	808
1932	1,950	686	181	241	842
1933	2,255	873	206	335	841
1934	2,163	942	157	361	703
1935	2,206	1,003	—	372	801
1936	2,287	1,078	—	363	846
1937	2,709	2,237	—	400	1,072
1929–31 average	1,590	459	(51)	256	824
1932–34 average	2,123	834	181	312	796
1935–37 average	2,399	1,116	(72)	378	833

Sources: Emergency relief expenditures from Emi [21], p. 203, and all others calculated from Okura Shō [106], p. 137.

but they were of great importance since they meant a temporary shift from the 1920s policy of focusing on cities to focusing on rural areas. But relief expenditures were not exclusive to the central government; local governments also engaged in large-scale spending for relief. Table 9.3 shows relief-related expenditures of prefectures and municipalities for the same period covered above. Between 1931 and 1932, public works, industrial promotion, and social expenditures rose almost ¥200 million in one stroke. Combined with central government expenditures, these funds played a vital role. In very gross terms the three years 1932–34 saw yearly expenditure increases of ¥130 million for the central government and ¥200 million for local governments, for a total of ¥330 million, much of which went to farm villages. Even if the multiplier were a moderate three, this spending would have created about ¥1.0 billion per year in increased income. The effects of fiscal expenditure were not minor.

Let us add a word on the revenues that supported all this. Takahashi's policies cannot be understood by looking at expenditure alone, and we must take an overall view of both central and local government revenues. Table 9.4 gives provisional estimates of net revenues of both. According to these numbers, total revenue rose from more than ¥3.36 billion in 1931 to ¥5.02 billion in 1933, a jump of ¥1.66 billion. Of this,

Table 9.3. Local Spending on Emergency Relief

	Prefectures			Villages			Total		
	A	B	C(%)	A	B	C	A	B	C(%)
1929	489	182	37.2	530	62	11.7	1,019	242	23.7
1930	478	182	37.9	498	62	12.5	976	242	24.8
1931	503	201	39.9	489	63	12.9	992	264	26.6
1932	625	315	50.5	544	134	24.7	1,169	264	38.4
1933	717	330	46.1	547	141	25.8	1,264	471	37.2
1934	659	302	45.9	540	119	22.0	1,199	421	35.1
1935	857	331	38.8	560	117	20.9	1,412	448	31.7
1936	1,013	333	32.9	571	101	17.7	1,584	434	27.4
1937	828	340	41.2	567	96	16.9	1,395	436	31.3
1929–31 average	490	188	38.4	506	62	12.3	996	249	25.0
1932–34 average	667	316	47.5	544	131	24.4	1,244	447	37.0
1935–37 average	899	335	37.3	566	105	18.6	1,464	439	30.0

Source: Okura Shō and Nihon Ginkō [109], pp. 241, 249.

Notes: A: Total spending; B: Public works, industrial promotion, and public welfare projects; C: = B/A.

¥ 1.46 billion was revenue from bond flotations. The large scale of these increases is attributable to the needs of relief projects.

But the problem was that Takahashi's fiscal policies came when the military was strengthening its political role. Takahashi at first acceded to demands of the armed services for higher military expenditures but later tried to restrain them. Yet in spite of his opposition they continued their rapid rise. Average military expenditures between 1929 and 1931 were ¥460 million but grew to ¥830 million between 1932 and 1934, a jump of ¥370 million. Military expenditures were far greater than relief expenditures for the central government, but if we add local government expenditures for relief into the total, relief exceeds military spending. Military expenditure began its largest increases only in 1937 under Finance Minister Baba.

Table 9.2 shows clearly how much pressure these expenditures put on fiscal policy. A substantial amount of the expenditures were indeed directed toward armaments. This gave a shot in the arm to the stagnating heavy and chemical industries, as is well known. But it would be a mistake to think that only military demand was behind the development of

Table 9.4. Composition of Central and Local Government General Account
Revenues (¥ million)

	Tax revenue (A)	Bond and loan revenue (B)	Other income (C)	Net total revenue (D)	National and local grants (not included) (E)	Ratio (A/D)	(B/D)	(C/D)
1928	1,584.5	610.4	1,761.5	3,956.4	241.8	40.0	15.4	44.5
1929	1,570.6	404.9	1,634.2	3,609.7	200.5	43.5	11.2	45.3
1930	1,447.0	516.5	1,459.6	3,423.1	193.4	42.3	15.1	42.6
1931	1,265.8	566.5	1,527.8	3,360.1	179.1	37.7	16.9	45.5
1932	1,217.5	1,220.8	1,547.2	3,985.5	346.4	30.5	30.6	38.8
1933	1,306.9	2,027.0	1,681.6	5,015.5	379.9	26.5	40.4	33.5
1934	1,439.2	1,590.0	1,634.8	4,664.0	346.4	30.9	34.1	35.1
1935	1,560.5	1,414.2	1,731.0	4,705.7	302.5	33.2	30.1	36.8
1936	1,723.8	1,847.2	1,915.7	5,485.7	279.4	31.4	33.7	34.9
1937	2,000.5	1,096.7	2,192.2	5,379.4	317.1	38.9	20.4	40.8
1938	2,687.8	1,085.8	2,406.4	6,180.0	366.7	43.5	17.6	38.9

Sources: Estimated from Okura Shō [106] and appendix table in Fujita [25].
Note: D is estimated as $A + B + C - E$.

heavy and chemical industries. As will be seen later, the expansion of
plant and equipment investment and the development of electrochemical industries were also important sources of demand for them.

But the early 1930s also saw significant financial problems. During the
years 1932–35 an extremely unusual monetary situation prevailed, almost unique in Japan's financial history. Because of the highly liquid
financial market the public bonds mentioned above were easily absorbed
(see table 9.5). Particularly from late 1931 to 1934 we see banks' total
deposits rising steadily while loans fell. But securities holdings rose
about the same amount as deposits. Nonbank financial institutions displayed the same trends but to a greater degree. Trust and insurance
companies' deposits grew faster than those of banks, and deposits in
financial institutions serving the general public—the Central Cooperative Bank for Agriculture and Forestry (Norin Chūō Kinko), industrial
co-ops, credit unions, mutual aid credit societies (*mujin-gyō*), and postal
savings and insurance—grew faster than bank deposits. In addition to
the implications of this trend for financial markets, there were implications for income distribution, which are discussed later.

Table 9.5. Financial Institutions: Principal Sources and Uses of Funds (¥ million)

	1930	1931	1932	1933	1934	1935	1936	1931–34 Net increase	1934–36 Net increase
Total for major financial institutions									
Deposits	17,763	17,996	18,574	20,059	21,542	23,251	25,437	3,546	3,895
Loans	13,178	13,262	12,928	12,324	12,090	12,587	13,402	−1,172	1,312
Securities	8,512	8,868	9,578	11,172	12,620	13,811	15,045	3,752	2,425
All banks									
Deposits	11,332	10,843	11,089	11,651	12,335	13,120	14,093	1,492	1,758
Loans	10,030	9,888	9,578	9,438	8,830	9,011	9,509	−1,058	679
Securities	4,591	4,496	4,759	5,341	5,946	6,598	7,038	1,450	1,092

Trust banks, life and casualty insurance

Deposits	3,437	3,322	3,487	3,886	4,297	4,738	5,189	975	892
Loans	1,353	1,430	1,504	1,518	1,470	1,615	1,672	40	202
Securities	1,409	1,495	1,563	1,855	2,308	2,622	3,123	813	815

Central Cooperative Bank for Agriculture and Forestry; industrial and credit co-ops; mutual aid finance societies; and postal savings, annuities, and life insurance

Deposits	4,568	4,996	5,462	6,047	6,453	6,870	7,398	1,457	945
Loans	2,464	2,321	2,277	2,125	2,146	2,314	2,639	−175	493
Securities	2,512	2,877	3,256	3,976	4,366	4,591	4,883	1,489	517

Sources: Aggregated from Chō [17], p. 234.

Note: Central Cooperative Bank for Agriculture and Forestry is the Nōrin Chūō Kinkō. Overlapping accounts mean that the appropriate figures in the last three categories do not necessarily equal the corresponding figure in the total category. Differences are as follows.

	1930	1931	1932	1933	1934	1935	1936
Deposits	1,574	1,165	1,464	1,525	1,543	1,477	1,243
Loans	669	377	431	757	356	353	418
Securities	0	0	0	0	0	0	1

Interest rates showed a strong downtrend in these years (see table 9.6). At the time of strong anti-yen speculation in 1931 Finance Minister Inoue had raised the discount rate, but between the spring and summer of 1932 the discount rate was lowered repeatedly, heralding an age of "unprecedented low interest rates." The low interest policy was taken not only to stimulate plant and equipment investment but to lower the burden to the government of bond flotation. In 1933, the year that local and national bond flotation hit its peak with a combined total of ¥2 billion, interest rates were lowered drastically.

But how are these events to be interpreted? Borrowing Yoshio Suzuki's model [142], let us analyze the financial mechanism of fiscal expenditure. Suzuki poses the problem as follows. From a macro viewpoint, any independent rise in effective demand should, ceteris paribus, produce an expansion of income with the same multiplier, but on the financial side differences will arise based on whether the new effective demand originates as corporate investment or as fiscal expenditure.

Table 9.6. Interest Rates

	Bank of Japan Year-end discount rate on commercial bills (%/year)	National bond yield*	Time deposit (aver. for Dec.)	Unconditional call money (Tokyo)	
				High	Low
1929	5.5	5.0	5.3	5.8	1.8
1930	5.1	5.0	5.3	5.8	1.8
1931	6.6	5.0	5.2	9.1	1.5
1932	4.4	5.0	5.0	8.0	2.0
1933	3.7	4.9	4.5	3.7	2.4
1934	3.7	4.8	4.2	4.0	2.5
1935	3.3	4.7	4.1	4.4	2.5
1936	3.3	n.a.†	3.6	4.4	2.5
1937	3.3	n.a.	3.6	3.3	2.5
1938	3.3	4.0	3.5	2.9	2.3

Source: Okura Shō Rizai Kyoku, Kinyū Jikō Sankōshō, various years.

*Equals interest payments by government divided by current value of bonds outstanding.

†Not applicable.

Omitting formal presentation of the model, we can summarize the assumptions and conclusions as follows.

1. A given amount of increase in effective demand will produce a given increase of total income regardless of whether the demand originates in fiscal expenditure (case A) or in corporate investment (case B).
2. With household marginal propensity to save, marginal tax rates, marginal liquidity preference, and marginal rates of income distribution to households out of national income all fixed, cases A and B will cause identical increases in household savings, cash balances, and savings deposits.
3. Let us assume that the marginal tax rate on firms is fixed. In case A an original increase of corporate cash deposits coming with a rise in national income will yield, in the end, a total rise in corporate deposits of

$$dY \, (1 - MDH) \, (1 - MTF),$$

   where dY is the increase in income, MDH the marginal rate of income distribution to households, and MTF the marginal tax rate on firms.
4. In case B the amount of investment is first financed by decreases in firms' cash deposits, and even as national income rises and firms' deposits increase, firms' net cash deposits fall on balance.
5. For fiscal policy, case A results in government deficit and case B in government surplus. (For details of the model, see Suzuki [142], pp. 96, 104. Suzuki finds, for the period from the latter part of the 1950s onward in Japan, instances of case A in 1955 and 1962–63. In this author's opinion, however, the classic case A situation occurred in the early 1930s.)

For cases A and B a rise in fiscal spending increases the level of firms' deposits and the financial market becomes easy, but in case B with lower corporate deposits, the financial market tightens. In 1932–33 the Bank of Japan underwrote a great part of the debt as fiscal expenditure rose, so an easing of the financial market was only natural. And the export expansion that followed had the same effect as fiscal expansion, i.e., raising income and firms' cash deposits along with household deposits to a level corresponding to that of international reserves. Indeed, the bonds underwritten by the Bank of Japan were sold at opportune times by commercial financial institutions, but in the early 1930s even this did not absorb enough money to tighten up the financial market. And of course export expansion can never put pressure on the financial markets as bond sales can. Moreover, plant and equipment investment in these years was financed largely by equity. These, then, were the financial conditions that made possible the easy money and low interest rates of the era. As plant and equipment investment did pick up, these conditions gradually changed but only after 1936.

EXPORTS AND PLANT AND EQUIPMENT INVESTMENT

As mentioned earlier, exports were also a major source of demand in the early 1930s. Table 9.7 presents data on exports and world trade during this era. The reason that Japanese exports grew in an era when nominal world trade fell and real world trade stagnated was the decline in relative prices of Japanese goods on world markets—which was in turn due to the fall of the yen after abandonment of the gold standard in 1931. But the devaluation also had the effect of quickly halting the fall of domestic prices. Relative prices as seen from Japan did not seem to be worsening, and the corporate sector's desire to export was strongly stimulated. The devaluation was not done all at once but rather throughout 1932, so the full effects did not become clear until the last half of that year, but exports were rising at the rate of ¥500 million per year until 1935. With a multiplier of three, this means a rate of increase in income of ¥1.5 billion per year.

Another widely held opinion on the reason for export growth is that domestic industries, particularly cotton, had been pursuing rationalization, which was beginning to bear fruit at that time in the form of greater international competitive strength. According to this view the devaluation was merely the occasion for the start of export expansion. The increased competitiveness of Japanese industry is undeniable. But at the same time, Japan was almost alone in seeing exports increase; this would have been difficult during the world depression without the drastic devaluation of more than 40%. In this sense the export expansion was indeed a result of Takahashi's policies.

After a lag, private plant and equipment investment gained strength, touched off by fiscal and export expansion. Private investment began rising only after 1933 but from then until 1936 rose ¥200–300 million per year. Still, its share of GNP was less than 8% in 1932 and less than 12% in 1936. Because of this factor the expansion of the 1930s must be seen as based on fiscal expenditure and exports, with investment playing a comparatively minimal role. On the other hand the scale of investment in 1935–36 was quite large, and this combined with expansion of military industry to worsen the balance of payments situation, as will be described below. But let us also look at the composition of investment as seen in table 9.8. The estimation method used for this table differs slightly from that used for national income data so the total here is slightly high, but the data are useful for studying relative composition. The so-called military industries, defined here as metals, machinery shipbuilding, and chemicals, did not have such a large share of investment. Certainly the amounts they invested in 1934 and 1935 were large but their increase in share was not particularly large. Rather, textiles (the nation's main export industry), electricity and gas, and transportation saw the largest increases in investment. These facts suggest that much of the military industry expansion up to 1935 was carried out through utilizing excess productive capacity or by using subcontractors with low capital coefficients. Investment increases in military industries became quite apparent in 1936–37 but this only testifies to the fact that full-scale military investment began in an effort to catch up with demand generated by the burgeoning military budget.

A large part of the private investment of the early and mid-1930s was funded internally or by the sale of equities. But in 1936 the proportion funded by borrowing rose. This meant that financial markets were tightening, but government policy tried to counter this trend by lowering interest rates and making fund raising easier. The inconsistency of policy is well represented by the lowering of interest rates at a time of deterioration in the balance of payments.

However, the low share of heavy and chemical industries in plant and equipment investment in the first half of the 1930s did not mean that their share of production or sales growth was low. In fact growth of heavy and chemical industry was remarkable in the first half of the 1930s. As seen from the industry statistics in table 6.15, the share of heavy and chemical industry in total value of product advanced from 36% in 1930 to 49% in 1935. Yasuba's indexes of production for 1935, taking 1930 = 100, are: for metals 180, machinery 174, chemicals 183, textiles 148, and food products 108; i.e., the heavy and chemical industries were higher. Plant and equipment investment was low in the heavy and chemical industries despite expanding production. An increase in those industries' share of total production occurred because tremendous excess capacity existed during the world depression as a result of plant expansions during the 1920s. Production was increased up to 1935 by utilizing existing capacity. Expansion of investment in 1936 and after reflected the fact that these industries were operating at or near capacity and had to expand in order to meet growing demand.

But where did demand for heavy and chemical products come from? One opinion is that the source was military demand or demand arising from the prosperity generated by military spending. But as seen previously, military demand as evidenced in the military budget was not all that high in the first half of the 1930s. This can be seen in the data in table 6.17 on sources of demand for steel, and in similar data continuing

Table 9.7. Japanese Exports and World Trade Indicators

	Nominal commodity exports (¥ million) (1)	Real commodity exports (¥ million) (2)	Japanese export prices (1934–36=100) (3)	U.S.$ per 100 ¥ (4)	World trade volume ($100 million) (5)	Unit price of world imports (1934–36=100) (6)	Index of world import volume (1934–36=100) (7)	Relative prices within Japan (8)	Japan's relative price in foreign currency terms (9)
1924	2,036	998	204.0	42.000	295.5	149	92.5	1.65	1.98
1925	2,559	1,212	211.2	40.750	338.1	159	99.6	1.51	1.87
1926	2,313	1,273	181.7	46.875	328.1	149	102.9	1.55	1.97
1927	2,266	1,412	160.5	47.375	344.4	145	111.2	1.53	1.81
1928	2,306	1,497	154.0	46.500	353.3	143	116.1	1.48	1.73
1929	2,513	1,665	150.9	46.070	363.2	139	121.8	1.53	1.72
1930	1,800	1,602	112.4	49.367	296.1	122	113.6	1.38	1.57
1931	1,426	1,596	89.4	48.871	211.3	94	104.7	1.43	1.60
1932	1,720	1,903	90.4	28.120	141.9	74	89.2	1.25	1.18
1933	2,278	2,145	106.2	25.227	162.0	83	91.8	1.20	1.11
1934	2,713	2,705	100.3	29.511	203.9	101	95.1	1.05	1.01
1935	3,183	3,291	96.8	28.570	210.9	99	100.4	.96	.96
1936	3,492	3,437	101.6	28.951	226.7	102	104.7	.98	.99
1937	4,094	3,494	117.2	28.813	281.9	112	119.1	1.05	1.04
1938	3,924	3,298	119.0	28.496	250.2	106	110.4	1.04	1.11

Sources: Columns 1, 2, 3 from Ohkawa et al. [O], tables A26, A28, A30, respectively; col. 4 from Nihon Ginkō Tōkei Kyoku [85]; columns 5–7 from Maddison [H].

Notes: Column 8 is the ratio of yen-based Japanese export prices to yen-based Japanese import prices, from Ohkawa et al. [O], table A30. Column 9 is the ratio of the dollar-based Japanese export price index, calculated from columns 3 and 4, and the index of world import prices, column 6.

Table 9.8. Funding of Plant and Equipment Investment (¥ million)

	By industry									By source of funds				
	Mining industries	Metals industries	Machinery Industries	Shipbuilding	Chemical industries	Electricity and gas	Spinning and other mfg.	Transport and communications	Total (including others)	Stocks	Bond flotations	Borrowing	Profits	Total
1932	17	10	13	13	40	56	118	113	511	209	70	70	162	511
	(3.3)	(2.0)	(2.5)	(2.5)	(7.8)	(11.0)	(23.6)	(22.1)	(100.0)	(40.9)	(13.7)	(13.7)	(31.7)	(100.0)
1933	64	60	34	49	141	105	219	128	917	493	63	125	237	917
	(7.0)	(6.5)	(3.7)	(5.3)	(15.4)	(11.5)	(23.9)	(14.0)	(100.0)	(53.7)	(6.8)	(13.6)	(25.9)	(100.0)
1934	116	108	94	24	158	160	275	304	1,386	699	239	152	296	1,386
	(8.4)	(7.8)	(6.8)	(1.7)	(11.4)	(11.6)	(19.8)	(21.9)	(100.0)	(50.4)	(17.2)	(11.0)	(21.4)	(100.0)
1935	208	156	92	10	232	147	387	230	1,632	723	236	226	447	1,632
	(12.7)	(9.6)	(5.6)	(0.6)	(14.2)	(9.0)	(23.6)	(14.1)	(100.0)	(44.3)	(14.5)	(13.9)	(27.4)	(100.0)
1936	222	193	141	23	285	304	414	326	2,164	910	258	414	522	2,104
	(10.6)	(9.2)	(6.7)	(1.1)	(13.5)	(14.4)	(19.6)	(15.5)	(100.0)	(43.3)	(12.3)	(19.7)	(24.8)	(100.0)
1937	474	263	319	40	547	522	434	364	3,260	1,933	136	590	601	3,260
	(14.6)	(8.1)	(9.8)	(1.2)	(16.7)	(16.0)	(13.3)	(11.2)	(100.0)	(59.5)	(4.2)	(18.1)	(18.4)	(100.0)

Source: Sanroku Izumiyama's estimates in "Saikin Go-ka-nen-kan Hompō Sangyō-betsu Seisan Shihon Tōka-gaku Ichiranpyō" (Summary of Capital Investment in the Last Five Years by Major National Industries), which are virtually the same as corporate investment.

Note: Figures in parentheses are percentage shares of total.

to the end of the war shown in table 9.9. The table demonstrates that in the first half of the 1930s military and government demand for steel was not strong, only a bit above 10% of the total. The principal demand came from civil engineering construction and from industries such as machinery, shipbuilding, and steel itself. Clearly, the effects of Takahashi's fiscal policies were being felt, but to conclude that the demand was military is problematical. The role of military demand became conspicuous only starting in 1936.

If not military demand, what then were the reasons for the expansion of heavy and chemical industry demand? Fiscal expenditure certainly supported expansion but there were in turn several reasons for this. One was the growth of subsidy policies, an example being the Subsidy Facility for Improvement of Ships (*Senpaku Kaizen Josei Shisetsu*) of 1932–37. Ships more than 25 years old were scrapped and subsidies for up to half the number scrapped were given for new ships, the amount depending on the speed of the new ship. Under this program, 119 ships of 500,000 gross tons were scrapped, and 48 new ships of 300,000 gross tons were built, accounting for about 30% of the 1,029,000 gross tonnage built between 1933 and 1938 (Tōyō Keizai Shimpo Sha [156], p. 257). Shipbuilding is of course only an assembly industry but extension of aid to it meant that heavy industry in general was affected. Other reasons for heavy and chemical industry expansion in the early 1930s were the revival of demand that had been suppressed since the late 1920s, and technological progress that facilitated the domestic production of goods formerly imported. Large-scale electric equipment, spinning and weaving machinery, machine tools, and industrial machinery are examples. A third reason was development and introduction of new products: aluminum, magnesium, synthetic fibers, automobiles, and—entirely tied to military demand—aircraft. In addition to these reasons for expansion the heavy and chemical industries grew because of plant and equipment investment and growth in other sectors since heavy and chemical products are the raw materials and intermediate goods of so many industries.

Thus, the heavy and chemical industries expanded rapidly in the early 1930s. Although the mood was one of expanding military demand, the scale of actual demand was limited. Firms in the heavy and chemical industries, while hoping to do some military-related business, were not concentrating all their efforts in that area. Rather, these industries, having withstood the rigors of introduction into Japan and of competition since World War I, were able to show a profit for the first time and grasped the opportunity to expand without outside assistance. In fact the conditions for the full-scale heavy and chemical industrialization of the first half of the 1950s were gradually ripening during this period.

Table 9.9. Consumption of Ordinary Steel and Steel Products (Thousands of tons)

	Military and other government demand	Railways	Civil engineering and construction	Shipbuilding	Machinery industries	Oil, gas, electricity, and waterworks	Mining	Steel	Chemicals	Other	Total
1932	a	232	621	159	662	60	38	b	a	413	2,185
1933	a	212	730	275	1,009	132	65	b	a	266	2,690
1934	a	319	792	330	1,003	70	130	b	a	404	3,048
1935	400	255	846	321	1,090	81	71	b	a	82	3,145
1936	450	281	1,198	567	886	187	96	b	a	95	3,761
1937	1,000	320	1,590	755	1,256	131	217	b	a	249	5,518
1938	1,000	168	608	350	1,256	120	139	b	a	130	3,771
1939	1,364	201	212	199	1,548	131	121	397	38	41	4,253
1940	1,422	193	140	196	1,221	115	127	300	31	74	3,820
1941	1,616	147	128	276	1,470	140	168	87	21	24	4,077
1942	1,845	112	23	363	353	56	66	228	91	448	3,514
1943	2,172	158	3	986	191	51	102	275	4	505	4,447
1944	1,060	138	a	940	103	13	31	89	10	211	2,594
1945	?	45	2	21	8	11	7	4	2	71	171

Source: Tōyō Keizai Shimpō Sha [156].

a: Included in other.

b: Included in machinery industries.

THE EFFECTS OF SPENDING

The fiscal and monetary policies of the early 1930s induced several important changes in the economy. Among the most important were shifts in the structure of monopoly and income distribution.

Changes in the Structure of Monopoly

Expansionary fiscal policy brought not only a rise in income but also an extraordinary easing of financial markets and lowering of interest rates, as well as change in interclass and interregional income distribution. These changes in turn altered certain aspects of monopoly. As previously seen, the economy between the end of World War I and the abandonment of the gold standard in 1931 saw a near completion of one stage of zaibatsu takeover of industries. Methods of takeover can be distinguished as follows. First came the control of major sources of profits, which were in banking, trust companies, insurance, other financial industries, commerce, and mining. Table 7.9 shows Mitsui companies in these fields (the Mitsui Bank, the Mitsui Trust Company, Mitsui Life Insurance, Mitsui & Company [the main trading company], Mitsui Mining, the Hokkaido Colliery and Steamship Company) accounting for ¥100.6 million, or 88% of received dividends of the holding company between 1932 and 1936. The Mitsubishi holding company, Mitsubishi Gōshi, took ¥41.9 million, or 71% of dividends received, from the Mitsubishi Bank, Mitsubishi Trust, Tokio Marine and Fire, Mitsubishi Trading, and Mitsubishi Mining. Mitsubishi Heavy Industries contributed only ¥9.1 million, or 15%. (See *Mochikabu Gaisha Seiri Iinkai* [68], pp. 42, 45.) Mitsui & Company in turn owned many firms in the industrial sector (Tama Shipbuilding, Tōyō Rayon) while Mitsui Mining owned the Omuta industrial complex used for the dye-making sector and in other activities. But despite ownership of secondary sector industries by tertiary ones, the largest portion of zaibatsu profits still came from finance and commerce and from the primary sector. The second method of extension of zaibatsu power was that used in the 1920s, i.e., use of financial pressure to extend the network of zaibatsu influence to the various industrial sectors by means of their control over funds. Tokyo Power & Light, Shiomizu Bay Sugar, the Fuji–Minobu Railway, Gōdō Woolens, and Japan Match are examples (Shibagaki [122], p. 245). The merger of Fuji Paper (associated with Oji Paper) and Karafuto Kōgyō was based on the backing of financial interests. A third method was for trading companies, classically Mitsui & Company, to expand zaibatsu control by not only establishing subsidiaries but also obtaining sole agent agreements with existing companies.

But in the 1930s extensive growth became difficult for the zaibatsu. Such things as criticism of anti-yen speculation in the fall of 1931 and the terrorism by radical activists that aimed for an "about face of the zaibat-su," e.g., the Ketsumeidan murders and the May 15 Incident, did help restrain zaibatsu activity. However, structural changes in the economy, such as shifts in the level of economic growth, financial markets, and income distribution, also played a major role in the changed environment. Let us look at the reasons from several viewpoints.

First, zaibatsu banks, faced with controls on the funds supply side, had trouble absorbing firms. The formation in 1932 of the Electric Power Federation at the initiative of the Big Five banks announced a suspension of the aggressive acquisition policy of the zaibatsu. In fact, even the position of the great zaibatsu banks within the financial world slipped. In terms of total deposits, Mitsui and Mitsubishi fell from first and fourth place, respectively, in June 1931 to fifth and sixth in December 1933 (see table 9.10). Mitsui's own *Eighty-Year History of the Mitsui Bank (Mitsui Ginko 80-nen Shi* [65]) says this slippage was due to a paucity of branches, and to their not extending business to medium-sized firms or to sub-contractors of large firms. But more important reasons were shifts of the industrial structure toward sectors where zaibatsu were not strong and shifts of income distribution toward sectors that were not oriented to zaibatsu banks.

A second reason for relative weakening of zaibatsu was easier mone-tary policy and its consequent low interest rates. With easy money and low interest it became advantageous to issue stock and float bonds. Firms' internal fund-raising capability recovered, and funds became more readily available from government financial institutions such as the Deposits Bureau (disburser of Postal Savings) and the Industrial Bank of Japan—all of which worked to the detriment of the big zaibatsu banks. Financial data in tables 9.5 and 9.8 and data on the asset composition of financial institutions reflect this. Fund demand fell as paid-up capital and retained profits rose, and with the recovery of corporate performance, financial institutions' power to control weakened. Deposits increased but usage of funds shifted from loans to the retirement of

Table 9.10. Comparison of Deposits in the Big Six Banks (¥ million)

	Mitsui	Mitsubishi	Daiichi	Sumitomo	Yasuda	Sanwa
June 1931	710	647	659	684	610	—
June 1932	620	616	648	679	607	—
End of 1933	715	661	787	798	740	1,025
End of 1937	945	932	1,120	1,152	1,089	1,340

Source: Mitsui Ginkō [65].

government securities. If we take the class of ordinary banks as an example, loans regained their year-end 1930 level only in 1936, in contrast to the growth seen in deposits. This lower leverage over the corporate sector could only weaken banks' power over firms.

Third, although an industrial investment boom could certainly be expected in the environment of the 1930s, the areas of greatest growth were in the heavy-and chemical-related industries, precisely where the share of zaibatsu funds was relatively low. The so-called new zaibatsu were in electrochemical, soda, aircraft, and automotive industries, e.g., Japan Nitrogen, Japan Soda, Showa Denkō, Nissan, Nakajima Aircraft, and Toyota. Electric machinery makers such as Hitachi and Yasukawa also began to expand. The old zaibatsu were slow to enter these fields. With a few exceptions such as Mitsubishi Heavy Industries, Mitsubishi Electric, Tōshiba, and Fuji Electric, the old zaibatsu were not seen in these new areas until about 1936. Moreover, even firms that earlier had been within the old zaibatsu groups, such as Japan Nitrogen in the Mitsubishi group, Showa Denkō in the Yasuda group, and Toyota in the Mitsui, gradually moved away from group control during these years. Thus, in overall terms, the great age of old zaibatsu control passed in the 1930s, and conditions were being created for the emergence of oligopolistic competition.

To summarize, the turning points for the changes in monopoly structure were (1) improvement of general economic conditions, (2) rise of demand for heavy and chemical industry products, (3) technological progress within heavy and chemical industries, and (4) strengthening of interdependence among industries. Japan Nitrogen and Nissan were perfectly suited to these conditions and thus served as pioneers for such post-World War II successes as Hitachi, Tōshiba, and Matsushita.

Of course old zaibatsu too expanded into heavy and chemical industries, which were linked to military demand. But they did not recover their former power. Production control passed into the hands of the military and the bureaucracy, and the old zaibatsu were no longer able to force concentration of production on their own initiative. Although able to achieve their profit-making goals, they lost their voice in political and other affairs and headed for post-World War II dissolution. The erosion of old zaibatsu power was another key change of the early 1930s.

Changes in Income Distribution
As seen above, the emergency expenditures of Takahashi's fiscal policies shifted the center of economic attention—although only temporarily—from urban areas to rural. Money for public works eventually went into the pockets of the farm population and thus had something of an income redistribution effect. There are no data to show the overall change

Table 9.11. Fluctuations of Deposits in Ordinary Banks by Region (¥ million)

Deposits outstanding	1930 Year-end	1932 Year-end	1934 Year-end	1936 Year-end	1937 Year-end
Tokyo	2,412	1,981	2,339	2,888	3,435
Osaka	1,674	1,523	1,759	1,999	2,350
Subtotal	4,086	3,504	4,098	4,887	5,785
Other regions	4,652	4,813	5,340	6,121	6,649
Nation	8,738	8,317	9,438	11,008	12,434

Increase or decrease	1930–32	1932–34	1934–36	1936–37
Tokyo	−531	358	549	550
Osaka	−151	236	240	351
Subtotal	−582	594	789	901
Other regions	161	527	781	525
Nation	−421	1,121	1,570	1,426

Source: Okura Shō Ginkō Kyoku [110], various years.

but partial evidence is available. For example, table 9.5 above shows composition of deposits by financial institution. Liquidity went up for institutions catering to small depositors, e.g., the Nōrin Chūō Kinko, (Central Cooperative Bank for Agriculture and Forestry), industrial co-ops, credit co-ops (Shinyō Kyōdō Kumiai), and Postal Savings. On the other hand the stagnation of deposits in ordinary banks corroborates the assertion of a rise in total income of the lower income classes. Moreover, as seen in table 9.11, the amount of ordinary bank deposits outstanding in Tokyo and Osaka fell between 1930 and 1932 while that in other areas rose. The level of deposits in Tokyo did not recover to its 1930 level until after 1935. The combined share of Tokyo and Osaka in total deposits descended rapidly between 1930 and 1932 from 46.8% to 37.2%, then recovered to 43.5% in 1934 and 44.4% in 1936. Their share recovered its 1930 level only in 1937 at the outbreak of war in China (April 1937). Although this is indirect evidence, we can surmise that distribution of income, and thus the regional distribution of financial assets also, changed around 1932.

TWO PROBLEMS

Aside from political problems, Takahashi's stimulative fiscal policies contained two economic problems. One was that despite the strength of exports the balance of payments did not improve. The other was that domestic productive capacity became fully used; the effectiveness of further spending soon became marginal and inflation began to accelerate. The next chapter deals with the problems caused by the plunge into a wartime economy under these conditions but here we shall only point out the facts behind them.

Worsening Terms of Trade and the Balance of Payments

The rise of Japan's exports was due, as seen above, to declining relative prices and worsened terms of trade resulting from the devaluation of the yen. But the weak currency also had disadvantageous effects on the Japanese economy, including the higher prices and decreased quantities of imports that accompany declining terms of trade. Table 9.12 presents data on the matter.

First of all, degrees of dependence, as expressed by ratios of nominal trade to GDP, were roughly the same for exports and imports. In the 1920s the ratios were about 18%, fell to about 15% during the worst of the depression, rose to 23–24% in 1935–37, and fell again slowly as the war proceeded. But real figures show quite different trends. Exports increased 2.7 times between 1926 and 1936—2 times of which was be-

Table 9.12. Dependence on Trade and Real Exports and Imports

	Nominal GDP exports (%)	Nominal GDP imports (%)	Index of real export volume (1934–36 = 100)	Index of real import volume (1934–36 = 100)
1926	18.7	21.1	40.0	71.4
1927	18.3	19.1	45.2	74.3
1928	18.4	19.2	47.8	76.0
1929	20.3	19.8	53.2	81.8
1930	16.9	16.2	53.8	74.5
1931	15.3	15.8	55.2	84.0
1932	18.1	18.2	66.3	85.3
1933	20.2	20.2	70.8	88.0
1934	21.1	21.5	86.8	95.5
1935	22.7	21.8	103.6	98.7
1936	23.7	22.7	109.6	105.8
1937	23.7	26.2	112.1	133.2
1938	20.2	22.4	108.0	129.4
1939	20.2	19.9	100.4	118.0

Source: Calculated from Ohkawa et al. [100] (or Ohkawa et al. [O], tables A1, A3).

tween 1930 and 1936. Real imports, however, rose only 48% over these ten years, almost all the growth coming after 1930. In other words, with declining relative prices and worsening terms of trade, balance in the international trade accounts required nominal dependence on exports to rise substantially—or, from another viewpoint, required real dependence on imports to decline. If Japan had not exported so strongly as to be charged with dumping, it would have been difficult to secure imports. And, as is well known, strong opposition arose abroad in the form of tariff barriers against Japanese exports.

But even in purely domestic terms there were still other problems. Japan managed to cut import dependence (and its troublesome implications) by several means. One was reduction of imports of finished products and substitution of raw materials and semifinished goods for intermediate use. Thus, within ten years import substitution of many products began (see table 9.13). For example, increasing sugar production in the colony of Taiwan and domestic development of machinery and woolen weaving substituted for imports of sugar, machinery, and woolens. Meanwhile, ginned cotton, wool, natural rubber, and steel imports rose and became the basic materials for industries that developed at the time.

But the shift to raw materials imports also had its disadvantages, even for the strongest export product, cotton textiles. Because declining terms of trade underlay the export expansion, raw cotton imports rose along with increased textile exports, thus lowering the rate of value added and lowering the industry's ability to earn foreign exchange. Table 9.14 depicts the ratio of value of raw materials to that of total output for the cotton yarn and cotton weaving industries. The ratio jumped in the depression of 1930–31, and the reversal of this with higher value added in Japan in 1932–33 reflects worsened foreign markets for textile products. But from 1934 to 1937 the ratio rose every year, and the rate of value added dropped. An upturn in the ratio of raw materials cost to product means an equivalent loss of foreign exchange earning power. For example, with the ratio at 43%, ¥100 million of exported cotton textiles meant that ¥57 million of foreign exchange could be used for non-raw materials purposes, but with a rate of 65% only ¥35 million would be available.[1] As seen from this example, the declining terms of trade did stimulate exports but on the other hand increased the pay-

1. The decline in income accompanying a fall in the terms of trade has been pointed out by Miyohei Shinohara. He has said that in an economy engaged in intermediate trade for reexport, "there occurs," with a decline in the terms of trade, "a phenomenon of increased relative prices of imported raw materials, while exports sag by comparison." Even if labor productivity rises, "part of the gains go abroad, in the form of higher raw materials prices." (See Shinohara [128], p. 304.)

Table 9.13. Composition of Imports (Total imports = 100)

	Category						Major products								
	Total	Food products	Raw materials	Processed materials	Manufactures	Sundry goods	Rice, wheat, and soybeans	Sugar	Cotton	Wool	Lumber	Natural rubber	Crude oil	Steel	Machinery and parts
1926	100	14.7	56.4	15.0	13.3	0.6	8.0	3.5	30.5	3.6	4.3	1.7	1.3	5.7	3.8
1927	100	14.9	56.2	16.0	13.3	0.7	8.0	3.5	28.6	4.7	4.8	1.6	2.2	6.2	3.6
1928	100	13.6	53.1	17.4	15.1	0.8	6.9	3.0	25.0	3.4	5.0	1.3	3.5	6.8	4.2
1929	100	12.2	55.2	16.0	15.6	0.9	6.9	1.4	25.8	4.6	4.0	1.5	3.7	7.2	5.5
1930	100	13.5	53.6	15.3	16.5	1.2	5.7	1.7	23.4	4.8	3.4	1.2	5.3	6.1	5.5
1931	100	12.8	55.4	14.7	16.0	1.1	5.6	1.3	24.0	7.0	3.5	1.0	6.5	3.9	4.1
1932	100	11.2	58.6	14.1	15.3	0.8	6.6	0.2	31.2	6.1	2.4	1.0	6.4	4.5	4.2
1933	100	9.0	61.6	17.2	11.5	0.7	4.9	0.7	31.5	8.6	2.1	1.5	5.3	7.1	3.8
1934	100	7.6	61.9	18.2	11.5	0.7	3.6	0.4	32.0	8.2	1.8	2.5	5.0	7.5	4.3
1935	100	7.8	61.0	19.0	11.6	0.7	4.0	0.5	38.9	7.7	2.0	2.1	5.8	8.4	4.2
1936	100	8.4	62.9	17.2	10.7	0.9	3.6	0.8	30.7	7.3	2.0	2.6	6.2	6.9	3.3
1937	100	6.7	52.7	29.0	11.1	0.7	2.9	0.5	22.4	7.9	1.7	2.6	—	—	4.2

Sources: Tōyō Keizai Shimpō Sha [155] and Okura Shō and Nihon Ginkō [109].

Table 9.14. Raw Material/Product Ratios for the Cotton Industry

	Cotton spinning	Cotton weaving	Cotton yarn and cotton textiles
1929	61.3	60.7	37.3
1930	74.0	70.4	52.0
1931	67.6	77.7	52.6
1932	60.3	70.5	42.6
1933	63.3	77.1	48.9
1934	75.4	79.3	59.9
1935	79.3	80.8	64.1
1936	76.5	84.3	64.5
1937	76.4	88.9	67.9
1938	68.3	67.4	46.2

Source: Calculated from Tsūshō Sangyō Shō [161].

ments for imported raw materials needed to make them. Added to this was the rise in 1935–36 of metals, machinery, and petroleum imports for plant and equipment investment. The various advantages and disadvantages of exchange rate depreciation have been pointed out for many years. Japan's case in the 1930s is a classic example. Japan's devaluation was fairly large and so were the profits, but the losses were also great.

Adding more trouble was the structure of international payments under the bloc economy system. Japan's balance of payments is summarized in table 9.15. As is well known, Japan's pre-World War II trade balance was negative, but the nontrade accounts (see table 9.16), particularly shipping, were in surplus and the overall balance was in virtual equilibrium. But just at this time, the world economy separated into blocs and conditions changed as Japan tried to establish its independence in the rather small yen bloc. Not merely the overall balance but subbalances with third countries (notably the United States and the United Kingdom) had to be considered. With the world separated into areas in which settlements could be made in yen and those in which settlements had to be made in international currencies or gold, the balance vis-à-vis the entire world was not so important as that vis-à-vis non-yen-bloc countries. In the first half of the 1930s no big problems developed. The trade deficit vis-à-vis the non-yen bloc was ¥200–400 million per year, but the nontrade accounts, especially shipping, were able to earn enough foreign exchange to cover this. Japan's large trade surplus with Manchuria was settled in yen but this money flowed back into Manchuria as investment. Still, these two bilateral imbalances on the trade account reveal that Japan's balance of payments structure was substan-

Table 9.15. Balance of Payments by Region (A: total, B: yen bloc, C: third countries)

		Trade account				Nontrade accounts			
		Exports	Imports	Trade balance	Current account balance	Temporary payments	Investment in Manchuria	Gold outflow	Overall balance
1929		2,221	2,388	-167	187	-92		-1	-73
1930		1,520	1,681	-160	133	-147		286	111
1931		1,180	1,321	-140	83	-232		388	98
1932	A	1,466	1,524	-58	102	-100	(97)	112	55
	B	175	175	0					
	C	1,291	1,349	-58					
1933	A	1,439	2,017	-78	109	-20	(151)	20	31
	B	351	230	121					
	C	1,588	1,787	-199					
1934	A	2,270	2,401	-131	144	-183	(272)	1	-169
	B	459	260	199					
	C	1,811	2,141	-330					
1935	A	2,828	2,698	130	178	-371	(379)	-0	-63
	B	488	291	699					
	C	2,340	2,403	-67					

1936	A	2,797	2,925	-128	233	-269	(263)	-0	-164
	B	631	410	221	23	-3			-22
	C	2,166	2,515	-349	209	-267			-142
1937	A	3,318	3,953	-635	-18	-565	(341)	866	-1,129
	B	795	469	326	-119	-547			-340
	C	2,252	3,485	-963	99	-19			-883
1938	A	2,895	2,835	60	-797	-41	(431)	660	-778
	B	1,234	637	597	-767	-175			-345
	C	1,661	2,198	-537	-31	134			-434
1939	A	3,929	3,126	803	-977	-1,148		663	-1,322
	B	1,838	728	1,110	-841	-1,028			-759
	C	2,091	2,398	-307	-136	-121			-564
1940	A	3,656	3,453	203	-789	-1,300		320	1,887
	B	1,867	756	1,111	} -1,968	} -122		857	
	C	1,789	2,697	-908					1,030
1941	A	2,651	2,899	-248	-1,342	-1,444		152	3,035
	B	1,659	855	804	} -2,659	} -128			1,855
	C	992	2,043	-1,051					1,179

Sources: For 1929–35, data for A are from Okura Shō [106] and data for B, C, and Manchurian investment from Nihon Keizai Renmei Kai [86]. Data for 1936–41 are from Hara [30]. Yen bloc is Japan and Manchuria for 1932–35 and Japan, Manchuria, and North China for 1936–41.

Table 9.16. Structure of Nontrade Accounts

	Current items					Temporary items			
	Interest and dividends	Business and labor remittances	Freight and insurance	Government payments balance	Total (including other)	Foreign capital	Foreign investment	Total	Actual investment in Manchuria
1930	−80	90	125	−14	133	−28	−120	−148	—
1931	−71	77	2	−30	83	−217	−17	−233	—
1932	−96	145	107	−87	102	−105	5	−100	97.2
1933	−116	157	134	−120	109	20	−41	−21	151.2
1934	−101	176	167	−135	144	−4	−180	−183	271.7
1935	−107	201	187	−141	178	−17	−354	−372	378.6
1936	−85	196	208	−129	232	−101	−168	−269	263.0
1937	2	90	230	−393	−17	−51	−514	−567	341.3
1938	39	89	196	−978	−796	659	−701	−41	431.0
1939	17	49	−22	−1,015	−976	−71	−1,077	−1,148	—
1940	−18	194	45	−1,087	−789	4	−1,034	−1,300	—
1941	130	273	55	−1,890	−1,342	32	−1,477	−1,445	—

Sources: Okura Shō [107]. Data for actual investment in Manchuria from Nihon Keizai Renmei Kai [86].

tially different from what the overall numbers appear to show. Thus, when the trade deficit with non-yen-bloc countries expanded after 1936, balance of payments problems suddenly became worse.

Expansion of Productive Capacity and Inflation

The major part of the labor made idle by the world depression was not absorbed back into employment until 1936, and the major part of idle capacity was not utilized again until then. But even this statement must be qualified by definition of employment and utilization. For example, employment in factories of more than five operatives rose by 950,000 between year-end 1930 and year-end 1936 to a total of 2.88 million (see Tsūshō Sangyō Shō [161]). According to Mataji Umemura's estimates, agricultural population in these years was stable. The overall numbers of employed increased about 2.0 million, so the expansion of employment was of a slightly different character from that of the 1920s. While employment in secondary industry, primarily manufacturing and public works, did indeed rise, expansion of tertiary industry also was vigorous. But simultaneously, demand from military industries put pressure on the labor market, and openings were filled by temporary workers. Some say, however, that the availability of temporary labor at all proves that there was continued slack in the market (see Sumiya [139], p. 97). Skilled labor was in particularly short supply and raiding other firms was common. Thus, given the social conditions of the time, most of the labor that could be absorbed without creating friction was already absorbed. In this respect the situation resembled that of the post-World War II era before 1958–59.

We can conclude the following. First, given the agricultural technology of the 1930s, maintaining and raising agricultural production in the face of large outflows of agricultural labor would not have been possible—this being contrary to experience after World War II. Second, an outflow of agricultural population in the 1930s would have weakened the source of supply for the military and would have made self-sufficiency in food impossible. Thus, a rapid shift in the composition of the labor force to the industrial sector, as occurred in the 1960s, was not possible in the 1930s. And in turn, promotion of rapid population shifts based on an economically rational growth mechanism was not possible in the 1930s.

In this sense the labor market of the time was approaching full employment. On the other hand a strange disequilibrium existed in capital equipment markets. Although output and plant and equipment investment rose rapidly between 1931 and 1935, restrictions on production continued (table 9.17). In 1935 and 1936 there was a great expansion of investment in the heavy and chemical industries, where an investment fever led by military demand prevailed. At the same time, however, this

Table 9.17. Investments by Industry and Rates of Production Restriction
(¥ million)

Increases in investment

	Heavy and chemical industries	Light industries	Other industries	Total
1932	76	118	317	511
1933	284	219	414	917
1934	384	275	727	1,386
1935	580	387	665	1,632
1936	612	414	1,048	2,104
1937	1,169	434	1,657	3,260

Rates of production restriction

	Spinning	Rayon	Lime and nitrogen	Sulfuric acid	Western-style paper	Cement	Steel
1931	31.4	30.0	40.0	50.0	55.0	57.0	38.0
1935	33.8	30.0	40.0	25.0	43.7	53.0	30.0

Sources: Data for increases in investment from Nihon Kindai Shiryō Kenkyū Kai [87]. Data for rates of production restriction from Nihon Ginkō [84], appendix table.

investment was in anticipation of expanded military demand and did not conform to the current demand structure. This meant that the economy could not meet domestic consumer demand, which eventually rose as a result of income generated by this investment. Moreover, the fact that the cartels for the most part retained production restrictions while production increased markedly indicates that such restrictions were not aimed at limiting current production so much as checking the expansion of plant and equipment. This is evidence that oligopolistic competition was strengthening.

Thus, the economy of this era saw the exhaustion of the balance of payments surplus, establishment of overall supply and demand equilibrium, and the absorption of excess productive capacity. It was not generally recognized at the time, although it is clear now, that with the addition of any further demand, this equilibrium would be destroyed both on the international payments side and on the supply/demand side with the onset of inflation. Or, even if this fact was realized at the time by some, it was ignored because of political pressures.

Ten □ The Beginning of Wartime Economic Controls

THE ECONOMIC ENVIRONMENT OF 1936–37

As seen in the previous chapter, Japan's economy in the first half of the 1930s was characterized by the accumulation of classic multiplier effects. The turning point was abandonment of the gold standard in December 1931, the impact of which became apparent with the sudden increase in government expenditure in 1932 and the increase in exports stemming from the decline in the value of the yen. Production continued to rise through 1934–36. Employment showed a sudden advance, and plant and equipment investment became brisker. However, the ceiling imposed by the balance of payments was lowered. Had normal policy been possible, tightening would have been expected under such circumstances. But instead the military proposed the Five-Year Plan for Key Industries (*Jūyō Sangyō Go-ka-nen Keikaku*).

Let us first look in some detail at the economic situation of 1936–37. Balance of trade developments are seen in table 10.1 (quarterly data, at monthly rates, seasonally adjusted, moving averages). Through 1934 raw materials imports (e.g., raw cotton and wool) rose but in 1935 imports were stable. Exports were expanding so the trade account was improving. But in 1936, although exports continued strong, imports from non-yen-bloc countries rose faster and the deficit thus suddenly began to widen. In late 1936 and early 1937 this deterioration accelerated, and the nontrade current payments surplus could not cover the trade deficit. In March 1937 the Bank of Japan had no choice but to begin shipping gold abroad. Although this trend was apparent in late 1936, Finance Minister Baba still drafted a budget of more than ¥3.0 billion, thus ignoring all canons of fiscal and monetary policy.

Let us also look at the rise in imports (see table 10.2). The ratio of imports to GNP was about 22% in the mid-1930s. But import volume rose substantially in 1936 and 1937 to levels that have been called excessive. To see if import volume was in fact excessive, let us regress import

Table 10.1. Trends in the Trade Account (¥ million)

		Total value of trade			Trade with third countries			Trade with the yen bloc			Nontrade current balance	Investment in Manchuria
		Exports	Imports	Trade balance	Exports	Imports	Trade balance	Exports	Imports	Trade balance		
1934	I	174.2	185.0	−10.8	143.3	169.8	−25.5	29.9	15.2	14.7		
	II	180.0	194.6	−14.6	147.8	179.0	−31.2	32.2	15.6	16.6	12.0	22.7
	III	190.5	207.9	−17.4	156.0	191.6	−35.6	34.5	16.3	18.2		
	IV	200.1	216.1	−16.0	164.3	199.3	−35.0	35.8	16.8	19.0		
1935	I	206.8	216.2	−9.4	171.1	199.2	−28.1	35.7	17.0	18.7		
	II	213.8	217.1	−3.3	178.0	199.5	−21.5	35.8	17.6	18.2	14.9	31.4
	III	217.9	221.4	−3.5	181.7	202.6	−20.9	36.2	18.8	17.4		
	IV	219.6	228.1	−8.5	182.1	208.5	−26.4	37.5	19.6	17.9		
1936	I	222.1	235.5	−13.4	183.1	217.0	−33.9	39.0	18.5	20.5		
	II	228.6	241.6	−13.0	187.8	221.8	−34.0	40.8	19.8	21.0	19.4	24.4
	III	238.4	253.8	−15.4	196.0	233.6	−37.6	42.4	20.2	22.2		
	IV	252.5	281.5	−29.0	208.7	260.3	−51.6	43.8	21.2	22.6		
1937	I	267.0	301.3	−34.3	221.0	290.6'	−69.6	46.0	10.7	35.3		
	II	274.6	316.3	−41.7	224.0	303.6	−79.6	50.6	12.7	37.9	14.9	28.4
	III	271.2	313.5	−42.3	214.7	285.1	−70.4	56.5	28.4	28.1		

Source: Calculated from Nihon Keizai Renmei Kai [86].

Note: Data are average monthly rates for quarter, seasonally adjusted using four-quarter moving averages.

Table 10.2. Indexes of Production and Import Volume

	Manufacturing production	Import volume
1930	62.7	74.6
1931	64.1	81.6
1932	68.8	81.1
1933	77.4	84.9
1934	89.1	94.9
1935	102.2	98.5
1936	108.6	106.5
1937	117.3	129.5

Source: Ohkawa et al. [O], tables A21, A29.
Note: Indexes have base 1934–36 = 100.

volume (M) on industrial production (IP). The equation using data from 1930–35 to estimate coefficients is

$$M = 42.612 + 0.560(IP) \qquad R^2 = .932.$$
$$(t=8.05) \qquad (t=8.27)$$

This equation would predict, using the actual values of IP for 1936 and 1937, values of 103.4 and 108.3 for M for those two years. The actual values of M were 106.5 and 129.5, higher in both cases and extraordinarily so for 1937. (Similar results hold even when data from 1930–37 are used to estimate coefficients and derive predictions.) A Bank of Japan research department publication noted at the beginning of 1936 that "soaring wool prices and increased demand for military-related products" (Nihon Ginkō Chōsa Geppō, Apr. 1936) were raising imports and that "poor markets in cotton, silk cloth, and silk thread" (ibid., May 1936) were hurting exports. Even at this early date balance of payments deficits were foreseen. Summer brought an upturn in exports and the holding back of imports, but "despite the continued prosperity of sales of various products, declines in important products have blunted the rising trend in exports, while import increases have been unavoidable due to the cost of raw materials for flourishing domestic production. The result has been a trade deficit of ¥130 million" (ibid., Dec. 1936). As will be seen, large trade deficits surfaced only when speculative imports stimulated by the FY (fiscal year) 1937 budget occurred; however, the conditions for the deficits had been ripening for some time. In 1937 the trade deficits became progressively worse and measures were taken to support the foreign exchange market, e.g., the strengthening of exchange controls in January and gold shipments in March. By this time the research bulletin no longer had to speak of the deficit; all observers recognized that concrete balance of payments policies were needed for the economy.

A second factor in the 1936–37 economic environment was Finance Minister Baba's policies. In the FY 1936 budget the Finance Ministry had opposed the Army's demands for an increased budget, and the symbol of this opposition, Finance Minister Takahashi, said in a speech to the cabinet that military expenditures exceeding the ability of the country to pay would not enhance true defense. Takahashi's assassination in the February 26 Incident of 1936 is said to have been caused in part by the anger of young officers at Takahashi's attitude. The Hirota cabinet, taking over after the incident, was formed only after the composition of the cabinet had been approved by the army. The new finance minister, Eiichi Baba, agreed to raise military expenditure. This was to be financed by tax reform, tax increases, and bond flotations, for which purpose interest rates were to be lowered. In March Postal Savings rates and the Bank of Japan discount rate were lowered, and a tax reform draft bill was made public in September. The bill proposed income tax increases of 80% for corporations and 30% for individuals, along with a 100% increase in inheritance taxes. Other proposals included an assets tax and increased indirect taxes while local taxes, such as the household tax (kosū-wari), were slated for cuts or abandonment. In November the FY 1937 budget of ¥3.0 billion was formulated, of which ¥1.4 billion went to army and naval expenses. This was an increase of ¥730 million over the previous year. Even after efforts to cover this amount with tax increases of ¥420 million and with tariffs and other revenues, a whopping ¥980 million bond flotation was still required (up ¥200 million from the previous year). Behind this budget was, in Nobuteru Aoki's words, the "twelve-year plan of the army to strengthen the national defense. During the first half of the plan period, with expenditure of about ¥3 billion, the goal was to improve and expand the modern armament arsenal, especially the air force, while the navy got its Third Enhancement Plan costing ¥770 million. Both plans were approved by the cabinet, and incorporated in the 1937 budget" (Aoki [5] pp. 263–64). The Ministry of Finance promised money for the "Six-year Plan for Armament Enhancement" for the army (41 divisions and 142 air squadrons, i.e., a considerable level of strategic resource preparedness), while the navy's Third Enhancement Plan, a five-year program, called for increases of 66 ships totaling 270,000 tons and 14 companies of marine troops.

Thus, the military won the opportunity to enact its armaments enhancement program with little modification. However, reaction in Japanese financial circles was quite severe and criticism of Baba's policies was vehement. Moreover, after the budget was implemented, the worsening of the balance of payments in conjunction with the already rising imports became obvious to all. On top of this, military demand and low interest rate policies raised plant and equipment investment, and the growth rate of overall industrial production hit 12.6%. Imports of raw materials and capital goods not directly related to military demand also rose, and, with strong domestic demand, exports fell. Identical conditions, when they occurred after World War II, naturally induced tight monetary policy and lower government expenditure. But owing to Baba's very large budget, the balance of payments was simply allowed to suffer temporarily. International reserves held by the Yokohama Specie Bank hit their trough in December 1936, and in January 1937 the Ministry of Finance revised a regulation based on the Foreign Exchange Control Act to make import payments subject to Ministry of Finance approval. Still, import increases did not subside, and the Yokohama Specie Bank's outstanding borrowings abroad exceeded ¥200 million at the end of February, close to its ¥310 million borrowing limit. These were the developments that forced the Bank of Japan to resume gold shipments for the first time since 1932. (See Okura Shō [112].) Nevertheless, imports continued to rise, and the balance of payments went further into deficit, requiring a total of ¥449 million in gold shipments through July.

Among those who sympathized strongly with the policies that had died with Takahashi was Eigo Fukai. On his resignation as governor of the Bank of Japan in January 1937, Fukai summarized the situation as follows in a speech to the Tokyo Clearing House. "The days of easy increase of production by raising capacity utilization are gone. From now on, strenuous efforts should be expended to expand production, but at the same time we must endeavor to conserve material resources in all manner of ways, in the broadest sense. . . . In monetary policy, while there is no reason to avoid funds creation by the power to print money when needed for reasons of state management, we should preserve as much as possible the equilibrium between production on one hand and currency and funds provision on the other. To this end, we must encourage savings, and increase the amount of fund raising carried on through normal financial channels. In order to do this, thrift at home in consumption also becomes desirable" (Fukai [26], p. 331).

Fukai warned of the inflation that would come with investment to meet military demand. He seemed to be resisting expansion of production for military demand, which was trying to move forward while ignoring the deterioration of financial conditions and of the balance of payments. But his desire to impose a more realistic approach to military spending inevitably met with frustration. At the peak of a boom, invest-

ment was spurred further; autumn 1936 to spring 1937 saw demands
for expansion of productive capacity made in the name of the military.

THE THOUGHT OF ISHIHARA

In August 1935 the planner and promoter of the Manchurian Incident,
Colonel Kanji Ishihara, became Chief of Operations at General Staff
Headquarters and began his plans for the defense of Manchuria. "It has
come to our attention that a major gap in armaments between Japan and
the Soviet Union is developing in Northern Manchuria. We must trans-
fer a substantial force to Northern Manchuria, and expand our armaments with a view to achieving armament balance with the Soviets, and
also mechanize the military, particularly through air power. But we were
surprised by the lack of research and coordinated judgment on economic strength in both government and private circles. After some
thought, we gained the understanding of the Southern Manchurian
Railway Company, and relying on Mr. Masayoshi Miyazaki, of the company's Tokyo office, we [established] in the autumn of 1935 the Japan-
Manchuria Finance and Economics Research Society" (Shimada and Inaba [124], p. 703).

Ishihara's ideas on this problem may be summarized as follows: "We
can prepare for war with the Soviets by 1941." At the time, the military
balance between Japan and the Soviet Union in Manchuria was rapidly
deteriorating, with Japan's strength falling precipitously. Ishihara
planned to expand the production capacity of industry enough to support an army in Manchuria 80% the size of the Soviet force. He wished
to expand "the air force and armaments stationed in Manchuria" and,
"within the area of Japan, Manchuria, and North China (northern
Hopei and Southeastern Chahar)," actively develop industry. In wartime, from the start of the offensive to its conclusion, military goods
would be supplied by continental areas. Thus, "economic power is to be
enhanced as much as possible, and necessary reforms made of political
and economic structure; henceforth we shall prepare for fundamental
reforms." In the event of economic confusion, "fundamental reforms
will be made rapidly, and there will be formed a political structure that
can lead the way to a new era." During these years Ishihara counseled
against opening hostilities, and, should they start, material was to be
obtained from England and the United States, while cooperation from
Germany and Poland also was sought. (See Shimada and Inaba [124], p.
682, "Sensō Junbi Keikaku Hōshin," of general headquarters, Department
2, July 19, 1936.) Ishihara was attempting to use military preparations
against the Soviet Union and the development of Manchuria as a springboard for a "Showa Restoration" presumably to be as epoch-making as

the Meiji Restoration (see the untitled piece on current policy published near the end of 1935 by Ishihara, printed in Nihon Kokusai Seiji Gakkai [88], p. 215).

The Ishihara plan was constructed as the actual policy framework of an overall plan focused on expanded armaments to be promoted as government policy. Military pressure on the government had been strong previously but had not gone outside the bounds of demands for larger military budgets, denouncement of the theory of the emperor as "organ" of state, and thought control amnesty issues. It was indeed epoch-making that the army revealed its desire for an overall economic policy extending into overall political and economic structure reorganization. The military needed a concrete plan to renovate the domestic political and economic structure, to promote economic development abroad in Manchuria, and to expand military preparedness against the Soviet Union. Masayoshi Miyazaki, who drafted the plan, had studied in the Soviet Union at the time of its revolution, and later, as a member of the research department of the Southern Manchurian Railway, had helped plan the Manchurian Incident for the Kwantung Army. He pushed for national economic controls and a Japan–Manchuria economic bloc when he set up economic plans for the newly established Manchukuo. A close associate of Ishihara, with whom he confided, Miyazaki was entrusted with the writing of the new plans. To promote the necessary research, Ishihara pumped secret general headquarters funds (estimated at ¥100,000 per year [apparently there was an extra ¥100,000 from the Southern Manchurian Railroad]) into the Japan––Manchuria Finance and Economic Research Society (hereafter called the Miyazaki group). Leaving analysis of the plan itself to the next section of this chapter, for now let us examine the evolution of the plan.

On February 22, 1936, general headquarters had presented its "Fiscal Objectives in the Future of the Empire Relating to Military Expenses." The Miyazaki group used this to construct its "Five-year Plan for 1937–41 for Imperial Revenues and Expenditures (with an Outline for Emergency Policy Implementation)" (see Nihon Kindai Shiryō Kenkyū Kai [87], pp. 19–89). This contained plans for distributing military industry in Japan and Manchuria—with a ratio of about 7 to 3 in Japan's favor—and the fiscal plans and monetary policies to be promoted in tandem with plans to improve administrative structures. We shall leave economic plans for later and here limit ourselves to a summary of administrative structure reform plans, using Miyazaki's own words.

The cabinet system should be discarded, and a Liaison Council (Kokumu-In) established for administration. The council would consist of a Prime Minister and four others. The five ministers would be men well versed in current affairs, true statesmen cooperating in a spirit of solidarity. The prime minister would place ministers in each ministry who would conduct affairs according to his dictates. A General Affairs Agency (Sōmuchō) would be established as a direct organ of the National Affairs Committee, to plan and oversee integrated, unified, and strengthened politics. (The General Affairs Agency would comprise a planning bureau, a budget bureau, and three other bureaus). There would also be established new ministries of defense industries, trade, aviation, and unions. These are the main points of the plans. (Miyazaki [66], p. 179)

The close resemblance of Manchukuo's government to that in the plan bears witness to the influence of Ishihara's and Miyazaki's ideas and backgrounds. The part of the original plan devoted to the expansion of military industries was changed slightly to become the "Plan for the Establishment and Expansion of Military Industries in Manchuria" (Sept. 1936) and then the "Imperial Military Industries Expansion Plan" (Nov. 1936). Plans for Manchuria were quickly taken up by the Kwantung army, revised by Nobusuke Kishi, Naoki Hoshino, and others, and in 1937 began implementation as the "Five-year Plan for Manchurian Industrial Development." On the other hand, general headquarters presented the plans to the Ministry of the Army, which revised them into the "Five-year Plan for Integrated Expansion of Military Industries in Japan and Manchuria" of May 1937. In June of that year the army endorsed its "Outline of the Five-year Plan for Key Industries" with two appendixes by the Miyazaki group, "Outline of Policy Concerning Implementation of the Plan" and "Explanatory Materials to Accompany the Outline." (See Nihon Kindai Shiryō Kenkyū Kai [87].)

Just after completion of the plans, associates of Ishihara, Miyazaki, Kenzō Asahara, Shinji Sogō, and others presented the plan to important members of political and financial circles, e.g., Fumimarō Konoe, Shigeaki Ikeda, Toyotarō Yūki (Industrial Bank of Japan), Shingo Tsuda (Kanebō), Yoshisuke Ayukawa (Nissan), Jun Noguchi (Japan Nitrogen), Kiyoshi Gōko (Mitsubishi), Koshirō Shiba (Mitsubishi), and Masatsune Ogura (Sumitomo). Members of military circles such as General Senjurō Hayashi also received it. In political and financial circles Konoe and Ikeda were particularly positive, whereas it looks as if those associated with Mitsubishi interests were passive. Konoe himself pointed the plan out to Kōichi Kidō.

In mid-September 1937 both army and naval ministers proposed political and administrative structure reforms to the prime minister, and the Hirota cabinet agreed to study the matter on October 23. The military plan called for placing a national policy integration organ beneath the prime minister, including an intelligence commission. An organ to integrate and reform personnel and administration was also to go directly beneath the prime minister, along with merger of the Foreign Affairs and Colonial Affairs ministries, of Agriculture with Commerce and Industry, of Railways with Communications, and so on. Much of this resembled the Miyazaki plan. (See Nihon Ginkō Chōsa Kyoku [83].)

Let us now quote from the famous Harada diary, an important source of off-the-record opinions of major figures of the time. On November 26, 1936, he writes of a conversation with Konoe: "The backbone of the army is at this time mostly pro-England and America, since they think the only way to defend against Russia is to use England and America; so, there is mostly opposition to what the Kwantung Army is now doing in North China" (Harada [32], p. 195). The following is from a November 29 conversation with Ikeda: "Fiscal and monetary plans these days are actually just a product of collaboration between the Kwantung Army and the rest of the military. I am concerned that this will assuredly have a bad influence on financial circles" (ibid., p. 198). The first of these segments shows that the Ishihara and general headquarters plans had been revealed to Konoe. The second shows that the Miyazaki group's plans (especially the "Five-year Plan for 1937–41 for Imperial Revenue and Expenditures") had been presented to Ikeda, and the passage confirms that Ikeda expressed an opinion on the plan. In fact the actual budget for fiscal 1937 and that proposed in Miyazaki's plan were of almost the same amounts and resembled each other in plans for bond flotation, tax increases, and large-scale military expenditure increases (see table 10.3). It is said that Baba's budget turned "emergency" policy

Table 10.3. Comparison of Miyazaki Plan and Original FY 1936 and FY 1937 Budgets (¥ 100 million)

	FY 1936 original budget	FY 1937 original budget	First Miyazaki plan
Export total	22.7	30.4	30.2
New bond flotations	6.8	8.1	11.0
Taxation	—	14.2	—
Military expenditure	10.6	14.1	16.0
Army	5.1	7.3	—
Navy	5.5	6.8	—

Sources: Nihon Ginkō [83] and Nichi-Man Zaisei Keizai Kenkyū Kai, "Shōwa 12-nendo Ikō 5-nenkan Sainyū Oyobi Saishutsu Keikaku Tsuki Kinkyū Jisshi Kokusaku Taikō" (Outline of National Policies for Emergency Implementation Appended to the Revenue and Expenditure Plan for the Five Years from FY 1937), dated Aug. 17, 1936.

into "quasi-war" policy, and in fact Baba did approve most of the military's requests.

In December 1936 there began a movement to install General Senjurō Hayashi as prime minister of a cabinet that would promote planning. In January, 1937 the Hirota cabinet resigned, and General Ugaki was not able to form a new cabinet due to the army's unwillingness to nominate a minister of the army. General headquarters, with the approval of the chief of staff, attached the following conditions on the participation of a minister of the army in the new cabinet: "(1) full provision for armaments and equipment, (2) creation of an aviation industry within five years that will surpass the world standard, and (3) creation of a self-sufficient economy in the area of Japan and Manchuria by 1941, to secure a base for the prosecution of war" (See Sambō Honbu, "*Naikaku Kōtetsu no Baai Rikugun Daijin no Nyūkaku Jōken to shite Yōbō Subeki Jikō,* approved by Chief of Staff, Jan. 23, 1937, in Hata [34], p. 300).

Hayashi did become the new prime minister once general headquarters views were recognized. Shigeaki Ikeda recommended Toyotarō Yūki as finance minister, and Ikeda himself became governor of the Bank of Japan. Ikeda told Harada what had transpired with regard to the Ishihara plan, adding that full provision for the national defense just as the military desired was necessary due to international conditions, and that "the basis of the present economic structure must not be destroyed" (Harada [32], p. 254). But just after taking office, at a news conference Ikeda announced a plan for direct provision of industrial funds by the Bank of Japan. The plan never went into effect due to Ikeda's short tenure in the job but he had decided to implement it. Moreover, in April Ikeda called on Sanroku Izumiyama of the Mitsui Bank's research department to participate in the Miyazaki group in order to "create without delay a five-year plan for military industries." He also said, "The military is to be the core of the plan, and when the military speaks the cabinet cannot do anything [else]." Furthermore, he said that the plan was to "make a ring of Japan, Manchuria, and China" and that Konoe, Ishihara, and he "would take responsibility for such a plan" (Izumiyama [46], pp. 106–107). Ikeda also brought into the Miyazaki group Shingo Tsuda of Kanebō (with Kiyoshi Inoue as his representative), Yoshisuke Ayukawa of Nissan (with representatives Genshichi Asahara and Yoshiaki Yazaki). Ikeda tended to accept the demands of the military, commit himself to the plans, and then try to adjust them from the inside. Then in June, Ishihara claimed in public that financial circles were asking for even more than the rightists, and for this he was placed under surveillance by right-wing elements (see note of Izumiyama to Ikeda, June 1937).

With the participation of Izumiyama, Asahara, and others, the

Miyazaki group drew up on May 15, 1937, its "Five-year Plan for Integrated Military Industry Expansion in Japan and Manchuria" (*Nichi-Man Sōgō Gunju Kōgyō Kakujū Go-ka-nen Keikaku*). But the plan did not touch on the amount of military demand planned for FY 1941 and "swallowed completely" the military's plans. But "for the achievement of the plan a necessity will be the addition of an item in the plan on general machinery industries," said the report. Thus, in expectation of rising prices the amount originally planned for machinery was raised from ¥7.2 to 8.5 billion, although this did not change the basic plan substantially (see Sanroku Izumiyama, "Kyōgi ni Motozuku Shūsei to Sono Jōkō," University of Tokyo). As will be seen later, Izumiyama had some misgivings about the plan but the situation would allow no basic changes. Also on May 15 general headquarters decided, in consultation with the Ministry of the Army, on its "Outline of a Five-year Plan for Key Industries" (*Jūyō Sangyō Go-ka-nen Keikaku Yōkō*), and the plan was immediately presented to the government. Commerce and Industry Minister Takuo Godō of the Hayashi cabinet spoke as early as May 28 of the urgent necessity for "expansion of productive capacity."

In this atmosphere it appears that the government was preparing its own plan even before presentation of the military's. Just after the Hayashi cabinet's crushing defeat in the general election in May 1937, the Southern Manchurian Railway office in Tokyo reported to the home office that "P. M. Hayashi has entrusted Finance Minister Yūki and Commerce and Industry Minister Godō with the preparation of a basic plan for creating a five-year plan for production capacity expansion, with the aim of forming a planned economy. The aim is a plan for general outlines of a renovationist policy by the time the special Diet session meets, and particularly to correct the unsatisfactory results of individual control measures hitherto used for the basic industries sector." The office's report continued, "Both ministries [of Yūki and Godō], once plans are finished, will aim at establishing a new planning agency to discuss and adjust various policies and be a stage in developing national policy." (See Minami Manshū Tetsudō Kaisha Chōsa Bu, [61], p. 327). The plan called for the Ministry of Commerce and Industry to play the major role and to pursue first the parts relating to mining and manufacturing sectors. For the steel industry the ministry in March 1937 established a "Five-year Plan for Expanding Steel Production" with a planned increase in steel product output from 5 to 6.5 million tons between FY 1937 and FY 1941. These numbers are quite small compared to the army's plan for 10 million tons in 1941, and on July 20 the ministry explained the revised 10 million-ton plan to the first subcommittee of the Price Committee. The ministry, however, could see little possibility of using so much steel in peacetime and included a plan to export 3 million tons in the absence of hostilities (Shiina [123], pp. 200–01). Authorities soon came up with plans for other materials, and by May 15 rough first draft plans were ready for aluminum, magnesium, sulfuric acid, soda ash, caustic soda, industrial salt, pulp, staple fiber, ammonium sulfate, phosphate rock, natural rubber, automobiles, machine tools, cotton, wool, and hemp—sixteen products in all (but excluding iron, coal, and liquid fuels). The plan was very much a creature of the Ministry of Commerce and Industry, with two consumer demand-oriented items, staple fibers and ammonium sulfate, taking about half the funds, i.e., ¥1.5 and ¥3.0 billion, respectively, of the plan's ¥9.3 billion total. (See Minami Manshū Tetsudō Kaisha Chōsa Bu [61], pp. 328–77.)

But the real significance of the Ministry of Commerce and Industry plan was not its consumer orientation but rather the fact that it was formally presented as official national policy. On one hand, in May 1937 the Cabinet Research Office was expanded and reorganized into the Planning Agency, with responsibility for investigating, coordinating, and drafting major policies. But simultaneously the Central Economic Conference was established to "form integrated, basic economic policy for both home islands and colonies" and "to decide on implementation plans." It was through this organ that the army's "Plan to Expand Productive Capacity" came to the forefront of national policy.

In June 1937 the Konoe cabinet succeeded the Hayashi cabinet, with Okinori Kaya as Finance Minister and Shinji Yoshino as Minister of Commerce and Industry. The new cabinet of course promoted the army plan but the actual responsibility for implementation fell on these two, who were former vice-ministers of the two ministeries. Kaya had considered, at the time of the large Baba budget, the worsening balance of payments and the necessity for a controlled currency. He also had had difficulty telling military leaders that, with rising prices and import difficulties, even a large budget could not guarantee availability of material, and thus that imports of each item would have to be calculated separately. (See Aritake [12], p. 233.) Moreover, while vice-minister under Yūki, Kaya had thought that supporting the economy when large increases in military spending were unavoidable would require economic controls, and that, as a formula for control, the three principles of "accommodation of supply and demand conditions for goods, balance of payments equilibrium, and expansion of productive capacity" should be established. Realizing the need for close cooperation with the Ministry of Commerce and Industry, Kaya had advocated Yoshino for that portfolio during negotiations for the new cabinet's formation because he felt Yoshino the right type of person to facilitate such a tie-up (see Aritake [12], pp. 293–94).

The "Kaya–Yoshino Three Principles," as they came to be known, were the basic platform of the Konoe cabinet. Broad, direct economic controls were probably already a necessity. An internal memo dated June 7, 1937, in the Ministry of Finance (see Ōkura Shō [112]) went as follows. First, as an "Outline of Current Economic Conditions" came the following points:

Due to international conditions, and in order to establish a basis for development of our nation, the first priority of national policy should be supplementing the national defense. To this end, various economic policies should not be denied adequate consideration, namely those toward:
(1) Achieving, to the greatest degree possible, of course, supplementation of the national defense, while simultaneously,
(2) sustaining stability in the lives of the populace.
However, by "stability in the lives of the populace" we mean that, while increases in living standard are not ruled out, there should be avoided to the greatest extent possible disruption in those aspects of the national life that form the basis of national defense. Thus, the cardinal elements of economic policies toward achieving these two great objectives of national policy are not only securing supply of goods and materials needed for supplementing the national defense and stabilizing the lives of the populace, but also smooth raising of funds for these purposes.

Second, on classification of economic policies by their direct objectives: Naturally the many policies that must be established and implemented on the basis of conditions mentioned above are highly interrelated, but still can be classified, as follows, by direct objective.
(1) Balance of payments accommodations (maintenance of the market for foreign exchange) and control of exchange transactions (control of trade)
(2) Expansion of productive capacity
(3) Regulation of use of materials and goods
(4) Improvement of distribution of national income
(5) Prevention of pernicious inflation
(6) Financial policies needed to implement the above, e.g.
    (a) appropriate interest rates
    (b) appropriate supply of money
    (c) absorption of national bonds
    (d) suppression of speculation
    (e) encouragement of savings
Moreover, appropriate consideration should be given to
(7) Balance in fiscal expenditures and revenues to the greatest extent possible.

The Kaya–Yoshino Three Principles were the first three of the above seven points and became the means toward supplementing national defense and so-called stabilization of the lives of the populace. In particular the "accomodation to the balance of payments [pressures]" was "the axis around which other policies revolved," and "whether the balance of payments accommodations occurred [i.e., maintenance of the exchange rate at a fixed level] determine[d] the extent and speed of progress of all other policies." The reason was that, should the value of the yen fall, exports would be postponed, but speculative imports would flood into the nation for a time," so a worsening of the balance of payments would bring a further fall in the value of the yen. Even with exchange control and import control, "shortages of materials and goods would develop, and an attitude of hoarding would start." This would bring steep price increases and invite vicious inflation. Thus, the exchange rate had to be maintained. "Therefore, both for government consumption through the budget and of course for general consumption, the amounts of goods and materials supplied must be limited to amounts consistent with balance of payments equilibrium." In this way direct controls became an absolute requirement.

These policies became a framework for the army's demand in that they combined setting of limits within which policy consideration was carried out and the formation of the basis for strengthening and rationalization of direct controls based on the demands for "enhancing the national defense." Thus, the war in China only speeded the arrival of strengthened controls: the policy of control itself already existed. The ideas for laws passed after the outbreak of war in China, e.g., the "Temporary Funds Adjustment Law" (*Rinji Shikin Chōsei Hō*) and the "Temporary Import–Export Grading Measures Law (*Yushutsu-nyū Hintō Rinji Sochi Hō*), were to be found in the Ministry of Finance's documents. The war in China thus had two effects on the economy. The first was the acceleration and embodiment of large-scale expansion of direct controls due to the needs of vastly expanded military demand and diversion of imports toward military demand. The other was that the war made impossible the realization of the production capacity expansion plans because of current demand from the unexpected hostilities. The war promoted and brought implementation of controls aimed at capacity expansion but prevented actual expansion.

THE FIVE-YEAR PLAN FOR KEY INDUSTRIES

Given the economic conditions described above, what did the "Five-year Plan for Key Industries" (Jūyō Sangyō Go-ka-nen Keikaku), which the military had demanded of Prime Ministers Hayashi and Konoe, bring the Japanese economy (see Shimada and Inaba [124])? Originally the plan's authors had intended five years without war, so the outbreak of war in China at the start of the plan gave rise to inconsistencies. However, even without war, implementation of the plan would have caused suffering for the people similar to that of wartime years. *If* is usually a forbidden word in historical analysis, but let us nevertheless ask what the plan's effects would have been on the Japanese economy if the war had not occurred.

A general outline of the Five-Year Plan is given in table 10.4. This particular version is the third (the *Nichi-Man Shūgō Gunju Kōgyō Kakujū Go-ka-nen Keikaku*), the one just previous to the final plan. This version is used here because it is more detailed and convenient. Table 10.4 was constructed by Sanroku Izumiyama, who participated in the preparation of the final plan, and the table fully outlines the plan. The plan foresaw, for the five years from 1937 to 1941, the following large expansions. Steel products output was to expand 2.6 times (to 12.0 million tons), pig iron production 3.7 times (11.5 million tons), electric power 1.7 times (to 12.57 million kilowatts), and shipbuilding 1.9 times (to 930,000 tons). Moreover, weapons, the focus of military demand, were to expand 2.1 times in value (to ¥960 million), aircraft to 10,000 units (figures in the original table are in index form, the actual number being classified). Total funding was ¥8.5 billion, of which ¥6.1 billion was aimed for Japan and ¥2.4 billion for Manchuria. Moreover, according to Izumiyama, total demand for funds was forecast to reach ¥19.2 billion, the composition of which is seen in table 10.5.

Now let us touch for a moment on the method by which the plan was constructed. No document on the concrete methods is available but the following summary of how goals were set is possible:

1. Goals for weapons, aircraft, and military transportation equipment were taken directly from the military.
2. Levels of production for steel, coal, electric power, aluminum, magnesium, and other basic materials were determined through previous trends of demand growth and growth rates of government and military expenditure.
3. Levels of funds needed are estimated by multiplication of the amount of capacity expansion needed (goal levels minus existing levels) and estimated unit costs of plant and equipment.
4. Necessary government expenditures and revenues (including new taxes and bond flotations) were computed based mainly on the military budget and related industrial subsidies.
5. Levels of national saving required were derived from the amounts needed for industrial funds and bond absorption.
6. As to trade, the amount of imports required by the plan was estimated, and then export levels were determined to find these imports; a balance of payments surplus was planned for the last half of the plan period.
7. A great shortage of skilled labor existed, so the plan included provisions for manpower training.
8. Various government policies would also be needed, e.g., monetary,

Table 10.4. Summary of the Five-Year Plan for Japan–Manchuria Integrated Military Industry Expansion

Sector	Category	Unit	Wartime demand		
			Japan	Manchuria	Total
Steel industry	Steel materials	1,000 tons	8,000	4,000	12,000
	Pig iron	1,000 tons	8,500	4,000	12,500
	Iron ore	1,000 tons	15,300	7,200	22,500
	Total	1,000 tons			
Liquid fuels	Crude oil	1,000 tons			
	Synthetic oil	1,000 tons			
	Anhydrous alcohol	1,000 tons			
	Total	1,000 tons	11,750?	900?	12,650
Mining	Coal	1,000 tons	86,000	28,000	114,000
	Gold	kg	—	—	—
Light metals	Aluminum	tons	65,000	20,000	85,000
	Magnesium	tons	900	2,000	5,000
	Total				
Armaments	Arms	¥1,000	89,000	70,000	961,000
	Aircraft	index	86	119	976
	Military vehicles	index	50	500	1,000
	Total				
Manufacturing industries	Ordinary automobiles	number	145,000	5,000	150,000
	Railway cars	number			
	General machinery	¥1,000			13,000,000*
	Machine tools	¥1,000			1,000,000*
	Ships	1,000 tons	860	70	930
	Total				
Electric power		1,000 kw	11,170	1,400	12,570
Chemical industries	Soda	1,000 tons	550	3	553
	Paint	1,000 tons	70		70
	Pulp	1,000 tons	1,800		1,800
	Total				
	Grand total				

Note: J, Japan; l, liquid; s, solid; t, target; m, maximum.
*Total five-year production.

trade, price policies, along with industrial control, technical, labor, livelihood adjustment, fiscal, and an administrative restructuring policy including a new cabinet consultative body, the liaison conference (Kokumu-In).

All these elements are in the schematical diagram of the plan outline given in figure 10.1. The figure puts the military's policy goals at the top and depicts with arrows the policy's hierarchy of effects. To achieve the

Table 10.4 (*continued*)

Projected	Production target (A)			Current capacity (B)		
Imports (i) or Exports (e)	Japan	Manchuria	Total	Japan	Manchuria	Total
North China	8,000	4,000	12,000	4,400	450	4,850
		500(J)				
1,000(i)	7,000	4,500	11,500	2,260	850	3,110
		2,800(J)				
6,500(i)	6,000	10,000	16,000	1,230	2,700	3,930
	2,000		2,000	490		490
		1,500(l)			{ 14(l)	
	1,675	1,000(s)	4,175	25	{ 140(s)	179
	280	56	336	30	15	45
		1,655(J)				
6,139(i)	3,955	2,555	6,510	545	169	714
		10,000(J)				
	76,000	38,000	114,000	42,000	13,560	55,560
	80,000	20,000	100,000	40,000	2,800	42,800
	65,000	20,000	85,000	21,000	0	21,000
	3,000	2,000	5,000	500	0	500
	891,000	70,000	961,000	450,000	10,000	460,000
25(e)	850	150	1,000	95	5	100
	500	500	1,000	100	0	100
	145,000	5,000	150,000	37,000	0	37,000
		3,400			400	
{ 2,000,000(i) { 1,700,000(e)			{ 11,000,000(t) { 2,750,000(m)	1,480,000	20,000	1,500,000
250,000(i)			{ 750,000(t) { 180,000(m)	43,000	0	43,000
	860	70	930	500	0	500
	11,170	1,400	12,570	6,750	458	7,208
117(e)	598	72	670	410	36	446
20(e)	40		40	18		18
570(i)	1,110(J)	120	1,230	880	70	950
		120				

goals, equilibrium had to be maintained in each of the lower areas but, of course, achieving the various equilibria required control of elements further down. Thus, among policy goals those hurt most by controls and suppression were consumer goods, especially private goods. This was the basic form of the wartime controls that were soon to emerge.

Of course, the method of constructing this plan was far from exact. Military and aircraft goals were taken just as the military desired, while basic industry demand was estimated on extrapolation of trends, with

Table 10.4 (*continued*)

Sector	Category	Unit	Japan	A/B	Manchuria	A/B	Total	A/B
			Expansion plan					
Steel industry	Steel materials	1,000 tons	3,600	1.8	3,550	8.9	7,150	2.6
	Pig iron	1,000 tons	4,740	3.1	3,650	5.3	8,390	3.7
	Iron ore	1,000 tons	4,770	4.9	7,300	3.7	12,070	4.1
	Total	1,000 tons						
Liquid fuels	Crude oil	1,000 tons	1,510	4.1			1,510	4.1
					{1,486(l)			
	Synthetic oil	1,000 tons	1,650	67.0	860(s)	16.2	3,996	23.3
	Anhydrous alcohol	1,000 tons	250	9.3	42	3.7	291	7.5
	Total	1,000 tons	3,410	7.3	2,388	15.1	5,799	9.1
Mining	Coal	1,000 tons	34,000	1.8	24,440	2.8	58,440	2.1
	Gold	kg	40,000	2.0	17,200	6.7	57,200	2.3
Light metals	Aluminum	tons	44,000	3.1	20,000		64,000	4.1
	Magnesium	tons	2,500	6.0	2,000		4,500	10.0
	Total							
Armaments	Arms	¥1,000	441,000	2.0	60,000	9.0	501,000	2.1
	Aircraft	index	755	9.0	145	30.0	900	10.0
	Military vehicles	index	400	4.0	500		900	10.0
	Total							
Manufacturing	Ordinary automobiles	number	108,000	3.9	5,000		113,000	4.1
industries	Railway cars	number			3,000	8.3	3,000	?
	General machinery	¥1,000	1,170,000	1.8	80,000	5.0	1,250,000	1.8
	Machine tools	¥1,000	107,000	3.5	30,000		137,000	4.2
	Ships	1,000 tons	360	1.7	70		430	1.9
	Total							
Electric power		1,000 kw	4,420	1.7	942	3.1	5,362	1.7
Chemical	Soda	1,000 tons	188	1.5	36	2.0	224	1.5
industries	Paint	1,000 tons	22	2.2			22	2.2
	Pulp	1,000 tons	230	1.3	50	1.7	280	1.3
	Total							
	Grand total							

fiscal expenditure growth kept in rough balance. Taking one example, steel products, we see four methods of estimate used for demand in 1941.

1. Extrapolation of the average growth rate of 7.88% from 1926 to 1936 yielded a level of 6.08 million tons for 1941;
2. Extrapolating the 1930–36 average growth rate of 17.6% yielded 9.39 million tons;
3. For 1937–41 expected annual budget growth was 13.6%, implying 8.02 million tons for 1941;
4. Expected average annual military expenditure growth for 1937–41 was 18.2% per year, implying 9.52 million tons for 1941.

Table 10.4 (*continued*)

		Funds required		
Japan		Manchuria		Total
¥ 1,000	Unit cost	¥ 1,000	Unit cost	¥ 1,000
504,000	140	497,000	140	1,001,000
		97,500	65	97,500
38,160	8	58,400	8	96,500
542,160		652,900		1,195,000
100,000	66			100,000
597,500	362	620,820	418	1,325,400
		107,100	125	
75,000	300	11,412	272	86,400
772,500		739,382		1,511,800
476,000	141	293,280	12	769,200
144,000	3.6	41,540	2.4	185,500
79,200	1,800	62,000	3,100	141,200
7,000	2,800	7,120	3,060	14,100
86,200		69,120		155,300
441,000		60,000		501,000
302,000		72,000		374,000
40,000		100,000		140,000
783,000		232,500		1,015,500
146,000	1,352	6,750	1,350	102,000
		28,100		28,000
585,000		40,000		625,000
107,000		30,000		137,000
108,000	300	21,000	300	129,000
946,000		125,850		1,071,800
2,210,000	500	266,800	283	2,476,000
18,800	100	4,900	136	23,000
33,000	1,500			33,000
80,500	350	17,500	350	98,000
132,300		22,400		100,000
6,092,160		2,443,772		8,535,000

Using these four estimates, Izumiyama chose 8.0 million tons.[1] As can be seen from this one example, the consistency of such a plan is very much in doubt. No check on whether the scale of production in each of the industries was actually achieved without going over or under the plan has been carried out; also there are no estimates of output outside the basic industries and military demand catagories. But we may well suppose that production in the consumer and nonmilitary industries was

1. Nichi-Man Zaisei Keizai Kenkyū Kai, "Jūyō Sangyō Go-ka-nen Keikaku Setsumei Shiryō," from Nihon Kindai-shi Shiryō Kenkyū-Kai [87]. However, the rates used for extrapolation are the simple averages of the various years' individual growth rates. Compounded, the rates would be, for (2) 20%, for (3) 11%, for (4) 7%.

Table 10.5. Sources and Uses of Funds Data Summary (¥100 million)

Sources	
Japan central government deficit bonds	62
Private	125
(Within current plan)	(70)
(Outside current plan)	(55)
Subtotal for Japan	187
Manchurian government	5
Total	192
Uses	
Expansion under current plan	85
(Japanese government funds)	(10)
(Manchurian government funds)	(5)
(Japanese private funds)	(70)
Outside current plan	55
Japanese government fiscal expenditure	52
Total	192

held down to give a cushion so that basic sectors could achieve their goals.

Moreover, the military's goals expanded as the planning process reached later stages, and they further intensified the degree to which private demand was to be suppressed. As seen in table 10.6, the goal levels for output grew successively larger, particularly for such basic goods as steel, coal, and electric power.

But even Sanroku Izumiyama, who helped frame the plan, acknowledged in a letter to Shigeaki Ikeda that "depending on one's point of view, there are problems of how to get out of the paper plan stage, or rather of formulating an implementation plan" (Izumiyama, "Kyōgi ni Motozuku Shūsei to Sono Jōkō," in "Sanroku Izumiyama Papers," cited above). Moreover, Izumiyama noted the following points under "Remaining Problems." First, "resource adjustment problems" had hardly been considered, that is, there were almost no "places in the plan touching on the inter-relations of shortages and surpluses of various materials in the plan." Second, there were doubts about availability of an "additional supply of laborers." Third, there were questions over ability to raise funds. Fourth, "difficulties of implementation" were cited and were explained as follows:

> The plan's major goal is the expansion of plant and equipment, so obtaining materials for the plant and equipment is the first problem. But under present conditions if there were already an insufficiency of supply, particularly of

machine tools and general machinery, it is clear that complete implementation of the plan in the various sectors can not be expected from expansion of domestic capacity alone. It is inevitable that machinery imports of ¥2.2 billion to ¥2.3 billion will be required by the plan. Thus, not only will deterioration of the trade account be a problem, but there are grave doubts that such levels of imports can actually be made. Thus, when thinking of completion of the plan which creates what in peacetime would seem like excess capacity, since of course the plan is based on wartime needs, there remain the fiscal problems of course, but also serious problems of trade and how to use the excess productive capacity [in peacetime].

Izumiyama's observation was certainly a point of basic, economic common sense.

The policy outline of the plan was exactly the one drafted by the Miyazaki group, but some of the numbers differ a bit from the iterated "Outline of the Five-year Plan for Key Industries." The policy outline considers in a general way the interrelationships and hierarchy of the policy described above but even in a strictly technical sense still contains several contradictions. The first concerns trade. The outline foresaw aggregate Japanese–Manchurian imports rising from ¥4.7 billion in 1937 to ¥5.5 billion in 1941, with exports going from ¥4.1 billion to 5.9 billion and the balance of payments turning positive after 1939. But the

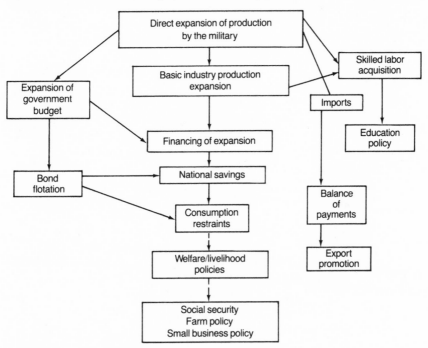

Figure 10.1. Schema of Planning Hierarchy.

Table 10.6. Comparison of Production Capacity in Draft Plans (Total capacity for Japan and Manchuria)

		First draft	Second draft	Third draft	Plan approved by the army
Steel	Steel products (thousand tons)	12,000	8,200	12,000	10,000
	Pig iron	8,300	8,700	11,500	11,500
	Iron ore	13,500	11,200	16,000	22,500
Liquid fuels	Crude oil (thousand tons)	2,000	2,000	2,000	Benzine 3.3 (10,000 kl)
	Synthetic oil (thousand tons)	5,000	5,025	4,175	Alcohol 500 (10,000 kl)
	Anhydrous alcohol (thousand tons)	250	330	336	Benzol 200 (10,000 kl)
					Heavy oil 2350 (10,000)
Coal (thousand tons)		82,000	86,600	114,000	110,000
Gold mining (tons)				100	
Aluminum (tons)		70,000	70,000	85,000	10,000
Magnesium (tons)		5,000	5,000	5,000	9,000
Arms (¥ million)			951	961	
Aircraft				10,000	
Military vehicles (number)					10
Autos (number)		163,000	155,000	150,000	(10,000)
Railway cars (number)		1,750	14,071	3,400	100,000
Machine tools (thousands)				2,750	(10,000) 50
Ships (thousand tons)				930	930
Electric power (1,000 kW)		9,400	10,800	12,570	12,570
Soda (thousand tons)		447	546	670	
Dyes (tons)			40,000	40	
Pulp (thousand tons)		1,020	1,230	1,230	

Sources: First draft: "Manshū ni Okeru Gunju Kōgyō Kensetsu Kakujū Keikaku (Dai-ichiji Chūkan An)" Plan for Establishment and Expansion of Military Industries in Manchuria, First Interim Draft (3 Sept. 1936). Second draft: "Teikoku Gunju Kōgyō Kakujū Keikaku (Dai-ichiji Shian)" (Imperial Military Industries Expansion Plan, First Draft) (11 Nov. 1936). Third draft: "Nichi-Man Sōgō Gunju Kōgyō Kakuju Go-ka-nen Keikaku" (Five-year Plan for Integrated Military Industry Expansion in Japan and Manchuria) (1 May 1937). Plan approved by the army: "Jūyō Sangyō Go-ka-nen Keikaku Yōkō" (Outline for Five-Year Plan for Key Industries). All plans are listed in Nihon Kindai Shiryō Kenkyū Kai [87].

plan also estimated that production in basic industries would double and that national income would "rise from the current ¥20 billion to ¥30 billion or more." But only a 20% increase in imports probably would not have been enough; even if exports expanded according to the plan, the balance of payments deficit could only have widened. And this would have destroyed the entire plan. A reduction of the reliance on imports would have been impossible without controls on materials use and suppression of consumption such as were in force during wartime. The authors of the plan indeed foresaw that inflation would inevitably accompany the plan, saying that "due to the rise in demand for goods during the plan, price increases during the plan period of an average of about 10% are estimated" (Shimada and Inaba [124], p. 741). Price controls to prevent this inflation from hurting exports were included in the policy, but overcoming these difficulties and increasing exports 50% to achieve a trade surplus in the five years of the plan was impossible.

The second major problem with the plan was the intention to have general and direct controls on industry by the state. This would have involved (1) the strengthening of industrial aid policies and payment of subsidies, loss indemnities, profit subsidies, and a system of separate industrial laws; (2) scrapping or reduction of certain production facilities, along with government guidelines on production, sales, labor, and other managerial policies, as well as government approval of profit distribution; and (3) price controls. These seem much like the ideas stated in the national mobilization law passed later, but no such direct controls, even with the country controlled by the military, would have been possible without the war in China. On one hand the ensuing Sino–Japanese War indeed prevented the expansion of capacity intended by the military, but on the other hand the catastrophic, crisis situation that the war brought also made possible the controls that the military had wanted. This was the basic contradiction in the plan: Its implementation required conditions that would ensure its failure.

As pointed out correctly by commentator Kamekichi Takahashi, the blueprint given here "was not implemented as government policy.... But the largest part of the fiscal and economic policies carried out by the various cabinets after the February 26 Incident were within the rough outlines of the military's plans, as seen from the results of actual plans, and from the political conditions of the time."

THE START OF WARTIME ECONOMIC CONTROLS AND INDUSTRIAL PLANNING

War in China forced Japanese economic and fiscal policy to turn to direct controls. Hawks in the army used the war as an excuse to send troops and to sever the five provinces of northern China from the control of Chinese leaders. Moreover, in 1936, following the battles in Suiyuan province of Mongolia (in which Nationalist Chinese defeated Japanese-supported Mongolians [November]) and the Sian Incident (in which Chiang Kai-shek was kidnapped by Chinese political rivals [December]), China became hardened in its opposition to Japan. And in this environment the war could do nothing but expand. In July 1937, with the battle lines growing in North China, the government appropriated ¥500 million in war expenses for North China, and after the battle spread to Shanghai in September, ¥2.1 billion more was appropriated for temporary military expenses. Previous to this, the large Baba budget of ¥3.04 billion had been formulated, though succeeding Finance Minister Yūki had cut this to ¥2.87 billion in the final version adopted. Still, in one stroke the war in China almost doubled the size of the budget. To pay for all this, there was nothing to depend on but bond flotations.

The new budget caused two major economic problems. The first was that the multiplier effects of the fiscal expenditures lead to an inflationary gap and the possibility of soaring prices. Moreover, the increase in military expenditures directly brought even more aggregate demand and an expansion of imports—and hence a wider deficit in the balance of payments. In both monetary and trade policy direct controls were the only choice.

Moreover, the economy's imports were growing at an accelerated pace in 1937 (see table 10.7). In the first half of the year total imports were ¥2.14 billion (of which ¥1.88 billion were from non-yen-bloc countries), with exports of only ¥1.53 billion (¥1.18 billion of which were outside the yen bloc), leaving required gold shipments at ¥310 million. But for the year, gold shipments were ¥860 million, indicating accelerated deterioration (gold shipment data from Nihon Keizai Renmei Kai [86]). This situation made direct controls imperative even at the start of war in China, which was expected to end in quick victory. And just at this time, U.S. industrial production, which had been rising through 1935 and 1936, turned downward and continued falling for an entire year, from May 1937 to June 1938, for a total decline of 30%. The world business cycle, which had been on the mend since the early 1930s, once again met reversal. Japanese exports also peaked in the summer of 1937, partly due to the poor world environment and partly to the supply shortages brought on by war demand and domestic price increases. The exports to non-yen-bloc countries dropped very sharply.

Thus, Japan's wartime economy began under the disadvantageous circumstances of a peak in the domestic business cycle, with consequent deterioration of the balance of payments and a fall-off in the world business cycle, and with domestic inflation weakening international com-

Table 10.7. Quarterly Movements in the Wartime Trade Balance (¥ million)

		Value of all trade			Trade with the yen bloc			Trade with third countries		
		Exports	Imports	Trade balance	Exports	Imports	Trade balance	Exports	Imports	Trade balance
1937	III	1,036	1,197	−161	159	258	−99	877	939	−62
	IV	982	1,072	−90	200	244	−44	782	828	−46
1938	I	925	956	−31	264	225	39	661	731	−70
	II	899	894	5	345	201	144	554	694	−60
	III	906	901	5	400	191	209	506	710	−204
	IV	948	915	33	436	198	238	512	717	−205
1939	I	1,035	931	104	494	208	286	541	723	−182
	II	1,137	960	177	555	221	334	582	739	−157
	III	1,224	1,008	216	614	234	380	610	774	−164
	IV	1,292	1,046	146	670	242	428	622	804	−182
1940	I	1,302	1,067	235	677	247	430	625	820	−195
	II	1,250	1,117	133	641	251	390	609	866	−257
	III	1,196	1,143	53	601	254	347	596	889	−293
	IV	1,158	1,152	6	557	263	294	602	889	−287
1941	I	1,079	1,147	−68	533	273	260	545	874	−329
	II	949	1,046	−97	543	281	262	407	766	−359

Source: Okura Shō, "Gaikoku Bōeki Geppō," volumes for 1937–41, December issues.
Note: Data given are moving averages of quarterly figures.

petitiveness. Fiscal and commercial authorities quickly adopted direct control policies in order to pursue the war and attempted to push the various effects onto consumer goods industries and onto consumption, both of which were considered "inessential and unnecessary." The promptness of the policy response indeed prevented the collapse of monetary and fiscal policy during the war years, but as then Finance Minister Kaya pointed out later, they also made a long war possible and opened the road to war with the United States (Kaya [50], p. 250).

In September 1937, when it was clear that the war in China would be protracted, another special session of the 72d Diet was convened, and there were enacted, simultaneous with the ¥2.1 billion in temporary military expenditures, two other laws, the Temporary Funds Adjustment Law (*Rinji Shikin Chōsei Hō*) and the Temporary Import–Export Grading Measures Law (*Yushutsu-nyū Hin tō Rinji Sochi Hō*). These two laws marked the real start of direct economic controls in Japan. The National General Mobilization Law (*Kokka Sōdōin Hō*) was enacted in May 1938 at the regular session of the 73d Diet. Of course, the Foreign Exchange Control Law and the Capital Flight Prevention Law had been passed in 1932. The former established a system of prohibitions and controls by the government on acquisition, disposition, and ten other categories of transactions concerning foreign exchange. The latter suspended convertibility of yen for foreign exchange, in effect preventing the flow of yen out of the country after the bitter lesson of the fall of the yen following the abandonment of the gold standard in 1931. Although these laws did add controls over capital transactions with foreigners, their intent was to prevent speculation, and their effects on the domestic business cycle were not great. Instead, effects were limited to financiers and traders.

But the two laws of 1937 affected the entire economy. The Temporary Funds Adjustment Law set controls over loans for new plant and equipment, stock and bond underwriting, establishment of companies, or increase of capital. Also, for the implementation of this law, industries were divided into three groups (military-priority, essential, and inessential), intending to force change in the direction of fund flows. The Temporary Import–Export Grading Measures Law directed prohibition or controls on import and export of specific goods and controlled consumption, manufacturing, and processing of trade-related goods. Virtually no good could escape control under it. These two laws became the basis for direct control of the economy in both the financial and the commodities markets.

Moreover, an old law, the 1918 Military Industry Mobilization Law (*Gunju Kōgyō Dōin Hō*) came into play. This law provided, in times of war or incidents, for government "control, use, or expropriation" of factories or workplaces of military industries, for government use, expropriation or prohibition of consumption, movements, or distribution of military goods, for impressment of labor, and for mandatory reporting from owners of military industries. Simultaneous with enactment of the two laws mentioned earlier, a Law Concerning Implementation of the Military Industries Mobilization Law (*Gunju Kōgyō Dōin Hō no Tekigō ni Kan Suru Hōritsu*) was passed. Enforcement orders such as the Factories and Workplaces Control Order (*Kōjō-Jigyōjō Kanri Rei*) were promulgated, and the 1918 law was enforced for the first time since its passage.

When the National General Mobilization Law was debated by the Diet in 1938, many felt that it was a product of Nazi-style control ideology. Indeed, many new bureaucrats held views supporting such controls, and it is undeniable that they expected realization of long-hoped-for controls through the use of a military incident. (For example, in the bill for national management of electric power, the views of bureaucrat Kiwao Okumura are striking.) But such ideological debate was hardly necessary. The Japanese economy in 1937 already faced a catastrophic balance of payments position. To finance the large military-related import requirements related to the war in China, it was already apparent that the indirect control methods would not be sufficient and hence that drastic, swift controls were needed.

But even after imposition of the controls the state of the economy could not improve. In 1938 and 1939 the trade controls did have some effects, with imports being held down and exports maintaining a good level. A trade surplus was even recorded but this was due to trade with the yen bloc and particularly to export expansion related to Manchurian projects in the Five-Year-Plan. Trade with non-yen-bloc countries remained in substantial deficit, and the de facto deficits were not erased; gold shipments continued and the means of payment to foreign countries reached the verge of exhaustion.

Given these new circumstances, how did the group that had drafted the Five-Year Plan for Key Industries react? At first Kanji Ishihara was in favor of improving and increasing the nation's power and had called it foolish to fight a war of attrition in China. But the war in China continued to expand and finally in September Ishiwara was replaced. General headquarters (especially the War Direction Section and later the War Direction Team, where Ishihara's influence was strong), tried to bring an early end to the fighting in China first through showing its strong desire for peace negotiations using the German ambassador to China, Oskar Trautmann, as intermediary, then by opposing the January 1938 communiqué of nonrecognition of the Kuomintang government of China. However, these schemes failed. In the background was impatience over the lack of progress in basic industries and the slowness of war preparations versus the Soviet Union.[2]

The controls of these years grew broader and broader in coverage and as a system became stronger and stronger. The logic of the system may be summarized as follows. (1) There are certain necessities for adequate military expansion, so limited funds must be preferentially channeled toward the proper industries. Thus, funds control became unavoidable. (2) There then arises the need for an import control system to ensure imports for direct military manufacturing and for facilities of the key industries that support military production. (3) These imports must be paid for within the limits of resources provided by exports, non-merchandise receipts, gold shipments, sales of foreign bonds, and other emergency measures. (4) The most important exports are cotton textiles and other light manufactures, so there is a necessity to secure imports of the raw materials for these industries. (5) Thus, the amount of imports available for privately used goods is only the amount left over after military import needs and export-industry raw material needs are sub-tracted from total import ability. A *"Materials Mobilization Plan"* (*Busshi Dōin Keikaku*) is imperative; furthermore, to channel resources to mili-tary related goods, fund controls are also needed. (6) Production of goods for consumption must be cut down, or otherwise prices will rise and not only imperil the people's livelihood but also have a deleterious effect on exports. Hence, along with adjustment of demand and supply, price controls are imperative. If the above mechanism is continued, (7) an organization for control of distribution of goods will become neces-sary. This is the reason for control companies and associations. (8) To maintain productive capacity, labor must be secured. Since the labor force has already been reduced by conscription, maintaining production requires that a new class of workers be added to the labor force. To this end "labor mobilization" and "national conscription" are needed. These points are identical with those in the "policy outline" described above but are also one degree more serious because the policy outline saw mea-sures such as improvement of national livelihood, improvement of edu-cation, provision of social security, and dealing with problems of farms and small business not as war-related measures but only as a means of raising production.

Once economic controls started in one sector, the resultant chain reac-tion forced controls on all other sectors. But the final burden devolved on private consumption (see table 10.8). Data on national income and on

---

2. For an account of the specifics of objections to the China War, see Nakamura and Hara [77], pp. 3–57.

Table 10.8. Wartime Economic Indicators

	Real GNP*	Real personal consumption expenditure†	Gross domestic fixed private capital formation*	Government purchases of goods and services*	Industrial production index (manufacturing) (1960 = 100)				Bank of Japan wholesale price index†	Retail price index, including estimate of black market prices†	Real wages†
					Total	Steel	Machinery	Textiles			
1930	135	109	10	22	21.3	9.4	9.5	45.6	88.5	—	105.9
1931	139	108	12	27	19.1	8.1	7.2	48.2	74.8	—	109.1
1932	141	108	10	31	20.2	10.0	6.5	52.2	83.0	—	105.9
1933	147	108	14	30	24.7	13.7	9.4	59.8	95.1	—	104.9
1934	162	111	24	31	26.4	16.6	9.4	65.8	97.0	—	102.9
1935	166	107	26	31	27.9	19.5	9.0	70.0	99.4	101	98.7
1936	172	110	29	31	31.5	21.9	11.4	74.9	103.6	—	97.6
1937	212	115	40	48	37.2	25.3	15.3	85.3	125.8	—	99.0
1938	219	114	41	62	38.2	29.0	16.8	70.4	132.7	—	105.0
1939	221	108	52	55	42.4	31.1	20.6	70.4	146.6	139	93.4
1940	208	97	51	57	44.3	32.4	25.0	63.7	164.1	180	81.9
1941	211	94	53	70	45.8	33.4	28.8	51.5	175.8	210	79.1
1942	214	90	57	73	44.5	35.3	29.9	40.7	191.2	273	65.9
1943	214	85	49	84	45.0	39.5	32.8	26.7	204.6	321	65.8
1944	206	70	54	84	46.2	36.9	38.6	14.2	231.9	401	60.0
1945	—	—	—	—	19.6	13.1	16.4	5.5	250.3	703	41.2

Sources: Nihon Ginkō [85], national accounts data are from Economic Planning Agency, industrial production from Ministry of International Trade and Industry, and price data from Bank of Japan, retail price index data estimates by Yūzō Morita (Cohen [15], vol. 2, p. 129). Real wage data are estimates by Junzō Yamada (Aihara [1], p. 97).

*1934–36 prices, in ¥100 million.

†1934–36 = 100.

real wages show this clearly. Even compared to the experience of Nazi Germany, the decline in consumption in Japan was quite steep. In Germany production of goods for consumption did not fall until 1941, and some products, particularly foods, even saw production rise between 1940 and 1941 (see Millward [K], p. 28). This was because Hitler's war strategy was based on blitzkriegs and on an existing military-industrial base. Moreover, in addition to the absence of a need to suppress consumption, the basic capacity of the German industrial structure was higher and technology such as liquefaction of coal allowed a lower dependence on foreign resources.

The reasons that economic controls in Japan had to be strengthened so quickly were not only those of basic underlying factors but also those of unfortunate circumstances that followed one after another. We observed above that the depression in the United States became more serious simultaneously with the outbreak of war with China. Promulgated only early in 1938, the Materials Mobilization Plan was revised in June of that year, with total import capacity lowered from ¥3.0 to 2.42 billion (see Nakamura and Hara [77], p. 305). As a result the controls on imported goods tightened sharply. The supply of cotton fabric for domestic uses was forbidden, and as of July 1 raw cotton distribution was limited to use for export products using the so-called linkage system. Similar provisions were made for leather, rubber, and other goods. Black markets naturally developed with tightened controls, and skyrocketing prices made price controls a dire necessity. Indeed, control begat control.

In 1939 economic conditions improved in the United States, but "in western Honshu, northern Kyushu, Shikoku, and Korea there occurred drought, while in Taiwan and North China floods occurred, meaning great disruptions to the production and transport of goods" (Testimony of Planning Agency Governor Takeuchi, Feb. 28, 1940, cited in Nakamura and Hara [77], p. 461). Moreover, as a result of the decline in rice production ¥100 million of foreign rice had to be imported, and even with this the shortage of rice still became serious. By December Tokyo grain dealers were reduced to less than one day's supply (Nakamura and Hara [77], p. 698). Thus, distribution and control of food products also became a real issue, and after June 1941 a ticket rationing system was begun for rice and matches.

Moreover, again according to Takeuchi, "As for coal and electric power problems, a severe drought has caused a large increase in the demand for coal of power generation grade. But the fall in supply both from the home islands and from Karafuto [Sakhalin] coupled with lower production in the yen bloc, particularly Manchuria, along with lower quality of coal—all these seriously affect all the nation's industries"

(Nakamura and Hara [77], p. 462). As a result, coal distribution controls were strengthened and electric power was rationed. Furthermore, the outbreak of war in Europe in 1939 further constrained all imports, and some were cut off completely. Prices of goods that could still be imported soared, and despite the rise in price for silk and other exportables government plans were disrupted tremendously. Under such circumstances the Materials Mobilization Plan was reformulated; new supply controls proliferated and all controls were strengthened.

In 1940 the effects of the previous year's abrogation of the United States–Japan Treaty of Commerce and Navigation surfaced. In May, with the German attack on Paris and the fall of Dunkirk, Japanese policy suddenly focused on the occupation of Southeast Asian territories in the policy of "Advance to the South" (Nanshin). Owing to the expected cut-off of all resource imports from the United States, Great Britain, and the Dutch East Indies (a major source of oil), an "Outline of Basic National Policy" (Kihon Kokusaku Yōkō) was adopted on July 26, along with an "Outline for Dealing with the Current Emergency" (Jikyoku Shori Yōkō); on July 27, former Colonial Minister Kuniaki Koiso was dispatched to the Dutch East Indies, and later followed by Minister of Commerce and Industry Ichizō Kobayashi. In preparation for the eventual controls on trade with the area, a plan was formulated in August 1940 to make emergency imports of strategic materials. Even a year earlier, in August 1939 the government had used ¥300 million (of which ¥200 million was gold from the Bank of Japan) on advance imports; this time ¥600 million was spent on gasoline and nonferrous metals among other items. In the process the gold reserves at the Bank of Japan hit rock bottom, and the difficulties of scraping together new funds from within the yen block for payments continued.

The freezing of Japanese assets in July 1941 by the United States, Great Britain, and the Netherlands was symbolic of Japan's difficulties. On hearing of the freezing of the assets, Kikusaburo Okada, then chief of the War Preparations Division of the Ministry of the Army, thought that war was the only road open to Japan. He told his division of his thoughts and ordered final preparation for war. With the embargo on oil, Okada said that "in at most two years we will not have the power to defend our position against the strong countries, ... and we will be in a position of choosing either a declining destiny for our nation or finding salvation in fighting to the death" (Nakamura and Hara [77], p. 144). It is noteworthy that the embargo brought the materials control bureaucrats, who had been "passive about understanding the nation's weak point in foreign policy," to the conclusion that war was unavoidable. It was precisely at this time that the Ministry of Commerce and Industry established a special organ "to take all measures possible to prepare various areas to deal with emergency situations," so that a bill could be enacted "to complete the preparation measures, i.e. the Ministry's troop dispatch, so to speak." These included plans for materials mobilization and production capacity expansion beginning with ocean transport, production controls, merger and rationalization of firms, repair and use of nonworking or idle capacity, preparation of substitutes for goods in shortages, rationalization of distribution structures, consumption controls, recovery of resources, and transportation policy. These plans were actually implemented one after another after the outbreak of the Pacific War.

A simple, broad sketch has been presented of wartime economic trends and the inevitability of the strengthening of economic controls, along with the effects these had on the economy, for the years up until the outbreak of the Pacific War. We shall now survey, again simply, the system of controls itself and the conditions under which it progressed.

THE DEVELOPMENT OF ECONOMIC CONTROLS

At the time of the outbreak of the war in China, the army felt that hostilities would be relatively short-lived, and even with a postponement of the capacity expansion plans the army put its powers to work expanding essential military goods supplies. This was the reason for invoking the Military Industries Mobilization Law. With mobilization there was a shortage of rifles and bullets, and the exigency of emergency imports of rifles from Italy shows the urgency of the need to expand production. Moreover, there was dire need for increases in temporary military expenditures, production increases, and stockpiling of military goods. A very large portion of military expenses of the China war, e.g., in the case of the army more than ¥2 billion between 1937 and 1942 (see Okura Shō, [111], p. 122), was applied to war materials, with military production taking a quantum leap. Such increases in production made mobilization of certain goods imperative, and for that purpose the Planning Office (Kikaku In) was established in October 1937.

The Planning Office had actually begun work in May 1937 as the Planning Agency (Kikaku Chō), but at the strong insistence of the army it was soon merged with the Office of Resources (Shigen Kyoku) and reorganized. The Planning Office was to be the "central organ for national mobilization" and was "to plan for expansion of production, adjustment of supply/demand balances, improvement of distribution, and equilibrium achievement for the balance of payments, by which processes it is expected that expansion and application of the nation's aggregate power will occur without miscalculation" (Nihon Ginkō Chōsa Kyoku, "Kokka Sōdōin Jisshi ni Kan Suru Naikaku Junrei" in [84], p.

477). Moreover, the Office of Resources, which was an organ of the Prime Minister's Office that had been established in 1927, was responsible for "preparing plans to fulfill private and military demand through the controlled application of all resources" in wartime. When the Plan for Times of Total Mobilization for wartime had to be formulated, personnel from both the army and the navy participated as administrators in the Office of Resources, which was in charge of goods mobilization for the Provisional Principles of the Plan for Times of Total Mobilization of 1932, the Emergency General Mobilization Plan of 1933, and the Second General Mobilization Plan of June 1936.

In May 1937 the Ministry of the Army requested the Office of Resources to study a general mobilization law, and a draft was produced in September. Owing to the shortness of the diet then in session, presentation was postponed until the special session of the 72d Diet, and the newly formed Planning Office combined the draft with its Production Capacity Expansion Plan and carried on the work. With Masao Taki as governor and Kazuo Aoki as vice-governor, the new Planning Office was staffed by members of the Office of Resources, the old Planning Agency, and officials from various ministries including the military, but the main roles in formulating the general mobilization law and the materials mobilization plans were played by military officers on active duty. Three committees were formed in the Planning Office, the First Committee for materials mobilization plans, the Second Committee for "investigating Japan's war-making capability based on resource considerations," and the Third Committee to "plan for economic construction in concert with military activities in China." (For details see Aritake [12], p. 382.)

The Planning Agency's first tasks were the creation of materials mobilization plans and of a general mobilization law. The Second General Mobilization Plan of the Office of Resources in 1936 included outline plans for food, iron products, nonferrous metal products, and oil. Also included were tables on supply/demand balances and plans for shortage amelioration, similar complete plans for shipping, import plans, plans for labor provision (including skilled workers, operatives, and miners), plans for transport operators, scientific mobilization, and enforcement plans. The Planning Office's plans were, for resources, the successors of the Office of Resources plans and even retained similar names. Labor, funds allocation, and trade plans were revised after the 1939 materials mobilizations, but even these revisions were actually Planning Office plans in different clothing.

But when it came time to implement the plans, the deficit in the balance of payments (as seen above) bad become serious, and consideration had to be given to allocation within import limits to direct army and navy demand on one hand and to private demand (including raw materials, equipment, and goods for production expansion for military and public sector demand) on the other. Thus, when the Materials Mobilization Plan went into effect, it took on the character of a plan to allocate important materials that in turn depended on imported raw materials. After import capability became an issue, restrictions on transportation capacity emerged and, with each passing year, economic conditions undercut the increasingly wishful plans. As seen in table 10.9 for the case of steel products, the original plan, effected plan, and actual performance grew further and further apart with every year. Capacity to supply could go nowhere but down, and original plans always had to be revised when time for implementation came. Even this simple table shows quite well the distress within the materials mobilization plans.

The National General Mobilization Law prepared by the Office of Resources was reexamined by the Planning Office, and on February 19, 1938, it was submitted to the 73d regular session of the diet after cabinet approval; it became law on March 24. The law established extremely broad national controls over labor, materials, facilities, firms, prices, and publishing, thus creating a mandate of "reliance on establishment by imperial order" for all details. The first clause of the National General Mobilization Law provided that "in times of conflict including cases of incidents which correspond to war, there shall be controlled application of all human and physical resources in such a way as to demonstrate the most efficiency in use of the total power of the nation for the purpose of achievement of national defense." The second clause dealt with materials, and the third with activities under general mobilization, with extremely broad boundaries for the definition of materials and activities. Even so, the law still provided for additional controls on materials and activities "necessary for national general mobilization" on a volitional basis through imperial order.

Clauses 4–27 provided categories of national controls by the government. A few of the essential ones follow. The fourth clause allowed impressment of the populace when needed for general mobilization, and the fifth ordered popular cooperation with general mobilization activities. The sixth made labor conditions such as wages and employment subject to official order. Clause 8 made production, repair, allocation, disposal, use, consumption, possession, and movement of materials all subject to command. Clause 9 allowed control of foreign trade, with imposition, raising, or lowering of tariffs. The tenth allowed use or expropriation of materials. The eleventh forbade or limited corporate formation, fund raising, or mergers and gave orders on the distribution of profits, management practices, and use of funds from financial institutions subject to command. Clause 13 forbade, limited, and gave orders concerning construction, expansion, and improvement of capital

Table 10.9. Planned and Actual Materials Mobilization of Ordinary Steel Products (Thousand tons)

		Supply		Allotments	
		Demand production	Total (including other)	Total military demand	Total private demand
1938	(a)	5,036	5,431	1,557	3,874
	(b)	4,523*	4,725*	1,179*	3,550*
	(c)	4,890	—	—	—
1939	(a)	5,498	6,247	1,429	4,818
	(b)	5,193	5,474	1,263	3,840
	(c)	4,657	5,096	1,157	3,539
1940	(a)	5,200	5,453	1,250	4,223
	(b)	4,613	4,825	1,381	3,422
	(c)	4,560	4,774	1,436	3,380
1941	(a)	4,645	5,054	1,803	2,952
	(b)	4,566		1,834	2,843
	(c)	4,303	4,251	2,021	2,655
1942	(a)	4,979	5,054	2,000	3,054
	(b)	4,135	—	—	—
	(c)	4,180	4,251	1,937	2,080
1943	(a)	4,122	4,220	2,100	2,937
		616†	917†		
	(b)	4,122	—	—	—
	(c)	4,196	—	—	—
1944	(a)	4,386	4,350	820	2,730
					440†
	(b)	2,791	3,348	1,403	1,937
					180†
	(c)	2,681	—	—	—
1945	(b)	403	413	248	154
1st half	(c)	325	—	—	—

Source: Keizai Antei Honbu Sangyō Kyoku [53].
*1938 revised figure.
†Supplementary drawdowns from inventories.
Notes: (a) Original plan, (b) implemented plan. (c) actual performance.

equipment. Clause 17 controlled cartels. The eighteenth ordered the formation of industry associations to aid control of firms, with participation mandatory. The nineteenth allowed command of prices, freight rates, storage charges, and insurance fees. Clause 20 limited topics and forbade sales or distribution of publications. Clause 21 ordered reporting of labor capacity. And clause 32 set penalties for noncompliance.

Prince Saionji, the only remaining elder statesman of the Meiji period, said that "the bill ignores the constitution" and advocated its defeat (see Harada [33], p. 249). And indeed, the government used the bill to try to get rights equivalent to a comprehensive enabling act. The government thereafter was able to control the economy through imperial orders. Along with promulgation of the law (on April 1) and enforcement (from May 5), the old Military Industries Mobilization Law and the laws applying it to the China Incident (as the war in China was called) were rescinded, and the Factory and Workplaces Control Order (an imperial order), based on the general mobilization law, was enforced. The Temporary Funds Adjustment Law and the Temporary Import–Export Grading Measures Law remained in force, and further tightening of materials mobilization aimed at strengthening controls was based primarily on the latter law. In this sense the National General Mobilization Law was, until about 1940, of less importance than is generally believed.

Because there is not space here for a detailed description concerning the broadening and strengthening of controls, let us list some of the main ones promulgated between the outbreak of war in China and the end of 1941. Most of the early imperial orders implemented under the general mobilization law dealt with labor. But the April 1939 employment controls and the July 1939 national impressment order were epoch-making in their migration and redistribution provisions. Most notable was the large number of people who were forced to change jobs due to carte-blanche call-up orders. In November 1938 the army pressed for the implementation of both profit ceilings and forced loans as provided for in clause 11, and this occasioned a bitter exchange between Finance Minister Shigeaki Ikeda and the Minister of the Army. Ikeda was strongly opposed to both measures. In the end a compromise emerged whereby profits were limited to a maximum of 10% and the issue of forced loans was set aside for further study. (See Nihon Ginkō [83], pp. 610–11.) Moreover, under the sixth and nineteenth clauses, a wage/price freeze was ordered as an anti-inflation move in October 1939 with wages and prices not to rise above the level of September 18. But the measure was so strong that it was highly criticized. However, these steps were only the beginning, and after 1940 the network of direct controls was broadened.

On one hand the pressures of supply and demand due to the materials mobilization program made direct control over industry inevitable and the Temporary Import–Export Grading Measures Law became the basis for these controls. The process of enforcement of the law is made clear in the Time Line of Economic Controls (appendix to this chapter). Looking at the time line, we see that the controls were at first applied only to cotton, wool, rubber, copper, steel, and other such imported raw materials but soon expanded and became generalized to cover fertilizer, oil, and finally fodder and leather. With the proliferation of controls, authority over those not complying became an inevitable problem, and in the last half of 1938 the "economic police" made their debut.

Nevertheless, as the disequilibria caused by progressions of controls became more violent, it was only normal for black market activity to increase. Malignant varieties of this activity were prevalent, and there was even a case of some Osaka cotton wholesalers who, after the cotton manufacturers sales ban of June 29, 1938, chartered a ship to hide the forbidden items by sailing through the Inland Sea for three months hoping to escape the watch of the economic police (see Arisawa [10], p. 339). But there were also many pitiable cases when the regulations were simply not known and the police still cracked down hard on violators. In the bitter words of Judge Takeshi Osatake, "Difficult and unclear controls are promulgated which ignore national conditions and trade practices, and which go against the logic of supply and demand. These are enforced on the populace without enough time having been provided to inform people and to make preparations to comply, but with stiff penalties to force compliance. These circumstances can certainly not be blamed merely on aiming at the perfection of the controls" (Nakamura and Hara [77], p. 705).

Another problem that developed in this era was controls over funding under the Temporary Funds Adjustment Law. Its enforcement began after October 1937 and lasted until the Pacific War years. The boundaries of control under this law included loans by financial institutions, flotations by securities companies, establishment of enterprises, capital increase or merger, and change of objective for corporations. The amounts of funds affected were ¥ 1.3 billion in 1937, 2.8 billion in 1938, 4.5 billion in 1939 and 1940, 4.4 billion in 1941, 5.5 billion in 1942, 11.6 billion in 1943, and 10.3 billion in 1944. Furthermore the skewing of allocations under the law to Class A, i.e., military or related fields, was obvious, with 67.7% of the total approved between September 1937 and March 1940 going to them, with 25.2% going to Class B priority industries, and a mere 6.1% going to Class C industries. Looking by industrial sector at the funds going from financial institutions to industry during the same period, machinery and equipment industries received 30.7%, metals industries 20.8%, chemical industries 10.7%, and weapons and parts industries 5.7% (subtotal of 67.9%); meanwhile, textiles received 4.8% and foods 1.2% (see Hara [31], pp. 70–73).

As can be seen from the above description, the controls were not so much plans as ex post facto responses to conditions, and there were many cases where controls had no positive reason for existing. The final result of these policies was that actual performance dropped below levels planned in the materials mobilization plans, as reflected in the continued diminution of the scale of planned output levels.

What most clearly demonstrates the conditions of the times is the sad

Table 10.10. Production Capacity Expansion: Plans and Performance

		Ordinary steel products (thousands)	Synthetic oil (kiloliters)	Aluminum (tons)
1938	(a)	4,615	38,000	19,000
	(b)	4,615	38,000	19,000
	(c)	4,891	23,082	22,118
1939	(a)	5,630	74,000	29,200
	(b)	5,719	68,274	33,448
	(c)	4,657	29,436	30,840
1940	(a)	6,280	159,000	39,100
	(b)	5,200	88,700	46,854
	(c)	4,560	40,202	41,889
1941	(a)	7,260	536,000	126,400
	(b)	4,710	73,300	73,917
	(c)	4,303	57,567	71,747
1942	(a)	—	—	—
	(b)	4,979	162,000	124,110
	(c)	4,135	78,879	103,075
1943	(a)	—	—	—
	(b)	4,250	160,200	151,869
	(c)	4,196	107,589	141,084
1944	(a)	—	—	—
	(b)	2,992	—	126,744
	(c)	2,681	122,523	110,343
1945	(a)	—	—	—
	(b)	—	53,620	16,000
	(c)	—	—	8,896

Source: Keizai Antei Hombu Sangyō Kyoku [53].
Note: (a) Four-year plan, (b) implemented plan, (c) actual performance (total empire).

fate of the Production Capacity Expansion Plan (*Seisanryoku Kakujū Keikaku*), which had been inaugurated with such fervor under the Five-Year Plan for Key Industries. After a preliminary plan was formulated by the Ministry of Commerce and Industry during the Hayashi cabinet, the Planning Office took over and produced a draft plan in January 1938, completed its First Production Capacity Expansion Plan (draft) in April 1938 and a second draft in October. In December a final plan was finished, and it was adopted by the cabinet in January 1939. But in the year and a half that passed during the process, the environment surrounding the plans changed greatly. That is, materials mobilization plans were implemented and constraints on capacity expansion plans were added by shrinking import capability.

The army's plans were criticized by the Ministry of Commerce and Industry as having a scale of production of military goods that was too large, with levels of production that could not be maintained in peacetime. With the prospect of war and of shortages of productive capacity for military goods, controls based on import constraints strengthened further. Let us end this chapter by simply showing, in table 10.10, the changes in target levels of the Production Capacity Expansion Plan and mourning the large scale of the decreases.

Once started, the economic controls that began under the three principles of Kaya and Yoshino could not, particularly when combined with the lengthening of the war, follow any course except self-perpetuating expansion and strengthening. But even so, the plans did enable Japan, with no help from abroad and an extremely poor position both in natural resources and in productive capacity, to endure a war that lasted from 1937 to 1945. In this sense the controls did enjoy a measure of "success." But this was the same process that destroyed the lives of the people. Hiromi Arisawa, doyen of Japanese economists of the time, has written about 1936:

> I often got together with [political journalist] Tsunego Baba and [freelance writer] Nyozekan Hasegawa in seminars and such, and they would say it was economists' job to tell when expanded military expenditures just could not expand anymore. But I used to say that an economy has a lot of flexibility, and that, for example, a 10% cut in the national living standard could squeeze out about ¥1.5 billion for military expenditures, so the limits could not be drawn so strictly. The real question was whether people could endure the lowered living standard, and this was a political problem: unless politicians stood firm there would be no solution. (Arisawa [6], pp. 162–63)

This prediction proved unfortunately accurate, and the "flexibility" of the livelihood of the people was surprising. This flexibility was the secret of success for controls, but a tragedy for the Japanese people.

APPENDIX TO CHAPTER 10: □ TIMELINE OF ECONOMIC CONTROLS AFTER THE CHINA INCIDENT

Note: All dates are given in the form year/month/day.

1937	8	3	Promulgation and enforcement of Revised Usury Control Order
	9	10	Promulgation of Revised Foreign Exchange Control Law (ordering sale to Bank of Japan of gold, foreign exchange, and so forth.)
			Promulgation and Limited enforcement (with full enforcement from 38/2/27 of the Temporary Funds Adjustment Law and the Temporary Import/Export Grading Measures Law
	10	11	Promulgation and enforcement of temporary import and export approval rules
			Promulgation and enforcement of wool and staple fiber mixing rules
			Promulgation and enforcement of·approval rules for use of steel in construction
	11	6	Promulgation (with enforcement from 37/11/10 of copper use control rules
	12	3	Rubber Manufacturers' Association enforces natural rubber distribution controls (using a stamp system)
	12	27	Promulgation of cotton and staple fiber mixing rules (enforced 38/2/1 and abandoned 38/6/29
1938	1	7	Establishment of Raw Cotton Import Control Association
	1	15	Promulgation and enforcement of Temporary Fertilizer Distribution Control Order
	1	17	Activation of the Military Industry Mobilization Law, with military taking control of some factories
	2	11	Promulgation of orders from the Ministry of Commerce and Industry on plant and equipment investment in the textile industry (approval system for new investments)
	3	1	Promulgation and enforcement of rules to control cotton thread distribution (stamp system)
	3	7	Promulgation and enforcement of rules directing sales of kerosine and heavy oil (stamp system)

3 30 Promulgation of Feed Distribution Control Law (enforced from 38/10/15

4 1 Promulgation of Total National Mobilization Law (enforced from 38/5/5)
Promulgation and enforcement of controls on distribution and increased production of ammonium sulfate

4 6 Promulgation of Electric Power Administration Order and Japan Electric Power Transmission Company Law (creating national control of electric power)

4 22 Establishment of export approval system (i.e., de facto export termination) for phosphoric acid (*karinsan*), lime nitrate (*ishibai chisso*), distributed fertilizer, synthetic fertilizer, and potassium chloride (*kari-en*)
Promulgation of Price Committee Order and beginning of Price Committee activities

4 25 Promulgation of rules controlling manufacture of steel and pig iron castings (enforced from 38/5/14)

5 4 Promulgation and enforcement of the Factories and Workplaces Control Order (activation of clause 13 of the Total National Mobilization Law)

5 17 Activation of controls over the Lightbulb Exporters Association

5 20 Promulgation of rules directing sales prices for cotton thread (enforced from 38/5/22, with effective administered price)

6 13 Enforcement for light and sundry industries of the export linkage system (whereby imported raw materials were distributed only for use in export products)

6 15 Promulgation of rules directing sales prices for staple fiber and thread

6 29 Promulgation of rules to control and direct production, processing, and sales of cotton products in order to secure cotton thread for export
Promulgation of textile product pricing control rules

7 1 Enforcement of export linkage system in cotton fabrics
Promulgation and enforcement of rules controling use of leather, sales prices of leather products, and distribution of leather (latter enforced from 38/8/1)

7 9 Promulgation and enforcement of rules controlling sales prices of commodities (i.e., beginning of blanket administered price system)

			Promulgation and enforcement of Rubber Distribution Control Order and of conditions on controls of use of rubber
	7	20	Promulgation and enforcement of rules concerning machine tool supply controls
	8	3	Ministry of Welfare announces unemployment of 390,000 as result of materials mobilization plans
	8	24	Promulgation and enforcement of School Graduate Use Control Order (activating clause 6 of the Total National Mobilization Law)
	8	27	Activation of controls on export of silk thread
	9	19	Promulgation of Coal Distribution Control Rules (enforcement from 38/10/1)
	11	2	Enforcement of fertilizer distribution controls
			Establishment of Scrap Iron Distribution Control Association
	11	18	Activation of clause 11 of Total National Mobilization Law, controlling profit distribution by firms, with up to 10% freely distributed and constraints thereafter
	11	21	Promulgation of rules controlling scrap iron distribution (enforced from 38/12/1)
	11	22	Promulgation of white rice control rules (enforced from 39/1/1)
	11	25	Promulgation of Wool Weaving Control Order (enforced from 38/12/20)
	12	16	Promulgation and enforcement of feed import control rules
1939	1	7	Promulgation of National Occupation Abilities Notification Order (enforced 39/1/21, according to clause 21 of Total National Mobilization Law)
	1	10	Enforcement of new rules on delivery of documents on export related raw materials and of rule banning other use of raw materials originally meant for export goods (special export linkage system)
	1	23	Promulgation of thread distribution rules (enforced from 39/2/1, with abolition of cotton thread distribution control rules)
	1	30	Promulgation and enforcement of Seamen's Occupational Capability Notification Order (clause 21 of Total National Mobilization Law)
	2	8	Ministry of Commerce and Industry reports unemployment of 374,600 in sacrificed industries, of whom 22,500 had changed jobs, changed occupations, or returned to farms

2   7   United States enforces embargo on aluminum shipments to Japan

3   30   Activation of clause 6 in Total National Mobilization Law, with promulgation of rules on industrial employment and hiring control orders
Activation of clause 22 in Total National Mobilization Law, with promulgation of School Skills Cultivation Order and Factory and Workplace Skills Cultivation Order

4   1   Promulgation and enforcement of Corporate Profits Distribution and Fund Raising Order (ordered funding system), according to clause 11 of the Total National Mobilization Law

4   12   Promulgation of Rice Distribution Control Order (enforced from 39/5/1)

4   14   Enforcement by Ministry of Finance of forced savings system through paycheck deductions at all factories

4   27   Decision on price control network by the Central Price Committee, with the objectives of lowering prices to international levels and of augmenting and rationalizing administered prices

5   31   Promulgation of scrap and powdered rubber distribution control system (enforced 6/1/39)

6   19   Establishment of the Federation of Industrial Associations for Wool Weaving Adjustment

6   23   Revision and strengthening of Ministry of Commerce rules concerning textile industry investment

7   1   Promulgation of Total Mobilization of Operations and Enterprise Investment Order, according to Total National Mobilization Law clause 16 (enforced from 39/7/10)

7   8   Promulgation of the National Draft Order (Total National Mobilization Law clause 4, enforced from 39/7/15)

7   26   Establishment of rules controlling steel industry investment (with an approval system for small producers; enforcement from 39/8/10), based on clause 28 of Total National Mobilization Law

7   27   United States announces six months' notice for abrogation of United States–Japan Commerce and Navigation Treaty

8   5   Promulgation of rules controlling distribution of industrial sweet potatoes (used as alcohol raw material) (enforced from 39/8/20)

8   16   Promulgation of rules on coal sales controls

8   19   Activation of Dividends Control Order (strengthening controls on firm management)

8   14   Enforcement of nationwide controls on electric power supply in response to a worsening coal and power shortage

8   25   Activation of clause 14 of the Rice and Grains Distribution Control Law to control rice prices

8   30   Determination of enforcement framework for price controls

9   23   Promulgation of rules on oil controls and establishment of Cooperative Oil Sales Corporation

9   27   Promulgation of rules on control of materials production

9   28   Promulgation of rules on control of steel distribution

10   3   Promulgation and enforcement of the Temporary Fertilizer Distribution Control Law

10   18   Promulgation of the Military Goods Industries and Workplaces Examination Order (enforced 39/10/20, in accordance with clause 19 of the Total National Mobilization Law)

Promulgation of the Electric Power Adjustment Order (enforced 39/10/20, in accordance with clause 8 of the Total National Mobilization Law)

Promulgation of the Price Control Order (enforced 39/10/20; the order forbade raising prices, wages, and so forth above the level of 39/9/18 and was in accordance with clause 19 of the Total National Mobilization Law)

Promulgation of the Temporary Wage Measures Order and the Temporary Employee Compensation Measures Order (enforced from 39/10/20, pegging wages at 39/9/18 levels, in accordance with clause 6 of the Total National Mobilization law)

11   21   Promulgation and enforcement of the Marine Navigation Skills Cultivation Order (based of clause 22 of the Total National Mobilization Law)

12   6   Promulgation of the Tenancy Fee Control Order (enforced 39/12/11, pegging fees at the 39/9/18 level, in accordance with clause 19 of the Total National Mobilization Law)

12   8   Strengthening of trade controls, with 70 more export items and 54 more import items placed under control

12	16	Promulgation of the Mobilization Materials Use and Expropriation Order (enforced 39/12/20, in accordance with clause 10 of the Total National Mobilization Law)
12	20	Promulgation of rules controlling charcoal distribution (enforced 39/12/25)
12	27	Promulgation of the Rice Distribution Adjustment Order
12	29	Promulgation of the Factories and Workplaces Use and Expropriation order and of the Land and Structures Administration, Use, and Expropriation Order (enforced 40/2/1, in accordance with clause 13 of the Total National Mobilization Law)
1940	1	9	Promulgation and enforcement of rules controlling distribution of silk thread
	2	1	Promulgation of the Land Transport Control Order (enforced 41/11/20)
			Promulgation and enforcement of the Marine Transport Control Order (clauses 3, 8, 16, and 19 of the Total National Mobilization Law)
			Promulgation of the Youth Employment Control Order (enforced 40/3/1, based on clause 6 of the Total National Mobilization Law)
	2	9	Promulgation of rules on controlling distribution of textile products (partially enforced from 40/2/26)
			Public pricing of soda ash and caustic soda
	2	13	Promulgation and enforcement of rules controlling rice distribution
	3	13	Promulgation of production controls rules on ammonium sulfate
	3	15	Promulgation of rules on soda industry chemicals distribution (enforced from 40/3/20)
	3	30	Promulgation of rules for steel supply and demand control (enforced from 40/4/10)
			Promulgation of the Law Creating the Special Account for Charcoal Supply and Demand Adjustment (enforced 40/4/1)
	4	1	Creation of the Price Countermeasures Commission and the Price Formation Committee (and abolition of the Central Price Committee)
	4	8	Promulgation of the Coal Distribution Control Law (enforced 40/4/12)
	4	10	Activation of the Rice Control and Shipments Order

6   1   Establishment of a stamp system for sugar and matches
Start of distribution controls on beer to private houses

6   10   Promulgation and enforcement of rules on controlled distribution of wheat products

7   3   Promulgation of the Steel-Use Raw Materials Import Distribution Control Order (enforced from 40/7/8, based on clause 8 of the Total National Mobilization Law)

7   6   Promulgation of rules controlling sale and manufacture of luxuries

7   8   Promulgation of rules controlling distribution of scrap textiles

7   10   Promulgation and enforcement of rules controlling distribution of fruits

7   13   Promulgation of rules controlling distribution of wheat (enforced from 40/7/20)

7   30   Promulgation of Household Fuel Materials Supply and Demand Adjustment Rules (enforced 40/8/5)

7   31   Promulgation of Coal Distribution Adjustment Rules (enforced 40/10/1)

8   8   Promulgation of rules controlling distribution of wheat flour (enforced 40/8/20)

8   20   Promulgation of temporary rules controlling distribution of rice (enforced 40/9/10)

9   21   Promulgation of rules controlling distribution of bicycles, bicycle parts, and bicycle accessories (enforced 40/11/10)

10   4   Promulgation of rules controlling distribution of sugar and matches (enforced 40/10/15)

10   19   Promulgation of revised Wage Control Order and the Seamen's Compensation Control Order (enforced 40/10/20, based on clause 11 of the Total National Mobilization Law)
Promulgation of Corporate Management Order and the Bank Funds Application Order (enforced 40/10/20, based on clause 11 of the Total National Mobilization Law)

10   21   Promulgation of the Land and Housing Rent Control Order (enforced 40/10/20, based on clause 19 of the Total National Mobilization Law)
Promulgation of the Seamen's Draft Order (enforced

40/10/22, based on clause 4 of the Total National Mobilization Law)

10   24   Promulgation of rules on rice administration (enforced on 40/11/1, meaning national administration of rice)

10   25   Promulgation and enforcement of rules controlling distribution of eggs

10   29   Promulgation of rules controlling distribution of soybeans and soybean oil (enforced 40/11/5)

11   9   Promulgation of Employee Movement Prevention Order (enforced 40/11/20, based on clause 6 of the Total National Mobilization Law)

11   14   Promulgation and enforcement of rules controlling distribution of non-rice grains

11   21   Promulgation of the Residential Construction Price Control Order (enforced 40/11/25, based on clause 19 of the Total National Mobilization Law)

1941   3   7   Promulgation of the National Labor Passbook Law (enforced 41/10/1)

3   13   Promulgation of the Silk Thread Industry Control Law and the Lumber Materials Control Law (enforced 41/6/1)

3   31   Promulgation of the Essential Commodities Control Order

4   1   Enforcement of rice distribution ration book system in Tokyo and Osaka
Promulgation of fish distribution control rules
Promulgation of distribution controls on charcoal used for gas

5   14   Promulgation of the Trade Control Order (enforced 41/5/15, based on clause 9 of the Total National Mobilization Law)

6   1   Enforcement of rules controlling distribution of hardened oil

6   9   Promulgation and enforcement of new rules controlling distribution of wheat
Enforcement of general administration of sales of wheat

7   2   Establishment of the Fish Control Federation

7   11   Promulgation of rules controlling distribution and manufacture of wheat flour

7   15   Revision of rules controlling usury (banning tie-in sales and hoarding)

9   15   Enforcement of national administration of rice, with government purchase of all administered rice

9   17   Promulgation of Port Transport Industry Controls (enforced 41/9/20, based on clause 18 of the Total National Mobilization Law)

9   20   Promulgation of rules controlling the distribution of foods

10   4   Promulgation of rules controlling the distribution of grains

10   8   Controls on the use of male youth (i.e., indication of jobs for which female labor was to be used)

11   22   Promulgation of the National Patriotic Labor Association Order (enforced 41/12/1, based on clause 5 of the Total National Mobilization Law)

12   8   Promulgation of the Labor Adjustment Order (enforced 41/1/10, based on clause 6 of the Total National Mobilization Law)

12   11   Promulgation of the Corporation Approval Order (enforced 41/12/13, based on clause 16 of the Total National Mobilization Law)

12   13   Promulgation and enforcement of the Newpaper Firms Order (based on Clauses 16 and 18 of the Total National Mobilization Law)

12   16   Promulgation and enforcement of the Materials Control Order (based on clause 8 of the Total National Mobilization Law)

Publications Cited

WESTERN LANGUAGE SOURCES

A. Cassel, G. *The Downfall of the Gold Standard*. Clarendon Press, 1936.

B. Department of Commerce (U.S.). *Historical Statistics of the United States*, 1976.

C. Dore, Ronald. *Education in Tokugawa Japan*. Routledge and Kegan Paul, 1965.

D. Hirschmeier, J. *The Origins of Entrepreneurship in Meiji Japan*. Harvard University Press, 1964.

E. Imlah, A. H. "British Balance of Payment and Export of Capital 1816–1913. *Economic History Review*, 5, no. 2 (1952): 208–39.

F. Kuznets, S. "Quantitative Aspects of Economic Growth of Nations, VII— The Share and Structure of Consumption. *Economic Development and Cultural Change* 5 (1961): 3–92.

G. Maddison, Angus, *Economic Growth in Japan and USSR*. George Allen and Unwin Ltd., 1969.

H. _____. "Growth and Fluctuation in the World Economy, 1870–1960." Banca Nazionale del Lavoro, 1962.

I. Mitchell, B. R. *Abstract of British Historical Statistics*. Cambridge University Press, 1962.

J. _____. *European Historical Statistics*. McMillan, 1975.

K. Milward, Allan S. *The German Economy at War*. Athrone Press, 1962.

L. Moulton, Harold G. *Japan: An Economic and Financial Appraisal*. Brookings Institution, 1931.

M. Nakamura, James. *Agricultural Production and the Economic Development of Japan 1873–1922*. Princeton, 1966.

N. Ohkawa Kazushi. *The Growth Rate of Japanese Economy since 1878*. Kinokuniya Book Store, 1957.

O. Ohkawa, Kazushi, and Shinohara, Miyohei, with Larry Meissner. *Patterns of Japanese Economic Development: A Quantitative Appraisal*. Yale University Press, 1979.

JAPANESE LANGUAGE SOURCES

1. Aihara, Shigeru, ed. *Kindai Nihon Shihonshugi Taikei IV Rōdō* (Outline of Modern Japanese Capitalism, vol. IV, Labor). Kōbundō, 1958.

2. Akimoto, Hiroya. "Hagi-han no Zaisei to Keizai Seisaku" (Public Finance

and Economic Policy of Hagi Province). Shakai Keizai Shigaku, February 1977.

3. Akita Ginkō (Akita Bank). *Akita Ginkō Hachi-jū-nen Shi* (An Eighty Year History of the Akita Bank), 1959.

4. Ando, Yoshio, ed. "Kindai Nihon Keizai Shi Yōran" (A Handbook of Modern Japan Economic History). Tōkyō Daigaku Shuppan Kai, 1975.

5. Aoki, Nobuteru. *Baba Eiichi Den* (A Biography of Eiichi Baba). Eiichi Baba Memorial Society, 1945.

6. Arisawa, Hiromi. *Gakumon to Shisō to Ningen to* (Scholarship, Thought, and Acquaintances). Mainichi Shimbun Sha, 1957.

7. _____, ed. *Gendai Nihon Sangyō Kōza II* (Studies in Contemporary Japanese Industry, vol. II). Iwanami Shoten, 1959.

8. _____, ed. *Gendai Nihon Sangyō Kōza III* (Studies in Contemporary Japanese Industry, vol. III), appendix table. Iwanami Shoten, 1960.

9. _____, ed. *Gendai Nihon Sangyō Kōza V* (Studies in Contemporary Japanese Industry, vol. V). Iwanami Shoten, 1960.

10. _____, ed. *Nihon Sangyō Hyaku-nen Shi* (A Hundred Year History of Japanese Industry). Iwanami Shoten, 1966.

11. _____ and Nakamura, Takafusa. *Kokumin Shotoku* (National Income). Chūō Keizai Sha, 1955.

12. Aritake, Shūji. *Shōwa Okura Shō Gaishi, Chū-kan* (A History of the Ministry of Finance, middle volume), 1969.

13. Asakura, Kōkichi. *Meiji Zenki Nihon Kinyū Kōzō Shi* (A History of Japanese Financial Structure in the Early Meiji Period). Iwanami Shoten, 1961.

14. Asakura, Kōkichi, and Nishiyama, Chiaki. *Nihon Keizai no Tsūkateki Bunseki: 1868–1970* (Monetary Analysis of the Japanese Economy, 1868–1970). Sobun Sha, 1974.

15. Cohen, J. B. (trans. Ōchi Hyōe). *Senji, Sengō no Nihon Keizai.* Originally published in English as *The Japanese Economy in War and Reconstruction* (University of Minnesota Press, 1949). Iwanami Shoten, 1950–51.

16. Chiang, Ping-Kun. *Taiwan Chiso Kaisei no Kenkyū* (A Study of Land Tax Reform in Taiwan). Tōkyō Daigakn Shuppan Kai, 1974.

17. Chō, Yukio. *Nihon Keizai Shishō Shi Kenkyū* (Studies in the History of Economic Thought of Japan). Mirai Sha. 1963.

18. Dai-Nippon Bōseki Rengō Kai (All Japan Spinning Federation). *Menshi Bōseki Jijō Sankō Sho* (Reference Materials on Conditions in Cotton Spinning), various years.

19. Denda, Isao. *Kindai Nihon Keizai Shisō no Kenkyū* (Studies in the Economic Thought of Modern Japan). Mirai Sha, 1962.

20. Ehime Ken (Ehime Prefecture). Ehime Ken Tōkei Sho (Statistical Yearbook of Ehime Prefecture), 1918, 1920.

21. Emi, Kōichi. "Meiji, Taishō, Shōwa no Zaisei Seisaku" (Fiscal Policy in the Meiji, Taishō and Shōwa Eras). In Tachi Ryūichirō and Watanabe Tsunehiko, eds., *Keizai Seichō to Zaisei Kinyū* (Economic Growth and Fiscal and Monetary Policy). Iwanami Shoten, 1965.

22. Emi, Kōichi, and Shionoya, Yūichi. *Zaisei Shishutsu* (Fiscal Expenditure). Tōyō Keizai Shimpō Sha, 1966 (Long-Term Economic Statistics [LTES 7]).

22a. Fujino, Shōzaburō. Keizai Kenkyū Shiryō 41–4: Kikai Kōgyō no Junkan-teki Hendō to Hatten no Bunseki (Economic Research Materials 41–4: Analysis of Development and Cyclical Fluctuation in the Machinery Industry). Published by Kikai Shinkō Kyōkai Keizai Kenkyū Sho (Economic Research Institute of the Machinery Promotion Society), 1967.

23. Fujino, Shōzaburō. Nihon no Keiki Junkan—Junkanteki Hatten Katei no Rironteki, Tōkeiteki, Rekishiteki Bunseki (Business Cycles in Japan—Theoretical, Statistical, and Historical Analysis of the Cyclical Growth Process). Keisō Shobō, 1965.

24. _____, and Ono, Akira. Sen-i Kōgyō (Textile Industry). Tōyō Keizai Shimpō Sha (LTES 11), 1978.

25. Fujita, Takeo. Shōwa Zaisei Shi XIV, Chihō Zaisei (Shōwa Period Fiscal History, vol. XIV, Local Finance). Tōyō Keizai Shimpō Sha, 1954.

26. Fukai, Eigo. Kaiko Shichi-jūnen (A Retrospective on Seventy Years). Iwanami Shoten, 1941.

27. Furushima, Toshio. Sangyo Shi III (History of Industries III). Yamakawa Shuppan Sha, 1966.

28. Gifu Ken (Gifu Prefecture). Gifu Ken Tōkei Sho (Statistics Book of Gifu Prefecture), 1913, 1921.

29. Gotō, Shinichi. Nihon no Kinyū Tōkei (Financial Statistics of Japan). Tōyō Keizai Shimpō Sha, 1970.

30. Hara, Akira. "Nikka Jihen Ki no Kokusai Shūshi" (The Balance of Payments during the China Incident). In Shakai Keizai Shigaku 34, no. 6 (1969): 44–77.

31. Hara, Akira. "Shikin Tōsei to Sangyō Kinyū—Nikka Jihenki ni Okeru Seisan Kakujū Seisaku no Kinyūteki Sokumen" (Funds Control and Industrial Finance—The Financial Aspects of Production Expansion Policy during the China Incident). In Tochi Seido Shi Gakkai (Society of Land System History), Tochi Seido Shi Gaku no. 34, 1967, pp. 52–74.

32. Harada, Kumao (as told by), Saionji-Kō to Seikyoku, Dai-go Kan (Prince Saionji and Political Affairs, vol. 5). Iwanami Shoten, 1951.

33. _____. Saionji-Kō to Seikyoku, Dai-roku Kan (Prince Saionji and Political Affairs, vol. 6). Iwanami Shoten, 1951.

34. Hata, Ikuhiko. Gun Fashizumu Undō Shi (A History of the Military Facism Movement). Kawaide Shobō, 1962.

35. Hayami, Akira. Kinsei Nōson no Rekishi Jinkōgakuteki Kenkyu (Historical Demography of Early Modern Farm Villages). Tōyō Keizai Shimpō Sha, 1973.

36. Henmi, Kenzō. "Nōgyō Yūgyō Jinkō no Tōhata Suikei" (Estimates of Agriculturally Employed Population). In Seiichi Tōi, Kazushi Ohkawa, and Shigeto Kawano, eds., Nihon no Keizai to Nōgyō (The Economy of Japan and Agriculture). Iwanami Shoten, 1956.

37. Hirano, Yoshitarō. Nihon Shihonshugi Shakai no Kikō (Mechanisms of Japanese Capitalist Society). Iwanami Shoten, 1934.

38. Hotta, Shōsō. Kannō Kinnosuke Jūkō Shigeyuki (The Hard Road of Kanno Kinnosuke). Kanno Kinnosuke Biography Compilation Society, 1940.

39. Hyōgo Ken (Hyōgo Prefecture). Hyōgo Ken Tōkei Sho (Statistical Yearbook of Hyōgo Prefecture), 1922, 1929.

40. Ibaraki Ken (Ibaraki Prefecture). *Ibaraki Ken Tōkei Sho* (Statistical Yearbook of Ibaraki Prefecture), 1921.
41. Imaizumi, Kaichiro. *Tetsukuzu Roku* (Annals of Scrap Iron). Kōseikai Shuppan Bu, 1930.
42. Inoue, Junnosuke. *Inoue Junnosuke Ronsō, Dai 1 Kan* (Treatises of Inoue Junnosuke, vol. I). Inoue Junnosuke Compilation Committee, 1933.
43. Ishikawa, Junkichi. *Sōgō Kokusaku to Kyōiku Kaikaku* (A General National Policy and the Education Reform Bill). Shimizu Shotō, 1960.
44. Ishizaki, Tadao. "Sangyō Kōzō to Shūgyō Kōzō" (Industrial Structure and Employment Structure). In Shōwa Dōjin Kai, *Kōyō no Igi to Taisaku* (Full Employment for Japan and Policies to Achieve It). Shōwa Dōjin Kai, 1956).
45. Itō, Mitsuharu. "Nijū Kōzō Ron no Tenbō to Hansei" (Prospects and Critiques of the Dual Structure Theory). In Kawaguchi Hiroshi, ed., *Nihon Keizai no Kiso Kōzō* (Basic Structures of the Japanese Economy, Shujūsha, 1963.
46. Izumiyama, Sanroku. *Tora Daijin ni Naru Made* (To Become a Drunken Minister). Shi Kigensha, 1953.
47. Kagawa Ken (Kagawa Prefecture). *Kagawa Ken Tōkei Sho* (Statistical Yearbook of Kagawa Prefecture), 1918, 1925.
48. Kajinishi, Mitsuhaya; Oshima, Kiyoshi; Katō, Toshihiko; and Ōuchi, Tsutomu. *Nihon Shihonshugi no Seiritsu* (The Establishment of Japanese Capitalism). Tokyo Daigaku Shupan Kai, 1955.
49. Kanda, Kōhei. "Denso Kaikaku Kengi" (A Proposal of Rice Field Tax Reform). In Hyōe Ōuchi and Nobuo Tsuchiya, *Meiji Zenki Zaisei Keizai Shiryō Shūsei, Dai Nana Kan* (A Collection of Sources on Early Meiji Period Finance and Economics, vol. 7). Meiji Bunken Shiryō Kankō Kai, 1963.
50. Kaya, Okinori. *Watashi no Rirekisho, Dai-19-shū* (My Personal History, vol. 19). Nihon Keizai Shimbun Sha, 1963.
51. Kayō, Nobufumi, ed. *Nihon Nōgyō no Kiso Tōkei* (Basic Statistics of Japanese Agriculture). Nōrin Suisan Gyō Seisansei Kōjō Kaigi, 1963.
52. Kazahaya, Yasoji. *Nihon Shakai Seisaku Shi* (A History of Social Policy in Japan). Nihon Hyōron Sha, 1937.
53. Keizai Antei Hombu Sangyō Kyoku (Economic Stabilization Headquarters, Industrial Office). *Ji Shōwa Jūsan Nendo Shi Shōwa Nijū Nendo Busshi Dōin Keikaku Sōkatsu Hyō* (General Tables on Materials Mobility Plans from F.Y. 1938 to F.Y. 1945), 1951.
54. Keizai Kikaku Chō Tōkei Ka (Statistics Division, Economic Planning Agency). *Nihon no Keizai Tōkei* (Economic Statistics of Japan). Shisei Dō, 1964.
55. Kinukawa Taiichi, *Hompō Menshi Bōseki Shi, Dai-Yon Kan* (A History of the National Cotton Spinning Industry, vol. 4). Nihon Mengyō Kurabu, 1939.
56. Kinyū Kenkyū Kai (Financial Research Society). *Waga Kuni ni Okeru Ginkō Gōdō no Taisei* (The Trend to Bank Mergers in the Nation), 1935. Included as part of Nihon Ginkō Chōsa Kyoku (Bank of Japan Research Department) *Nihon Kinyū Shi Shiryō Shōwa Hen Dai 24 Kan* (Sources of Japanese Financial History, Showa Edition), vol. 24, 1969.
57. Kōgaku Kai (Industrial Studies Society). Nihon Kōgyō Taikan (Overview of Japanese Industry). Kōsei Kai Shuppan Bu, 1925.

58. Kokusai Renmei Iinkai (League of Nations Committee) (trans. League of Nations Secretariat, Tokyo Office). Sekai Nōgyō Kyōkō (World Agricultural Panic), 1931.

59. Komiyama, Takuji. *Nihon Chūshō Kōgyō Kenkyū* (Studies of Small and Medium Industry in Japan). Chūō Kōron Sha, 1941.

60. Mayet, Paul. *"Nihon Nōmin no Hihei Oyobi Sono Kyūjisaku"* (The Impoverishment of Japanese Farmers and Policies for Their Relief). In Sakurai Takeo, ed., *Meiji Nōgyō Ronshū* (Papers on Meiji Era Agriculture). Sōgen Sha, 1955.

61. Minami Manshū Tetsudō Kaisha Chōsa Bu (Southern Manchurian Railway Company, Research Department). Papers relating to a bill for a five-year plan for Manchuria, 1st ed., vol. 1, *Manshū Go-ka-nen Keikaku Gaiyō* (Outline of a Five-year Plan for Manchuria), 1937.

62. Minami, Ryōshin. *Nihon Keizai no Tenkanten.* Sōbunsha, 1970. Published in English as *The Turning Point in Economic Development: The Case of Japan.* Kinokuniya, 1973.

63. _____. *"Nōringyō Shūgyōsha-sū no Suikei"* (Estimates of Employment in Agriculture and Forestry). In Hitotsubashi Daigaku, *Keizai Kenkyū,* vol. 17, no. 3, pp. 275–78.

64. _____. *Tetsudō to Denroyoku* (Railways and Electric Power). Tōyō Keizai Shimpō Sha, 1965 (LTES 12).

65. Mitsui Ginkō (Mitsui Bank). *Mitsui Ginkō Hachijūnen Shi* (An Eighty Year History of the Mitsui Bank), 1957.

66. Miyazaki, Masayoshi. *Tōa Renmei Ron* (A Theory of East Asian Integration). Kaizō Sha, 1938.

67. Mizoguchi, Toshiyuki. *Taiwan Chōsen no Keizai Seichō* (Economic Growth in Taiwan and Korea). Iwanami Shoten, 1975.

68. Mochikabu Gaisha Seiri Iinkai (Stockholding Adjustment Committee). *Nihon no Zaibatsu to Sono Kaitai* (Japanese Combines and Their Dissolution), 1950.

69. Morikawa, Hidemasa. "Meiji-ki Membō Kaisha ni Okeru Torishimariyaku Sō no Henka" (Changes in the Director Class in Meiji Era Cotton Spinning Companies). In Hisao Ozuka, Yoshio Ando, Toshio Matsuda, and Hisayuki Sekiguchi, eds. *Shihonshugi no Keisei to Hatten* (Formation and Development of Capitalism). Tokyo Daigaku Shuppan Kai, 1968.

70. Morita, Yūzō. *Jinkō Zōka no Bunseki* (An Analysis of Population Increase). Nihon Hyōron Sha, 1944.

71. Naikaku Tōkei Kyoku (Cabinet Statistical Office). *Ishin Ikō Teikoku Tōkei Zairyō Isan Dai-ni-shū, Genzai Jinkō Seitai ni Kan Suru Tōkei Zairyō* (Imperial Statistical Compilations Since the Restoration, vol. II: Sources Relating to the Current State of Population), 1913.

72. _____. "Nihon Teikoku Jinkō Seitai Hyō, 1898" (Tables on the State of Population of Imperial Japan). In *Nihon Teikoku Seitai Jinkō Tōkei 1903–1918* (Stationary Population Data for the Japanese Empire 1913–1918).

73. _____*Rōdō Tōkei Jitchi Chōsa* (Labor Data from Onsite Surveys), 1924, 1927, 1930, 1933.

74. Nakamura, Takafusa. *Keizai Seisaku no Unmei* (The Destiny of Economic Policy). Nihon Keizai Shimbun Sha, 1967.

75. ———. *Senzenki Nihon Keizai Seichō no Bunseki* (Japanese Economic Growth in Prewar Period). Iwanami Shoten 1971.

76. ———. "Zairai Sangyō no Kibō to Kōsei—Taisho 4-nen Kokusei Chōsa o Chūshin ni" (Scale and Composition of Traditional Industry—with Focus on the 1920 Census). In Mataji Umemura, Hiroshi Shinpo, Shunsaku Nishikawa, and Akira Hayami, eds., *Sūryō Keizai Shi Ronshū 1 Nihon Keizai no Hatten* (Studies in Quantitative Economic History 1: Development of the Japanese Economy). Nihon Keizai Shimbun Sha, 1976.

77. ———, and Hara, Akira. *Gendai Shi Shiryō 43, Kokka Sōdōin 1* (Sources of Contemporary History vol. 43, National Mobilization part 1). Misuzu Shobō, 1970.

78. ———, and Kumon, Toshihira. "Nihon to Roshia no Keizai Hatten no Ruigata" (Types of Economic Development in Japan and Russia). In *Keizai Hyōron*, 1967, no. 2.

79. Namiki, Masayoshi. "*Sangyō Rōdōsha no Keisei to Nōka Jinkō*" (Formation of Industrial Workers and Farm Family Population). In Tōi Seiichi and Uno Kōzō, eds., *Nihon Shinonshugi to Nōgyō* (Agriculture and Japanese Capitalism). Iwanami Shoten, 1959.

80. Nawa, Tōichi. *Nihon Bōseki-gyō to Genmen Mondai* (The Japanese Spinning Industry and the Raw Cotton Problem). Daidō Shoin, 1937.

81. Nihon Ginkō. *Nihon Ginkō Enkaku Shi* (The History of the Bank of Japan). Dai Isshū, vol. III, 1913.

82. Nihon Ginkō, Chōsa Kyoku (Bank of Japan Research Department). *Nihon Kinyū Shi Shiryō Meiji, Taishō Hen, Dai Nijuni Kan* (Sources of Japanese Financial History, Meiji and Taishō Era Edition, vol. 22).

83. "*Nihon Ginkō Chōsa Geppō (Chū), Showa 9-16 Nen*" (Bank of Japan Research Monthly [middle vol., 1934–41]), from Okura Shō Insatsu Kyoku. Also included in Nihon Ginkō Chōsakyoku (Bank of Japan Research Department). *Nihon Kinyū Shi Shiryō Shōwa Hen, Dai-Hachi Kan* (Sources of Japanese Financial History, Shōwa Edition), vol. 8, 1964.

84. Nihon Ginkō, Chōsa Kyoku Tokubetsu Chōsa Shitsu (Bank of Japan, Research Office Special Research Department). *Manshū Jihen Ikō no Zaisei Kinyū Shi* (A History of Fiscal and Monetary Affairs Since the Manchurian Incident), 1948. Included in Nihon Ginkō Chōsa Kyoku (Bank of Japan Research Department), *Nihon Kinyū Shi Shiryō Shōwa Hen, Dai Nijūshichi Kan* (Sources of Japanese Financial History, Shōwa Edition), vol. 27, 1970.

85. Nihon Ginkō Tōkei Kyoku (Bank of Japan Statistics Department). *Meiji Ikō Hompō Shuyō Keizai Tōkei* (Hundred Year Statistics of the Japanese Economy), 1966.

86. Nihon Keizai Renmei Kai (Japan Economics Federation). *Kin Yushutsu Saikinshi Irai no Waga Kuni Zaisei Keizai Suii no Katei* (The Processes of Financial and Economic Trends in the Nation Since Leaving the Gold Standard), 1939.

87. Nihon Kindai Shiryō Kenkyū Kai (Association for Studies of Modern Jap-

anese History). *Nichi-Man Zaisei Keizai Kenkyū Kai Shiryō I* (Sources of the Japan–Manchuria Finance and Economics Society, vol. 1), 1970.

88. Nihon Kokusai Seiji Gakkai (International Politics Society of Japan). *Taiheiyō Sensō e no Michi, Bekkan Shiryō-hen* (The Road to the Pacific War, Appendix Volume on Sources). Asahi Shimbun Sha, 1963.

89. Nihon Tōkei Kenkyūsho (Japan Statistics Institute). *Nihon Keizai Tōkei Shū* (A Collection of Statistics on the Japanese Economy). Nihon Hyōron Sha, 1959.

90. Niigata Ken, Mishima Gun (Niigata Prefecture, Mishima District). *Niigata Ken Mishima Gunze* (This is the Mishima District of Niigata Prefecture). Niigata Ken, Mishima Gun, 1918.

91. Nishihara, Kamezō. *Yume no Shichi-jū-amari Nen* (Seventy Years and More of Dreams). Heibonsha, 1965.

92. Nishikawa, Shunsaku, and Akimoto, Hiroya. "Bōchō Ichien Keizai Hyō Josetsu" (Introduction to the 'tableau economique' in the Bōchō Area). In Shakai Keizai Shi Gakkai (Social Economic History Association). *Atarashi Edo Jidai Zō o Motomete* (Looking for a New Picture of Edo Period). Tōyō Keizai Shimpō Sha, 1977.

93. Nomura, Kentarō. *Mura Meisai Chō no Kenkyu* (On the Village Concise Report). Yūhikaku, 1941.

94. Nōrin Shō (Ministry of Agriculture and Forestry). *Fukkaku-ban Nōka Keizai Chōsa Hōkoku* (Reproduction of Report on the Survey of the Economy of Farm Families), 1956.

95. Nōshōmu Shō (Ministry of Agriculture and Commercial Affairs). *Chingin Tōkei Hyō* (Statistical Tables on Wages), various years.

96. _____. *Kinji Nihon Nōgyō Hensen* (Transition of Modern Japanese Agriculture), 1913.

97. _____. *Kōgyō Iken Kan-ni* (Views on Encouraging Enterprise, vol. 2). Included as no. 1 of vol. 18 of *Meiji Zenki Zaisei Keizai Shiryō Shūsei* (A Collection of Historical Sources on Early Meiji Era Finance and Economics), in reproduced form, published by Meiji Bunken Shiryō Kankō Kai (Meiji Era Documents and Sources Publication Society), 1964.

98. _____, Nōshōmu Shō Tōkei Hyō (Statistical Tables from the Ministry of Agriculture and Commercial Affairs), various years.

99. Ohkawa, Kazushi, ed. *Bukka* (Prices). Tōyō Keizai Shimpō Sha, 1967 (LTES 8).

100. _____; Takamatsu, Nobukiyo; and Yamamoto, Yūzo. *Kokumin Shotoku* (National Income). Tōyō Keizai Shimpō Sha, 1974 (LTES 1).

101. _____. *Nihon Keizai Bunseki* (Analysis of the Japanese Economy). Shunjūsha, 1962.

102. _____. "Tanki Junkan to Chōki Hadō" (Short Cycles and Long Waves). In *Nihon Keizai Bunseki—Seichō to Kōzō* (Analysis of the Japanese Economy—Growth and Structure). Shunjūsha, 1962.

103. _____ et al. *Shihon Sutokku* (The Capital Stock). Tōyō Keizai Shimpō Sha, 1966 (LTES 3).

104. _____, and Rosovsky, H. "Kindai Keizai ni Okeru Zairaiteki Yōso" (Tradi-

tional Factors in Modern Economies). In Kazushi Ohkawa, *Nihon Keizai Bunseki* (Analysis of the Japanese Economy). Shunjūsha, 1962.

105. Okayama Ken (Okayama Prefecture). *Okayama Ken Tōkei Sho* (Statistical Yearbook of Okayama Prefecture), 1918.

106. Okura Shō (Ministry of Finance). *Okura Shō Hyaku-nen Shi Bekkan* (One Hundred Year History of the Ministry of Finance, appendix volume), 1969.

107. _____. *Zaisei Kinyū Tōkei Nempō* (Statistical Annual on Fiscal and Monetary Affairs), 1948.

108. Okura Shō, Rizai-Kyoku (Ministry of Finance, Financial Office). *Doitsu Zaisei Keizai Tōkei Yōran* (Statistical Elements of German Financial and Economic Affairs), 1927.

109. Okura Shō, Nihon Ginkō (Ministry of Finance and Bank of Japan). *Zaisei Keizai Tōkei Nempō* (Statistical Annual on Economics and Finance), 1948.

110. Okura Shō, Ginkō Kyoku (Ministry of Finance Bank Office). *Ginkō Kyoku Nempō* (Statistical Annual of Bank Office) Okura Shō Ginkō Kyoku.

111. Okura Shō, Shōwa Zaisei Shi Henshūshitsu (Ministry of Finance, Editorial Office on Showa Period Fiscal History). *Shōwa Zaisei Shi XI, Kinyū (Ge)* (Showa Period Fiscal History, vol. XI, Finance, part II). Tōyō Keizai Shimpō Sha, 1957.

112. Okura Shō Rizai-Kyoku (Ministry of Finance Financial Office). *Kokusai Shūshi Tekigō ni Kan Suru Shiryō* (Sources Relating to International Payments Adjustment), 1937.

113. Oshima, Kiyoshi, *Nihon Kyōkō Shiron Jō, Ge* (A Treatise on Japanese Panics, vols. I and II). Tōkyō Daigaku Shuppan Kai, 1952, 1955.

114. Ōuchi, Hyōe. *Shōwa Zaisei Shi I Sōsetsu* (A History of Shōwa Fiscal Policy, vol. I, Overview). Tōyō Keizai Shimpō Sha, 1965.

115. Ōuchi, Tsutomu. *Nihon ni Okeru Nōmin So no Bunkai* (Dissolution of the Agricultural Class in Japan). Tokyo University Press, 1970.

116. Rōdō Undō Shiryō Hensan Kai (Labor Movement Sources Compilation Committee). *Nihon Rōdō Undō Shiryō, Daijū Maki, Tōkei Hen* (Sources on the Japanese Labor Movement, vol. 10, Statistics), 1959.

117. Saito, Osamu. "Ōsaka Oroshiuri Bukka Shisū" (Ōsaka Wholesale Price Index). Mita Gakkai Zasshi no. 10, vol. 69, pp. 63–70.

118. Sampei, Takako. *Nihon Orimono Shi* (A History of Japanese Weaving). Yuzankaku, 1961.

119. Sato, Seizaburo. "Seiō no Shōgeki e no Taiō—Kawaji Toshiakira no Baai" (Dealing with Western Impact—The Case of Kawaji Toshiakira). In Hajime Shinohara and Taichirō Mitani, eds., *Kindai Nihon no Seiji Shidō Seiji-ka Kenkyu* (Political Leadership of Modern Japan). Tōkyō Daigaku Shuppan Kai, 1965.

120. *Seitetsu-gyō Sankō Shiryō* of 1932 and 1937. (Steel Industry Reference Data). Shōkō Shō, 1932, 1937.

121. Sekiyama, Naotarō. *Kinsei Nihon no Kinkō Kōzō* (Population Structure of Medieval Japan). Yoshikawa Kobun Kan, 1958.

122. Shibagaki, Kazuo. *Nihon Kinyū Shihon Bunseki* (An Analysis of Japanese Financial Capital). Tōkyō Daigaku Shuppan Kai, 1965.

123. Shiina, Eisaburō. *Senji Keizai to Bukka Chōsei* (The Wartime Economy and Goods Adjustments). Sangyō Keizai Gakkai, 1941.

124. Shimada, Toshihiko, and Inaba, Masao, eds. *Gendai Shi Shiryō (8) Nitchū Sensō I* (Sources of Contemporary History (8), the [Second] Sino–Japanese War, vol. I. Misuzu Shobō, 1964.

125. Shimoyama, Saburō. "Meiji Jū-nendai no Tochi Shoyū Kankei o Megutte" (On Land Proprietary Relationships in the Second Ten Years of the Meiji Era). In *Rekishigaku Kenkyū*, no. 176, pp. 1–15.

126. Shinohara, Miyohei. *Kō kōgyō* (Mining and Manufacture). Tōyō Keizai Shimpo Sha, 1972 (LTES 10).

127. _____. *Kojin Shōhi Shishutsu* (Private Consumption Expenditure). Tōyō Keizai Shimpō Sha, 1967. (LTES 6)

128. _____. *Nihon Keizai no Seichō to Junkan* (Growth and Cycles in the Japanese Economy), Sōbun Sha, 1961.

129. _____. *Sangyō Kōzō* (Industrial Structure). Shunjūsha, 1959.

130. _____. "1874–1940 Nenkan no Kōgyō Seichō—Seichō-ritsu Junkan to Kōzō Henka" (Industrial Growth between 1874 and 1940—Growth Rate Cycles and Structural Change). In Hitotsubashi Daigaku, *Keizai Kenkyū* vol. 20, no. 4, pp. 289–97.

131. _____. "Senzen-no Keizai Seichō to Chōki Hadō" (Prewar Economic Growth and Long Waves). In Miyohei Shinohara, *Nihon Keizai no Seichō to Junkan* (Growth and Cycles in the Japanese Economy). Sōbun Sha, 1961.

132. _____. "Shihon Shūchū Kasetsu Hihan ni Kotau" (In Answer to Criticism of the Capital Concentration Hypothesis). In Miyohei Shinohara, *Keizai Seichō no Kōzō* (The Structure of Economic Growth). Kunimoto Shobō, 1964.

133. Shiomi Saburō, *Kokumin Shotoku no Bunpai* (The Distribution of National Income). Yuhikaku, 1946.

134. _____. "Shotoku Bunpu to Ruishinzei" (Income Distribution and Progressive Taxation). In Nihon Tōkei Gakkai. *Kokumin Shotoku to Sono Bunpu* (National Income and Its Distribution). Nihon Hyōron Sha, 1944.

135. Shionoya, Yūichi. "Nihon no Kōgyō Seisan Shisū—1874–1940-nen" (Japanese Industrial Production Indicies—1874–1940). In Miyohei Shinohara, *Sangyō Kōzō Ron* (Theories of Industrial Structure), appendix. Chikuma Shobō, 1966.

136. Shōkō Shō (Ministry of Commerce and Industry). *Hompo Kōgyō no Sūsei Gojunen-shi* (Fifty Years of Trends in the National Mining Industry). Okura Shō, Insatsu Kyoku, 1963.

137. _____. *Meiji Sanjūsan-nen Naishi Shōwa Yon-nen Chingin Tōkei Hyō* (Wage Statistics Tables from the 33rd Year of Meiji to the 4th Year of Shōwa), 1930.

138. Shōwa Dōjin Kai. *Waga Kuni Chingin Kōzō no Shi-teki Kōsatsu* (A Historical Consideration of the National Wage Structure). Shiseidō, 1960.

139. Sumiya, Mikio. *Nihon no Rōdō Mondai* (Labor Problems in Japan). Tōkyō Daigaku Shuppan Kai, 1964.

140. _____. "Rinji Kō Mondai no Seisei to Saisei" (The Development and Recurrence of Temporary Worker Problems). In Ichio Okochi and Masuru

Naitō, eds., *Nihon no Keizai—Senzen, Sengō* (The Economy of Japan, Prewar and Postwar). Tōyō Keizai Shimpō Sha, 1963.

141. Suzuki, Takeo. *En* (The Yen). Iwanami Shoten, 1963.

142. Suzuki, Yoshio. *Nihon no Tsūka to Bukka* (Currency and Prices in Japan). Tōyō Keizai Shimpō Sha, 1964.

143. Takagi, Naofumi. "Senzen, Sengō ni Okeru Nōson Jinkō no Toshi Shūchū ni Kan Suru Tōkei-teki Kansatsu" (A Statistical Survey of Urban Concentration of Farm Village Population, Prewar and Postwar). In Seiichi Tōi, ed., *Nōson ni Okeru Senzai Shitsugyō* (Latent Unemployment in Farm Villages). Nihon Hyōron Shinsha, 1956.

144. Takahashi, Kamekichi. *Nihon Keizai Tōsei Ron* (A Theory of Economic Control in Japan). Kaizō Sha, 1933.

145. _____. *Nihon Zaibatsu no Kaibō* (A Dissection of Japanese Zaibatsu). Chūō Kōron Sha, 1930.

146. Teishinshō (Ministry of Communication). *Denki Jigyo Yōran* (Survey of Electricity Concerns), various years.

147. Tetsudo In (Railways Office). *Hompō Tetsudō no Kaisha Oyobi Keizai ni Oyobaseru Eikyō* (Effects of the Nation's Railways on Firms and the Economy), 1916.

148. Tōkai Ginkō (Tokai Bank). *Tōkai Ginkō Shi* (A History of the Tōkai Bank), 1961.

149. Tōkei In (Statistics Office). *Kainokuni Genzai Jinbetsu Shirabe* (Survey of Contemporary Population in Kainokuni), 1882. Reprint. Hōbun Kaku, 1968.

150. Tokyo Shi (City of Tokyo). *Tokyo Shisei Chōsa* (Census Survey of Tokyo), 1908, 1920.

151. Tonomura, Shigeru. *Ikada* (Raft). Shincho Bunko, 1960.

152. Tōyō Bōseki Kabushiki Kaisha (The Tōyōbō Company, Limited). *Tōyō Bōseki Nana-jū-nen Shi* (A Seventy Year History of the Toyobo Company), 1953.

153. Tōyō Keizai Shimpō Sha. *Jigyō Kaisha Keijō Kōritsu no Kenkyū* (Studies of Operating Efficiency of Concerns and Firms), 1932.

154. _____. *Meiji Taishō Kokusei Sōran* (Overview Census for the Meiji and Taishō Eras), 1926.

155. _____. *Nihon Bōeki Seiran* (Survey of Japanese Trade), 1934.

156. _____. *Shōwa Sangyō Shi, Dai-ikkan* (History of Shōwa Industry, vol. I), 1950.

157. _____. *Shōwa Sangyō Shi, Dai-san Kan* (History of Shōwa Industry, vol. III), 1950.

158. Tsuchiya, Takao, ed. *Chihō Ginkō Shōshi* (A Short History of Local Banks). Chihō Ginkō Kyōkai, 1961.

159. _____. *Nihon Shihonshugi no Keiei Shi-teki Kenkyū* (Historical Studies of the Management of Japanese Capitalism). Misuzu Shobō, 1954.

160. _____, and Yamaguchi, Kazuo. *Nihon Keizai Keiei Shi Nenpyō* (A Timeline of Japanese Economic and Management History). Nihon Keizai Shimbun Sha, 1968.

161. Tsūshō Sangyō Shō Chōsa Tōkei Bu (Ministry of International Trade and

Industry, Research and Statistics Department), *Kōgyō Tōkei Gojū-nen Shi, Sangyō Hen* (A 50-Year History of Industrial Statistics, Industry vol.), 1961.

162. Tu-Chiao-Yen, *Nihon Teikokushigi Ka no Taiwan* (Taiwan under Japanese Imperialism). Tōkyō Daigaku Shuppan Kai, 1975.

163. Umemura, Mataji. *Chingin, Kōyō, Nōgyō* (Wages, Employment, Agriculture). Daimeido, 1961.

164. _____. *"Chingin Kakusa to Rōdō Shijō"* (Wage Differentials and the Labor Market). In Shigeto Tsuru and Kazushi Ohkawa, eds., *Nihon Keizai no Bunseki, Daini Kan* (An Analysis of the Japanese Economy, volume II). Keisō Shobō, 1955.

165. _____, ed. *Nōrin-gyō* (Agriculture and Forestry Industries). Tōyō Keizai Shimpōsha, 1966 (LTES 9).

166. _____. "Rōdō Shijō Kōzō to Nōgyō—Meiji Nenkan o Chūshin ni" (Labor Market Structure and Agriculture—with Focus on the Meiji Years). In Tōkei Kenyū Kai, *Rōdō Tōkei Shiryō* (Statistical Sources on Labor), vol. 28.

167. _____. "Sangyō Betsu Kōyō no Hendō: 1880–1980" (Changes in Employment by Industry). In *Keizai Kenkyū*, vol. 24, no. 2, pp. 107–13. (Ohkawa et al. [O], p. 392).

168. _____. "Shūgyōsha-sū no Shinsuikei: 1871–1920-nen" (New Estimates of Numbers of Employed: 1871–1920). In Hitotsubashi Daigaku Keizai Kenkyū Sho, *Keizai Kenkyū*, vol. 19, no. 4, pp. 322–29.

169. Wada, Hideko. *Tomioka Kōki* (Postscript on Tomioka). Shinano Kyōiku Kai (Education Society of Shinano), 1931.

170. Yamada, Moritarō. *Nihon Shihonhugi Bunseki* (An Analysis of Japanese Capitalism). Iwanami Shoten, 1934.

171. Yamaguchi, Kazuo. *Meiji Zenki Keizai no Bunseki* (An Analysis of Japanese Capitalism). Tōkyō Daigaku Shuppan Kai, 1953.

172. _____, ed. *Nihon Sangyō Kinyū Shi Kenkyū, Bōseki Jigyō Hen* (Studies in the History of Industrial Finance in Japan: Spinning Concerns). Tōkyō Daigaku Shuppan Kai, 1970.

173. Yamaguchi, Kazuo, ed. *Nihon Sangyō Kinyū Shi Kenkyū, Seishi Jigyō Hen* (Studies in the History of Industrial Finance in Japan: Silk Reeling Concerns). Tōkyō Daigaku Shuppan Kai, 1967.

174. Yamanashi Ken (Yamanashi Prefecture). *Yamanashi Ken Tōkei Sho* (Statistical Yearbook of Yamanashi Prefecture), various years.

175. Yanagida, Kunio. *Teihon Yanagida Kunio Shū, Daijūroku Kan* (The Standard Yanagida Kunio, vol. 16). Chikuma Shobō, 1962.

176. Yanaihara, Tadao. *Teikokushugi-ka no Taiwan* (Taiwan under Imperialism). Iwanami Shoten, 1929.

177. Yasuba, Yasukichi. "Senzen Nihon ni Okeru Kōgyō Tōkei no Shimpyōsei ni Tsuite (On the Credibility of Production Statistics in Prewar Japan). In *Osaka Daigaku Keizaigaku*, vol. 17, nos. 2 and 3, pp. 76–95.

178. _____. "Nihon no Kōgyō Seisan Shisū 1905–1935 Nen" (Japanese Industrial Production Indicies). In Kenichi Inada and Tadao Uchida, eds., *Keizai Seichō no Riron to Keisoku* (Theory and Measurement of Economic Growth). Iwanami Shoten, 1966.

179. Yokohama Shiritsu Daigaku Keizai Kenkyū Sho (Economic Research In-

stitute of Yokohama City University). *Yokohama Keizai Bunka Jiten* (A Dictionary of Economic Culture in Yokohama), 1958.

180. Yokomizo, Mitsuteru, ed. *Sakaguchi Yoshio no Shōgai* (The Life of Sakaguchi Yoshio). Nihon Sen'i Kōgyō Kabushiki Kaisha (Japan Textile Industries, Company, 1961.

181. Yoshida, Tōgo. *Ishin Shi Hakkō* (Eight Lectures on the History of the Restoration). Toyama Shobō, 1918.

182. Yukisawa, Kenzō. "Ishin Seifu to Shihon Chikuseki" (The Restoration Government and Capital Accumulation). In Kiyoshi Matsui, ed., *Kindai Nihon Bōeki Shi* (A History of Modern Japanese Trade). Yūhikaku, 1959.

Index

agriculture: crop mix in, 50, 51, 213; growth of, 2–3, 55, 119–24; income in, 142, 145–47, 213–14, 236–37, 252–53; labor and wages in, 112, 119, 130, 214; prices, 16–18, 213; population in, 112, 115–18; reform of, 54; role of, in economic growth, 49, 58–59, 86; technical change and, 62, 261

balance of payments, 29, 173, 257; exchange rate and, 31, 254; foreign asset position, 140, 152, 173; in 1930s, 257, 262, 275–76, 289, 295–96. See also currency; gold reserves; gold standard; money; yen

banking: concentration in, 97–99, 203–05, 229; early days of, 60–61, 105–06; structural weakness in, 61, 203; ties to industry, 97, 99, 205, 239

Bank of Japan, 29, 61, 233, 243, 265, 272

bonds: electric power, 208; in late 1930s, 266, 288; municipals, 167; stipend commutation, 60–61, 105; Takahashi policy and, 233, 237–42

Bōseki Renmei (Federation of Spinners), 196

capacity, 178, 189, 245, 261

capital, physical, 4, 11, 13, 71–73; farm role in accumulation of, 54, 58, 104, 108. See also investment

capital/labor ratio, 13, 70–73

capital/output ratio, 13, 157

cartels, 153, 178, 194, 200, 226, 228, 262. See also concentration; monopoly

chemical industry, 189. See also heavy and chemical industry

coal, 62, 292–93

colonies, 36–41, 143, 152, 213

concentration, 194, 196–99. See also monopoly

consumption: in GNP, 4, 144; in 1930s, 236, 275, 279, 288, 290–92, 301; patterns of, 51, 86, 213

controls: course over time, 35, 285, 294, 299; evaluation, 289, 301; responses to, 292–94; structure of, 288–90, 294. See also planning

corporate finance, 153, 205, 245, 251–52, 288, 299. See also equities

corporate form, 62–66, 104, 106–08, 110

cotton industry, 35, 62–63, 71, 95, 106–08, 244, 255, 265, 292, 299

currency, 53, 60–61. See also money; yen

cycles: Juglar, 8, 11; Kitchin, 8; Kondratieff, 8; Kuznets, 8, 9, 11, 161

demography, 11, 115–18, 147; Edo period, 45–47

dual structure, 27–29, 114, 134–36, 213, 220, 224, 228

earthquake of 1923, 156

Edo period economy, 45–53

education, 48, 104

electric power: early development of, 73–74, 175, 184; finance of, 205, 251; growth after World War I, 151, 161, 175, 202; heading, 173; relation to other industries, 184, 185–90

employment, 18–22, 125–28, 194, 261; growth of, 22–23, 147, 178; sectoral composition of, 25–27, 51, 114–15, 119, 147, 218, 261

England, 36, 103, 139

equities, 173, 175, 243, 299. See also corporate finance

exchange rate, 144, 244, 254, 255